POLITICAL PROBLEMS

POLITICAL PROBLEMS

EDITED BY

STEVEN M. CAHN

CITY UNIVERSITY OF NEW YORK GRADUATE CENTER

ROBERT B. TALISSE

VANDERBILT UNIVERSITY

Prentice Hall
Boston Columbus Indianapolis New York San Francisco Upper Saddle River
Amsterdam Cape Town Dubai London Madrid Milan Munich Paris Montreal Toronto
Delhi Mexico City Sao Paulo Sydney Hong Kong Seoul Singapore Taipei Tokyo

Editor in Chief: Dickson Musslewhite
Publisher: Nancy Roberts
Editorial Project Manager: Sarah Holle
Editorial Assistant: Nart Varoqua
Director of Marketing: Brandy Dawson
Senior Marketing Manager: Laura Lee
   Manley
Marketing Assistant: Pat Walsh

Production Manager: Fran Russello
Cover Manager: Jayne Conte
Cover Designer: Axell Designs
Full-Service Project Management:
   Suganya Karuppasamy/GGS Higher
   Education Resources, PMG
Printer/Binder: Courier Corporation, Inc.
Text Font: Palatino

Credits and acknowledgments borrowed from other sources and reproduced, with permission, in this textbook appear on pages 303–304.

Library of Congress Cataloging-in-Publication Data
Political problems/edited by Steven M. Cahn, Robert B. Talisse.
   p. cm.
 ISBN-13: 978-0-205-64247-2
 ISBN-10: 0-205-64247-0
 1. United States—Politics and government—1989- I. Cahn, Steven M. II. Talisse, Robert B.
JK1726.P63 2011
320.60973—dc22

                                                    2009053071

10 9 8 7 6 5 4 3 2 1

Prentice Hall
is an imprint of

www.pearsonhighered.com

ISBN 10:   0-205-64247-0
ISBN 13: 978-0-205-64247-2

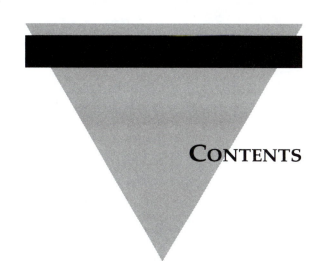

CONTENTS

SECTION 3   PORNOGRAPHY   43

SECTION 4   SAME-SEX MARRIAGE   67

SECTION 5   DRUG LEGALIZATION   95

ABOUT THE AUTHORS

WILLIAM F. BAXTER

William F. Baxter (1929–1998) was Professor of Law at Stanford University. He argues that it is impossible to eradicate pollution without severely harming people, a result to be avoided.

TOM L. BEAUCHAMP

Tom L. Beauchamp is Professor of Philosophy and Senior Research Scholar at the Kennedy Institute of Ethics of Georgetown University. He argues that certain forms of affirmative action are needed to overcome discrimination.

HUGO ADAM BEDAU

Hugo Adam Bedau is Austin B. Fletcher Professor Emeritus of Philosophy at Tufts University. He argues that the death penalty is not an effective deterrent and thus is unjustified.

STEVEN M. CAHN

Steven M. Cahn is Professor of Philosophy at the City University of New York Graduate Center. He argues that affirmative action is not justified either as compensation for past injustice or as a contribution to future diversity but might be a last resort to overcome present-day prejudice.

JOSEPH H. CARENS

Joseph H. Carens is Professor of Political Science at the University of Toronto. He argues that freedom of movement is a fundamental liberty and thus immigration can be restricted only under special circumstances.

NOËL CARROLL

Noël Carroll is a Professor of Philosophy at the City University of New York Graduate Center. Carroll argues that although art plays an important moral role in society, state support for the arts can undermine those forms of art that do not appear to be socially useful.

RONALD DWORKIN

Ronald Dworkin is Professor of Philosophy and Frank Henry Sommer Professor of Law at New York University. He argues that the liberal state can support the arts because it has a legitimate interest in protecting and sustaining culture.

JOEL FEINBERG

Joel Feinberg (1926–2004) was Regents Professor of Philosophy and Law at the University of Arizona. He argues that legal restriction of pornography would be justified only if compelling evidence demonstrated a causal connection between consuming pornography and committing violence against women; he believes such evidence has not been produced.

SAMUEL FREEMAN

Samuel Freeman is Avalon Professor of Humanities at the University of Pennsylvania. He argues that drug use erodes an individual's capacity for rational moral agency and thus should be prohibited.

ERNEST VAN DEN HAAG

Ernest van den Haag (1914–2002) was John M. Olin Professor of Jurisprudence and Public Policy at Fordham University. He defends the death penalty on the grounds that it deters would-be murderers.

JEFFREY R. HENIG

Jeffrey R. Henig is Professor of Political Science and Education at Teachers College, Columbia University. Henig argues that proposals for school choice over-simplify or ignore the complex empirical questions concerning schooling that any responsible program for reform should address.

DANIEL J. HILL

Daniel J. Hill is Lecturer in Philosophy at the University of Liverpool. He argues that torture is never morally justified.

THOMAS E. HILL, JR.

Thomas E. Hill, Jr. is Kenan Professor of Philosophy at the University of North Carolina, Chapel Hill. He argues that admirable human character traits entail a love of nature.

TODD C. HUGHES

Todd C. Hughes teaches Philosophy at the State University of New York, Geneseo. He argues that a legal ban on firearms contradicts core principles of liberalism.

LESTER H. HUNT

Lester Hunt is Professor of Philosophy at the University of Wisconsin, Madison. He argues that a legal ban on firearms contradicts core principles of liberalism.

DOUGLAS N. HUSAK

Douglas N. Husak is Professor of Philosophy at Rutgers University. He argues that legal prohibitions on recreational drug use are unjust because they violate liberal neutrality.

JEFFREY JORDAN

Jeffrey Jordan is Professor of Philosophy at the University of Delaware. He argues that state recognition of same-sex marriage is tantamount to moral approval of homosexuality, and because society is divided over the morality of homosexuality the state should avoid taking a stance that indicates moral approval of it.

HUGH LAFOLLETTE

Hugh LaFollette is Cole Chair in Ethics at the University of South Florida in St. Petersburgh. He concludes that a legal ban on guns would be unwise but suggests instead holding gun owners strictly liable for the harms caused by their guns.

HELEN E. LONGINO

Helen E. Longino is Clarence Irving Lewis Professor of Philosophy at Stanford University. She argues that the production and distribution of pornography threatens women and therefore should be legally restricted.

LIONEL K. MCPHERSON

Lionel K. McPherson is Associate Professor of Philosophy at Tufts University. He argues that if, as many philosophers allege, war is sometimes justifiable, then so too is terrorism.

HENRY SHUE

Henry Shue is Senior Research Fellow at Merton College, Oxford University. He argues that although interrogational torture might be justified under very specific conditions, these conditions are almost never realized, and so legal prohibitions against torture are justified.

JOSEPH S. SPOERL

Joseph S. Spoerl is Professor of Philosophy at St. Anselm College in New Hampshire. He argues that the current system of public education severely limits parental liberty, and thus a justice requires a voucher system of education.

MICHAEL WALZER

Michael Walzer is Professor Emeritus at the Institute for Advanced Study at Princeton University. In "Terrorism: A Critique of Excuses," he argues that terrorism is a distinctive kind of violence that cannot be morally justified. In "The Distribution of Membership," he argues that a country has the right to control immigration, though it is morally required to admit immigrants under certain conditions.

RALPH WEDGWOOD

Ralph Wedgwood is Professor of Philosophy at Merton College of Oxford University. He argues that because justice requires social institutions to be open to all, a ban on same-sex marriage is unjust.

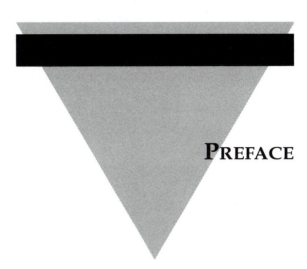

PREFACE

Just as moral philosophy includes the history of ethics, modern ethical theory, and contemporary moral problems, so political philosophy includes the history of political philosophy, modern political theory, and contemporary political problems. History and theory are the focus of most anthologies in political philosophy, whereas this volume is intended to explore practical problems of our day, each of which centers on determining the appropriate use of governmental authority in a contested area of concern.

By including extended, mostly unabridged essays defending competing positions, we have sought to do justice to the complexities of the debates. Which side has the stronger arguments in each case is for the reader to decide. To help clarify the issues in dispute, we have provided questions at the end of each of the twelve sections in order to stimulate discussion and suggest possible topics for papers.

We appreciate the support of our editor, Nancy Roberts, and we thank the staff of Prentice Hall for assistance throughout production. For help in preparing the manuscript for publication, we are grateful to Jennifer Jeavons, Sarah Holle, Mary Butterfield and Suganya Karuppasamy.

We would also like to thank the reviewers who provided us with some valuable feedback during the development of the manuscript.

Max Pensky
Florida State University
Tallahassee, FL

Dena Hurst
Binghamton University
Binghamton, NY

Jonathan Anomaly
University of Virginia
Charlottesville, VA

Coleen Murphy
Texas A&M
College Station, TX

Dave Reidy
University of Tennessee
Knoxville, TN

Zev Trachtenberg
University of Oklahoma
Norman, OK

SECTION 1

SCHOOL VOUCHERS

JUSTICE AND THE CASE FOR SCHOOL VOUCHERS

Joseph S. Spoerl

Two serious injustices plague the American system of primary and secondary education. The first injustice is that children in poor school districts are frequently denied the funding necessary to provide them with a decent education.[1] The second injustice is that parents, especially less affluent parents, are unnecessarily denied the freedom they ought to have in choosing schools for their children, for government school districts typically have a quasi-monopoly over the education of children within their boundaries.[2] I will argue in this paper that the introduction of a voucher system is the best way of eliminating both injustices.

The voucher system I have in mind would operate roughly as follows. The duty to fund education would be taken from municipalities and given to states, with poorer states receiving aid from the federal government. States in turn would distribute educational funds directly to parents in the form of checks or vouchers which could only be cashed by schools that

have contracted to educate the children. Schools would have to meet certain minimal standards to cash the vouchers, but would be given as much autonomy as possible. Vouchers would be worth as much as state legislatures deemed necessary to educate children at various grade levels, with larger vouchers going to children with documented learning disabilities or other serious handicaps. For reasons that will become clear in what follows, justice requires that religious schools be allowed to cash vouchers, but I shall not address the question of whether this would be allowed by the U.S. Constitution.[3]

The thesis of this paper, then, is that justice requires that our current system of government schooling[4] in the United States be replaced with a voucher system. Two further preliminary remarks are in order, however, before I begin to develop the argument for this thesis. First, I will focus primarily on the voucher system as a solution to the second of the two injustices mentioned above, the injustice of unnecessarily restricting parental choice. The injustice of gross disparities in funding

From *Public Affairs Quarterly*, vol. 9, no. 1 (January 1995), pp. 2–14.

across school districts, after all, could be eliminated in less radical ways, for example by increasing state or federal aid to poor school districts. Moreover, most Americans do not sufficiently appreciate the injustice of restricting parental choice in education. This injustice needs to be demonstrated, and I shall attempt to demonstrate it by appealing to values that most Americans share. The second preliminary remark is that my argument for a voucher system will be an argument from justice, not an argument from utility or efficiency. Many, perhaps most, defenders of school vouchers argue for their position by attempting to show that a voucher system would educate students far more efficiently than does our current system.[5] These authors bear the heavy burden of proving that the educational benefits of a voucher system would be so superior to the benefits of the current system that they justify the cost of wholesale educational reform. I, however, do not bear this burden of proof. My position is that even if our current system is, on balance, as academically effective as a voucher system would be, respect for justice nonetheless requires that we replace our current system with a voucher system.

The argument for the thesis has eleven main steps. I will state each step and then briefly explain it before moving on to the next one, numbering each main step and drawing the relevant conclusions as I proceed.[6]

> 1. Parents have the duty to promote the well-being of their children and the right to make the principal decisions concerning the fulfillment of that duty.

That parents have a duty to promote the well-being of their children follows from four considerations. First, as a rule parents voluntarily bring children into the world. Second, human well-being is complex, comprising physical, emotional, social, intellectual, moral, and spiritual elements, and can only be attained with the extensive help and cooperation of others over a period of years. Third, children need the special love and affection that parents (and especially biological parents) are best able to provide. Fourth, parents were themselves children at one time and cannot coherently deny that they would wish to be loved and nurtured if their and their children's roles were reversed.

That parents have the *right* to make the *principal decisions* concerning the fulfillment of this duty is slightly more difficult to demonstrate but no less true. Human well-being consists in participating freely in important human goods such as friendship, knowledge, beauty, play and religion. The activities in which human flourishing consists—loving a friend, apprehending truth, enjoying a well-played game for its own sake, appreciating beauty, worshipping God[7]—cannot be coerced. Moreover, the basic goods that form the raw material of human flourishing can be participated in and realized in indefinitely many ways: one person's friendships, games and projects may be very different from, though no less good than, another's. Indeed, given the wide variety of human tastes, talents and opportunities, we should expect human flourishing to take many different forms. Freedom is therefore essential to human flourishing. But human flourishing ought to be promoted. Therefore, human beings ought to be granted as much freedom in the pursuit of their own well-being as is consistent with the flourishing of all. But one of the most important components of human flourishing is family life. Parents are perfected by the activities of pro-creating and raising children; children are perfected by the love of their parents. Therefore, parents ought to be granted as much freedom in having and raising children as is compatible with the flourishing of all. Now it is compatible with the general flourishing of society that parents should make the principal decisions about the well-being of their children, for parents generally know and care more about their children than do strangers. Therefore parents ought to have the liberty to make the principal decisions concerning the well-being of their children (while they are children, that is, in their formative years). This, in turn, implies that parents have a legitimate moral claim to the noninterference of others in the principal decisions concerning the well-being of their children. But having a legitimate moral claim against others is precisely what it means to have a moral right. Therefore, parents have a moral right to make the principal decisions concerning the well-being of their children.

> 2. The way in which children are educated has a profound influence on every dimension of their well-being.

This premise is obvious enough that it needs little by way of explanation and defense. Education affects the physical development of the child at least in the trivial sense that schools must guarantee the physical safety of their students.[8] The moral tone of the student body and the discipline inculcated by teachers and principals affects the moral development of a child. So do the values informing teachers' discussions of human sexuality, history, politics, warfare, human relationships as portrayed in literature, and so forth. Pedagogy clearly affects a child's intellectual development, as do factors as basic as how big a school is[9] or whether it is co-educational or single-sex.[10] A teacher's subtle biases for or against religions or denominations can affect a child's religious development. Some parents may judge that an entirely secular school may harm their child's religious development

by suggesting to the child that religion is not something that ought to guide and permeate every aspect of the believer's life. In all of these ways, a child's education deeply affects his or her well-being.

> 3. Therefore, parents have the right to make the principal decisions concerning the education of their children. (from 1 + 2)
> 4. Parents can exercise this right fully only if they have the liberty to select schools that they judge to be appropriate for their children.

For those who do not or cannot homeschool, selecting an appropriate means of educating one's child means selecting schools that will promote the child's well-being as the parents conceive it. Parents may judge a school unacceptable for a variety of reasons. The school may fail to guarantee the physical safety of the child. It may subject the child to morally corrupting influences such as promiscuous or violent peers, sexual education programs that parents consider immoral, condom distribution without parental consent, teachers or textbooks that glorify what the parents regard as unjust wars, a materialistic milieu, or rampant drug and alcohol abuse. Parents may judge that only a certain type of school will adequately promote their child's academic growth, for instance a Montessori school or a single-sex school or a school that specializes in subjects for which their child shows a special aptitude. Parents may prefer to avoid schools with tenure systems that make it nearly impossible for administrators to dismiss incompetent or morally corrupt teachers.[11] Religiously committed parents may consider it very important that their child learn about history or science or sexuality from teachers who sympathize with, or at least are not biased against, their faith. Parents who consider morality to be inseparable from religion will consider that a purely secular school will threaten their child's moral development. Some parents may consider it very important that their child *not* be taught that creationism is as convincing a theory as evolution. Because there are so many ways in which a school can harm or fail to promote a child's well-being as the parents understand it, the full exercise of the right to determine their child's education requires that parents have fairly broad liberty in the choice of schools.

> 5. It is unjust to restrict the liberty people need to exercise moral rights unless the common good requires such a restriction.

Liberty is valuable because it is essential to human flourishing. The necessary link between liberty and human flourishing, and the general duty to promote human flourishing, together entail that humans have rights, or legitimate moral claims, to certain liberties. Nonetheless, restrictions on liberty are often justifiable because necessary for the common good. ("Common good" here means the set of conditions necessary for the members of society to achieve a reasonable level of well-being with relative ease and efficiency.) The outbreak of a serious and highly contagious disease might lead the authorities to prohibit public gatherings, including, for example, attendance at religious services. Laws against child abuse limit the liberty of parents, yet are entirely appropriate. Taxation limits the freedom to do as one pleases with one's money yet is justifiable, within the limits of economic prudence, because of the public goods it makes possible. Environmental regulations are essential to the protection of human health. In each case, the common good requires a restriction of liberty: it is impossible for all to flourish if contagious diseases or uncontrolled pollution damage human health; abuse of children can destroy or seriously harm their well-being; without

some taxation, the poor would lack necessities and the state would be unable to maintain the order necessary for everyone's well-being.

Now justice requires that we give every person his or her due; that is justice is a matter of respecting the legitimate moral claims of others. But legitimate moral claims are grounded in the more basic duty to promote human flourishing, and freedom is essential to human flourishing. Therefore, it is unjust to restrict freedom, unless doing so is necessary for securing the flourishing of all.

> 6. Therefore, it is unjust to restrict the liberty of parents to select appropriate schools unless the common good requires such restriction. (from 3 + 4 + 5)
> 7. Government schooling in its current form severely limits the liberty of parents to select appropriate schools; moreover, many less affluent parents lack this liberty altogether.

Under our current system of government schooling, parents who are dissatisfied with their local government schools have three options. They may move to a new school district, or send their children to a non-government school, or work to reform their government schools. Moving to a new school district, however, is expensive, especially since the better government schools in the U.S. tend to be located in areas with high property values. This option is simply unavailable to millions of less affluent American parents, as is the option of sending one's children to non-government schools. Working to reform government schools is a difficult and lengthy process and, even if successful, is unlikely to benefit one's own children, who will frequently have graduated long before the reforms are implemented. Moreover, government schooling in the U.S. is run democratically.[12] In a democracy, the majority wins and the minority loses. Parents with minority views are therefore likely to be stymied in any attempt to reform their children's schools. Even if a politically astute minority succeeds in reforming the schools, perhaps by exploiting the indifference or ignorance of the majority, the result will be offensive to many or most other parents in the community.[13] Our current educational system therefore imposes serious restrictions on the liberty of parents to select schools for their children that they judge to be appropriate.

> 8. The common good does not require this limitation of parental liberty in the selection of schools.

The severe restriction of parental liberty that is built into our current system of government schooling is not a necessary means for securing the flourishing of all members of society. It is not necessary to secure equal access for all students to a decent education, for (a) the current system already fails to do this, and (b) the voucher system described at the beginning of this paper would provide equal access to quality education even more effectively than does our current system. Nor can our current system of government schooling be justified as a necessary means of binding our diverse society together and creating a citizenry with a common commitment to democracy and civil rights,[14] for private schools in the United States have historically done this as effectively as government schools. Some argue that, by giving freedom of choice to parents, a voucher system would lead to grade inflation and the deterioration of primary and secondary education, since students and parents alike will flock to less demanding schools. Those who argue this way frequently point to the grade inflation at private colleges and universities, which they attribute to the competition for students among these schools.[15] However,

competition for students cannot be the only, or even the main, reason for grade inflation, since private colleges and universities were competing for students long before grade inflation began in the early 1970s. Moreover, primary and secondary schools that must compete for students—private schools and government schools serving affluent parents who could afford to move or sent their children to private schools—are at least as academically rigorous as government schools serving poor families who cannot afford to take their business elsewhere. Restrictions on parental choice also cannot be justified on the grounds that parents are ignorant of pedagogy and must therefore hand over all pedagogical decisions to teachers and administrators if their children are to be educated properly. Parents generally are far more intimately acquainted with the unique capacities of their children, and are far more concerned about the well-being of their children, than are strangers. Moreover, as noted above, schools that must be highly sensitive to parental preferences—private schools and government schools serving affluent parents who could afford to send their children elsewhere—tend to be at least as effective as schools that need not be sensitive to parental preferences, e.g. government schools serving captive markets in impoverished areas. I conclude, therefore, that the standard reasons given in defense of restricting parental choice in education do not stand up to critical scrutiny. The common good simply does not require such restriction.

> 9. Therefore, the American system of government schooling is unjust. (from 6 + 7 + 8)
>
> 10. A voucher system is the best means of guaranteeing parents the liberty that the current system denies them while are the same time providing adequate educational funding for all children regardless of family income.

It is obvious enough that a voucher system would grant wide autonomy to parents in selecting schools for their children. It is less obvious that a voucher system is the *best* means of granting such autonomy to parents. After all, there are many ways of granting parents the freedom to choose their children's schools, for example magnet schools, charter schools, and open enrollment.[16] Nonetheless, all of these reforms suffer from the same flaw: in all of them, ultimate authority over schools remains in hands of democratically elected officials. "The structures of democratic authority remain in place, and, if they become occupied by people with different beliefs or constituencies, the same public authority that liberated the schools could then be used to regain control over them."[17] The virtue of a voucher system is that it embodies the principle that the parent, not the state, has the primary responsibility for the education of the child. The state's role in education should be restricted to the subsidiary role of ensuring equal access to decent education for all children and preventing obvious and egregious forms of child abuse. Justice requires that the state fulfill this function, but justice also forbids the state to supplant the parent as the one who bears primary responsibility for educating the child. Because our current system of government schooling is profoundly unjust, and because its replacement with a voucher system is the best way of eliminating this injustice, my final conclusion follows:

11. Therefore, justice requires that we replace our current system of government schooling with a voucher system. (from 9 + 10)

That completes the argument for my thesis. I would like now to raise and answer some common objections to the introduction of a voucher system.[18]

Objection 1: "In a pure voucher system, if schools are free to reject applicants and expel students, then some young people will end up not being able to enroll in any school at all."

Reply: There may well be a need for some state-operated schools to educate such students. However, if students with special cognitive or emotional problems were given supplementary vouchers, as in justice they ought to be, then this alone would create a market for schools that specialize in educating students with special needs.

Objection 2: "Vouchers could perpetuate or exacerbate existing inequalities between rich and poor students. If a voucher will pay only for an inferior level of education, then that is what the poor will get, while rich parents will use the voucher as a subsidy for private-school tuition that they would have paid anyway. Moreover, the rich will have the transportation necessary to select from a wide array of schools, while the poor will be geographically isolated. Furthermore, the rich will know far more about the options available to them, while the poor and recent immigrants with limited or no English will be at a serious disadvantage."

Reply: It is unclear why we should assume that vouchers would only pay for an inferior education, especially if they were to replace altogether funding based on local property taxes. If the problem envisioned in the objection were to arise, however, one possible solution would be to allow schools to cash vouchers only if their tuition did not exceed the voucher's value, or did not exceed it by a certain percentage. This would give all parents, rich and poor alike, an incentive to ensure that vouchers be adequate to cover the cost of a decent education. This is an example of a restriction on parental freedom that could be required by the common good.[19]

As for the problem of transportation, it is possible that most parents would prefer to send their children to neighborhood schools anyway. Moreover, many parochial schools exist in America's inner cities, and many more would exist if more inner-city parents could afford to send their children to such schools.[20] There is, therefore, little reason to fear that inner-city parents will have trouble finding decent schools for their children under a voucher system. The problem of transportation may be more acute for the rural poor, but presumably the money being spent busing these students to school under our current system could be put to the same use under a voucher system. Finally, with regard to the disadvantages some parents will face in selecting an appropriate school for their children, it would no doubt be important for the state to set up some sort of clearinghouse or system of local information offices to distribute brochures and application forms and perhaps counsel parents about the options available to them, showing appropriate sensitivity to their linguistic needs.

Objection 3: "A voucher system will be even more racially segregated than our current educational system, for it will give whites even more freedom to flee from schools with substantial minority populations."

Reply: If the 40 years since *Brown v. Board of Education of Topeka* prove anything, they prove that integration does not work if imposed on parents by the state. In spite of massive forced busing programs, American schools are only somewhat less segregated today than they were in 1954.[21] The most effective means of promoting integration has been, not forced busing, but the use of magnet schools in which parents voluntarily enroll their children.[22] The success of parochial schools in achieving integration also suggests the importance of respecting parental freedom of choice in designing desegregation strategies.[23] There is therefore ample evidence that the introduction of a voucher system would not increase racial segregation in the U.S., but might actually reduce it.

Objection 4: "The argument given for the thesis grants a host of absurd privileges to parents. Surely no one will disagree that parents should have extensive freedom to raise their children as they see fit. The state has no business telling parents they may not raise their children as Hasidic Jews, Hindus, Catholics, or atheists, for example. Yet there are limits to the positive claims parents may make against the state for assistance in raising their families. The state has no obligation to help Jewish parents teach Judaism, or even Yiddish or Hebrew, to their children. Nor may Amish or Quaker parents reasonably demand state support for the teaching of pacifism to their children. Sensitivity to parental preference can be taken too far: if the state should accommodate parents who prefer Montessori schools or Catholic schools for their children, should it also accommodate schools that cater to witches, or homosexuals, or white supremacists, or nudists? The state's duty is to provide young people with the basic academic and vocational skills they need to become self-sufficient adults; the common good requires no more than this, and it is therefore unreasonable for parents to demand more."

Reply: The central flaw in this argument is its naive assumption that schools can merely provide students with "basic academic and vocational skills" without at the same time profoundly affecting their moral, social and religious development. It is impossible for a school to adopt a disciplinary system without thereby affecting the social and moral development of its students. It is impossible to send a child to a school without thereby subjecting the child to the moral influence of that school's student body. It is virtually impossible to teach students about history, literature, science or human sexuality without insinuating into textbooks and class discussions certain assumptions about morality, human nature and cosmology. The objection also naively assumes that providing students with "basic academic and vocational skills" is a straightforward matter for educational professionals who need not show any special sensitivity to parental preferences. Yet what works for one child may not work for another, and large, heavily bureaucratized government school systems tend not to have the flexibility necessary to handle the diverse pedagogical needs of schoolchildren. Moreover, public employees in large state bureaucracies like government school systems tend to protect themselves with unions and tenure rules that make it extremely difficult to discipline even those who are clearly incompetent.[24] A decentralized voucher system would give more power to parents and principals, for the marketplace would penalize those schools that failed to discipline inept teachers or maintain order.[25] Finally, the objection fails to acknowledge the very real burdens that our current system imposes on parents. State law typically requires parents to keep their children in school for up to a decade. Yet many parents have little or no choice over the schools their children attend. At the same time, many of our government schools cannot guarantee the physical safety of their students, fail to educate effectively, and frequently threaten the moral and spiritual well-being of children as understood by their parents. To demand greater parental autonomy in education is not to demand absurd privileges for eccentric tastes; it is, rather, to demand relief from the morally intolerable burdens that our current educational system imposes on parents.

The objection does contain a kernel of truth, however. There clearly must be some limits to the parental preferences accommodated within a voucher system. The common good, as defined above, is the key to determining such limits, and there is a virtually universal consensus in the U.S. that certain practices and ideologies threaten the common good. The Ku Klux Klan, the Aryan Nations, and the American Nazi Party, for example, would unjustly deny to African-Americans, Jews, and others the conditions necessary for their flourishing. It therefore seems legitimate for the state to refuse to accommodate the educational preferences of parents belonging to such groups. However there are other issues on which our society lacks a consensus on what is conducive to human fulfillment. Is corporal punishment necessary for the proper moral development of children? Amish and Hutterite parents would say yes, while others classify all corporal punishment as child abuse. Are homosexual activity and pre-marital sex legitimate means to personal fulfillment? Many contemporary moral philosophers would answer yes, while traditional Catholics, Protestants and Jews would answer with an emphatic no. Because of the deep moral and religious differences within our society, if we were to implement a voucher system, we would have no choice but to use the moral consensus that does exist to fashion restrictions on the schools that will qualify for vouchers, and then learn to live with the diversity that results. Tolerating such diversity is the price we will have to pay for taking seriously our own rhetoric about the importance of individual liberty.

In conclusion: I have argued in this paper for a thesis that most Americans will find surprising, namely that the traditional system of government schooling in the

United States is seriously unjust and ought to be radically reformed. Yet I have argued for this conclusion by appealing to values and principles with which most Americans sympathize, in particular the principle that freedom is essential to human flourishing and therefore ought not to be restricted except as required by the common good. If American voters were consistent in their moral thinking, they would cease to regard vouchers as a dangerous innovation and would instead see them as the natural expression of values that are central to the American political tradition.

Notes

1. See Jonathan Kozol, *Savage Inequalities* (New York: HarperCollins, 1991).
2. While liberals like Kozol have focused on the first injustice, they have been largely blind to the second. Religiously committed parents and their spokespersons have been more sensitive to the injustice of restricting parental choice. See, for example, "A School for the President's Daughter," *America*, Feb. 6, 1993, p. 3; "Politics and School Reform," *America*, Sept. 5, 1992, p. 99; "A Very American Proposal," *America*, Nov. 16, 1991, p. 355; Quentin L. Quade, "Prochoice on Schools," *Commonweal*, April 10, 1992, p. 5; John J. Conley, S.J., "Educational Right," *America*, Oct. 3, 1992, pp. 203–4; James D. Foster, "Parental Choice: Will Vouchers Solve the School Crisis?" *Christianity Today*, Aug. 19, 1991, pp. 27, 29.
3. For a detailed, though slightly different account of how a voucher system could work, see John E. Chubb and Terry M. Moe, *Politics. Markets and America's Schools* (Washington, DC: The Brookings Institution, 1990), pp. 215–26.
4. I shall use the expressions "government schooling" and "government schools" instead of "public education" and "public schools," because non-government schools, far from serving narrowly "private" interests, serve the general public as well as government-operated schools do. For example, many non-Catholic inner-city parents choose to send their children to Catholic schools. Moreover, the graduates of non-government schools go on to make the same sorts of contributions to society as do the graduates of state-operated schools.
5. See, for example, Milton and Rose Friedman, *Free to Choose* (New York: Avon, 1980), pp. 140–65; Thomas Sowell, *Black Education: Myths and Tragedies* (New York: David McKay Co., Inc., 1972), pp. 242–50; Dwight R. Lee and Robert L. Sexton, "The Government School Lobby vs. Educational Vouchers," *USA Today* (magazine), Sept. 1988, pp. 79–81; Chubb and Moe, *op. cit.*; Gary S. Becker, "School Finance Reform: Don't Give Up On Vouchers," *Business Week*, Dec. 27, 1993, p. 25.
6. For a more detailed exposition of the general moral theory that I employ in this paper, see John Finn is *Natural Law and Natural Rights* (Oxford: Clarendon Press, 1980), and Germain Grisez, *The Way of the Lord Jesus*, Vol. I, *Christian Moral Principles* (Chicago: Franciscan Herald Press, 1983), Vol. II, *Living a Christian Life* (Quincy, IL: Franciscan Press, 1993).
7. I am not presupposing the existence of God here. Rather, my point is that if one believes in God, then a major component of one's well-being will be to bring one's life into harmony with the will of God as one understands it.
8. On the physical threats to children in New York City's government schools, as contrasted with the relative security of the city's parochial schools, see David Gonzalez, "Poverty Raises Stakes for Catholic School," *The New York Times*, April 17, 1994, Section 1, pp. 1, 32.
9. For evidence that large, impersonal schools are less effective in teaching students, see Sam Dillon. "Thirty New High Schools Report First-Year Success," *The New York Times*, May 15, 1994, Section 1, p. 35, and Lynda Richardson, "St udent Anonymity Fuels the Truancy: Grim Product of Factory Schools," *The New York Times*, June 19, 1994, Section 1, pp. 23, 27.
10. Recent research indicates that girls and young women do better academically at all-female schools. See Susan Estrich, "Separate is Better," *The New York Times Magazine*, May 22, 1994, pp. 38–9.

11. The teacher tenure system in New York State, for example, makes it extremely difficult for schools to dismiss even teachers who are convicted drug dealers. See Sam Dillon, "Teacher Tenure: Rights vs. Discipline," *The New York Times*, June 28, 1994, pp. Al, B3.

12. Some might argue that our current educational system is not democratic since educational bureaucracies wield far more power than do voters. If this is so, then the restrictions on parental choice under our current system of government schooling are even more severe than I suggest in the argument that follows.

13. Consider the success of fundamentalist Christians in gaining control of many local school boards even though they constitute a minority of parents: the result is frequently the adoption of policies that are offensive to other parents. See, e.g., Larry Rohter, "Battle over Patriotism Curriculum: Critics Vow to Overturn Pro-United States Policy in Florida." *The New York Times*, May 15, 1994, Section 1, p. 22.

14. See Paul D. Houston, "School Vouchers: The Latest California Joke," *Phi Delta Kappan*, Sept. 1993, pp. 61–74.

15. See Albert Shanker, "Competing for Customers," *The New York Times*, June 27, 1993, Section 4, p. 7, and "Students as Customers," *The New York Times*, Aug. 8, 1993, Section 4, p. 7. For a recent discussion of the problem of grade inflation at American colleges and universities, see "Making the Grades," *The New York Times*, June 5, 1994, Section 4, p. 16.

16. For a concise survey of recent reforms aimed at increasing parental autonomy, see Chubb and Moe, *op. cit.*, pp. 206–15. The authors omit the recent phenomenon of charter schools, however; on the charter school movement, see Chris Pipho, "Bipartisan Charter Schools," *Phi Delta Kappan*, Oct. 1993, pp. 102–3.

17. Ibid., pp. 214f. Chubb and Moe are speaking here of the most radical parental choice reform implemented to date in the U.S., that of New York City's District No. 4 in East Harlem. For a powerful argument showing how a school system controlled by a democratic state tends to become heavily bureaucratized and hence immune to parental control, see Chubb and Moe, Chapter 2.

18. In answering these objections, I will in effect be supplementing the arguments given above for premise 8.

19. Milton and Rose Friedman oppose any restrictions on the parents' right to supplement vouchers: *op. cit.*, pp. 156–8. However, the Friedmans fail to appreciate that without some such restriction, wealthy parents lose a powerful incentive to ensure the adequacy of the vouchers given to poorer parents.

20. See David Gonzalez, *art. cit.*

21. See Kozol, *op. cit.*, on the persistence of segregation in American government schools. See also William Celis 3d, "40 Years After Brown, Segregation Persists," *The New York Times*, May 18, 1994, pp. Al, B7.

22. Celis, *art. cit.*

23. On the superior record of New York State's Catholic schools in achieving integration, see Donohue, *art. cit.*

24. See Dillon, *art. cit.*

25. For a persuasive argument for this point, see Chubb and Moe, *op. cit.*, Chapter 2.

READING

2

RETHINKING SCHOOL CHOICE

Jeffrey R. Henig

Sheltering under the broad umbrella of the word choice are a number of policy options that could take quite distinct concrete forms. . . .

While nominally recognized, these differences often are given short shrift in the contemporary debate over education policy. These are matters of detail that, it naturally is assumed, can safely be put off until later. Once we decide whether to move in the direction of choice, specifying its precise form is a simple matter. This has worked to the advantage of those who favor privatization and market-based reforms in at least two ways. It has helped inflate the movement for choice by allowing groups with different basic interests and visions temporarily to coalesce. And it has made it easier for proponents of market-based proposals to sidestep serious questions about whether the institutional and social

frameworks that their models presume can be developed and sustained.

But the devil, they say, is in the details. The surface meaning of this old saying is familiar. Decisions about details matter. While some differences among school-choice plans may indeed be technical matters that could be worked out later, others have consequences potentially so great that they represent variations of the same policy in name only. . . .

The Devil in the Details: Choosing Among Varieties of School Choice

Contemporary debate about educational reform is muddied and misdirected because of basic confusion about what school choice would entail in specific terms. . . . Given a broad commitment to the abstract notion of educational choice, it remains to be determined what decisions the nation is likely to make in order to translate that commitment into specific program alternatives. Choice programs may vary in several key ways, among them

From Henig, Jeffrey; *Rethinking School Choice.* Copyright © 1994 by Princeton University Press. Reprinted by permission of Princeton University Press.

12

regulation, redistribution, level of support, and scope.

The Extent of Regulation

Among the specific questions about regulation that must be answered in fashioning a workable program of school choice are these:

- *Curriculum requirements:* Will participating schools be required to provide at least some base level of instruction in key subjects such as math and science? What about geography and government? How demanding and detailed will such standards be? Will any subjects or ideas be proscribed? For example, should schools be free to teach creationism as fact, to advocate racial separatism, to assign sexually suggestive literature, to include abortion counseling in health classes?

- *Teacher qualifications:* Should teachers in participating schools be required to have graduate degrees in education? take graduate-level coursework in education or the area of their teaching expertise? have college degrees? Should they be required to pass competency tests? What about background checks for criminal records? Should any regulations regarding teacher qualification be illegal for participating schools? For example, should schools be free to require teachers to belong to a particular religion, sign a national loyalty oath, submit to mandatory drug testing, join (or not join) a union?

- *Admissions and discipline:* Should participating schools be free to accept or reject applicants according to whatever criteria they deem relevant? Should they be required to hold a certain proportion of spaces for low-income students? minorities? children from the surrounding neighborhood? Should they be prohibited from rejecting applicants based on certain criteria? For example, should they be permitted to refuse admission to students based on

racial or ethnic compatibility? prior disciplinary record? prior academic record? parents' religion? parents' criminal record? parents' educational attainment or profession? older siblings' academic and disciplinary record? parents' willingness to provide a donation to the school? What about regulations regarding discipline and expulsion? Should participating schools be allowed to suspend or expel students based on their failure to "fit in," or should more precise grounds for acceptable action be legislatively specified? Should procedures for due process be defined and enforced? Should any forms of discipline be prohibited? For example, should participating schools be allowed to inflict corporal punishment? impose long-term isolation? encourage systematic hazing?

- *Health and safety:* Will participating schools be required to provide a minimal ratio of restrooms per person? Must facilities be gender-specific, with the proper ratios figured separately? What about access for the disabled? Should participating schools be required to provide lunch? If so, what, if any, nutritional standards will be required? How about regulations regarding refrigeration and food handling intended to reduce the risk of disease? Will there be building-code requirements relating to fire safety, lead paint, asbestos, ventilation, and sunlight? Will access to medical services be required, and, if so, how strict will the requirements be? Should participating schools be required to acquire insurance to cover liabilities incurred due to injuries to students or staff?

- *Tuition and fees:* Should participating schools be allowed to charge as much in tuition and fees as the market will bear? Should they be required to limit tuition to the face value of publicly funded vouchers? Should they be allowed to charge different tuitions to different types of students? For example, should they be allowed to offer reduced tuition to students from low-income families? to academically talented students? to athletes? Should they be required to provide scholarships for low-income students? Should they be required to charge lower fees to neighborhood applicants? to those living within the district or state?

- *Order and stability:* Markets are dynamic. They can also be disruptive. Historically, one of the frequent catalysts for government regulation is pressure from citizens, workers, and employers to moderate harsh cycles and maintain services when market forces withdraw, Should participating schools be completely free to retract previously advertised programs, replace teachers in midyear with substitutes willing to work at lower pay, or relocate or close without considering the impact on the surrounding neighborhood? Should the state or district guarantee that no area will be left without a school within a specified distance? What about participating schools whose labor practices result in frequent or lengthy strikes? Should they be forced to refund a portion of the tuition to parents? Should they refund the value of the vouchers to the government? Should they be barred from the choice program?

- *Intrafamily disputes:* Should the right of choice be invested in the parent, or should the child at some age gain a formal role? How will disagreements be mediated? Should there be conditions under which school officials can challenge a parent's decision if they believe that it is injurious to the child's well-being?

- *Data collection and repotting:* What, if any, information will participating schools be required to collect regarding the characteristics and performance of their students? What information must they provide about their internal decisions and practices? Will they be required to collect data on race? on religion? on place of residence? Will they be required to administer standardized tests? to record graduation rates? to keep track of drop-outs

and transfers? to monitor the racial characteristics of disciplinary cases? What, if any rules will govern disclosure of such information? Will it be published and disseminated through specified outlets? Will schools be required to make such data available, upon student request, to other schools or employers? What information about their revenues and expenditures will schools be required to keep and make available? What information about their teachers and administrators will they be required to keep and make available?

- *Truth in advertising:* Will advertisement practices or outlets be regulated? Will participating schools be permitted to air appeals on television or radio shows watched primarily by young children? Will they be restricted at all in the types of appeals and claims they can make? For example, will they be permitted to claim that their students are less likely to use illegal drugs, or more likely to obey their parents? that their graduates will make more money, or be happier, or live longer? What, if any, substantiation will they be required to offer?

The boundaries of regulation are set informally as well as formally. Elaborate regulations will mean little if they are disregarded and cannot be enforced. Linked to the question of the extent and specificity of regulation, then, are additional questions regarding the capacity of the public sector to monitor behavior, its political will and financial capacity to pursue enforcement, and the readiness of the judicial sector to view such regulations as acceptable exercises of the public authority.

The Commitment to Redistribution

Consider the difference between two voucher programs. One offers modest vouchers worth about fifteen hundred dollars to every child in the state. The other sets the amount of the voucher in inverse proportion to the child's educational disadvantages; low-income, homeless, or physically or emotionally disturbed children may qualify for vouchers of as much as sixty-five hundred dollars, while the majority of healthy, middle- and upper-class children receive a base level voucher worth five hundred dollars. If poorer districts cannot afford to finance these vouchers, the state supplements their revenues with taxes raised in other communities.

These two programs would be strikingly different in educational and political impact. Providing a fixed but modest universal grant to all students might be akin to offering ten free driving lessons to any teenagers purchasing a new car; those who are already advantaged are in a much better position to take full advantage of the offer. A grant of sixty-five hundred dollars might truly be sufficient to entice schools actively to pursue students who are difficult to educate, and to entice suburban districts to accept transfers from inner-city schools; a voucher of five hundred dollars most likely would not.

As with regulation, the full distributory effects of choice proposals would depend on more than formal and open decisions about the size and progressivity of vouchers or "scholarships." Other key factors include whether parents are permitted to supplement vouchers with their own money, whether family costs are given special tax status and whether they are treated as credits (progressive) or deductions (regressive), and whether or not free transportation is provided to children who opt for schools outside their normal attendance zone.

Footing the Bill

Proposals for school choice can differ dramatically depending on whether they are accompanied by increased, stable, or decreased public financial support. Experience has shown that making educational choice work can be an expensive proposition . . . . [M]agnet schools and other initiatives for choice often have depended on substantial subsidies from external sources. In spite of hopes that such expenses could be limited to an initial start-up phase, it so far appears to be the case that continued investment usually is necessary in order to maintain meaningful distinctions among schools, to ensure a continuing flow of information to succeeding generations of families, and to counteract resegregation tendencies rooted partly in residential patterns.

The Scope of Choice

School-choice systems can differ according to the types of schools they include, the jurisdictions they include, and the students they include. One question relating to the types of schools to be included concerns grade level: should choice be offered at all grade levels, or restricted to secondary schools where students are more mature and where curricular specialization may be more appropriate? Another question concerns whether to include private schools and, if so, which ones? Should only non-profit, secular private schools be included, or should for-profit entrepreneurial schools and parochial schools be included as well?

The most pressing question about jurisdiction is whether schools-choice programs will be restricted to schools within district borders or will allow cross-district transfers. If cross-district transfers are involved, decisions must be made about whether a district's participation in the program is to be mandatory or voluntary.

School-choice programs also can differ in the breadth of the eligibility criteria applied to students. In one scenario, assignment of a student to a "home" school could be the default for those who fail to exercise their option to change. In another, designations of home schools could be eliminated, and all students required to make an affirmative choice, as is nominally the case in Cambridge. Should choice be universal, or restricted to certain categories of students—perhaps those defined by race, income, academic interest, academic ability, or the availability of adequate programs at the home school?

The scope of choice, as implemented, may be affected by informal as well as formal provisions. For example, if free transportation is not provided, the formal extension of choice across district boundaries will be relatively meaningless for many students, who will be able to afford neither the time nor the expense that would be involved in taking advantage of the theoretical possibility of transferring. The same is true if parents are not provided with adequate and understandable information about the available options and the procedures for pursuing them. . . .

As this discussion makes apparent, a jurisdiction does not face a simple yes-or-no decision about whether to move in the direction of expanding educational choice. It faces, rather, a series of ongoing decisions. Being clear about the distinctions among school-choice plans can help citizens and policy-makers shape a plan that meets their needs and aspirations. . . .

Choice as a Tool—Not a Solution

Moving from a broad rethinking of the nature of social learning, public institutions, and schools to a more concrete set of proposals for education reform calls for an intermediate step. One of the most troublesome aspects of the contemporary movement for market-based school choice is the willingness of some partisans to present choice as a panacea: a solution that fits all times and places and that has the power to solve all problems completely on its own. . . . Such zealous presentation of choice as a universal and exclusive solution hampers clear thinking about reform in at least two ways. It encourages unreflective applications of choice, regardless of local circumstance. And it threatens to crowd off the public agenda a host of other reform possibilities—funding for preschools, smaller class sizes, extended school days—some of which, because they are more suited to local cultural, institutional, and political realities, may simply be more likely to work. Instead, choice should be regarded pragmatically as one tool among many, which citizens and officials should consider in seeking a workable education-reform strategy suited to their district's values, resources, and needs. This involves fitting choice to the context, considering opportunity costs, and appreciating modest victories.

Fitting Choice to the Context

Like the street vendor offering T-shirts with a sign claiming "one size fits all," some proponents of school choice offer legislative models as universal recipes for reform. Yet, there are dramatic differences among the more than fifteen thousand school districts in the United States. Some districts are dense, urban, and heterogeneous, while others are sparsely populated with little ethnic or racial variation. Some are compact; some cover many square miles. Some contain high proportions of students whose parents have the resources and desire to provide, at home, a supportive climate that complements the mission of the schools; others have too many children living in households so ravaged by economic hardship, drugs, and disease that learning takes second place to bare survival. Some communities have traditions of racial harmony; some bear scars of lengthy racial conflict. Some boast property wealth that provides a rich pool of resources for funding public initiatives; some are desperately underfunded. Some have well-developed public-transportation systems that make it feasible for students to move readily from home to school; others are dependent on automobiles. Some are dotted with well-regarded private schools; others have few of even minimal quality. Some districts are governed by effective leaders kept on their toes by a mobilized citizenry. In other districts, inept and part-time officials run systems in a relatively unmonitored and unaccountable fashion.

Differences such as these can have a tremendous effect on the way school choice would unfold. Considering choice as a tool, rather than a universal solution, means taking these differences into account. It means tailoring school-choice plans to meet the circumstances. In some cases it may mean delaying experimentation with choice until some of the preconditions can be put in place. School-choice plans for rural districts where students and schools are far apart, for example, might have to include quite different provisions from those for dense urban areas and those effectively served by mass transit. To the extent that viable programs require a threshold number of students; rural areas may simply be unable to accommodate the full range of choices sustainable in an urban area. For logistical reasons, choices may have to be structured as alternative programs or concentrations within schools (rather than between schools). School-choice plans in systems in which demographic changes have resulted in excess school capacity might need provisions different from those needed in growing areas where there are no empty seats in school.[1]

One Tool among Many

A hammer can be invaluable for some tasks and in some hands. But a hammer is no help in repairing a broken dish, and it can be dangerous if wielded in the dark or by a child. Those who use a tool have a responsibility to make sure that it is used when the time and the place are right. Because choice can have destructive consequences under some conditions, those who propose school choice as a policy priority have the responsibility to do the same. They also have a responsibility to consider other tools that might be available.

Choice is by means the only weapon in the arsenal available to school officials. Those who insist on nothing short of a radical restructuring of the entire system obscure this point with their undifferentiated charges of educational breakdown. Public officials at all levels of government have undertaken a vast array of school-reform initiatives over the last ten years. These have included tougher graduation requirements, more challenging curriculums, more sophisticated measurements of student performance, teacher competency testing, longer school days, longer school years, merit pay for teachers, school-based management, and school-finance reform. The blanket charge that these have failed simply is not substantiated by the evidence. By some indicators . . . school performance has actually improved. More to the point, there have been far too few of the controlled and careful studies that might more accurately sort through the web of nonschool factors that bear on performance to let us assign, with confidence, either congratulations or blame.

A pragmatic approach calls for evaluating school choice in relation to these alternatives. In some cases, the relationship may be complementary. In others, limited resources or underlying inconsistencies mean that pursuit of choice will make other options less possible. Choice can entail substantial expenses. Making transportation available to transferring students, for example, could mean having to settle for higher student/teacher ratios, or fewer advanced-placement courses, or less-competitive teacher salaries. Because different people emphasize different values, increasing the scope of parental choice require scaling back on efforts to expose all students to a common core of knowledge or significantly encroaching on traditions of local control. After public deliberation, based on the best available evidence, we might conclude that these are opportunity costs worth taking on. But they should not be ignored

Note

1. Even in older cities undergoing population loss, the supply of available seats may be insufficient to accommodate demand. Lewis and Taylor, *Options Without Knowledge,* for example, concluded that, of the roughly 14,700 empty seats, nearly two-thirds were in the worst schools; only 5,228 empty seats were in schools where quality was high enough that "student 'consumers' might improve by 'purchasing' them—i.e., changing enrollment" (16). Since over 164,000 students attended the lowest-quality elementary schools, the Urban League reasoned that at most one child in fifty who might benefit from choice would really have the opportunity to do so.

The notion that new schools can fill such vacuums is one of the most problematic assumptions of the advocates of market

choice; at least we can be certain that the likelihood of this occurring will depend on other conditions: the size of vouchers or scholarships, the extent of regulation, the intensity of crime, other costs of doing business, and so forth. In Milwaukee, where low-income students are eligible for vouchers that can be applied to private schools, ten private schools expressed an interest in participating, only seven enrolled any applicants, and only five accounted for over 92 percent of the placements. Over one-third of those who applied were refused admission because of lack of space. The second year the number of participating schools was even lower, with only four private schools accounting for over 92 percent of the placements . . .

Study Questions for Section 1

1. At the end of his essay, Spoer considers four objections to his proposal. Which of these objections is most compelling? Are Spoer's replies convincing?

2. Henig argues that choice is but one tool among many for structuring an effective system of education and calls for a "pragmatic" approach in which education systems should be fit to particular contexts in which they operate. Does the suggestion that the American education system might be structured differently in different parts of the country raise questions concerning justice and equality?

3. To what extent does the issue concerning school vouchers rest on empirical (sociological, economic, political) considerations of the kind that Henig raises? If, as Spoer alleges, the question is one of justice and parental liberty, then do the empirical details matter?

SECTION 2

GOVERNMENT SUPPORT FOR THE ARTS

CAN A LIBERAL STATE SUPPORT ART?

Ronald Dworkin

My topic in this essay is art and the humanities and how far the public should support these to make them excellent and fecund. People have discussed this subject endlessly, and discussion always begins by opposing two methods of study: the economic and the lofty approaches to the matter.

The economic approach—I use a rather generous definition—takes as its premise that a community should have the character and quality of art that it wishes to buy at the price necessary to secure it. The lofty approach, in contrast, turns its back on what the people think they want; it concentrates instead on what it is good for people to have. It insists that art and culture must reach a certain degree of sophistication, richness, and excellence in order for human nature to flourish, and that the state must provide this excellence if the people will not or cannot provide it for themselves.

Reprinted by permission of the publisher from "Can a Liberal State Support Art?" in *A Matter of Principle* by Ronald Dworkin, pp. 221–233, Cambridge, MA: Harvard University Press. Copyright © 1985 by Ronald Dworkin.

These two approaches are generally thought to be opposed as well as different, because it seems at first blush that the economic approach would commend either no public support for the arts, or very little. The argument goes this way. The *market* is the most effective instrument for deciding how much and what kind of culture people want at the necessary price. Would people contemplate Aristotle contemplating Homer if they had to pay the full cost of that opportunity, including their share of the cost of maintaining a museum, buying that painting from foreign owners, insuring and guarding it, and paying taxes on the property on which the museum sits? There is only one way to discover this. Let a museum charge people an admission price that reflects all these costs; then we shall see whether the museum was right in thinking that this is what enough of the people wanted badly enough. If art is left to the market in this way—and the same holds for universities providing courses in the humanities—then the public automatically will have exactly the art it really does want at the price it is willing to pay. But if public support enters this picture—if the public treasury subsidizes part of the true cost of space in front of a Rembrandt so that the museum's admission charges do no reflect the true cost—then this means that the public as a whole is spending more on art than it wishes to spend, at the expense of whatever the funds would otherwise have provided. The economic approach thus seems to rule out public subsidy almost by definition.

The lofty approach seems a much more promising avenue to pursue if we begin, as many of us do, by wanting to find some justification for a generous level of state support. We should decide how much collectively to spend on art by asking how much is necessary to make our culture excellent. The economic approach seems too mundane, almost Philistine, in contrast.

But before embracing the lofty approach, we must at least pause to notice its warts. First, experience teaches that those who would benefit most from subsidies to universities and museums and other cultural institutions are, on the whole, people who are already very well off, because they have been taught how to use and enjoy art. It seems unfair to provide, under the cover of some ideal of human flourishing, further and special benefits to those who already flourish more than most. Would it not be better to divert funds from rich museums to poor clinics and subsidized medical care? Second, the lofty approach seems haughtily paternalistic. Orthodox liberalism holds that no government should rely, to justify its use of public funds, on the assumption that some ways of leading one's life are more worthy than others, that it is more worthwhile to look at Titian on the wall than watch a football game on television. Perhaps it is more worthwhile to look at Titian; but that is not the point.

More people disagree with this judgment than agree with it, so it must be wrong for the state, which is supposed to be democratic, to use its monopoly of taxing and police power to enforce judgments only a minority accepts.

These difficulties in the lofty approach send us back to the economic approach, this time to study it more sympathetically and carefully. Perhaps it can furnish some support for state aid to the arts after all. I suggested that the economic approach must reject subsidy because only a market uncontaminated by subsidy can discover the public's true preferences about how its funds should be spent. But that was a simplification: the connections between market prices and people's true preferences are not always so tight. What someone is willing and able to spend on something depends on how much he has to spend altogether: If wealth is very unequally distributed in a community, then the fact that a rich man buys caviar while a poor man goes without bread does not mean that the community as a whole values the caviar more than the bread. For this reason, market prices and transactions will not always be a fair measure of what the community as a whole really wants.

I offer this only as a reasonably clear qualification of my original dictum about the market; unfortunately it offers no help in using the economic approach to justify subsidy to the arts. It can furnish an argument for a subsidy—for bread, for example—only if those who lack what is to be subsidized are relatively poor. But this is not true (or so it seems) of those who could not afford to go to the opera unless the opera were subsidized, but could afford it and would go if it were. They belong for the most part to the middle classes; indeed that was the basis of one of my initial objections to the lofty approach.

There is, however, another well-known qualification to the dictum that the market is a fair test of what the community wants for what it has to spend. This one is much more promising, for it might support an argument that art and the humanities, properly understood, are what the economists call "public goods" and for that reason must be supported from the public treasury rather than only from private purses.

Public goods are those whose production cannot efficiently be left to the market because it is impossible (or very difficult or expensive) to exclude those who do not pay from receiving the benefit and so riding free. People have no incentive to pay for what they will receive anyway if others buy it. Military defense is a common and useful example. Suppose an army could be raised only by private subscription. If I think my neighbors will purchase, together, an army large enough to repel an invasion, then I have no incentive to pay my share, because they cannot exclude me from the benefit they have bought. There is no way their army can protect them without also protecting me. Environmental benefits provide another example. If my neighbors spend enough to purify the air they breathe, they will also purify the air I breathe; they cannot exclude me from that benefit if I have not paid my share. So even though I might be anxious to pay my fair share of the cost of an army or of clean air if this were necessary in order for me to have these benefits, I nevertheless have a strong reason not to pay my share in the hope that others will buy the army or clean the air. But since everyone else will have the same reason, there is a lively danger that we will not, collectively, spend the sum we would be willing to spend if we each thought this necessary; so we will, perversely, end by not spending what we collectively want to spend.

In these circumstances, according to orthodox economic theory, the best remedy is for the state to calculate what the public would be willing to spend if necessary, and to spend that sum itself, gathered from taxes which the public is required by law to pay. Notice that the lofty approach plays no role in this kind of argument for state support. There is no assumption that the people should have military security or fresh air whether they want it or not; but just the very different assumption that they do want it, at the price that will provide it, so that state intervention is merely a tactical solution to a technical problem.

Such an analysis assumes that public officials can know, or at least have a respectable opinion about, how much the people would spend collectively if this were necessary. Economists have puzzled a great deal not only about how the state could discover this information but also about the more fundamental question of what exactly it means to say, of someone, that he would pay a particular price for something under circumstances that in fact never arise. They have offered various theories of what this should be taken to mean and of how the state can form some idea of what that hypothetical price is. All these theories are complex, and several are ingenious. But the important point here is that the usefulness of the public-goods approach depends on the availability of a reasonably plausible device for deciding what the public really wants to pay for whatever it is that the market, for technical reasons, cannot provide.

Particular cultural experiences, like the opportunity to hear a particular performance of a particular opera, are not public goods because it is easy to exclude those who will not pay. But the public-goods problem can arise in a partial or mixed way when private transactions have spillover effects which others value and from which they cannot be excluded. Consider vaccination. If someone pays the price necessary to be vaccinated, he secures for himself a special kind of protection from which those who do not pay are excluded; but if enough people are vaccinated, then even those who are not themselves vaccinated will benefit to a lesser degree because the risk of disease will be reduced for them. This "free-clinger" problem may also produce the perverse result, if production were left to the market, that society will not have what it wants at the price it would be willing to pay. Enough people might decide not to buy vaccination, in the hope of having much of the benefit anyway, so that overall protection drops below the level the community as a whole really wants. Once again state provision of vaccination in one form or another, rather than leaving vaccination to the market, would be justified on that ground, as wholly compatible with the economic approach to the matter.

Perhaps art should be regarded as at least a mixed public good, like vaccination, and some state subsidy justified on that ground. This suggestion assumes that when some people buy art and culture—by buying books or visiting fee-charging museums or attending concerts or studying in universities—other people who do not engage in these transactions benefit to a significant degree. Plainly that assumption is justified to some degree, but the power of the suggestion turns on the character and significance of the free-rider benefit. How do transactions in culture benefit those who are not parties? A sizable economic literature has been devoted to that question. Most of it considers a kind of free-rider benefit we might call "extrinsic" because it is not of the same aesthetic or intellectual character as the benefits parties to the transactions receive. For

example, New Yorkers who never use the Metropolitan Museum benefit financially when tourists come to their city to visit the museum—and remain to spend money elsewhere. These New Yorkers may benefit in another way: through the pride they may feel when their community's culture is celebrated and renowned.

My sense of the literature, however, is that the sum of the extrinsic benefits of this sort, even generously defined, would not be high enough to justify any substantial level of public support for that reason alone. I also have a sense that any attempt to justify art as a public good by appealing to this extrinsic kind of benefit demeans the suggestion that art is a public good. The initial appeal of that suggestion, I believe, lies in our sense that art makes a general contribution to the community as a whole, not just to those who enter into special commercial transactions to enjoy it, a contribution that is not extrinsic to aesthetic and intellectual experience, but one that, on the contrary, is exactly of that character.

The sense I report—that art and culture have intrinsic benefits for the public as a whole—rests on an assumption that is familiar and sound: that culture is a seamless web, that high culture and popular culture are not distinct but influence one another reciprocally. By general culture I do not just mean, though I mean to include, popular novels and plays and music. I mean also the whole range of diction and trope and style available within a community, as these are displayed in every aspect of communication from reporting and televizing public and athletic events to advertising campaigns. I mean, in short, the general intellectual environment in which we all live.

The influence of high culture on general or popular culture is reciprocated; but we should concentrate on the influence the former exerts on the latter and notice the various dimensions of that influence. High culture provides popular culture with form: musical comedy and television thrillers alike exploit genres first developed in opera and novel. It provides popular culture with reference: the working vocabulary of our community is saturated with specific reference to Oedipus, Hamlet, Carmen. (Hair-curling equipment is called "Carmen," for example, and decorated with a rose and advertised on television through the Toreador Song.) As a complement, high culture provides general culture with resonance. Specific references, such as the reference to Carmen, supply not just a convenient set of ideas easily invoked, but a set of ideas valuable exactly because they are identified as belonging to high culture and therefore as having a distinct aesthetic value.

All this might be summarized in the familiar phrase: spillover. It seems an encouraging start to an argument whose end may be the justification of state support for high culture. Because high culture, like vaccination, provides spillover benefits to the public at large, most of whom do not engage in the specific commercial transactions that finance it, state support is necessary to prevent the community's having less than it really wants of high culture because of the freerider (or free-clinger) problem. Unfortunately there are grave flaws in this argument, which are, taken together, fatal to it in this original form.

The first is the problem of time lag. In the standard examples of public goods, like clean air and military defense, the people who will pay for these goods through their taxes, if the state supplies them, are for the most part the very people who will benefit. If the state supports high culture in order to secure spillover benefits

for the general intellectual culture of the community as a whole, on the other hand, we cannot be confident that those who will pay the cost will reap the benefit, for the impact may be long enough delayed so that the main beneficiaries belong to a different generation of taxpayers. This objection, by itself, need not be fatal to our argument. It might be countered by using the public-good argument to support, not a one-lime state contribution to art, paid for by those who do not receive the major benefit, but a continuing program of contribution, so that each generation might be said to pay for benefits to the next, and each will both give and receive.

The second problem compounds the first, however. This is the problem of indeterminacy. Public officials can predict, perhaps with some confidence, how any particular level of public expense on military defense will improve security and so give the public what collectively it wants, and how any particular device or program for combating pollution will affect the quality of the air people breathe. But though we know that a decision to have a great many more productions of grand opera or larger collections of Renaissance paintings or more advanced university courses in classical literature will affect the general intellectual climate a generation hence, we have no way of predicting, even roughly, what genres or tropes or references it will add to that climate. It is in the nature of the transfer from high to general culture that such effects depend on judgments and reactions and developments that would be worthless because mechanical if they could be predicted. This fact weakens my original public-good argument for state support for the arts in a fundamental way. If we cannot predict what impact a public program will have on people's lives in the future, how can we justify that program as helping to give them what they really want?

The third difficulty is more fundamental yet. Any public-good argument requires some degree of information about what the public would be willing to spend to secure the benefit in question. In conventional examples—military defense and clean air—economists have difficulty devising techniques for identifying this sum once the market has been dismissed as inaccurate. But they are encouraged to search for these techniques because they assume, reasonably enough, that the community as a whole does want military security and clean air at *some* substantial price. The difficulty is one of accuracy and refinement. The parallel assumption needed for a public-good argument for art—that the community wants a popular or general culture of a certain character—is not only problematical; it may well be incoherent.

The intellectual culture of a community exerts such a profound influence over the preferences and values of its members that the question of whether and how much they would prefer a different culture to the one they have becomes at best deeply mysterious. I can explain why by beginning with a dramatic and improbable example. Imagine some cultural tragedy in which whole types of aesthetic experience familiar to us have wholly disappeared: no one has any idea, for example, of combining music and drama in the form we call opera. We could not say that people living in that culturally impoverished state would mind. They could not, after all, miss opera or regret not having it. Part of their situation, an aspect of their impoverished culture, would be that they would not have the capacity to mind, miss, or regret. What sense does it make, then, to say that if we do not preserve opera for them, we would be denying them something they want?

We would certainly want to say that they are missing something, that their lives are impoverished in some way compared to ours. But that is very different. It is not their judgment about their lives, which is what the economic approach in general and the public-goods argument in particular requires, but rather *our* judgment about their lives. We might want to say: If they knew what they were missing, they would miss it. But that is saying that if they did want it, they would want it—which is true but unhelpful. Someone may say: They would in any case want pleasure, and they would have more pleasure if they had opera. But this won't do. Set aside the thorny question whether it is always (or ever) right to say that people want pleasure. Set aside the question whether we can measure pleasure in the way this suggestion assumes. How can we say that people whose culture has developed without opera, and is therefore different from ours in countless other ways, would have less pleasure from what their culture does provide than we have from our own? We, who know opera, take pleasure in it— or some of us do—and we would be pained at suddenly finding it unavailable. But this is because the structure of our culture has that consequence for people fully immersed in it, and we can draw no conclusions about the hedonic states of people whose culture is entirely different. A taste for opera is in this way unlike some raw material—oil—that future generations might have to do without. If we assume their desires are much like our own—they want heat and light and transportation— we can say that not having oil gives them less of what they want, even if they have never heard of oil. But we cannot make a parallel assumption about people whose culture is unlike ours: we cannot say their desires are otherwise like our own, because the desires now in question are those produced by and bound up in the culture we assume they do not have.

Nor does it help if we abandon speculating about future generations and simply ask whether we ourselves would be willing collectively to pay any particular price to retain some valued part of our culture. For very much the same problem arises anyway. Suppose we ask, for example, whether our community would rather have the present richness and diversity of its general culture or more and better public parks. We have no way of approaching this question intelligently. The value public parks have for us and the ways in which we find value in them depend greatly on our culture. Parks would have very different meaning and value for us if we had no cultural tradition of romantic landscape, for example, a tradition that began in high culture, though it is now carried largely by general culture, including advertising. So the choice just offered is spurious: we would be assuming our present culture in valuing something we could only have, by hypothesis, by giving that culture up. Since our intellectual environment provides the spectacles through which we identify experiences as valuable, it cannot sensibly be put on the scales as one of the experiences it identifies, to be weighed against others and found more or less valuable than they.

These are dramatic examples, but the point also holds when the aspects or features of culture supposedly being valued are less comprehensive, more a matter of tone or degree. Imagine opera, not disappearing entirely without a trace, but losing its edge and excellence and general seriousness, no longer being performed well or in state, no longer being thought a matter of the highest art worth enormous sacrifice to perfect, in short, no longer being taken so seriously. This would be at once a change in the quality of an art and also a change in how much people want quality in that art, and these would not be separate and distinct changes. We are no more able, just because the stakes are not so high, to separate what is being valued from the social and personal apparatus being used to value it. This is the final blow to efforts to construct a public-good argument on the spillover effects of high culture. That argument cannot work without some way to identify, or at least make reasonable judgments about, what people—in the present or future—want by way of culture; and culture is too fundamental, too basic to our schemes of value, to make questions of that kind intelligible. Our problem is not one of discovery but of sense.

This essay began with the familiar story of opposition between the economic approach and the lofty approach as alternate ways to puzzle about public support for the arts. I said that the economic approach, at first glance, seemed to argue against public support; but I undertook to consider whether, on a closer look, the economic approach might favor it instead. That hope was encouraged by an apparent analogy between the public benefits of private transactions in art and familiar examples of public goods like military defense and clean-air campaigns. The analogy failed, but not in a way that reinstates the economic approach as the opponent of public support. On the contrary, all the difficulties in the claim that economics smiles on public support are equally difficulties in the opposing claim, with which we began, that economics frowns on it. The difficulties are symmetrical for both the positive and the negative claim. Nothing I said about the three problems of time lag, indeterminacy, and incoherence indicates that the public does not want what it would receive through public support. Or that the market, uncontaminated by any subsidy, is the best test of what the public does want at the price. My argument, if sound, justifies a much more radical and interesting conclusion, which is that the economic approach is simply unavailable either way as a test of whether art should be publicly supported or at what level. The issue of public support lies beneath or beyond the kinds of tastes, preferences, and values that can sensibly be deployed in an economic analysis.

Where, then, do we stand? We began with two approaches, the economic and the lofty; the first is now deemed unavailable, so presumably we are left with the second. But my argument, particularly with respect to the indeterminacy of prediction, seems to challenge the usefulness of the lofty approach as well. Once we acknowledge that the main impact of any program of aid to high culture will be, for most people and in the long run, its impact on general culture, and also that it is next to impossible to predict the details of that impact, the argument that we must aid culture to make people's lives better lives seems a shot in the dark, an article of faith. It suddenly appears that we have no argument at all, either way, and it is time to regroup. It is time to notice a distinction I have so far left latent: the distinction between two consequences our culture has for us. It provides the particular paintings, performances, and novels, designs, sports, and thrillers that we value and take delight in; but it also provides the structural frame that makes aesthetic values of that sort possible, that makes them values for us. We can use this distinction to define an approach to the problem of public support for the arts that is not the economic, and yet is different from the more unattractive versions, at least, of the lofty.

My suggestion is this. We should identify the structural aspects of our general culture as themselves worthy of attention. We should try to define a rich cultural structure, one that multiplies distinct possibilities or opportunities of value, and count ourselves trustees for protecting the richness of our culture for those who will live their lives in it after us. We cannot say that in so doing we will give them more pleasure, or provide a world they will prefer as against alternative worlds we could otherwise create. That is the language of the economic approach, and it is unavailable here. We can, however, insist—how can we deny this?—that it is better for people to have complexity and depth in the forms of life open to them, and then pause to see whether, if we act on that principle, we are open to any objection of elitism or paternalism.

Now let me concentrate on the structure of culture, the possibilities it allows, rather than on discrete works or occasions of art. The center of a community's cultural structure is its shared language. A language is neither a private nor a public good as these are technically defined; it is inherently social, as these are not, and as a whole it generates our ways of valuing and so is not itself an object of valuation. But language has formal similarities to what I called a mixed public good. Someone can exclude others, by relatively inexpensive means, from what he or she writes or says on any particular occasion. People cannot, however, be excluded from the language as a whole; at least it would be perverse to exclude them because, from the point of view of those who use a language, free riders are better than no riders. And the private transactions in language—the occasions of private or controlled speech—collectively determine what the shared language is. The books that we write and read, the education we provide and receive, the millions of other daily trans-actions in language we conduct, many of them commercial, all of these in the long run determine what language we have. We are all beneficiaries or victims of what is done to the language we share.

A language can diminish; some are richer and better than others. It barely makes sense to say that people in later generations would prefer not to have had their language diminished in some particular way, by losing some particular structural opportunity. They would lack the vocabulary in which to express—that is to say, have—that regret. Nor does it make much more sense to say that they would prefer to have a language richer in opportunities than they now have. No one can want opportunities who has no idea what these are opportunities of. Nevertheless, it is perfectly sensible to say that they would be worse off were their language to lack opportunities that ours offers. Of course, in saying this, we claim to know what is in their interest, what would make their lives better.

Is this paternalism? Now we need more distinctions. Paternalism is primitive when those in charge act in defiance of the preferences of those they govern, though supposedly in their interests. The police make people wear seat belts or avoid unorthodox sexual associations, in spite of their driving or sexual tastes. Paternalism is more sophisticated when those in charge try, not to oppose preferences already established, but to create preferences they think desirable and avoid those they think harmful. This is the paternalism of much moral education, for example, and the justification of much censorship. Protecting language from structural debasement or decay is paternalism of neither of these sorts. It does not, like primitive paternalism, oppose anyone's preferences. Nor does it, like sophisticated paternalism, aim to

create or forestall preferences identified in advance as good or bad. On the contrary, it allows a greater rather than a lesser choice, for that is exactly the respect in which we believe people are better off with a richer than a poorer language. Our dislike of paternalism furnishes a reason for, rather than against, naming ourselves trustee of the structure of linguistic opportunity.

The connection between these obser-vations about language and our problem about art and the humanities is obvious. For the structural aspect of our artistic culture is nothing more than a language, a special part of the language we now share. The possibilities of art, of finding aesthetic value in a particular kind of representation or isolation of objects, depend on a shared vocabulary of tradition and convention. This part of our language could have been much poorer. Suppose no one had ever found value in narrative invention, that is, in a story. Our language would not then have had the complex resources it does to distinguish between a novel and a lie. Then no one could suddenly, just out of creative inspiration, write a novel. There would be no resources available for him to recognize value in a false narrative, for others to receive what he offered them in this mode. The same point obviously enough, can be made about painting and sculpture and music and painting. And, for that matter, about history and philosophy and other humane studies as well.

Though we cannot imagine our culture losing any of the basic vocabulary of art entirely—we can scarcely imagine losing the power to distinguish fiction from lie—we can all too easily imagine less dramatic adverse change. For example, we now have the conceptual equipment to find aesthetic value in historical and cultural continuity. We can, and do, find various forms of quotation from the history of our culture exciting; we find value in the idea that contemporary art reworks themes or styles of other ages or is rich in allusion to them, that the past is with us, reworked, in the present. But this complex idea is as much dependent on a shared practice as is the idea of narrative fiction. It can be sustained only so long as that practice continues in a lively form, only so long the past is kept alive among us, in the larger culture that radiates out from the museum and university into concentric circles embracing the experience of a much larger community. The very possibility of finding aesthetic value in continuity depends on our continuing to achieve success and interest in continuity; and this in turn may well require a rich stock of illustrative and comparative collections that can only or best be maintained in museums and explored in universities and other academies. If it is right that the community as a whole, and not just those who use these institutions directly, shares and employs the structural possibilities of continuity and reference, something like the public-good argument for state support of such institutions is rehabilitated.

The language of culture can grow impoverished in a second way, not by losing particular dimensions of value, like continuity, but by becoming less innovative, by ceasing to develop or elaborate new dimensions. Our own culture has had moments of particular originality, when a use of language or a kind of presentation is suddenly claimed for art, as valuable in the aesthetic dimension, and the claim succeeds. Our ability to innovate is based on tradition in two ways, or on two levels. We must have a tradition *of* innovation, and we must have particular forms of art sufficiently open-ended and amenable to reinterpretation so that continuity can be preserved *through* innovation, so that people can see what is new as nevertheless sufficiently connected to what they already

regard as a mode of art, sufficiently connected to be embraced as falling within the same overall mode of experience. These traditions can languish into an academic or conventionalist settlement when the boundaries of what can count as art are drawn too tightly, and art degenerates into what is merely familiar or only pretty or, worse still, what is useful for some nonaesthetic goal. The state of art in some tyrannies is a depressing reminder of what is possible by way of degeneration.

We have much less difficulty in imagining changes that count as the decay rather than the extinction of some main branch of culture. Our question was, Can there be any objection, in principle, to accepting the postulate and the program I have described: that people are better off when the opportunities their culture provides are more complex and diverse, and that we should act as trustees for the future of the complexity of our own culture? We have seen, but it bears repeating, that the economic approach and the democratic values that approach represents offer no objection. Using state funds in that way does not deny the future public what it wants. I noted two standing objections to the lofty approach to state support for the arts: paternalism and elitism. If state subsidy has as its purpose protecting structure rather than providing particular aesthetic events, the charge of paternalism is defused. So is the charge of elitism, because structure affects almost everyone's life, and in such fundamental and unpredictable ways that we lack the conceptual equipment to measure who benefits most from the various possibilities and ideas they generate.

Once, long ago in this argument, it looked black for state support for the arts. Now it suddenly looks too rosy. Can we really end the argument simply by announcing that the point of state support is to protect the structure of our intellectual culture? No, of course not. We must earn, not just claim, the structural description, then show what kind and level of support that description justifies in the circumstances. We have changed the terms of the argument, but not won it in advance.

How much state support can be justified in this way? One point needs to be made at once. The argument at best justifies public officials' placing the protection of culture among their goals; it does not justify their making it the main or most pressing goal. They must still fix priorities about how much to spend for art and the humanities as against competing claims that will include, for some, military defense and, for others, social justice. It is far beyond my subject to consider how these priorities should be arranged. But the choice between art and the rest is not the choice between luxury and necessity, grandeur and duty. We inherited a cultural structure, and we have some duty, out of simple justice, to leave that structure at least as rich as we found it.

My argument, however, is meant to show that art qualifies for state support, not to set floors or ceilings to that support. But art qualifies only on a certain premise: that slate support is designed to protect structure rather than to promote any particular content for that structure at any particular time. So the ruling star of state subsidy should be this goal: it should look to the diversity and innovative quality of the culture as a whole rather than to (what public officials take to be) excellence in particular occasions of that culture. The rest is strategy and tactics: maxims and rules-of-thumb made to be broken. In general, aid should be given in the form of indiscriminate subsidies, such as tax exemptions for donations to cultural institutions rather than as specific subsidies to particular institutions, though not when private donation turns out to work against rather than for diversity and innovation. When discriminations are made, they should favor forms of art that are too expensive to be sustained by wholly private, market transactions. If these include (as I think they do) expensive comprehensive collections of paintings or comprehensive studies that the market would not support, like much of the programs of great universities, then it can be no objection that only a relatively few people who are already privileged in various ways will benefit directly and immediately. I do not mean that we should be insensitive to the appeal of programs with other aims, in particular, programs that try to secure a wider audience for the arts and scholarship. That ambition remains important and urgent. It can be defended in many ways, including pointing out how this, too, helps protect the fragile structure of our culture.

CAN GOVERNMENT FUNDING OF THE ARTS BE JUSTIFIED THEORETICALLY?

Noël Carroll

The question addressed in this article—Can government art support be justified theoretically?—might elicit an abrupt response: "Perhaps not, but so what, that is, why should it require a theoretical justification?" If, in a democracy, the citizens favor public arts funding, then public arts funding is what we should have. But the suspicion is abroad that the citizenry does not favor the use of public money for arts funding. The likelihood that Americans may not endorse arts funding indicates that some justification, in terms of the right and proper activity of the state (i.e., a theoretical justification), would be demanded if state funding were to continue in a context of public disapproval. Of course, we cannot claim to know that the majority does disapprove of government arts funding. Rather, that prospect merely recommends that justifications be prepared. Furthermore, charges, quite plausible ones, have been

From: *Journal of Aesthetic Education*, vol. 21, no. 1, Spring 1987. Copyright © 1987 Board of trustees of the University of Illinois. Used with permission of the University of Illinois Press.

made that public arts funding primarily benefits the already advantaged. And this suggests yet another reason why a theoretical justification ought to be produced. The purpose of this article is to explore various avenues for justifying arts funding. Our results are mixed. Some grounds for government arts funding are found, but it is noted that in embracing these justifications untoward consequences may be incurred. Thus, it is urged that we refrain from government funding of the arts because the effects of such funding, when guided by the kinds of justifications available, would be deleterious to the art world. However, the conclusions of this article are provisional; there is no reason to believe that someone may not construct better justifications for government arts funding than those examined here.

The question, Are there theoretical grounds for government arts funding? is unwieldy and needs trimming. First, what does "funding" refer to? Funding can be either direct or indirect. One might say that there was government arts funding in this country before 1965 but that it took indirect forms, including land grants, tax exemptions to educational and cultural institutions such as museums, and tax advantages for private donations of art to the public.[1] Concern here is not with indirect funding but with the justification of direct state funding of the arts.

But still the scope is too broad to be manageable, because there are so many different kinds of arts-related activities with which direct state funding may be involved. Much government funding is aimed at what might be thought of as the preservation of culture. It supports museums and repertory companies and is intent on keeping our culture intact. Other objectives of government funding target community art centers, regional theaters, and school programs. And funding may also be directed to professional artists for the purpose of enabling them to produce new works of art. This latter type of funding is the sort with which this article is concerned. Whereas funding of museums looks to the past of our culture, funding artists is prospective. It is not a matter of preserving culture, but of *creating* culture. The preservation of culture, of course, is involved with education, which appears to be a legitimate realm of state activity. And, furthermore, though even more vaguely, art preservation keeps us aware of who we have been, which knowledge is relevant to us in our practical decisions about who we shall become. But it is not so easy to see the way in which prospective funding—i.e., support for the production of contemporary art—can be defended as educational in terms of the state's responsibilities in this arena in the way the preservation might be. Bluntly, contemporary art is not our heritage yet; nor is it clear how much of it will be. So even if funding for the purpose of preservation falls within the state's educational responsibilities, prospective arts funding calls for some other kind

of theoretical justification, that is, a justification in terms of the way in which prospective arts funding can be seen as implementing one or more of the proper functions of the state.

Clearly, commissioning artists to design stamps and government buildings is a legitimate government activity. So our question is whether state funding of the production of new art that is not connected to state projects is also legitimate. Admittedly, the great bulk of governmental funding of the arts is not directed to artists. But the question is how even this admittedly small expenditure is to be funded. (Hereafter, "arts funding" refers only to this issue.)

Before proceeding, a word or two about the use of "state" in this discussion is appropriate. . . . [O]ur question is addressed to pluralistic, democratic states which have fundamental commitments to protecting their citizens from harm—both foreign and domestic—and to securing the welfare of those within their boundaries, i.e., to providing some manner of generally economic assistance to individuals in need, where such needs are connected to the individuals' capacity to maintain a livelihood.[2] Such states are also committed to the protection of the civic institutions upon which democracy rests.

It is important to stress that the viewpoint of this essay is not based on opposition to the idea that states have responsibilities to the welfare of all persons within their borders. . . . Full acceptance of the principle that the state, in our conception of it, has welfare obligations needs to be emphasized here just because in discussions of art funding it is often assumed that if one has any doubts about the propriety of arts funding, one must also be skeptical about welfare. Welfare is a legitimate arena of state activity, but it is not clear that *all* prospective arts funding is . . . .

The discussion of proper state functions may suggest an avenue of justification for prospective arts funding, viz., welfare. If one agrees that the state has a responsibility to secure the welfare of its citizens, then one may be tempted to say that prospective arts funding is a means by which the state secures the welfare of those within its borders. But "welfare," as it applies to state activity, refers to assistance to individuals in need of the basic goods that comprise a livelihood. Is it plausible to suppose that prospective arts funding provides some such goods?

A conclusive answer would require a full theory of needs, which, unfortunately, we lack. But perhaps we can at least determine whether the products of prospective arts funding sound like the things we ordinarily think of as needs. On one reading, to say that someone needs X is to say that if she lacks it, she will suffer injury, sickness, madness, hunger, or avoidable death.[3] Does the production of contemporary artworks assist individuals in needful situations such as these? Would anyone be harmed, in any literal sense of the term, if prospective arts funding were discontinued? Am I harmed if painter X does not execute the series she would have created had she received a state grant?

Of course, defining basic needs in terms of harms has limitations. But suppose we define welfare needs in terms of the amount of goods and services sufficient to raise an individual from his present state to somewhere above the poverty line.[4] If this is how we conceive of the welfare jurisdiction of the state, then it is difficult to see how prospective arts funding has anything to do with welfare.

Undoubtedly, the picture presented thus far involves thinking of the welfare of nonartists. Our rhetorical questions really ask, "What nonartists will be harmed, in a basic, literal sense, if they do not have the opportunity to see so-and-so's planned series due to a lack of government funding?" Or, even more ridiculously, "What nonartist will fail to be raised above the poverty line should so-and-so's proposed series not be funded?" It may be charged that the case has been rigged. Haven't we forgotten about the welfare responsibilities of the state to artist so-and-so? Isn't it possible that artist so-and-so will fail to rise above the poverty line without funding?

The problem with these new questions, however, is that if artist so-and-so has a legitimate welfare need, then the state will have the responsibility to assist her. That is, if a state is meeting its basic welfare responsibilities to everyone, then there is no reason to propose prospective arts funding as a further aspect of the state's welfare function. Of course, this raises issues about the relation of welfare to the active promotion of employment by the state, and we will come back to that matter.

Some writers who attempt to connect state arts support to the state's welfare function introduce a concept of "aesthetic welfare." "Aesthetic welfare," in turn, is defined as "all the aesthetic levels of the experience of members of the society at a given time."[5] It is then suggested that there is a prima facie government duty to preserve the aesthetic wealth of society where that wealth—pictures, plays, and so forth—is what gives rise to aesthetic welfare. It is not certain, however, that this particular notion of aesthetic welfare helps the case for prospective arts funding since it may be that, if there were such a prima facie duty, retrospective arts funding might suffice to discharge it.

Also, one must question whether the connection between "aesthetic welfare" and the concept of welfare relevant to government activity is really unequivocal. First, "aesthetic welfare" doesn't correlate with definable needs, especially basic needs; nor does being below the poverty line imply being aesthetically disadvantaged. And clearly promoting individuals' aesthetic welfare will not raise them over the poverty line. Moreover, the state's welfare responsibility under this conception of aesthetic welfare doesn't seem to be directly connected to individuals but is a matter of ensuring that there will be a large number of aesthetic objects around so that people can have aesthetic experiences if they want them. The state is to ensure the permanent possibility of high levels of what is called aesthetic welfare but might better be called aesthetic well-being. This well-being is to be secured for society at large, construed additively, whereas the state's welfare responsibilities are discharged toward particular persons, viz., anyone in need. Thus the notion of "aesthetic welfare" appears not to refer to welfare of the kind that defines the state's proper domain of activity; it is merely a homonymous term that, though sounding like the concept employed in the discussion of the state's welfare responsibilities, is actually quite separate. Of course, we have not adequately dealt with the notion of aesthetic needs, but will turn to it shortly.

In the discussion of welfare, it may be objected that our perspective is too narrow. By speaking of basic needs and poverty lines, we have restricted the compass of the welfare activities of the state to aid in desparate situations and to matters of life support. But must the state's welfare jurisdiction be so constrained? It might be argued that apart from assisting those in need, the state's welfare function also includes benefitting the populace, supplying human goods even to people above the poverty line, thus enabling people to flourish. Were this the case, the defender of prospective arts funding could argue that such a practice would be justified in virtue of the state's responsibilities to benefit the populace, to promote as much good as possible.

First, if the state does have a responsibility to promote human goods over and above the responsibility to prevent harms, it is not obvious that this is best conceived of as part of its welfare responsibility. Perhaps it is rather an obligation to beneficence. Whether the state has such an obligation is an important question which we cannot answer now. Some might argue that the state has such obligations, but only after it has discharged all of its welfare obligations—no money for paintings until all the needy are assisted. Personally, I find this viewpoint compelling in our present circumstances.

There are, however, other arguments against state obligations to beneficence that also bear serious consideration. In pluralist societies—such as we envision modern democracies to be—that which constitutes human good over and above welfare goods is essentially contested. If the state, given conditions of scarce resources, promotes some goods rather than others, it is unjustifiably favoring the proponents of one good over the proponents of a rival good who may, in fact, deny that the good so favored is a good at all. Of course, the problem disappears if we think that the state's obligation to beneficence extends to promoting every human good, every kind of benefit that facilitates human flourishing or that is believed to contribute to human flourishing. But this seems implausible. Even if the state has legitimate obligations of beneficence, there remain questions of the extent of these obligations even where scarce resources are not at issue. Assuming an obligation of beneficence, we may still argue that the state is not obligated to administer every human benefit to its populace. . . .

The state, even supposing a legitimate function of beneficence, will not be expected to deliver every possible benefit to its citizenry. This observation, of course, is relevant to the question of prospective arts funding, because if the proponent of such funding invokes beneficence in defense of it, we shall still want some demonstration that art is the kind of benefit the state has a duty to supply. . . .

Of course, the preceding discussion of benefit will dissatisfy those who feel that art is not merely a benefit to human life, but that it satisfies a human need, call it an aesthetic need. Often this belief is advanced through environmentalist metaphors. In the first annual report of the NEA, it was proclaimed that "we need to make our open spaces beautiful again. We must create an environment in which our youth will be encouraged to pursue the discipline and craft of the arts. We must not only support our artistic institutions, both national and local, but we must also make the arts part of our daily life so that they become an essential part of our existence."[6]

The underlying spirit of this plan seems to suggest that just as the government has an obligation to forestall the deterioration of the ecosystem, so there is an obligation to reverse the deterioration of the aesthetic environment. Human animals have aesthetic needs; environments replete with aesthetic and expressive qualities satisfy them. Perhaps it will be argued that environments bereft of such qualities, or possessing them in miniscule degrees, result in some sort of psychic tension, ranging from irritation to alienation. Miles of gas stations, fast-food restaurants, used-car lots, body shops—the strip phenomenon—present an impoverished aesthetic habitat that has unsettling

psychic consequences. Similarly, the private sphere, flooded with tawdry, mass-produced consumer goods, is aesthetically deprived in a way that is psychically unnerving. Vigorous arts funding is urged as a countermeasure, including prospective arts funding, which presumably will provide some of the objects we need to restore or perhaps to create the kind of aesthetic environment that promotes our psychic health. Thus, prospective arts funding would be warranted on the grounds that it implements the state's obligations in regard to the health of its citizens.

This argument is not implausible. Of course, it requires "fleshing out." Before it can be accepted, research would have to be undertaken to show that we do indeed have aesthetic needs whose frustration results in some form of psychic discomfort. And if this could not be demonstrated, this particular argument would falter.

But suppose it is the case that there are such aesthetic needs. What would that suggest about prospective arts funding? It would imply that we should do further research in order to determine the kinds of art that satisfy whatever aesthetic needs the earlier research identified. We might then go on to fund the kind of programs and the kind of art that satisfies those needs. But note that this will not imply support for any kind of art whatsoever. It only grounds support for those projects which function to alleviate aesthetic needs or which we predict are probable to alleviate aesthetic needs. Not all art will have this causal capacity. For example, Duchamp's *In Advance of a Broken Arm* as well as much Punk Art will not have this capacity, nor will films like Buñuel's *The Andalusian Dog*. Thus, prospective arts funding of works such as these will not be justified by an aesthetic need argument.

The problem here, of course, involves what is meant by "aesthetic." It is not synonymous with "art." Generally, it is associated with the beautiful and the sublime, or it is associated with the qualitative appearance of things. An aesthetic need, under this reading, would be a need for experiences of the beautiful, the sublime, or for the experience of objects and environments with marked expressive qualities such as warmth, friendliness, or joyfulness. Much art, including, significantly, much contemporary art, is not dedicated to producing aesthetic experience. Indeed, much contemporary art is even avowedly anti-aesthetic. If an artist makes a junkyard piece to portray modern life, it seems curious that he should expect funding on the basis of alleviating aesthetic privations. Nor is it obvious that every expressive quality projectible by a work of art will have the equilibrating effect presumed by the aesthetic need argument. Works marked by turmoil, horror, anguish, and so on are not prima facie defensible under the aesthetic need argument. The point is that even if the aesthetic need argument is acceptable, it will not support prospective arts funding as we know it. It will only support funding of those prospective artworks with high probability of bringing about equilibriating aesthetic experiences. Nonaesthetic, anti-aesthetic, reflexive, and certain darkly expressive artworks will not be defensible in the name of aesthetic experience.

If the aesthetic need argument gives us the means for justifying prospective arts funding, it also seems to have the unfortunate consequence that it only warrants the funding of certain kinds of art—the art of the beautiful, the sublime, and that expressive of psychically equilibrating qualities. If no further justification can be found, the consequence of this is that the state can only fund a certain type of art. Artists pursuing certain nonaesthetic aims cannot be funded by the state. But proponents of art funding, lovers of art, and artists with nonaesthetic projects should be disturbed by this. For if the government places large investments behind one type of art, the evolution of the art world will undoubtedly be affected. Whole avenues of artistic development will appear less viable than the production of aesthetic art. And from the contemporary art world's point of view, this kind of prospective arts funding might be regarded as having a regressive effect overall.

At this point, it may be claimed that the relevant need to consider is not an aesthetic need but a need for art. All societies, it might be said, have artlike practices—i.e., symbolizing practices of some sort—which suggests that art of some type answers a human need. Next, the idea will be advanced that in modern industrial societies, art will disappear if the government does not support it. Thus, without government support the conditions necessary for satisfying our need for art cannot be sustained. Perhaps prospective arts funding can be endorsed as a corollary to this via the claim that the need for art includes a need for new art. And if the state does not fund new art, no one else will.

Of course, this is an empirical claim, and a dubious one at that. The arts flourished in democratic societies before the advent of direct public funding; there is no reason to suppose that they will disappear without the direct government funding of new artwork. Where people are interested in art, there will still be an audience to support new work. Were there no audience whatsoever, it would be difficult to determine on what basis the government would justify funding new art. Moreover, in advanced capitalist societies at least, big businesses are attracted to arts patronage because projecting the kind of upwardly mobile profile associated with interest in the arts attracts upwardly mobile investors. One could go on elaborating considerations that count against the disappearance-of-art thesis. But perhaps what is most important to say about it is that, at best, it is worried not about the disappearance of art per se, but only of certain types of art, viz., what for want of a better label we call high art. Popular art—movies, TV, pop music—will not disappear if prospective arts funding is discontinued. So it is not the case that our society will be deprived of art, including new art, without prospective arts funding. Hence if there is a need for art, it will not be frustrated. On the other hand, it is unlikely that there is a human need for our kind of high art. But, in any event, it is also unlikely that our kind of high art is about to disappear if prospective arts funding is halted, though the assumption that it will seems implicit in too many of the arguments of proponents of such funding. Of course, sans funding, high art might be produced at a diminished rate. But here the burden of proof rests with the proponent of funding to show what social evil results from a diminished rate of high art production.

One practical justification for arts funding is that it may function as an economic stimulant, promoting prosperity by, for example, attracting tourists. Insofar as prospective arts funding can be pegged to the state of the economy, it would appear to be a legitimate state operation, since the maintenance of a functioning economy is related to the state's welfare responsibilities. Needless to say, it is often difficult to imagine the way in which grants to individual artists for new works—as opposed to city art centers— can engineer economic well-being; but there is no reason to think that such a connection could not be made in principle. Of course, an economic stimulation argument identifies the value of arts funding not

with aesthetic or artistic value, but with economic instrumentality.[7] But despite this, the economic stimulation argument seems acceptable, although it can only be mobilized where certain constraints are respected. Where prospective arts funding is employed to stimulate tourism or some other form of economic activity in a given area, the state must be convinced that no alternative form of intervention of comparable cost would yield greater prosperity in that area. Furthermore, where national rather than local stimulation is at issue, the nation state must supply some rationale why it is undertaking to stimulate tourism in one geo-graphical region rather than another. But when these conditions can be met, no obvious barrier to prospective arts funding appears to remain, though it is uncertain how often these criteria can be satisfied.

Connecting prospective arts funding to economic policy suggests another means for justifying state support, viz., employment. If state funding is not forthcoming, then many artists will be unemployed. Unemployment is clearly a matter of concern for the state. The massive unemployment of black inner-city youths is one of the great tragedies of our society, and we must demand that the state do something about it. Many would be in favor of New Deal-type programs to alleviate the problem. Can we mount a similar argument in order to show that prospective arts funding can be seen as a way of averting massive unemployment among artist? My inclination is to think not. Artists do not seem to constitute a group that is comparable to black inner-city youths. Questions of justice and equal opportunity do not seem to bear on the issue of artistic unemployment. Moreover, the artistic unemployment we might envision involves artists' unemployment as artists rather than their unemployment simpliciter. That is, I may not be able to support my family as an unemployed poet; but that does not mean that I can't do it in another way, say, as a journalist or a copywriter. It does not seem to me that the state's responsibilities in regard to the unemployed extend to guaranteeing that everyone have the job he or she most desires. The case of artistic unemployment involves people not able to pursue the line of work they most covet, while innercity unemployment involves people excluded from the work force altogether. Our belief that the state has clear responsibilities in the case of inner-city unemployment cannot ground claims to similar duties in regard to artistic unemployment. If artists are unemployed, the state will have certain duties to them, though it is not clear that those duties include finding them employment as artists.

It may be suggested that a certain conception of fairness can be used to ground government art support. If a given government subsidizes the building of sports arenas, then, in all fairness, arts production should also be supported. If the government facilitates the pursuits of sports fans, then it should, as a matter of treating people equally, also facilitate the pursuits of arts fans, perhaps by means of supporting the creation of new art. Of course, this argument presupposes a context in which some leisure activity, such as sports, is being subsidized. But what, in such a context, justifies the subsidizing of sports? If nothing does, then perhaps what is required is that neither sports nor the arts be subsidized.

Insofar as one objects to sports subsidies, one must forgo art subsidies. Of course, a subsidy for a sport might be defended on the grounds that it stimulates the economy of an area; but then arts funding can, in principle, be similarly defended. Again, it does seem correct to

say that if a majority, call them sports fans, demand sports funding in the face of opposition by a minority, Call them arts lovers, then fairness urges that the leisure activity of the latter group also be supported, though perhaps not to the same extent. The deeper question, however, is whether any leisure activity should be supported. For if any is supported, then all should be in proportion to the allegiance to that leisure activity in the society. And yet this appears extreme. Suppose skateboard racers wanted a national stadium. Does that seem to be something for which the state should pay by levying taxes on the rest of us? Obviously, even wilder examples could be concocted—hop-scotch stadia, a coliseum for Bocci Ball, a national gallery of toothpick sculpture. The advancement of the leisure professions may just not be an area the state should enter at all.

One of the earliest arguments in favor of government support of the arts is that the arts perform a moralizing function. During the period of the Second Empire, in nineteenth-century France, the Orpheon, a working-class choral society, was sponsored by Napoleon's government on the grounds that it would introduce the proletariat to "moral amusements," which would not only cultivate their tastes but "moralize" them.[8] Similarly in this country in the nineteenth century the belief was widespread that through art the populace could be morally improved. These beliefs influenced both school reform and the founding of the great American museums.[9] In the era of state funding of the arts, faith in their potential to make people more moral—faith in the civilizing power of the arts—suggests a line of justification for the prospective funding of art. For surely the maintenance of the moral order in society is a legitimate state concern. Thus, if art can function as a means of improving morality, then the state is justified in supporting it. If art provides moral exemplars or deepens conscience, the state, it would seem, can avail itself of the devices of art to instill moral behavior in its populace.

One aspect of art that is related to its capacity to engender moral improvement is the tendency of certain kinds of art to develop our sympathies for others. Some art enables us to see the world from different points of view, thus promoting not only the acquisition of a formal requirement of morality, but also enabling us to grasp vicariously the situations of different classes, races, creeds, and genders. Art, then, can foster greater tolerance within society and thereby bolster the moral order. A strengthened moral order is a goal that the state legitimately pursues, given, among other things, its responsibility to prevent harm from befalling its populace. That is, one way to prevent harm is to prevent people from harming each other by making them more moral. If art can serve the accomplishment of this goal, then the prospective funding of such art seems justified.

But this argument for prospective arts funding does have certain unhappy consequences. The argument assumes that art increases moral sympathies. We have no reason to dispute the contention that *some* art has this capacity. But it seems unlikely that all art functions this way. If the state is to justify its funding of art on moralizing grounds, then only that art which we can reasonably predict will increase moral sympathies can be funded. This will probably require some empirical research into the moral efficacy of different kinds of art. Art, indeed whole categories of art, that afford no moral uplift cannot be funded on the basis of this argument. Art that works against any increase in moral sympathy will also be problematic. Art devoted, for instance, to outraging the

bourgeoisie or politically partisan art is likely to be debarred from funding insofar as it instills divisiveness rather than tolerance. That is, in mobilizing this functionalist justification for arts funding, only grounds for certain types of arts funding have been secured. This raises problems like those encountered in our earlier discussion of the aesthetic environment argument. If the state is justified in funding only certain kinds of art and it enters the art world, putting its immense resources behind only moralizing kinds of art, then there is a great danger that the development of the art world will be skewed in certain directions. This violates our intuitions that the realm of art should be pluralist and relatively independent of considerations of social utility. Thus, though the state may be justified in funding certain types of art, we may be loath to have it exercise this prerogative because of the damage it would wreak upon art as we know it. Nor does it seem practicable to meet this objection by saying that the state should fund every type of art in order to fund the kinds of art it is justified to fund. For this will result in a kind of self-defeating schizophrenia: supporting anti-aesthetic art in order to support aesthetic art; supporting divisive art in order to support art that expands moral sympathies.

A recent argument in favor of public art support has been advanced by Ronald Dworkin. He draws a distinction between two dimensions of culture. Culture "provides the particular paintings, performances, and novels, designs, sports, and thrillers that we value and take delight in; but it also provides the structural frame that makes aesthetic values of that sort possible and makes them values for us."[10] This structural frame includes a wealth of associations, references, images, and contrasts, which, like language, supply us with the tools with which we forge and map our common life. Dworkin insists that it is better for people to have a complex and multifarious cultural framework and that we owe future generations at least as rich a cultural framework as the one we inherited. Both these values can be achieved by promoting the creation of innovative art. Government support in this area is necessary because it "helps protect the fragile structure of our culture."[11] Admittedly, Dworkin uses this argument to endorse indirect rather than direct arts support by the government. But he does countenance situations in which government support could be direct. And someone other than Dworkin might attempt to use this argument in favor of direct support.

At least two problems, however, beset this approach. First, there is the assumption that the structure of culture is fragile. We have encountered this before. But as an empirical supposition we have argued that its truth is far from obvious. Moreover, when we look at the structure of culture, we note that it comprises many ingredients beside art—social dances, children's games, fashion, sports, religion, indeed the whole gamut of our symbolizing activities. When we think of the twenties, we recall the flapper and the Charleston; perhaps in the future people will think of the eighties in terms of punk haircuts and break-dancing. These images become part and parcel of our ways of thinking; they are the very weave of our common culture. But it seems dubious to consider them to be fit beneficiaries of public funding. Yet if art deserves public funding because of its contribution to our cultural framework, so does anything else

that similarly contributes, including, potentially, every sort of symbolizing activity, and notably some outlandish ones: hoola-hoops, comic books, Billy Graham, the Watergate break-in; and so on.[12]

One criticism that is apt to be directed at this essay is that we have repeatedly discussed prospective arts funding in terms of things other than art, i.e., in terms of some good consequences which would justify such funding. One may feel that this completely misses the point. Art is good in itself and does not require further validation in virtue of the further consequences it abets.[13] It may be true, though one has one's doubts, that art is intrinsically good. But even if the production of art is intrinsically good, that, in and of itself, would not warrant state funding of the arts. For the state does not and, in some cases, should not be taken to have a role in the production of whatever we conceive to be an intrinsic good or even of whatever is an intrinsic good (if there are such things). State intervention in these matters calls for justification.

In conclusion, there do appear to be theoretical justifications for prospective government funding of art. The two strongest justifications seem to be those concerning the aesthetic environment and the moralizing effects of the arts. However, though these arguments are available, it is not clear that they should be acted upon. For they endorse the funding of only certain types of act. Government support for the arts guided strictly by these arguments may indeed disturb the structure of artistic production and perhaps destroy the art world as we know it.

Notes

1. Edward Banfield, *The Democratic Music* (New York: Basic Books, 1984), p. 4.
2. Carl Wellman, *Welfare Rights* (Totowa, NJ: Rowman and Littlefield, 1984), p. 30.
3. Joel Feinberg, *Social Philosophy* (Upper Saddle River, NJ: Prentice Hall, 1973), p. 111.
4. Derived from Wellman, *Welfare Rights,* p. 136.

5. Monroe C. Beardsley, "Aesthetic Welfare, Aesthetic Justice, and Educational Policy," in *The Aesthetic Point of View*, ed. M. Wreen and D. Callen (Ithaca, NY: Cornell University Press, 1982), pp. 113–14. Originally published in the *Journal of Aesthetic Education 7*, no. 4 (October 1973): 49–61.

6. Quoted in Banfield, *The Democratic Muse*, pp. 68–69.

7. A similar point is emphasized by William J. Baumol in his remarks in "IV. Panel Discussion: Public Support of the Arts," *Art and Law 9*, no. 2 (1985): 214–28. One kind of economic argument in favor of arts funding concerns the technical notion of a public good. I have not broached this issue directly in the article. Ronald Dworkin has dealt with the epistemological problems involved in considering art in this light in

"Can a Liberal State Support Art?" in his *A Matter of Principle* (Cambridge, MA: Harvard University Press, 1985), pp. 221–33. (This article is reprinted in *Art and Law 9*, no. 2 [1985].) I agree with Dworkin on this matter; for a differing view, see Baumol, "Public Support of the Arts."

8. Howard Becket, *Art Worlds* (Berkeley: University of California Press, 1982), pp. 181–82.

9. Banfield, *The Democratic Muse*, chaps. 4 and 5.

10. Dworkin, "Can a Liberal State Support Art?" p. 229.

11. Ibid., p. 233.

12. R. Nozick makes a related point in *Art and Law 9*, no. 2 (1985): 162–67.

13. T. Nagel seems to follow this line in ibid., pp. 236–39.

Study Questions for Section 2

1. Dworkin refers to the "fragile structure of our culture." What does he mean by this phrase? Is our culture structurally fragile?

2. Carrol raises two concerns about Dworkin's argument for state support for the arts. Are Carrol's concerns compelling? How might Dworkin reply?

3. Carrol considers an argument for state-supported sports competitions. How is state-supported art different from state-supported skateboarding? Or is it?

SECTION 3

PORNOGRAPHY

PORNOGRAPHY, OPPRESSION, AND FREEDOM: A CLOSER LOOK

Helen E. Longino

Introduction

The much-touted sexual revolution of the 1960s and 1970s not only freed various modes of sexual behavior from the constraints of social disapproval, but also made possible a flood of pornographic material. According to figures provided by WAVPM (Women Against Violence in Pornography and Media), the number of pornographic magazines available at newsstands has grown from zero in 1953 to forty in 1977, while sales of pornographic films in Los Angeles alone have grown from $15 million in 1969 to $85 million in 1976.[1]

Traditionally pornography was condemned as immoral because it presented sexually explicit material in a manner designed to appeal to "prurient interests" or a "morbid" interest in nudity and sexuality, material which furthermore lacked any redeeming social value and which exceeded "customary limits of candor." While these phrases, taken from a definition of "obscenity" proposed in the 1954 American Law Institute's *Model Penal Code*,[2] require some criteria of application

to eliminate vagueness, it seems that what is objectionable is the explicit description or representation of bodily parts or sexual behavior for the purpose of inducing sexual stimulation or pleasure on the part of the reader or viewer. This kind of objection is part of a sexual ethic that subordinates sex to procreation and condemns all sexual interactions outside of legitimated marriage. It is this code which was the primary target of the sexual revolutionaries in the 1960s, and which has given way in many areas to more open standards of sexual behavior.

One of the beneficial results of the sexual revolution has been a growing acceptance of the distinction between questions of sexual mores and questions of morality. This distinction underlies the old slogan, "Make love, not war," and takes harm to others as the defining characteristic of immorality. What is immoral is behavior which causes injury to or violation of another person or people. Such injury may be physical or it may be psychological. To cause pain to another, to lie to another, to hinder another in the exercise of her or his rights, to exploit another, to degrade another, to misrepresent and slander another are instances of immoral behavior. Masturbation or engaging voluntarily in sexual intercourse with another consenting adult of the same or the other sex, as long as neither injury nor violation of either individual or another is involved, is not immoral. Some sexual behavior is morally objectionable, but not because of its sexual character. Thus, adultery is immoral not because it involves sexual intercourse with someone to whom one is not legally married, but because it involves breaking a promise (of sexual and emotional fidelity to one's spouse). Sadistic, abusive, or forced sex is immoral because it injures and violates another.

The detachment of sexual chastity from moral virtue implies that we cannot condemn forms of sexual behavior merely because they strike us as distasteful or subversive of the Protestant work ethic, or because they depart from standards of behavior we have individually adopted. It has thus seemed to imply that no matter how offensive we might find pornography, we must tolerate it in the name of freedom from illegitimate repression. I wish to argue that this is not so, that pornography is immoral because it is harmful to people.

What is Pornography?

I define pornography as *verbal or pictorial explicit representations of sexual behavior that,* in the words of the Commission on Obscenity and Pornography, *have as a distinguishing characteristic "the degrading and demeaning portrayal of the role and status of the human female . . . as a mere sexual object to be exploited and manipulated sexually."*[3] In pornographic books, magazines, and films, women are represented as passive and as slavishly dependent upon men. The role of female characters is limited to the provision of sexual services to men. To the extent that women's sexual pleasure is represented at all, it is subordinated to that of men and is never an end in itself as is the sexual pleasure of men. What pleases women is the use of their bodies to satisfy male desires. While the sexual objectification of women is common to pornography, women are the recipients of even worse treatment in violent pornography, in which women characters are killed, tortured, gang-raped, mutilated, bound, and otherwise abused, as a means of providing sexual stimulation or pleasure to the male characters. It is this development which has attracted the attention of feminists and been, the stimulus to an analysis of pornography in general.[4]

Not all sexually explicit material is pornography, nor is all material which contains representations of sexual abuse and degradation pornography.

A representation of a sexual encounter between adult persons which is characterized by mutual respect is, once we have disentangled sexuality and morality, not morally objectionable. Such a representation would be one in which the desires and experiences of each participant were regarded by the other participants as having a validity and a subjective importance equal to those of the individual's own desire and experiences. In such an encounter, each participant acknowledges the other participant's basic human dignity and personhood. Similarly, a representation of a nude human body (in whole or in part) in such a manner that the person shown maintains self-respect—e.g., is not portrayed in a degrading position—would not be morally objectionable. The educational films of the National Sex Forum, as well as a certain amount of erotic literature and art, fall into this category. While some erotic materials are beyond the standards of modesty held by some individuals, they are not for this reason immoral.

A representation of a sexual encounter which is not characterized by mutual respect, in which at least one of the parties is treated in a manner beneath her or his dignity as a human being, is no longer simple erotica. That a representation is of degrading behavior does not in itself, however, make it pornographic. Whether or not it is pornographic is a function of contextual features. Books and films may contain descriptions or representations of a rape in order to explore the consequences of such an assault upon its victim. What is being shown is abusive or degrading behavior which attempts to deny the humanity and dignity of the person assaulted, yet the context surrounding the representation, through its exploration of the consequences of the act, acknowledges and reaffirms her dignity. Such books and films, far from being pornographic, are (or can be) highly moral, and fall into the category of moral realism.

What makes a work a work of pornography, then, is not simply its representation of degrading and abusive sexual encounters, but its implicit, if not explicit, approval and recommendation of sexual behavior that is immoral, i.e., that physically or psychologically violates the personhood of one of the participants. Pornography, then, is verbal or pictorial material which represents or describes sexual behavior that is degrading or abusive to one or more of the participants in *such a way as to endorse the degradation*. The participants so treated in virtually all heterosexual pornography are women or children, so heterosexual pornography is, as a matter of fact, material which endorses sexual behavior that is degrading and/or abusive to women and children. As I use the term "sexual behavior," this includes sexual encounters between persons, behavior which produces sexual stimulation or pleasure for one of the participants, and behavior which is preparatory to or invites sexual activity. Behavior that is degrading or abusive includes physical harm or abuse, and physical or psychological coercion. In addition, behavior which ignores or devalues the real interests, desires, and experiences of one or more participants in any way is degrading. Finally, that a person has chosen or consented to be harmed, abused, or subjected to coercion does not alter the degrading character of such behavior.

Pornography communicates its endorsement of the behavior it represents by various features of the pornographic context: the degradation of the female characters is represented as providing pleasure to the participant males and, even worse, to the participant females, and there is no suggestion that this sort of treatment of others is inappropriate to their status as human beings. These two features are together sufficient to constitute endorsement of the represented behavior. The contextual features which make material pornographic are intrinsic to the material. In addition to these, extrinsic features, such as the purpose for which the material is presented—i.e., the sexual arousal/pleasure/satisfaction of its (mostly) male consumers—or an accompanying text, may reinforce or make explicit the endorsement. Representations which in and of themselves do not show or endorse degrading behavior may be put into a pornographic context by juxtaposition with others that are degrading, or by a text which invites or recommends degrading behavior toward the subject represented. In such a case the whole complex—the series of representations or representations with text—is pornographic.

The distinction I have sketched is one that applies most clearly to sequential material—a verbal or pictorial (filmed) story—which represents an action and provides a temporal context for it. In showing the before and after, a narrator or film-maker has plenty of opportunity to acknowledge the dignity of the person violated or clearly to refuse to do so. It is somewhat more difficult to apply the distinction to single still representations. The contextual features cited above, however, are clearly present in still photographs or pictures that glamorize degradation and sexual violence. Phonograph album covers and advertisements offer some prime examples of such glamorization. Their representations of women in chains (the Ohio Players), or bound by ropes and black and blue (the Rolling Stones) are considered high-quality commercial "art" and glossily prettify the violence they represent. Since the standard function of prettification and glamorization is the communication of desirability, these albums and ads are communicating the desirability of violence against women. Representations of women bound or chained, particularly those of women bound in such a way as to make their breasts, or genital or anal areas vulnerable to any passerby, endorse the scene they represent by the absence of any indication that this treatment of women is in any way inappropriate.

To summarize: Pornography is not just the explicit representation or description of sexual behavior, nor even the explicit representation or description of sexual behavior which is degrading and/or abusive to women. Rather, it is material that explicitly represents or describes degrading and abusive sexual behavior so as to endorse and/or recommend the behavior as described. The contextual features, moreover, which communicate such endorsement are intrinsic to the material; that is, they are features whose removal or alteration would change the representation or description.

This account of pornography is underlined by the etymology and original meaning of the word "pornography." *The Oxford English Dictionary* defines pornography as "Description of the life, manners, etc. of prostitutes and their patrons [from πορμη (porne) meaning "harlot" and γραφειμ (graphein) meaning "to write"]; hence the expression or suggestion of obscene or unchaste subjects in literature or art."[5]

Let us consider the first part of the definition for a moment. In the transactions between prostitutes and their clients, prostitutes are paid, directly or indirectly, for the use of their bodies by the client for sexual pleasure. Traditionally males have obtained from female prostitutes what they could not or did not wish to get from their wives or women friends, who, because of the character of their relation to the male, must be accorded some measure of human respect. While there are limits to what treatment is seen as appropriate toward women as wives or women friends, the prostitute as prostitute exists to provide sexual pleasure to males. The female characters of contemporary pornography also exist to provide pleasure to males, but in the pornographic context no pretense is made to regard them as parties to a contractual arrangement. Rather, the anonymity of these characters makes each one Every woman, thus suggesting not only that all women are appropriate subjects for the enactment of the most bizarre and demeaning male sexual fantasies, but also that this is their primary purpose. The recent escalation of violence in pornography—the presentation of scenes of bondage, rape, and torture of women for the sexual stimulation of the male characters or male viewers—while shocking in itself, is from this point of view merely a more vicious extension of a genre whose success depends on treating women in a manner beneath their dignity as human beings.

Pornography: Lies and Violence Against Women

What is wrong with pornography, then, is its degrading and dehumanizing portrayal of women (and *not* its sexual content). Pornography, by its very nature, requires that women be subordinate to men and mere instruments for the fulfillment of male fantasies. To accomplish this, pornography must lie. Pornography lies when it says that our sexual life is or ought to be subordinate to the service of men, that our pleasure consists in pleasing men and not ourselves, that we are depraved, that we are fit subjects for rape, bondage, torture, and murder. Pornography lies explicitly about women's sexuality, and through such lies fosters more lies about our humanity, our dignity, and our personhood.

Moreover, since nothing is alleged to justify the treatment of the female characters of pornography save their womanhood, pornography depicts all women as fit objects of violence by virtue of their sex alone. Because it is simply being female that, in the pornographic vision, justifies being violated, the lies of pornography are lies about all women. Each work of pornography is on its own libelous and defamatory, yet gains power through being reinforced by every other pornographic work. The sheer number of pornographic productions expands the moral issue to include not only assessing the morality or immorality of individual works, but also the meaning and force of the mass production of pornography.

The pornographic view of women is thoroughly entrenched in a booming portion of the publishing, film, and recording industries, reaching and affecting not only all who look to such sources for sexual stimulation, but also those of us who are forced into an awareness of it as we peruse magazines at newsstands and record albums in record stores, as we check the entertainment sections of city newspapers, or even as we approach a counter to pay for groceries. It is not necessary to spend a great deal of time reading or viewing pornographic material to absorb its male-centered definition of women. No longer confined within plain brown wrappers, it jumps out from billboards that proclaim "Live X-rated Girls!" or "Angels in Pain" or "Hot and Wild," and from magazine covers displaying a woman's genital area being spread open to the viewer by her own fingers. Thus, even men who do not frequent pornographic shops and movie houses are supported in the sexist objectification of women by their environment. Women, too, are crippled by internalizing as self-images those that are presented to us by pornographers. Isolated from one another and with no source of support for an alternative view of female sexuality, we may not always find the strength to resist a message that dominates the common cultural media.

The entrenchment of pornography in our culture also gives it a significance quite beyond its explicit sexual messages. To suggest, as pornography does, that the primary purpose of women is to provide sexual pleasure to men is to deny that women are independently human or have a status equal to that of men. It is, moreover, to deny our equality at one of the most intimate levels of human experience. This denial is especially powerful in a hierarchical, class society such as ours, in which individuals feel good about themselves by feeling superior to others. Men in our society have a vested interest in maintaining their belief in the inferiority of the female sex, so that no matter how oppressed and exploited by the society in which they live and work, they can feel that they are at least superior to someone or some category of individuals—a woman or women. Pornography, by presenting women as wanton, depraved, and made for the sexual use of men, caters directly to that interest. The very intimate nature of sexuality which makes pornography so corrosive also protects it from explicit public discussion. The consequent lack of any explicit social disavowal of the pornographic image of women enables this image to continue fostering sexist attitudes even as the society publicly proclaims its (as yet timid) commitment to sexual equality.

In addition to finding a connection between the pornographic view of women and the denial to us of our full human rights, women are beginning to connect the consumption of pornography with committing rape and other acts of sexual violence against women. Contrary to the findings of the Commission on Obscenity and Pornography, a growing body of research is documenting (1) a correlation between exposure to representations of violence and the committing of violent acts generally, and (2) a correlation between exposure to pornographic materials and the committing of sexually abusive or violent acts against women.[6] While more study is needed to establish precisely what the causal relations are, clearly so-called hard-core pornography is not innocent.

From "snuff" films and miserable magazines in pornographic stores to *Hustler*, to phonograph album covers and advertisements, to *Vogue*, pornography has come to occupy its own niche in the communications and entertainment media and to acquire a quasi-institutional character (signaled by the use of diminutives such as "porn" or "porno" to refer to pornographic material, as though such familiar naming could take the hurt out). Its acceptance by the mass media, whatever the motivation, means a cultural endorsement of its message. As much as the materials themselves, the social tolerance of these degrading and distorted images of women in such

quantities is harmful to us, since it indicates a general willingness to see women in ways incompatible with our fundamental human dignity and thus to justify treating us in those ways. The tolerance of pornographic representations of the rape, bondage, and torture of women helps to create and maintain a climate more tolerant of the actual physical abuse of women. The tendency on the part of the legal system to view the victim of a rape as responsible for the crime against her is but one manifestation of this.

In sum, pornography is injurious to women in at least three distinct ways:

1. Pornography, especially violent pornography, is implicated in the committing of crimes of violence against women.
2. Pornography is the vehicle for the dissemination of a deep and vicious lie about women. It is defamatory and libelous.
3. The diffusion of such a distorted view of women's nature in our society as it exists today supports sexist (i.e., male-centered) attitudes, and thus reinforces the oppression and exploitation of women.

Society's tolerance of pornography, especially pornography on the contemporary massive scale, reinforces each of these modes of injury: By not disavowing the lie, it supports the male-centered myth that women are inferior and subordinate creatures. Thus, it contributes to the maintenance of a climate tolerant of both psychological and physical violence against women.

Pornography and the Law

Congress shall make no law respecting the establishment of religion, or prohibiting the free exercise thereof; or abridging the freedom of speech, or of the press; or the right of the people peaceably to assemble, and to petition the Government for a redress of grievances.

—First Amendment, Bill of Rights of the United States Constitution

Pornography is clearly a threat to women. Each of the modes of injury cited above offers sufficient reason at least to consider proposals for the social and legal control of pornography. The almost universal response from progressives to such proposals is that constitutional guarantees of freedom of speech and privacy preclude recourse to law.[7] While I am concerned about the erosion of constitutional rights and also think for many reasons that great caution must be exercised before undertaking a legal campaign against pornography, I find objections to such a campaign that are based on appeals to the First Amendment or to a right to privacy ultimately unconvincing.

Much of the defense of the pornographer's right to publish seems to assume that, while pornography may be tasteless and vulgar, it is basically an entertainment that harms no one but its consumers, who may at worst suffer from the debasement of their taste; and that therefore those who argue for its control are demanding an unjustifiable abridgment of the rights to freedom of speech of those who make and distribute pornographic materials and of the rights to privacy of their customers. The account of pornography given above shows that the assumptions of this position are false. Nevertheless, even some who acknowledge its harmful character feel that it is granted immunity from social control by the First Amendment, or that the harm that would ensue from its control outweighs the harm prevented by its control.

There are three ways of arguing that control of pornography is incompatible with adherence to constitutional rights. The first argument claims that regulating pornography involves an unjustifiable interference in the private lives of individuals. The second argument takes the First Amendment as a basic principle constitutive of our form of government, and claims that the production and distribution of pornographic material, as a form of speech, is an activity protected by that amendment. The third argument claims not that the pornographer's rights are violated, but that others' rights will be if controls against pornography are instituted.

The privacy argument is the easiest to dispose of. Since the open commerce in pornographic materials is an activity carried out in the public sphere, the publication and distribution of such materials, unlike their use by individuals, is not protected by rights to privacy. The distinction between the private consumption of pornographic material and the production and distribution of, or open commerce in it, is sometimes blurred by defenders of pornography. But I may entertain, in the privacy of my mind, defamatory opinions about another person, even though I may not broadcast them. So one might create without restraint—as long as no one were harmed in the course of preparing them—pornographic materials for one's personal use, but be restrained from reproducing and distributing them. In both cases what one is doing—in the privacy of one's mind or basement—may indeed be deplorable, but immune from legal proscription. Once the activity becomes public, however—i.e., once it involves others—it is no longer protected by the same rights that protect activities in the private sphere.

In considering the second argument (that control of pornography, private or public, is wrong in principle), it seems important to determine whether we consider the right to freedom of speech to be absolute and unqualified. If it is, then obviously all speech, including pornography, is entitled to protection. But the right is, in the first place, not an unqualified right: There are several kinds of speech not protected by the First Amendment, including the incitement to violence in volatile circumstances, the solicitation of crimes, perjury and misrepresentation, slander, libel, and false advertising. That there are forms of proscribed speech shows that we accept limitations on the right to freedom of speech if such speech, as do the forms listed, impinges on other rights. The manufacture and distribution of material which defames and threatens all members of a class by its recommendation of abusive and degrading behavior toward some members of that class simply in virtue of their membership in it seems a clear candidate for inclusion on the list. The right is therefore not an unqualified one.

Nor is it an absolute or fundamental right, underived from any other right: If it were there would not be exceptions or limitations. The first ten amendments were added to the Constitution as a way of guaranteeing the "blessings of liberty" mentioned in its preamble, to protect citizens against the unreasonable usurpation of power by the state. The specific rights mentioned in the First Amendments—those of religion, speech, assembly, press, petition—reflect the recent experiences of the makers of the Constitution under colonial government as well as a sense of what was and is required generally to secure liberty.

It may be objected that the right to freedom of speech is fundamental in that it is part of what we mean by liberty and not a right that is derivative from a right to liberty. In order to meet this objection, it is useful to consider a distinction explained by Ronald Dworkin in his book *Taking Rights Seriously*.[8] As Dworkin points out, the word "liberty" is used in two distinct, if related,

senses: as "license," i.e., "the freedom from legal constraints to do as one pleases," in some contexts; and as "independence," i.e., "the status of a person as independent and equal rather than subservient," in others. Failure to distinguish between these senses in discussion of rights and freedom is fatal to clarity and understanding.

If the right to free speech is understood as a partial explanation of what is meant by liberty, then liberty is perceived as license: The right to do as one pleases includes a right to speak as one pleases. But license is surely not a condition the First Amendment is designed to protect. We not only tolerate but require legal constraints on liberty as license when we enact laws against rape, murder, assault, theft, etc. If everyone did exactly as she or he pleased at any given time, we would have chaos if not lives, as Hobbes put it, that are "nasty, brutish, and short." We accept government to escape, not to protect, this condition.

If, on the other hand, by liberty is meant independence, then freedom of speech is not necessarily a part of liberty; rather, it is a means to it. The right to freedom of speech is not a fundamental, absolute right, but one derivative from, possessed in virtue of, the more basic right to independence. Taking this view of liberty requires providing arguments showing that the more specific rights we claim are necessary to guarantee our status as persons "independent and equal rather than subservient." In the context of government, we understand independence to be the freedom of each individual to participate as an equal among equals in the determination of how she or he is to be governed. Freedom of speech in this context means that an individual may not only entertain beliefs concerning government privately, but may express them publicly. We express our opinions about taxes, disarmament, wars, social-welfare programs, the function of the police, civil rights, and so on. Our right to freedom of speech includes the right to criticize the government and to protest against various forms of injustice and the abuse of power. What we wish to protect is the free expression of ideas even when they are unpopular. What we do not always remember is that speech has functions other than the expression of ideas.

Regarding the relationship between a right to freedom of speech and the publication and distribution of pornographic materials, there are two points to be made. In the first place, the latter activity is hardly an exercise of the right to the free expression of ideas as understood above. In the second place, to the degree that the tolerance of material degrading to women supports and reinforces the attitude that women are not fit to participate as equals among equals in the political life of their communities, and that the prevalence of such an attitude effectively prevents women from so participating, the absolute and fundamental right of women to liberty (political independence) is violated.

This second argument against the suppression of pornographic material, then, rests on a premise that must be rejected, namely, that the right to freedom of speech is a right to utter anything one wants. It thus fails to show that the production and distribution of such material is an activity protected by the First Amendment. Furthermore, an examination of the issues involved leads to the conclusion that tolerance of this activity violates the rights of women to political independence.

The third argument (which expresses concern that curbs on pornography are the first step toward political censorship) runs into the same ambiguity that besets the arguments based on principle. These arguments generally have as an underlying assumption that the maximization of freedom is a worthy social goal. Control of pornography diminishes freedom—directly the freedom of pornographers, indirectly that of all of us. But again, what is meant by "freedom"? It cannot be that what is to be maximized is license—as the goal of a social group whose members probably have at least some incompatible interests, such a goal would be internally inconsistent. If, on the other hand, the maximization of political independence is the goal, then that is in no way enhanced by, and may be endangered by, the tolerance of pornography. To argue that the control of pornography would create a precedent for suppressing political speech is thus to confuse license with political independence. In addition, it ignores a crucial basis for the control of pornography, i.e., its character as libelous speech. The prohibition of such speech is justified by the need for protection from the injury (psychological as well as physical or economic) that results from libel. A very different kind of argument would be required to justify curtailing the right to speak our minds about the institutions which govern us. As long as such distinctions are insisted upon, there is little danger of the government's using the control of pornography as precedent for curtailing political speech.

In summary, neither as a matter of principle nor in the interests of maximizing liberty can it be supposed that there is an intrinsic right to manufacture and distribute pornographic material.

The only other conceivable source of protection for pornography would be a general right to do what we please as long as the rights of others are respected. Since the production and distribution of pornography violates the rights of women—to respect and to freedom from defamation, among others—this protection is not available.

Conclusion

I have defined pornography in such a way as to distinguish it from erotica and from moral realism, and have argued that it is defamatory and libelous toward women, that it condones crimes against women, and that it invites tolerance of the social, economic, and cultural oppression of women. The production and distribution of pornographic material is thus a social and moral wrong. Contrasting both the current volume of pornographic production and its growing infiltration of the communications media with the status of women in this culture makes clear the necessity for its control. Since the goal of controlling pornography does not conflict with constitutional rights, a common obstacle to action is removed.

Appeals for action against pornography are sometimes brushed aside with the claim that such action is a diversion from the primary task of feminists—the elimination of sexism and of sexual inequality. This approach focuses on the enjoyment rather than the manufacture of pornography, and sees it as merely a product of sexism which will disappear when the latter has been overcome and the sexes are socially and economically equal. Pornography cannot be separated from sexism in this way: sexism is not just a set of attitudes regarding the inferiority of women but the behaviors and social and economic rules that manifest such attitudes. Both the manufacture and distribution of pornography and the enjoyment of it are instances of sexist behavior. The enjoyment of pornography on the part of individuals will presumably decline as such individuals begin to accord women their status as fully human. A cultural climate which tolerates the degrading representation of women is not a climate which facilitates the development of respect for women. Furthermore, the demand for pornography is stimulated not just by the sexism of individuals but by the pornography industry itself. Thus, both as a social phenomenon and in its effect on individuals, pornography, far from being a mere product, nourishes sexism. The campaign against it is an essential component of women's struggle for legal, economic, and social equality, one which requires the support of all feminists.

Notes

1. *Women Against Violence in Pornography and Media Newspage,* vol. II, no. 5, June 1978; and Judith Reisman in *Women Against Violence in Pornography and Media Proposal.*

2. American Law Institute, *Model Penal Code,* sec. 251.4.

3. *Report of the Commission on Obscenity and Pornography* (New York: Bantam Books, 1979), p. 239. The Commission, of course, concluded that the demeaning content of pornography did not adversely affect male attitudes toward women.

4. Among recent feminist discussions are Diana Russell, "Pornography: A Feminist Perspective" and Susan Griffin, "On Pornography," *Chrysalis,* vol. I, no. 4, 1978; and Ann Garry, "Pornography and Respect for Women," *Social Theory and Practice,* vol. 4, Spring 1978, pp. 395–421.

5. *The Oxford English Dictionary,* Compact Edition (London: Oxford University Press, 1971), p. 2242.

6. Urie Bronfenbrenner, *Two Worlds of Childhood* (New York: Russell Sage Foundation, 1970); H. J. Eysenck and D. K. B. Nias, *Sex, Violence and the Media* (New York: St. Martin's Press, 1978); and Michael Goldstein, Harold Kant, and John Hartman, *Pornography and Sexual Deviance* (Berkeley: University of California Press, 1973).

7. Cf. Marshall Cohen, "The Case Against Censorship," *The Public Interests,* no. 22, Winter 1971, reprinted in John R. Burr and Milton Goldinger, *Philosophy and Contemporary Issues* (New York: Macmillan 1976), and Justice William Brennan's dissenting opinion in *Paris Adults Theater I v. Slaton,* 431 U.S. 49.

8. Ronald Dworkin, *Taking Rights Seriously* (Cambridge: Harvard University Press, 1977), p. 262.

The Feminist Case Against Pornography

Joel Feinberg

Until 1970 or so, the demand for legal restraints on pornography came mainly from "sexual conservatives," those who regarded the pursuit of erotic pleasure for its own sake to be immoral or degrading, and its public depiction obscene. The new attack, however, comes not from prudes and bluenoses, but from women who have been in the forefront of the sexual revolution. We do not hear any of the traditional complaints about pornography from this group—that erotic states in themselves are immoral, that sexual titillation corrupts character, and that the spectacle of "appeals to prurience" is repugnant to moral sensibility. The new charge is rather that pornography degrades, abuses, and defames women, and contributes to a general climate of attitudes toward women that makes violent sex crimes more frequent. Pornography, they claim, has come to pose a threat to public safety, and its legal restraint can find justification either under the harm principle, or, by analogy with Nazi parades in Skokie and K.K.K rallies, on some theory of profound (and personal) offense.[1]

It is somewhat misleading to characterize the feminist onslaught as a new argument, or new emphasis in argument, against the same old thing. By the 1960s pornography itself had become in large measure a new and uglier kind of phenomenon. There had always been sadomasochistic elements in much pornography, and a small minority taste to be served with concentrated doses of it. There had also been more or less prominent expressions of contemptuous attitudes toward abject female "sex objects," even in much relatively innocent pornography. But now a great wave of violent pornography appears to have swept over the land, as even the mass circulation porno magazines moved beyond the customary nude cheesecake and formula stories, to explicit expressions of hostility to women, and to covers and photographs showing "women and children abused, beaten, bound, and tortured" apparently "for the sexual titillation of consumers."[2] When the circulation of the monthly porn magazines comes to 16 million and the porno industry as a whole does $4 billion a year in business, the new trend cannot help but be alarming.[3]

There is no necessity, however, that pornography *as such* be degrading to women. First of all, we can imagine easily enough an ideal pornography in which men and women are depicted enjoying their joint sexual pleasures in ways that show not a trace of dominance or humiliation of either party by the other.[4] The materials in question might clearly satisfy my . . . definition of "pornography" as materials designed entirely and effectively to induce erotic excitement in observers, without containing any of the extraneous sexist elements. Even if we confine our attention to actual specimens of pornography—and quite typical ones—we find many examples where male dominance and female humiliation are not present at all. Those of us who were budding teenagers in the 1930s and '40s will tend to take as our model of pornography the comic strip pamphlets in wide circulation among teenagers during that period. The characters were all drawn from the popular legitimate comic strips—The Gumps, Moon Mullins, Maggie and Jiggs, etc.—and were portrayed in cartoons that were exact imitations of the originals. In the pornographic strips, however, the adventures were all erotic. Like all pornography, the cartoons greatly exaggerated the size of organs and appetites, and the "plot lines" were entirely predictable. But the episodes were portrayed with great good humor, a kind of joyous feast of erotica in which the blessedly unrepressed cartoon figures shared with perfect equality. Rather than being humiliated or dominated, the women characters equalled the men in their sheer earthy gusto. (That feature especially appealed to teenage boys who could only dream of unrestrained female gusto.) The episodes had no butt at all except prudes and hypocrites. Most of us consumers managed to survive with our moral characters intact.

In still other samples of actual pornography, there is indeed the appearance of male dominance and female humiliation, but even in many of these, explanations of a more innocent character are available. It is in the nature of fantasies, especially adolescent, fantasies, whether erotic or otherwise, to glorify imaginatively, in excessive and unrealistic ways, the person who does the fantasizing. When that person is a woman and the fantasy is romantic, she may dream of herself surrounded by handsome lovesick suitors, or in love with an (otherwise) magnificent man who is prepared to throw himself at her feet, worship the ground she walks on, go through hell for her if necessary—the clichés pile up endlessly. If the fantasizing person is a man and his reverie is erotic, he may dream of women who worship the ground *he* walks on, etc., and would do anything for the honor of making love with him, and who having sampled his unrivaled sexual talents would grovel at his feet for more, etc., etc. The point of the fantasy is self-adulation, not "hostility" toward the other sex.

Still other explanations may be available. "Lust," wrote Norman Mailer, "is a world of bewildering dimensions. . . ."[5] When its consuming fire takes hold of the imagination, it is likely to be accompanied by almost any images suggestive of limitlessness, any natural accompaniments of explosive unrestrained passion. Not only men but women too have been known to scratch or bite (like house cats) during sexual excitement, and the phrase "I could hug you to pieces"—a typical expression of felt "limitlessness"—is normally taken as an expression of endearment, not of homicidal fury. Sexual passion in the male animal (there is as yet little but conjecture on this subject) may be associated at deep instinctive or hormonal levels with the states that capture the body and mind during aggressive combat. Some such account may be true of a given man, and explain why a certain kind of pornography may arouse him, without implying anything at all about his settled attitudes toward women, or his general mode of behavior toward them. Then, of course, it is a commonplace that many "normal" people, both men and women, enjoy sadomasochistic fantasies from time to time, without effect on character or conduct. Moreover, there are pornographic materials intended for men, that appeal to their masochistic side exclusively, in which they are "ravished" and humiliated by some grim-faced amazon of fearsome dimensions. Great art these materials are not, but neither are they peculiarly degrading to women.

It will not do then to isolate the most objectionable kinds of pornography, the kinds that are most offensive and even dangerous to women, and reserve the label "pornographic" for them alone. This conscious redefinition is what numerous feminist writers have done, however, much to the confusion of the whole discussion. Gloria Steinem rightly protests against "the truly obscene idea that sex and the domination of women must be combined"[6] (*there* is a proper use of the word "obscene"), but then she manipulates words so that it becomes true by definition (hence merely trivially true) that *all* pornography is obscene in this fashion. She notes that "pornography" stems from the Greek root meaning "prostitutes" or "female captives," "thus letting us know that the subject is not mutual love, or love at all, but domination and violence against women."[7] Steinem is surely right that the subject of the stories, pictures, and films that have usually been called "pornographic" is not love, but it doesn't follow that they are all without exception about male domination over women either. Of course Steinem doesn't make that further claim as a matter of factual reporting, but

as a stipulated redefinition. Her proposal can lead other writers to equivocate, however, and find sexist themes in otherwise innocent erotica that have hitherto been called "pornographic"—simply because they *are* naturally called by that name. Steinem adopts "erotica" as the contrasting term to "pornography" as redefined. Erotica, she concludes, is about sexuality, but "pornography is about power, and sex-as-a-weapon," conquerors dominating victims. The distinction is a real one, but better expressed in such terms as "degrading pornography" (Steinem's "pornography") as opposed to "other pornography" (Steinem's "erotica").

At least one other important distinction must be made among the miscellany of materials in the category of degrading pornography. Some degrading pornography is also violent, glorifying in physical mistreatment of the woman, and featuring "weapons of torture or bondage, wounds and bruises."[8] The examples, alas, are abundant and depressing.

There are other examples, however, of pornography that is degrading to women but does not involve violence. Gloria Steinem speaks of more subtle forms of coercion: "a physical attitude of conqueror and victim, the use of race or class difference to imply the same thing, perhaps a very unequal nudity with one person exposed and vulnerable while the other clothed."[9] As the suggested forms of coercion become more and more subtle, obviously there will be very difficult line-drawing problems for any legislature brave enough to enter this area.

Yet the most violent cases at one end of the spectrum are as clear as they can be. They all glory in wanton and painful violence against helpless victims and do this with the extraordinary intention (sometimes even successful) of causing sexual arousal in male viewers. One could give every other form of pornography, degrading or not, the benefit of the doubt, and still identify with confidence all members of the violent extreme category. If there is a strong enough argument against pornography to limit the liberty of pornographers, it is probably restricted to this class of materials. Some feminist writers speak as if that would not be much of any restriction, but that may be a consequence of their *defining* pornography in terms of its most revolting specimens.[10] A pornographic story or film may be degrading in Steinem's subtle sense, in that it shows an intelligent man with a stupid woman, or a wealthy man with a chambermaid, and intentionally exploits the inequality for the sake of the special sexual tastes of the presumed male consumer, but if that were the *only* way in which the work degraded women, it would fall well outside the extreme (violent) category. All the more so, stories in which the male and female are equals—and these materials too can count as pornographic—would fall outside the objectionable category.

May the law legitimately be used to restrict the liberty of pornographers to produce and distribute, and their customers to purchase and use, erotic materials that are violently abusive of women? (I am assuming that no strong case can be made for the proscription of materials that are merely degrading in one of the relatively subtle and nonviolent ways.) Many feminists answer, often with reluctance, in the affirmative. Their arguments can be divided into two general classes. Some simply invoke the harm principle. Violent pornography wrongs and harms women, according to these arguments, either by defaming them as a group, or (more importantly) by inciting males to violent

crimes against them or creating a cultural climate in which such crimes are likely to become more frequent. The two traditional legal categories involved in these harm-principle arguments, then, are *defamation* and *incitement*. The other class of arguments invoke the offense principle, not in order to prevent mere "nuisances," but to prevent profound offense analogous to that of the Jews in Skokie or the blacks in a town where the K.K.K. rallies.

I shall not spend much time on the claim that violent and other extremely degrading pornography should be banned on the ground that it *defames* women. In a skeptical spirit, I can begin by pointing out that there are immense difficulties in applying the civil law of libel and slander as it is presently constituted in such a way as not to violate freedom of expression. Problems with *criminal* libel and slander would be even more unmanageable, and *group* defamation, whether civil or criminal, would multiply the problems still further. The argument on the other side is that pornography is essentially propaganda—propaganda against women. It does not slander women in the technical legal sense by asserting damaging falsehoods about them, because it *asserts* nothing at all. But it spreads an image of women as mindless playthings or "objects," inferior beings fit only to be used and abused for the pleasure of men, whether they like it or not, but often to their own secret pleasure. This picture lowers the esteem men have for women, and for that reason (if defamation is the basis of the argument) is sufficient ground for proscription even in the absence of any evidence of tangible harm to women caused by the behavior of misled and deluded men.

If degrading pornography defames (libels or slanders) women, it must be in virtue of some beliefs about women—false beliefs—that it conveys, so that in virtue of those newly acquired or reenforced false beliefs, consumers lower their esteem for women in general. If a work of pornography, for example, shows a woman (or group of women) in exclusively subservient or domestic roles, that may lead the consumer to *believe* that women, in virtue of some inherent female characteristics, are only fit for such roles. There is no doubt that much pornography does portray women in subservient positions, but if that is defamatory to women in anything like the legal sense, then so are soap commercials on TV. So are many novels, even some good ones. (A good novel may yet be about some degraded characters.) That some groups are portrayed in unflattering roles has not hitherto been a ground for the censorship of fiction or advertising. Besides, it is not clearly the *group* that is portrayed at all in such works, but only one individual (or small set of individuals) and fictitious ones at that. Are fat men defamed by Shakespeare's picture of Falstaff? Are Jews defamed by the characterization of Shylock? Could any writer today even hope to write a novel partly about a fawning corrupted black, under group defamation laws, without risking censorship or worse? The chilling effect on the practice of fiction-writing would amount to a near freeze.

Moreover, as Fred Berger points out;[11] the degrading images and defamatory beliefs pornographic works are alleged to cause are not produced in the consumer by explicit statements asserted with the intent to convince the reader or auditor of their truth. Rather they are caused by the stimulus of the work, in the context, on the expectations, attitudes, and beliefs the viewer brings with him to the work. That is quite other than believing an assertion on the authority or argument of the party making the assertion, or understanding the assertion in the first place in virtue of fixed conventions of language use and meaning. Without those fixed conventions of language, the work has to be interpreted in order for any message to be extracted from it, and the process of interpretation, as Berger illustrates abundantly, is "always a matter of judgment and subject to great variation among persons."[12] What looks like sexual subservience to some looks like liberation from sexual repression to others. It is hard to imagine how a court could provide a workable, much less fair, test of whether a given work has sufficiently damaged male esteem toward women for it to be judged criminally defamatory, when so much of the viewer's reaction he brings on himself, and viewer reactions are so widely variable.

It is not easy for a single work to defame successfully a group as large as 51 percent of the whole human race. (Could a misanthrope "defame" the whole human race by a false statement about "the nature of man"? Would every human being then be his "victim"?) Perhaps an unanswered barrage of thousands of tracts, backed by the prestige of powerful and learned persons without dissent might successfully defame any group no matter how large, but those conditions would be difficult to satisfy so long as there is freedom to speak back on the other side. In any case, defamation is not the true gravamen of the wrong that women in general suffer from extremely degrading pornography. When a magazine cover portrays a woman in a meat grinder, *all* women are insulted, degraded, even perhaps endangered, but few would naturally complain that they were *libelled* or *slandered*. Those terms conceal the point of what has happened. If women are harmed by pornography, the harm is surely more direct and tangible than harm to "the interest in reputation."[13]

The major argument for repression of violent pornography under the harm principle is that it promotes rape and physical violence. In the United States there is a plenitude both of sexual violence against women and of violent pornography. According to the F.B.I. Uniform Crime Statistics (as of 1980), a 12-year-oid girl in the United States has one chance in three of being raped in her lifetime; studies only a few years earlier showed that the number of violent scenes in hard-core pornographic books was as high as 20 percent of the total, and the number of violent cartoons and pictorials in leading pornographic magazines was as much as 10 percent of the total.[14] This has suggested to some writers that there must be a direct causal link between violent pornography and sexual violence against women; but causal relationships between pornography and rape, if they exist, must be more complicated than that. The suspicion of direct connection is dissipated, as Aryeh Neier points out,

> . . . when one looks at the situation in other countries. For example, violence against women is common in . . . Ireland and South Africa, but pornography is unavailable in those countries. By contrast violence against women is relatively uncommon in Denmark, Sweden, and the Netherlands, even though pornography seems to be even more plentifully available than in the United States. To be sure, this proves little or nothing except that more evidence is needed to establish a causal connection between pornography and violence against women beyond the fact that both may exist at the same time. But this evidence . . . simply does not exist.[15]

On the other hand, there is evidence that novel ways of committing crimes are often suggested (usually inadvertently) by bizarre tales in films or TV . . ., and even factual newspaper reports of crimes can trigger the well-known "copy-cat crime" phenomenon. But if the possibility of copy-cat cases, by itself, justified censorship or punishment, we would have grounds for supressing films of *The Brothers Karamozov* and the TV series *Roots* (both of which have been cited as influences on imitative crimes). "There would be few books left on our library shelves and few films that could be shown if every one that had at some time 'provoked' bizarre behavior were censored."[16] A violent episode in a pornographic work may indeed be a causally necessary condition for the commission of some specific crime by a specific perpetrator on a specific victim at some specific time and place. But for his reading or viewing that episode, the perpetrator may not have done precisely what he did in just the time, place, and manner that he did it. But so large a part of the full causal explanation of his act concerns his own psychological character and predispositions, that it is likely that some similar crime would have suggested itself to him in due time. It is not likely that non-rapists are converted into rapists *simply* by reading and viewing pornography. If pornography has a serious causal bearing on the occurence of rape (as opposed to the trivial copy-cat effect) it must be in virtue of its role (still to be established) in implanting the appropriate cruel dispositions in the first place.

Rape is such a complex social phenomenon that there is probably no one simple generalization to account for it. Some rapes are no doubt ineliminable, no matter how we design our institutions. Many of these are the product of deep individual psychological problems, transferred rages, and the like. But for others, perhaps the preponderant number, the major part of the explanation is sociological, not psychological. In these cases the rapist is a psychologically normal person well adjusted to his particular subculture, acting calmly and deliberately rather than in a rage, and doing what he thinks is expected of him by his peers, what he must do to acquire or preserve standing in his group. His otherwise inexplicable violence is best explained as a consequence of the peculiar form of his socialization among his peers, his pursuit of a prevailing ideal of manliness, what the Mexicans have long called *machismo*, but which exists to some degree or other among men in most countries, certainly in our own.

The macho male wins the esteem of his associates by being tough, fearless, reckless, wild, unsentimental, hard-boiled, hard drinking, disrespectful, profane, willing to fight whenever his honor is impugned, and fight without fear of consequences no matter how extreme. He is a sexual athlete who must be utterly dominant over "his" females, who are expected to be slavishly devoted to him even though he lacks gentleness with them and shows his regard only by displaying them like trophies. . .

Would it significantly reduce sexual violence if violent pornography were effectively banned? No one can know for sure, but if the cult of macho is the main source of such violence, as I suspect, then repression of violent pornography, whose function is to pander to the macho values already deeply rooted in society, may have little effect. Pornography does not cause normal decent chaps, through a single exposure, to metamorphoze into rapists. Pornography-reading machos commit rape, but that is because they already have macho values, not because they read the violent pornography that panders to them. Perhaps then *constant* exposure to violent porn might turn a decent person into a violence-prone macho. But that does not seem likely either, since the repugnant violence of the materials could not have any appeal in the first place to one who did not already have some strong macho predispositions, so "constant exposure" could not begin to become established. Clearly, other causes, and more foundational ones, must be at work, if violent porn is to have any initial purchase. Violent pornography is more a symptom of *machismo* than a cause of it, and treating symptoms merely is not a way to offer protection to potential victims of rapists. At most, I think there may be a small spill-over effect of violent porn on actual violence. . .

If my surmise about causal connections is correct they are roughly as indicated in the following diagram:

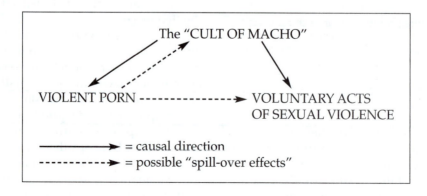

The primary causal direction is not from violent pornography to violent real-life episodes. Neither is it from violent pornography to the establishment and reenforcement of macho values. Rather, the cult of macho expectations is itself the primary cause *both* or the existence of violent porn (it provides the appreciative audience) and of the real-life sexual violence (it provides the motive). The dotted arrows express my acknowledgement of the point that there might be some small spill-over effect from violent pornography back on the macho values that spawn it, in one direction, and on real-life violence in the other, but the pornography cannot be the primary causal generator. Sexual violence will continue to fester so long as the cult of macho flourishes, whether or not we eliminate legal violent pornography.

How then can we hope to weaken and then extirpate the cultish values at the root of our problem? The criminal law is a singularly ill-adapted tool for that kind of job. We might just as well legislate against entrepreneurship on the grounds that capitalism engenders "acquisitive personalities," or against the military on the grounds that it produces "authoritarian personalities," or against certain religious sects on the ground that they foster puritanism, as criminalize practices and institutions on the grounds that they contribute to *machismo*. But macho values are culturally, not instinctively, transmitted, and the behavior that expresses them is learned, not inherited, behavior. What is learned can be unlearned. Schools should play a role. Surely, learning to see through machismo and avoid its traps should be as important a part of a child's preparation for citizenship as the acquisition of patriotism and piety. To be effective, such teaching should be frank and direct, not totally reliant on general moral platitudes.

It should talk about the genesis of children's attitudes toward the other sex, and invite discussion of male insecurity, resentment of women, cruelty, and even specific odious examples. Advertising firms and film companies should be asked (at first), then pressured (if necessary) to cooperate, as they did in the successful campaign to deglamorize cigarette smoking. Fewer exploitation films should be made. . . . Materials (especially films) should be made available to clergymen as well as teachers, youth counselors, and parole officers. A strong part of the emphasis of these materials should be on the harm that bondage to the cult of macho does to men too, and how treacherous a trap *machismo* can be. The new moral education must be careful, of course, not to preach dull prudence as a preferred style for youthful living. A zest for excitement, adventure, even danger, cannot be artificially removed from adolescent nature. Moreover, teamwork, camaraderie, and toughness of character need not be denigrated. But the cult of macho corrupts and distorts these values in ways that can be made clear to youths. The mistreatment of women, when its motivation is clearly revealed and understood, should be a sure way of eliciting the contempt of the group, not a means to greater prestige within it.

Rape is a harm and a severe one. Harm prevention is definitely a legitimate use of the criminal law. Therefore, if there is a clear enough causal connection to rape, a statute that prohibits violent pornography would be a morally legitimate restriction of liberty. But it is not enough to warrant supression that pornography as a whole might have some harmful consequences to third parties, even though most specific instances of it do not. "Communications from other human beings are among the most important causes of human behavior," Kent

Greenawalt points out, "but criminal law cannot concern itself with every communication that may fortuitously lead to the commission of a crime. It would, for example, be ludicrous to punish a supervisor for criticizing a subordinate, even if it could be shown that the criticism so inflamed the subordinate that he assaulted a fellow worker hours later."[17] An even stronger point can be made. Even where there is statistical evidence that a certain percentage of communications of a given type will predictably lead the second party to harm third parties, so that in a sense the resultant harms are not "fortuitous," that is not sufficient warrant for prohibiting all communications of that kind. It would be even more ludicrous, for example, for a legislature to pass a criminal statute against the criticism of subordinates, on the ground that inflamed employees sometimes become aggressive with their fellow workers.

A more relevant example of the same point, and one with an ironic twist, is provided by Fred Berger.

> A journal that has published studies often cited by the radical feminists . . . has also published an article that purports to show that the greater emancipation of women in western societies has led to great increases in criminal activity *by* women. Such crimes as robbery, larceny, burglary, fraud, and extortion have shown marked increase, as have arson, murder, and aggravated assault. But freedom of expression would mean little if such facts could be taken as a reason to suppress expression that seeks the further liberation of women from their secondary, dependent status with respect to men.[18]

Of course, one can deny that violent porn is a form of valuable free expression analogous to scholarly feminist articles, but the point remains that indirectly produced harms are not by themselves sufficient

grounds for criminalizing materials, that some further conditions must be satisfied.

Those instances of sexual violence which may be harmful side-effects of violent pornography are directly produced by criminals (rapists) acting voluntarily on their own. We already have on the statute books a firm prohibition of rape and sexual assault. If, in addition, the harm principle permits the criminalization of actions only indirectly related to the primary harm, such as producing, displaying, or selling violent pornography, then there is a danger that the law will be infected with unfairness; for unless certain further conditions are fulfilled, the law will be committed to punishing some parties for the entirely voluntary criminal conduct of other parties. . . . Suppose that A wrongfully harms (e.g., rapes) B in circumstances such that (1) A acts fully voluntarily on his own initiative, and (2) nonetheless, but for what C has communicated to him, he would not have done what he did to B. Under what further conditions, we must ask, can C be rightfully held criminally responsible along with A for the harm to B? Clearly C can be held responsible if the information he communicated was helpful assistance to A and intended to be such. In that case C becomes a kind of collaborator. Under traditional law, C can also incur liability if what he communicated to A was some kind of encouragement to commit a crime against B. The clearest cases are those in which C solicits A's commission of the criminal act by offering inducements to him. "Encouragement" is also criminal when it takes the form of active urging. Sometimes mere advice to commit the act counts as an appropriate sort of encouragement. When the encouragement takes a general form, and the harmful crime is recommended to "the general reader" or an indefinite audience, then the term "advocacy" is often used. Advocating criminal conduct is arguably a way of producing such conduct, and is thus often itself a crime. An article in a pornographic magazine advocating the practice of rape (as opposed to advocating a legislative change of the rape laws) would presumably be a crime if its intent were serious and its audience presumed to be impressionable to an appropriately dangerous degree.[19]

Violent pornography, however, does not seem to fit any of these models. Its authors and vendors do not solicit rapes; nor do they urge or advise rapes; nor do they advocate rape. If some of their customers, some of the time, might yet "find encouragement" in their works to commit rapes because rape has been portrayed in a way that happens to be alluring to them, that is their own affair, the pornographer might insist, and their own responsibility. The form of "encouragement" that is most applicable (if any are) to the pornography case is that which the common law has traditionally called "incitement." Sir Edward Coke wrote in 1628 that "all those that incite . . . set on, or stir up any other" to a crime are themselves accessories.[20] Thus, haranguing an angry crowd on the doorsteps of a corn dealer, in Mill's famous example,[21] might be the spark that incites the mob's violence against the hated merchant, even though the speaker did not explicitly urge, advise, or advocate it. Yet, a similar speech, twenty-four hours earlier, to a calmer audience in a different location, though it may have made a causal contribution to the eventual violence, would not have borne a close enough relation to the harm to count as an "incitement," or "positive instigation" (Mill's term) of it.

Given that "communication" is a form of expression, and thus has an important social value, obviously it cannot rightly be made criminal simply on the ground that it may lead some others on their own to act harmfully. Even if works of pure pornography are *not* to be treated as "communication," "expression," or "speech" (in the sense of the first amendment), but as mere symbolic aphrodisiacs or sex aids without further content[22]. . ., they may yet have an intimate personal value to those who use them, and a social value derived from the importance we attach to the protection of private erotic experience. By virtue of that significance, one person's liberty can be invaded to prevent the harm other parties might cause to *their* victims only when the invaded behavior has a specially direct connection to the harm caused, something perhaps like direct "incitement." Fred Berger suggests three necessary conditions that expected harms must satisfy if they are to justify censorship or prohibition of erotic materials, none of which, he claims, is satisfied by pornography, even violent pornography.

1. There must be strong evidence of a very likely and serious harm.
   [I would add—"that would not have occurred otherwise."]
2. The harms must be clearly and directly linked with the expression.
3. It must be unlikely that further speech or expression can be used effectively to combat the harm.[23]

Berger suggests that the false shout of "fire" in a crowded theatre is paradigmatically the kind of communication that satisfies these conditions. If so, then he must interpret the second condition to be something like the legal standard of incitement—setting on, stirring up, inflaming the other party (or mob of parties) to the point of hysteria or panic, so that their own infliction of the subsequent damage is something less than deliberate and fully voluntary. Their inciter in that case is as responsible as they are, perhaps even more so, for the harm that ensues. Surely, the relation between pornographers and rapists is nowhere near that direct and manipulative. If it were, we would punish the pornographers proportionately more severely, and blame the actual rapist (poor chap; he was "inflamed") proportionately less.

It may yet happen that further evidence will show that Berger's conditions, or some criteria similar to them, are satisfied by violent pornography. In that case, a liberal should have no hesitation in using the criminal law to prevent the harm. In the meantime, the appropriate liberal response should be a kind of uneasy skepticism about the harmful effects of pornography on third party victims, conjoined with increasingly energetic use of "further speech or expression" against the cult of macho, "effectively to combat the harm."

Notes

1. I do not wish to imply that there is one position about the punishability or censorship of pornography that all writers called "feminists" hold. Some, like Ann Garry in "Pornography and Respect for Women" (*Social and Practice,* vol. 4, 1978) deny that pornography is necessarily by its very nature degrading to women. Others, like Wendy Kaminer in "Pornography and the First Amendment: Prior Restraints and Private Actions" in *Take Back the Night: Women on Pornography,* ed. Laura Lederer (New York: William Morrow and Co., Inc., 1980), accept the analysis of pornography that I discuss in the text, but deny that it provides a sufficient ground for censorship. The view I attribute to "feminists" is simply one held by many leading radical feminists, and most frequently and plausibly defended by feminist writers in the 1970s and 80s.

2. Lisa Lehrman, Preface to the Colloquium on Violent Pornography: "Degradation of Women Versus Right of Free Speech," *New York University Review of Law and Social Change* 8 (1978–79), p. 181.

3. The figure estimates are from Sarah J. McCarthy, "Pornography, Rape, and the Cult of Macho," *The Humanist,* Sept./Oct. 1980, p. 11.

4. Ann Garry, *op. cit.* (footnote 1) is persuasive on this point:

Imagine the following situation, which exists only rarely today: two fairly conventional people who love each other enjoy playing tennis and bridge together, and having sex together. In all these activities they are free from hang-ups, guilt, and tendencies to dominate or objectify each other. These two people like to watch tennis matches and old romantic movies on TV, like to watch Julia Child cook, like to read the bridge column in the newspaper, and like to watch pornographic movies. Imagine further that this couple is not at all uncommon in society and that non-sexist pornography is as common as this kind of nonsexist relationship. The situation sounds fine and healthy to me. I see no reason to think that an interest in pornography would disappear in the circumstances. People seem to enjoy watching others experience or do (especially do well) what they enjoy experiencing, doing, or wish they could do themselves. We do not morally object to people watching tennis on TV: why would we object to these hypothetical people watching pornography? (p. 419)

I would qualify Garry's account in two ways. First, it is not essential to her point that the two people "love each other," provided only that they like and respect each other. Second, their pleasures will be possible only if the film is well done, in particular keeping at least minimal photographic distance from what is depicted. Otherwise it might arouse anti-erotic repugnance.

5. Norman Mailer, *The Prisoner of Sex* (New York: New American Library, 1971), p. 82.

6. Gloria Steinem, "Erotica and Pornography, A Clear and Present Difference," *MS,* November, 1978, p. 53.

7. *Ibid.*, p. 54. Susan Wendell proposes a similar definition according to which depictions of "unjustified physical coercion of human beings" with some exceptions will count as pornographic even if they are not in any way *sexual*. See David Copp and Susan Wendell, eds., *Pornography and Censorship, Scientific, Philosophical, and Legal Studies* (Buffalo, NY: Prometheus Books, 1983), p. 167. Pornography [all Pornography] is to Susan Brownmiller "the undiluted essense of anti-female propoganda"—*Against Our Will: Men, Women, and Rape* (New York: Simon & Schuster, 1975), p. 394. Lorenne Clark takes it to be essential to pornography that it portrays women "in humiliating, degrading, and violently abusive situations," adding that "it frequently depicts them willingly, even avidly, suffering and inviting such treatment." See her "Liberalism and Pornography" in the Copp-Wendell volume, *supra*.

8. Steinem, *op. cit.* (footnote 6), p. 54.

9. Steinem, *op. cit.* (footnote 6), p. 54.

10. The most extreme of these definitions is that of Andrea Dworkin in her "Pornography and Grief" in *Take Back the Night: Women on Pornography*, ed. Laura Lederer (New York: William Morrow and Co., 1980), p. 288— "The eroticization of murder is the essence of pornography. . ."

11. Fred R. Berger, "Pornography, Feminism, and Censorship" (Unpublished paper, Philosophy Department, University of California, Davis), pp. 17ff. I am greatly indebted to this scholarly and well-argued essay.

12. *Ibid.*, p. 18.

13. "Defamation [libel or slander] is an invasion of the interest in reputation and good name, by communications to others which tend to diminish the esteem in which the plaintiff is held, or to excite adverse feelings or opinions against him."—William L. Prosser, *Handbook of the Law of Torts* (St. Paul: West Publishing Co., 1955), p. 572.

14. The studies are cited by Berger, *op. cit.* (footnote 11), p. 38.

15. Aryeh Neier, "Expurgating the First Amendment," *The Nation*, June 21, 1980, p. 754.

16. *Loc. cit.*

17. Kent Greenawalt, "Speech and Crime," *American Bar Foundation Research Journal*, no. 4 (1980), p. 654.

18. Berger, *op. cit.* (footnote 11), pp. 23–24. The study cited by Berger is: Freda Adler, "The Interaction Between Women's Emancipation and Female Criminality: A Cross-cultural Perspective," *International Journal of Criminology and Penology*, 5 (1977): 101–12.

19. The Supreme Court's standards of seriousness and dangerousness have been so extraordinarily high, however, that even a magazine article advocating (in a general way) rape might escape constitutionally valid punishment unless it urged *imminent* action against precise victims. In the landmark case *Brandenburg v. Ohio*, 395 U.S. 444 (1969), the court ruled that advocacy of illegal violence may be proscribed only when the advocacy amounts to *incitement* of imminent lawless action. Two conditions must be satisfied for liability. The advocacy must be (1) "directed to inciting or producing imminent lawless action," and (2) likely to succeed in inciting or producing such action.

20. Edward Coke, Second Part of the *Institutes of the Laws of England*, p. 182.

21. John Stuart Mill, *On Liberty*, chap. 3, para. 1. Mill writes: "An opinion that corn dealers are starvers of the poor, or that private property is robbery, ought to be unmolested when simply circulated through the press, but may justly incur punishment when delivered orally to an excited mob assembled before the house of a corn dealer, or when handed about among the same mob in the form of a placard."

22. This interpretation is persuasively argued by Frederick Schauer in his article "Speech and 'Speech'—Obscenity and 'Obscenity': An Exercise in the Interpretation of Constitutional Language," *Georgia Law Review* 67 (1979).

23. Fred L. Berger, *op. cit.* (footnote 11), p. 28.

Study Questions for Section 3

1. Longino and Feinberg define pornography differently. Is either definition of pornography adequate?

2. Feinberg contends that "the cult of macho expectations" explains both the existence of violent pornography and acts of sexual violence against women. Is this account plausible?

3. How does the Internet and related technological developments, such as virtual worlds, affect the pornography debate?

SECTION 4

SAME-SEX MARRIAGE

SAME-SEX MARRIAGE: A PHILOSOPHICAL DEFENSE

Ralph Wedgwood

Introductory

In this paper, I give what I will call a "philosophical defense" of same-sex marriage. More precisely, I argue that the present system, which reserves the institution of marriage for opposite-sex couples, and excludes same-sex couples, is intolerably unjust.

I call my defense of same-sex marriage a "philosophical" defense for two reasons. My first reason is to emphasize that I am not arguing about any *constitutional* or *legal* questions—such as, for example, whether the constitution of Hawaii, or the United States Constitution, implies that same-sex couples have a legal right to civil marriage. These questions have been dealt with by other writers elsewhere.[1] I am arguing about a *political* question: about what sort of laws or social institutions we *ought* to have. My argument is designed to apply just as effectively to societies that lack constitutionally guaranteed civil rights, such

as Britain, as to societies that have such constitutional rights, such as the United States or South Africa.

My second reason for calling my argument a "philosophical defense" is to signal its most serious limitation—namely, the lack of any serious consideration of the relevant empirical questions, such as what the consequences of introducing same-sex marriage would be. My main focus throughout is not on these empirical questions, but on the fundamental values that are at stake—especially the values of justice and the common good, democracy, freedom, and equality. Of course, my argument will have to rely on empirical assumptions at certain points. I will carefully flag each of these assumptions when it first appears; but although I am convinced that these assumptions are true, I shall not try to defend these assumptions here.

The political question that I am concerned with, about whether the law should allow same-sex marriage, is clearly different from all the *ethical* questions that concern individual conduct, including the

From R. Baker, K. Wininger, and F. Elliston, eds., *Philosophy and Sex*, Third Edition, pp. 212–230.

question whether it is right or wrong (ethically speaking) for two people of the same sex to get married. Indeed, my argument for same-sex marriage is not just focused on a different issue from these ethical views about whether it is right or wrong to marry someone of one's own sex, it is *independent* of all such views.

My reason for making my argument independent of such ethical views is simply that all such views are intensely controversial. Some people believe that entering into a same-sex marriage would sometimes be the right thing to do, while others are firmly convinced that it would always be wrong. This disagreement about same-sex marriage is typically rooted in a disagreement about homosexuality, since it is generally assumed that marriage involves sexual relations.

The advantage of my neutral defense of same-sex marriage is that it allows us simply to *agree to disagree* about these disputed ethical questions, and to decide the political question on other grounds. "Agreeing to disagree" about a question involves finding a way to live and act together with the people with whom you disagree that is itself based on agreement. Agreeing to disagree on some question is easiest if the disputed question is simply *irrelevant* to the collective decisions that you have to make together. Even if the disputed question is not simply irrelevant, however, it may be possible to agree that other principles are more important in the context, and so to base your collective decisions on those shared principles. Finding ways to agree to disagree is extremely important in any pluralistic society that aspires to be democratic. Perhaps certain fervent atheists believe that society would be better off if religious belief were to die out. Still, they may be able to "agree to disagree" with religious believers if they accept that, in the context,

respecting freedom is more important than achieving their ideal of a postreligious society.

My argument then will rely, not on any disputed ethical view about homosexuality, but on the more widely held values of *democracy, freedom,* and *equality*. First, I argue that the values of freedom and democracy support a certain view of the essential rationale of the institution of marriage—that is, of the fundamental way in which marriage serves the common good (or at least would serve the common good if it were a just social institution). Assuming this account of marriage's rationale, I then argue that the ban on same-sex marriage conflicts with the value of equality and is for that reason seriously unjust. Finally, in arguing against some proposed justifications for the ban on same-sex marriage, I appeal again to the values of freedom and democracy.[2]

In principle then, even people who believe that homosexual relationships are deviant and inferior to traditional heterosexual marriages should find my defense of same-sex marriage convincing—so long as they also believe that it is more important for social institutions to respect the values of democracy, freedom, and equality, than for them to affirm this view of the moral superiority of heterosexuality. I have also tried to rely on the least controversial ideas about democracy, freedom, and equality, that I could. My goal is to construct a defense of same-sex marriage on the basis of the weakest assumptions possible. In this way, I hope that something like the argument presented here could be the basis for a widespread consensus in favor of same-sex marriage.

Besides its political utility, my argument may also have some philosophical interest. Many philosophers find the institution of marriage puzzling: why, after all, should the state become involved in people's intimate personal relationships? Many people assume that marriage necessarily involves the state's "legitimizing," or encouraging approval of, certain intimate relationships—implicitly by contrast with other, less favored relationships. But if this assumption is correct, marriage itself seems quite dubious, since it is doubtful that it is appropriate for the state to "legitimize" certain intimate relationships at all, let alone to do so at the expense of other relationships.[3] Although I do not offer a full defense of marriage (I argue only that the ban on same-sex marriage is unjust), I do propose an alternative view of marriage; and my alternative view may make marriage seem at least somewhat less dubious.

What is Marriage?

In spite of the large role that religion has played in its history, marriage is clearly not an essentially religious institution, since secular civil marriage is evidently a kind of marriage.[4] So what are the essential features of marriage?

It seems that marriage has always involved something like *marriage law*. In modern pluralistic societies, marriage law is part of civil law. In the past, marriage law was often part of religious law rather than civil law—such as Christian canon law, which was administered by the church courts, or Jewish religious law, which was administered by rabbinical courts. In those nonpluralistic societies, however, the religious authorities were just as much a valid source of law as the civil authorities. So it might seem that marriage is simply a *legal* institution, in the sense that its nature is entirely determined by the marriage laws that are laid down by some socially recognized authority.

This legalistic assumption has been common in recent discussions of same-sex

marriage; but it is, I think, a mistake. The legal character of marriage is not enough by itself to explain the institution's special centrality and importance in the lives of so many people. To explain why marriage plays this central role in people's lives, we must appeal, not only to marriage's legal character, but also to its *social meaning*, the web of shared assumptions about marriage that are common knowledge in society.

It is essential to marriage, it seems to me, that it has such a social meaning—that is, that it is an extraordinarily *familiar* social institution, which practically everyone has heard about and has some understanding of. For marriage to exist, it is not enough that there are certain laws on the books; these laws must also be surrounded by a familiar social practice of the appropriate kind. Imagine a society that had some laws on the books that defined a certain legal relationship, which in fact involved all the legal rights and obligations that marriage confers in our society, but which no one except a few legal theorists had ever heard of. Suppose that this society also recognized a relationship that had a different name, which was undergirded by generally recognized religious laws very similar to Roman Catholic marriage laws, and was universally familiar and understood, and generally favored by couples who wanted to share their lives together. In this society, it seems to me, it is the second relationship that is marriage, while the first, purely legal relationship is just some obscure sort of legal covenant.

So it is essential to marriage that it has a social meaning. This social meaning is a cultural phenomenon, consisting above all in the great familiarity of the institution, and the prevalence of certain shared understandings about what the institution involves. These shared understandings or assumptions vary over time and from place to place, but there is a basic core which seems essential to marriage.

First, marriage is understood to be a relationship between exactly two people.[5] It is, I think, always assumed that a married couple will normally be living together and have at least at some time had sex together; that they have shared finances, or at least will support each other economically if necessary; and that the two married people have a serious commitment to sustaining their relationship. It is generally assumed that both spouses will share in the activity of running their household (even if they play very different roles in that activity). In particular, it is assumed that if the married couple have children together, then they will share the responsibilities of parenthood.[6]

Marriage enables the married couple to make it public that they are in this sort of relationship, simply by exploiting these general assumptions about marriage: you can tell people "We are married," with the result that they will immediately come to expect that you are living together, have had sex, have shared finances, are committed to sustaining this relationship, and so on.

Saying "We are married" has this effect only because of the great familiarity of marriage. Suppose that I told you, "John and I went to the Odin-worshipping temple last week and had a ceremony to become each other's gloggle." You would have no idea what I meant. I would have to offer a lengthy explanation. Or suppose that I told you, "John and I became each other's domestic partner at City Hall last week." You would not have to be extraordinarily ignorant to wonder, "Do domestic partnerships expire every year unless they are renewed? Should I assume that you are lovers, or just that you are roommates who want to make sure that each of you can continue to rent the apartment in case the

other roommate dies? Have you made a commitment to support your domestic partner even if he loses his job, or do you just share the chore of buying groceries?" Again, I could not convey the information that I want to convey without a lengthy explanation.

This social meaning is, it seems to me, one of the essential features of marriage. But at least some of the legal aspects of marriage are no less essential, and closely bound up with its social meaning. The legal aspects of marriage fall into the following three categories.

First, it is the law that confers the marital status itself. When one learns that two people are married, one takes this to mean that those people have met all the legal requirements for being married. If people known not to be legally married say "We are married," they are understood to be speaking metaphorically or in jest. The fact that the marital status is conferred by law explains why it is not a controversial question whether or not two people are married. If two people are married, then there is typically general agreement that they are married, even among people who take very different views of those people and of the kind of life that they lead.

Second, marriage in many ways resembles a contract: each spouse has certain legally binding rights and obligations with respect to the other.[7] Many of these mutual rights and obligations have the function of assuring the spouses that they can rely economically on each other. Nowadays, these rights include, most notably, the right to spousal support; the right (in the event of divorce or separation) to alimony and an equitable division of property; and the right to inherit even if there is no will. Another group of mutual rights reflects the idea that spouses are each other's "next of kin." Nowadays, these rights include the legal authority to act for an incapacitated spouse; hospital visitation rights; and a right to priority in claiming human remains. These rights express the general assumption that spouses have a more intimate relationship with each other than with anyone else, and are committed to maintaining this relationship: hence, it is assumed, one's spouse will understand one's interests best, and is likely to have one's interests at heart; so one's spouse is best placed to act on one's behalf when necessary. The fact that marriage involves such legally binding obligations is crucial for reinforcing the assumption that married people have a serious commitment to maintaining their relationship.

Third, the state often provides certain special benefits for married couples over and above the marital status itself and the enforcement of spousal obligations. (In a similar way, many nongovernment organizations, especially employers, have a policy of giving certain special benefits to married couples, most notably health insurance.) Some of these special legal benefits reflect the expectation that the married couple have shared finances: under current law, married couples can file their taxes jointly, and property transfers between spouses are not taxed. Other such special legal benefits include the right to visit one's spouse in prison; the right not to be compelled to testify against one's spouse; and the right of a foreign spouse to receive preferential immigration treatment. These benefits reflect the expectation that marriage is a longterm intimate relationship: it would be thought unacceptably cruel to deny spousal visits to prisoners, to keep spouses apart through immigration barriers, or to compel anyone to testify against his or her spouse.

This third legal aspect of marriage—the benefits that the state (like certain other organizations such as employers) provides for married couples, in addition to the marital status itself and the enforcement of spousal obligations—is certainly an important aspect of marriage today. But these special legal benefits do not seem to be *essential* to the institution of marriage itself. Marriage would still exist if there were no tax breaks for married couples. What is really essential to marriage, I propose, is the legally conferred marital status, the legally binding mutual commitments, and the social meaning of the relationship.

The claim that these special legal benefits are not essential to marriage implies that a justification of marriage need not itself involve a justification of these special benefits. There ought to be a *separate* justification for attaching these special legal benefits to marriage. Such a justification would have to show that in attaching these benefits to marriage alone, the state is not unjustly discriminating against single people, or against unmarried couples. (The most plausible justification may be that these benefits are uniquely appropriate for couples who have a longterm intimate relationship involving economic and domestic cooperation; and rather than employing some intrusive test to determine whether a couple has a relationship of this kind, it is reasonable for the state simply to attach these benefits to marriage. But we need not consider this question here.)

The essential elements of marriage—the legally binding mutual commitments, the legally conferred marital status, and the social meaning of marriage—together form a coherent package. The legally binding mutual commitments of marriage are at least roughly standardized throughout society, and, when necessary, enforced, thus providing an assurance that these commitments will be fulfilled.[8] This reinforces and standardizes society's shared assumptions about marriage, since the mutual commitments of marriage clearly reflect these shared assumptions; thus, marriage has a clear social meaning that is understood, not just by a limited subculture, but by society as a whole. If the law attaches certain standardized rights and obligations to marriage, then the law must determine who counts as married and who does not; and the fact that the law determines who counts as married also ensures that there is general agreement about who is married and who is not, thus allowing a married couple to be regarded as married, not just by their circle of friends, but by society as a whole.

Consider what might happen if the law did not determine who was married and who was not. Suppose that individuals were free to form whatever legally binding contracts they wished, and nongovernment associations (such as religious organizations) were free to call any relationship a "marriage" if they wished; but no public authority made any attempt to determine which relationships counted as marriages and which did not. The risk is that this situation would lead to ever-increasing confusion about what the term "marriage" implies. Different associations might take very different views of what is required for a couple to be married: some associations might regard certain vows that are not legally binding as sufficient for marriage; some associations might allow polygamous marriages; some associations might allow marriages that expire every year unless renewed; and some of these "marriages" might become common between pairs of friends whose relationship is entirely nonsexual. This would confuse the social meaning of marriage so much that there would no longer be any clear shared understanding of marriage. Except within limited subcultures, saying "We are married" would convey little information. The point is not that such confusion is necessarily the most likely result

of this situation. The point is that if we are to be assured that marriage will not cease to have any clear social meaning in this way, then marriage must be insulated from the risk of such confusion; and the only effective way to insulate marriage from this risk is for marital status to be determined by law.[9]

For these reasons then, it is essential to marriage that it is undergirded by marriage law; and marriage law requires some generally recognized authority (such as the state or the religious authorities) as its source. In a pluralistic society, however, there is only one authority that is generally recognized as a valid source of law, namely, the state. So, in a pluralistic society, marriage law has to be part of the civil laws of the state.

In sum, marriage is a legally conferred relationship between two people, involving legally binding mutual commitments; the character of these commitments reflects society's shared understandings and assumptions about this relationship, assumptions that make this relationship uniquely familiar and well understood; and the core of these assumptions is that marriage involves both sexual intimacy and sharing the necessities of life.[10]

Why Marriage Might Further the Common Good

Several writers have argued that the chief justification for the institution of marriage is that it encourages married life, which tends (according to these writers) to be a particularly virtuous or valuable way of life.[11]

If this were the official justification for the institution of marriage, the government, in giving this justification, would have to appeal explicitly to this view about the value of married life—a view that we might call "conjugalism," perhaps. But the trouble is that this view, "conjugalism," is unnecessarily controversial. It is a view about the good life that many people quite reasonably reject. It seems far better for government not to take sides on controversial questions of this kind, if it can avoid it (just as it should take no sides in the dispute between Catholics and Protestants). The political process ought to involve a serious attempt to find ways of "agreeing to disagree," and of basing public policy decisions on the most inclusive possible consensus, since only then can such decisions be seen as collectively authorized by the people as a whole—that is, as democratically legitimate. The following principle encapsulates this point:

> Inclusive Democracy
> In a well-functioning democracy, the exercise of public authority should typically be adequately justified in public discussion on the basis of values that are as uncontroversial as possible.[12]

For example, wherever possible, laws and public policies should be justified by appeal to uncontroversial values like security, prosperity, freedom, and equality—not by appeal to controversial values about which there is deep, widespread, and intense disagreement. The controversial justification of marriage just considered will clearly conflict with *Inclusive Democracy* if there is an alternative justification of marriage that is less controversial. As I argue below, there is another, less controversial justification.

This controversial justification of marriage may also conflict with the value of freedom. This justification commits the state to promoting married life. But the existence of marriage will have the effect of encouraging married life only if a large proportion of the population desire to become and stay married—that is, presumably, only if it is widely believed that married life is a particularly good life to

lead. So, the government, in giving this controversial justification, would also be committing itself to *promoting* the view that married life is an especially good life to lead. If the government is really committed to promoting this view, it would have to encourage a social climate in which people are put under *pressure* to accept this view.[13] But in causing people to be pressured into accepting a controversial view of the best way to lead intimate and personal aspects of one's life, the government would be compromising people's power to lead their lives in the light of the beliefs, values, and choices that they develop through their own autonomous deliberation. In so doing, it would violate the following principle:

> Freedom
> Government should respect and protect people's power to lead their own lives in the light of their own beliefs, values, and choices (unless, perhaps, it is uncontroversial that compromising freedom in some way brings great benefits, while imposing only relatively trivial burdens).[14]

For these reasons then, the justification in question is misguided.

Not all proposed justifications of marriage are misguided for these reasons. Some writers have suggested that marriage is justified because it helps to cement stable relationships of a kind that tend to be highly beneficial both to those involved and, more indirectly, to a wider circle of people. Moreover, if unmarried people are discouraged from having children, then marriage will also help children to be brought up in stable families of this kind. These justifications of marriage do not obviously conflict with the principles of *Freedom* and *Inclusive Democracy*. They appeal to values that are relatively uncontroversial: practically everyone agrees that it is good for *some* couples to form stable unions, and that it is usually good for children to be brought up in a stable family of this sort.

It may well be that marriage does help to cement stable relationships. One reason for this may be that the community tends to support married couples' relationships more than unmarried couples'. Since the married couple have made a legally binding commitment, and have typically also made their commitment public, in a way that is especially readily understood, typically more people know about their relationship and regard the relationship as serious and likely to last; so if these people have goodwill toward the couple, they will tend to support their relationship. It has been claimed that empirical evidence about modern Western societies suggests that couples who marry are significantly more likely to stay together than couples who stay unmarried, and that stable relationships are on balance good for people: single people are apparently more likely to commit suicide, to fall sick, to become dependent on public assistance, and so on.[15]

Still, I shall argue that these justifications at best pinpoint beneficial *side effects* of marriage, not the essential rationale for the institution. The "essential rationale" for an institution, I assume, must be both necessary and sufficient to justify the institution, in any possible situation in which it is justified. But we can easily imagine that marriage might not have had these beneficial effects: perhaps married couples were no more likely to stay together than unmarried couples, people in stable relationships no happier and no healthier than single people, and children brought up by two parents no better off than children brought up by single parents. This would not by itself show that marriage was not a good social institution to have. So long as marriage had no positively harmful consequences, and so long

as people still wanted to be married, for reasons that were clearly serious and deserved to be respected, marriage would still be a good institution to have. On the other hand, if no one ever desired to marry, except perhaps for plainly frivolous or malicious reasons, then marriage would not be a good institution to have. So the essential rationale for marriage is simply that many people *want* to be married, for reasons that are clearly serious and deserve to be respected.

What do I mean by saying that people want to marry "for reasons that are clearly serious and deserve to be respected"? What I have in mind is that this desire is of a certain kind, such that it is generally agreed that there are strong reasons for public policy not to interfere with people's attempts to fulfill desires of this kind, and good reasons for public policy to support or assist people's attempts to fulfill such desires:[16] It is strong evidence that a desire is of this kind if the desire is extremely widespread and strongly held, and few people strongly resent those who succeed in fulfilling this desire.

It is plausible that the desire to marry is usually a serious desire in exactly this way. People want to get married in order to make a legally binding commitment, of a certain particularly familiar and widely recognized kind. This desire is both widespread and strongly held; and few people strongly resent those who satisfy this desire. Moreover, the typical reasons for wanting to marry all seem to be reasons that command respect. Some may want to get married as a gesture of love for their spouse; others because they wish to celebrate and share their happiness with their friends and family; others because they wish to cement their own relationship, by impressing on themselves their commitment to each other, and by enlisting the support of the community; and others may have the special legal benefits in view. All these reasons are clearly serious; none is frivolous or malicious.

Here is a plausible claim about one way in which social institutions can further the common good:

One way to further the common good
If a social institution is indispensable for enabling people to fulfill certain serious desires that they have, and if, at the same time, this institution does not impose any serious burdens on anyone else, and violates no principle of justice, then the institution furthers the common good.

Offhand, it seems plausible that marriage does further the common good in this way. People are impelled to marry by a serious desire to make a legally binding mutual commitment, of a certain uniquely familiar and well-understood kind: that is, people want some assurance that this commitment will have a clear social meaning of the relevant kind. As I argued in the previous section, we can only be assured that marriage will have a clear social meaning of this kind if marital status is determined by law. So legal marriage really is indispensable for enabling people to fulfill this serious desire that they have. Through undergirding the institution of marriage, the state provides a benefit that, in a pluralistic society, only the state can provide.[17]

Moreover, it might seem that marriage need not impose any burdens on anyone—not even on the taxpayer, since presumably the cost of maintaining the institution could be covered by the license fee (which could be means-tested to allow everyone to get married). So, on these assumptions, if the institution of marriage violates no principle of justice, it furthers the common good.

In the following section, however, I shall argue that marriage, in its present form, does not further the common good. This is because its present form involves a ban on same-sex marriage; and that ban violates a principle of justice.

The Demands of Equality

One might be tempted to argue that the ban on same-sex marriage is an unjustified restriction of freedom. The ban closes off a certain option, the option of marrying someone of one's own sex; surely people would be more free if this option were open to them. But, on second thoughts, it is not clear that failing to provide this option in itself limits people's freedom. It does not seem that a society that had never had the institution of marriage would thereby be less free than one that had it. So the most plausible objection to the ban on same-sex marriage is not that it denies an option that is essential to freedom, but that it denies an option to some that is *actually made available to others.* That is, the ban conflicts with the value of *equality.*

I am appealing here to the most basic and uncontroversial idea of equality—the idea that society, as a collective body, must treat all its members with equal respect. It must acknowledge that they are all equally members of society, and that they should not be impeded or obstructed in their participation in the life of society. I shall try to capture this idea with the following principle:

Minimal Equality
Every adult should have an equal, unabridged right to participate in the basic institutions of society (unless, perhaps, it is uncontroversial that a somewhat unequal or abridged right brings great benefits and imposes only relatively trivial burdens).

The basic point of this principle is to rule out certain unjust forms of discrimination.

Among the basic institutions of society are various political and economic institutions. So violations of *Minimal Equality* include the following familiar examples: denying women the right to vote; denying Roman Catholics the right to own land; a ban on Jews or atheists serving as members of Parliament; and the apartheid system in South Africa, which specifically excluded black South Africans from a large number of social institutions.

These examples, all familiar from history, involve discrimination on the basis of sex, race, or religion. But there could be many other examples. For example, in many societies only property-owners had the right to vote or to serve on juries. Or we could imagine a society in which people born into a certain caste were prohibited from filing civil lawsuits or pressing criminal charges in a court of law; or a society where widows, or redheads, or left-handed people were regarded as unlucky and so forbidden to work in a large number of occupations; or a mostly vegetarian society where people known to eat meat were forbidden to own or edit newspapers; and so on.

Marriage seems also to be one of the basic institutions of society. So, according to *Minimal Equality* everyone should have an equal unabridged legal right to participate in the institution: everyone should have an equal right to marry. But it might seem strange to claim that anyone is denied this right. After all, everyone, including those who wish to share their life with someone of the same sex, has the right to marry someone of the opposite sex (that, after all, is how many dictionaries define "marriage"); and no one has the right to "marry" someone of the same sex. So everyone has the same rights: no one is denied a right that is available to others.

But obviously a precisely parallel claim could be made about the ban on interracial marriage. You could say: everyone has the right to marry a member of her own race; and no one has the right to marry someone of a race different from her own. So everyone has the same rights: no one is denied a right that is available to others. But almost everyone today agrees that the ban on interracial marriages was an unjust form of discrimination.

This points to something important. Unless we impose some restrictions on how "rights to participate in society's basic institutions" are specified, then the demand for equal rights can be totally trivialized. Unless we impose some such restrictions, then any system of rights, no matter how unjust and discriminatory, could be specified in such a way that everyone can be said to have the same rights. Consider the old apartheid system, in which white South Africans could vote, while black South Africans could not. Suppose you say that the "form of political participation traditional for white South Africans" involved voting, running for office, and so on, while the "form of political participation traditional for black South Africans" consisted in holding political demonstrations until they were dispersed, often brutally, by the police. Then you could say that, under the apartheid system, everyone had an equal right to the form of political participation that was traditional for her ethnic group.

Clearly, this is outrageous. The rights in question have to be specified in the right sort of way. It was to signal this point that my formulation of *Minimal Equality* required that everyone's right to participate in society's basic institutions should be not only equal but also *unabridged*. But what does it mean for rights to be "unabridged" in this sense? What is the right way to specify such rights?

The key idea, I propose, is that each of the rights that we ought to have must be a right to something that is *desirable* or *worthwhile* in a certain way. Consider the right to participate in a certain social institution. Typically, it is part of the essential rationale of a social institution that there is something about participating in that institution that makes it an advantageous or worthwhile thing to do. If so, then the right in question must be specified in terms of the features of exercising the right that make it advantageous or worthwhile. Whatever exactly the rationale for a democratic political process may be, it is clear that the reason why participating in such a process is worthwhile has nothing to do with the fact that one is participating in the way that is traditional for one's ethnic group. That fact is incidental to what makes participation in the process desirable or worthwhile. So the right to political participation should not be restricted to political participation of the kind traditional for one's ethnic group. Such a restriction would be arbitrary at best.

Similarly, the essential rationale of civil marriage, I have argued, is that it enables couples to fulfill their serious desire to make a legally binding commitment to each other, of a certain uniquely familiar and widely understood kind. Getting married is worthwhile because it enables the married couple to fulfill this serious desire. But—I claim—many same-sex couples have exactly the same desire, to make such a commitment to each other, as opposite-sex couples. So the reason why getting married is worthwhile has nothing to do with the fact that one is marrying someone of the opposite sex; that fact is incidental to what makes getting married valuable or worthwhile for the married couple. So the right to get married should not be specified as the right to marry someone of the opposite sex. That is at best an arbitrary restriction of this right.

My claim, that many same-sex couples have exactly the same desire as opposite-sex couples, might be controverted. Someone might object that a traditional opposite-sex marriage and a so-called same-sex marriage are so different in their nature and their worth that the desires must also be quite different in kind. But whether two couples' desires count as "the same desire" should not be decided on the basis of such controversial ethical views. It should be decided on *empirical* grounds, by finding out whether our best empirical psychology needs to draw a sharp distinction between the desires of same-sex couples and those of opposite-sex couples, or whether more or less the same psychological theory is true of both. So my claim is in fact the first of the empirical assumptions on which my defense of same-sex marriage is based:

1. Many same-sex couples desire to get married for essentially the same kinds of reasons as opposite-sex couples; that is, they are motivated by desires that empirical psychology would hardly even need to treat differently, for theoretical or explanatory purposes.

As I warned at the outset, I am not going to defend this empirical assumption, although I am convinced that it is true. There is in my view ample evidence for this assumption, in the motives that move many same-sex couples to have "commitment ceremonies," or to enter registered domestic partnerships. But a full defense of the assumption would require a more extensive survey than I can undertake.

If this assumption is true, then we can see why anything less than full same-sex marriage is "separate and unequal." Commitment ceremonies, private contractual arrangements, and registered domestic partnerships are just not as familiar and well understood as marriage. They lack the resonance of marriage. Saying, "We had a commitment ceremony two years ago," or "We are registered domestic partners," signally lacks the social consequences of saying, "We are married." As a result, commitment ceremonies and registered partnerships are unlikely to be as effective as marriage for a couple who want to impress their commitment on themselves by affirming it publicly in a way that the community will readily understand, or to enlist the support of the community for their relationship. To fulfill the desires effectively, same-sex couples actually need to be able to *say that they are married*. The word "marriage" (or some word that means the same thing in the language of the community) is essential. Suppose that same-sex marriage had a different name—as it might be, "quarriage." Inevitably, would be fewer same-sex quarriages than opposite-sex marriages; so, even if the term became more familiar over the years, "quarriage" would always be less familiar and well understood than "marriage." Hence the arrangement would still be separate and unequal.

When the right to marry is properly specified, in its genuine, unabridged form, as the right to get married to the person who wishes to marry you, it is clear that not everyone has this right. Those who wish to marry members of the opposite sex have it, while those who wish to marry members of the same sex do not. Prima facie, this is a violation of *Minimal Equality*, and so an unjust form of discrimination.

In fact, the first and third of my three empirical assumptions are sufficient to show that the ban on same-sex marriage is unjust. But there is also an additional factor that makes this form of discrimination, not merely unjust, but intolerably unjust.

This is the second empirical assumption of my defense of same-sex marriage:

2. Many people are gay or lesbian: that is, they have an involuntary and effectively immutable homosexual orientation; they are, and will always be, sexually attracted only toward members of their own sex.

This point is sometimes denied; but it has been adequately confirmed by contemporary psychology. Sexual intimacy is typically an integral part of marriage. So gay and lesbian people have no hope of forming a satisfactory marriage except with a member of their own sex. Hence a ban on same-sex marriage excludes lesbian and gay people from marriage altogether. This makes the ban on same-sex marriage not just unjust, but intolerably unjust.

Still, I have formulated the minimal equality principle so that it allows for exceptions: if an unequal or abridged right uncontroversially brings great benefits, while imposing only relatively trivial burdens, it may be justified. For instance, it would be outrageous if people of Asian descent were denied driver's licenses. But it is not outrageous that blind people are denied driver's licenses. Denying blind people the right to drive does not deprive them of any benefit that they could realistically have, and is essential to maintaining road safety; so it is clearly justified. So, my defense of same-sex marriage also rests on a third empirical assumption:

3. The ban on same-sex marriage brings no uncontroversial benefits that could outweigh its obvious and serious burdens.

Many writers have claimed that same-sex marriage would have harmful effects. Typically, these writers allege that their claims are supported by empirical evidence;

and, as before, I shall not assess this alleged empirical evidence here. But some writers appear to believe that the ban on same-sex marriage can be justified directly on the basis of the view that homosexual acts and relationships are morally wrong, or at least greatly inferior to heterosexual acts and relationships. In the remainder of this section, I shall argue that the ban on same-sex marriage cannot be justified in this way.

Some people argue, on the basis of this moral view of the inferiority of homosexuality, that same-sex marriage must be banned in order to discourage homosexual acts and relationships, or at least to affirm this moral view of homosexuality. But this argument does not reveal any *uncontroversial* benefits of the ban on same-sex marriage, since this moral view of homosexuality is clearly intensely controversial. No appeal to such controversial "benefits" could justify an exception to the principle of *Minimal Equality.*

The requirement that only uncontroversial benefits can justify exceptions to the principle of *Minimal Equality* reflects the principle of *Inclusive Democracy,* together with the assumption that equality itself is a value that is basically uncontroversial. Practically everyone agrees that equality is an important value, while this moral view about homosexuality is intensely controversial. Since it is important, in a pluralistic society that aspires to be democratic, to find ways of "agreeing to disagree," it is preferable to base our decision about same-sex marriage on the relatively uncontroversial value of equality, rather than on such controversial moral views.

Moreover, there is a general objection to laws that aim to discourage homosexuality, or to affirm the superiority of heterosexuality; and this objection is also grounded in another relatively uncontroversial value—namely, *freedom.* Laws

that discourage homosexuality aim to put pressure on people to adopt a view that not only is highly controversial, but also concerns the best way to lead the most intimate and important aspects of one's life. This is connected with the fact that the kind of conduct stigmatized by this view consists of intimate interaction between *consenting adults*: while it is uncontroversial that nonconsensual sexual interactions are wrong, the consenting adults who engage in homosexual acts typically do not believe that these acts are wrong; indeed, they typically believe that their engaging in such acts is vital for their chances of living the best life that they can (even if they are wrong to believe this, this belief is clearly a considered, coherent part of their whole outlook on life). Laws that put pressure on people to adopt a view of this kind compromise people's power to lead their own lives in the light of their own beliefs, values, and choices. Thus, the principle of *Freedom* condemns all laws that aim to discourage or denigrate homosexuality. The ban on same-sex marriage cannot possibly be justified by any moral view of homosexuality.

By contrast, lifting the ban on same-sex marriage would not in itself express any ethical view about homosexuality. It is not plausible that marriage involves the state's expressing its approval of any particular relationship. After all, convicted wife-murderers, convicted child-abusers, and convicted rapists are all allowed to get married (indeed, they can even get married while in prison).[18] The state is not expressing approval of these relationships. So why should we think that if the state allows same-sex marriage, it is expressing any view about whether same-sex marriage is inferior to opposite-sex marriage? The state could even allow same-sex marriage while making a special proclamation that it values marriages that raise children properly, and has no position on whether or not same-sex marriages are inferior to opposite-sex marriages, no more than it has any official position on whether Christianity is better than Judaism or atheism.

The Role of Empirical Evidence

My "philosophical defence" of same-sex marriage is now complete. Before concluding, however, I shall briefly comment on the role of empirical evidence in answering the commonest objections to same-sex marriage.

My defense of same-sex marriage rested on three empirical assumptions: (1) same-sex couples typically want to get married for essentially the same sorts of reasons as opposite-sex couples; (2) the ban on same-sex marriage imposes intolerable burdens on some people; and (3) the ban brings no uncontroversial benefits. Of these three assumptions, the most controversial is the third. Clearly, further empirical investigation is needed to evaluate this assumption.

Still, it is not necessary to prove this third assumption beyond all reasonable doubt. It is fair to demand that we should be reasonably confident that introducing same-sex marriage will not cause serious harm. But the main burden of proof should be on those who wish to justify exceptions to *Minimal Equality* (although it may be arguable that there should also be some burden of proof on those who wish to achieve such equality by means of radical departures from the status quo).

Moreover, in assessing the empirical evidence for this third assumption, we need only consider whether there are any uncontroversial benefits that are *effectively inseparable* from the ban on same-sex marriage. Suppose for example—what seems to me almost certainly false[19]—that the empirical evidence shows that same-sex couples are bad parents. This does not show that the ban on same-sex marriage in itself brings any uncontroversial benefits, since it would always be possible to sever the connection between marriage and the legal right to adopt children. A ban on same-sex marriage would not be necessary in order to protect children, even if it were necessary to ban adoption by same-sex couples.

It might be thought that my account of marriage clearly supports the often-repeated claim that allowing same-sex marriage would weaken and undermine the institution of marriage. According to my account, it is essential to marriage that it has a clear and widely understood social meaning. But it is plainly part of the current social meaning of marriage that it is the union of one man and one woman. If you say, "I'm getting married," people will assume that you are getting married to someone of the opposite sex. So wouldn't allowing same-sex marriage confuse and destabilize the social meaning of marriage?

Introducing same-sex marriage would indeed *change* the social meaning of marriage. But the social meaning of marriage has already changed in many ways: most notably, it is now widely assumed that marriage ought to be a relationship of equals, whereas formerly it was assumed that the wife ought to be subordinated under the authority of her husband. Few people really want the social meaning of marriage to stay forever unchanged; what they fundamentally want is that marriage have a *clear* social meaning, involving a certain *basic core* of shared understandings about how marriage involves both intimacy and sharing the necessities of life. Introducing same-sex marriage would not change this basic core of marriage's social meaning, and it need not lead to great confusion about what marriage involves. So there is no need to fear that same-sex marriage would undermine or weaken marriage in this way.

My argument's reliance on these three assumptions also suggests a reply to the ever-popular "polygamy objection"—the objection that the arguments for same-sex marriage can be automatically adapted to support polygamy. To answer this objection, we should consider the empirical evidence for the three corresponding assumptions with respect to Polygamy. (1) Do those who are already married and want to acquire a second spouse typically want this for the same sorts of reasons as impel people to enter their first marriage? Or is the motivation for entering polygamous marriages typically quite different, from a psychological point of view? (2) Is there such a thing as a polygamous sexual orientation? is there any significant group of people whose only hope of a satisfactory marriage is to have more than one marriage at the same time? (3) Does the ban on polygamy bring any uncontroversial benefits? Would allowing polygamy cause serious harm? It is far from obvious that the answers to these questions will be the same as the answers to the corresponding questions about same-sex marriage.[20]

Conclusion

I have argued that if marriage is to be justifiable at all, it must be made available to same-sex couples as well as opposite-sex couples. I have also given an account of the essential rationale for the institution of marriage—that is, of the basic way in which marriage would further the common good, if it were a justifiable institution. I have not argued that marriage definitely would be a justifiable institution as soon as the ban on same-sex marriage is lifted. Perhaps marriage also violates a principle of justice in some other way (perhaps it still discriminates against women, for example); or perhaps people's reasons for wanting to get married are in fact typically frivolous or malicious, rather than serious reasons that deserve to be respected. By itself, however, my argument does nothing to suggest that marriage is marred by any such flaws. My argument poses no threat to the justification of marriage itself—only to the existing ban on same-sex marriage.

Notes

1. See William N. Eskridge, Jr., *The Case for the Same-Sex Marriage* (New York: Free Press, 1996); Cass R. Sunstein, "Homosexuality and the Constitution," in David Estlund and Martha Nussbaum, eds., *Sex, Preference and Family: Essays on Law and Nature* (New York: Oxford University Press, 1997); and Mark Strasser, *Legally Wed: Same-Sex Marriage and the Constitution* (Ithaca, NY: Cornell University Press, 1997).

2. The overall structure of my argument is similar to that of A. A. Wellington, "Why Liberals Should Support Same-Sex Marriage," *Journal of Social Philosophy* 26, 3 (Winter 1995): 5–32. There are many differences between our arguments, however: I give a quite different account of the nature of marriage and of its

essential rationale, and my appeal to equality is related to my account of marriage's rationale in a different way.

3. This argument has often been used to attack marriage; see, for example, Paula Ettelbrick, "Since When Is Marriage a Path to Liberation?" in Robert Baird and Stuart Rosenbaum, eds., *Same-Sex Marriage: The Moral and Legal Debate* (Amherst, NY: Prometheus Books, 1997).

4. Indeed, even in the past, as recent historians have pointed out, "although the church had been trying to control marriage since the twelfth century, it had only been partially successful in doing so" (John Gillis, *For Better, for Worse: British Marriages, 1600 to the Present* [New York: Oxford University Press, 1985], p. 15).

5. The existence of polygamy is no exception: the patriarch Jacob had a separate marriage with each of his two wives, not one "group marriage" in which all three of them married each other. Polygamy involves being in *more than one* marriage *simultaneously.*

6. Thus, if society draws a distinction between legitimate and illegitimate Children, the child of a married couple will count as legitimate (since both parents are expected to assume full parental responsibilities for the child). But it is not essential to marriage that society should draw any distinction between legitimate and illegitimate children.

7. Marriage need not strictly speaking *be* a contract, however. In the United States, for example, marriage is not covered by the constitutional rule that "no state shall pass any law impairing the obligation of contracts." The rights and obligations of marriage can be changed by new legislation even without the consent of the parties involved (just as these rights and obligations change if the married couple move to another state). Under American law then, marriage is a legal *status*, which is entered by means of a contract. For this point, and an account of the mutual rights and obligations of marriage, see Harry D. Krause, *Family Law in a Nutshell*, 3rd ed. (St. Paul, MN: West Pub. Co., 1995), pp. 88–90, and chapters 8, 25, and 26.

8. I say "roughly standardized," not only because of variations between the marriage laws of different states, but also because of the variations introduced by prenuptial agreements. Still, not all spousal rights and obligations can be waived by means of such agreements. For example, parties are not permitted to contract away their obligation to support their spouse during the marriage. There are numerous other restrictions as well; see Kraus, *Family Law in a Nutshell*, pp. 91–99.

9. Consider two social relationships and practices that are not undergirded by law, promising and friendship. Promising has a clear social meaning, but promising is a relatively simple social practice, defined by a clear social norm whose utility is generally understood. Marriage is a much more complex practice, serving many different functions; and the social norms surrounding marriage are often contested, in this respect, friendship resembles marriage: it too is complex, serves many different functions, and is often contested. Unlike marriage, friendship is not undergirded by law, and has little in the way of a clear social meaning. Saying, "We are friends" conveys remarkably little information (as Brecht's Mother Courage says, "I don't trust him— he's a friend of mine").

10. I owe this formulation to Richard Mohr, "The Case for Gay Marriage," in Baird and Rosenbaum, *Same-Sex Marriage: The Moral and Legal Debate*, pp. 91–92.

11. Andrew Sullivan, *Virtually Normal: An Argument about Homosexuality* (New York: Knopf, 1995), p. 182; see also his "Three's a Crowd," in Andrew Sullivan, ed., *Same-Sex Marriage: Pro and Con* (New York: Vintage Books, 1997), pp. 278–82.

12. Thus, every proposed public policy decision should be given the most uncontroversial justification possible; and if, out of two alternative public policy decisions, one can be adequately justified on the basis of much less controversial values than the other, then typically the first decision is preferable to the second. Whether one value is more or less controversial than another depends on at least three factors: how widespread the disagreement is (how many people disagree); how deep it is (whether it is a rational disagreement about basic values, or just a matter of detail); and how intense it is (how much reasonable resentment would be felt if the value were a basis for public policy). (For similar ideas, compare John Rawls, *Political Liberalism* [New York: Columbia University Press, 1993], Lectures IV and V; and Joshua Cohen's unpublished "Deliberative Democracy.")

13. This consequence is explicitly embraced by Jonathan Rauch, "For Better or Worse?" in Sullivan, *Same-Sex Marriage: Pro and Con*, pp. 169–81.

14. By this contrast between relatively "serious" and relatively "trivial" benefits and burdens, I have in mind something like T. M Scanlon's idea of "urgency"; see his "Preference and Urgency," *Journal of Philosophy* 82 (1975): 655–69, and "The Moral Basis of Interpersonal Comparisons," in Jon Elster and John Roemer, eds., *Interpersonal Comparisons of Well-Being* (Cambridge: Cambridge University Press, 1991). One burden is more "serious" than another if, other things equal, there are

stronger reasons against public policies imposing the first burden than the second.

15. The Editors of *The Economist*, "Let Them Wed," in Sullivan, *Same-Sex Marriage: Pro and Con*, pp. 181–85.

16. The general idea of desires that are serious and deserve to be respected is also related to Scanlon's idea of "urgency" (see n. 14 above).

17. Of course, some marriages turn out very badly for the people concerned. But the state can still described as "helping" these people, since they were harmed as the direct result of their own free choice, and the state was only enabling them to achieve their own freely chosen goals.

18. See William Eskridge, *The Case for Same-Sex Marriage*, pp. 106–108.

19. Compare the finding of Judge Kevin S. C. Chang in *Bachr v. Miike*, First Circuit Court, State of Hawaii, Civil Case No. 91–1394 (December 1946).

20. See Richard Posner, *Sex and Reason* (Cambridge, MA: Harvard University Press, 1992), pp. 253–60.

Is It Wrong to Discriminate on the Basis of Homosexuality?

Jeffrey Jordan

Is it wrong to discriminate against homosexuals—to treat homosexuals in less favorable ways than one does heterosexuals? Or is some discrimination against homosexuals morally justified? These questions are the focus of this essay.

In what follows, I argue that there are situations in which it is morally permissible to discriminate against homosexuals because of their homosexuality. That is, there are some morally relevant differences between heterosexuality and homosexuality which, in some instances, permit a difference in treatment. The issue of marriage provides a good example. While it is clear that heterosexual unions merit the state recognition known as marriage, along with all the attendant advantages—spousal insurance coverage, inheritance rights, ready eligibility of adoption—it is far from clear that homosexual couples ought to be accorded that state recognition.

From Jeffrey Jordan, "Is It Wrong to Discriminate on the Basis of Homosexuality?" *Journal of Social Philosophy* 26, no. 1 (Spring 1995): 39–52. Copyright © 1995, Blackwell Publishers.

The argument of this essay makes no claim about the moral status of homosexuality per se. Briefly put, it is the argument of this essay that the moral impasse generated by conflicting views concerning homosexuality, and the public policy ramifications of those conflicting views justify the claim that it is morally permissible, in certain circumstances, to discriminate against homosexuals.[1]

The Issue

The relevant issue is this; does homosexuality have the same moral status as heterosexuality? Put differently, since there are no occasions in which it is morally permissible to treat heterosexuals unfavorably, whether because they are heterosexual or because of heterosexual acts, are there occasions in which it is morally permissible to treat homosexuals unfavorably, whether because they are homosexuals or because of homosexual acts?

A negative answer to the above can be termed the "parity thesis." The parity thesis contends that homosexuality has the same moral status as heterosexuality. If the parity thesis is correct, then it would be immoral to discriminate against homosexuals because of their homosexuality. An affirmative answer can be termed the "difference thesis" and contends that there are morally relevant differences between heterosexuality and homosexuality which justify a difference in moral status and treatment between homosexuals and heterosexuals. The difference thesis entails that there are situations in which it is morally permissible to discriminate against homosexuals. . . .

A word should be said about the notion of discrimination. To discriminate against X means treating X in an unfavorable way. The word "discrimination" is not a synonym for "morally unjustifiable treatment." Some discrimination is morally unjustifiable; some is not. For example, we discriminate against convicted felons in that they are disenfranchised. This legal discrimination is morally permissible even though it involves treating one person unfavorably different from how other persons are treated. The difference thesis entails that there are circumstances in which it is morally permissible to discriminate against homosexuals.

An Argument for the Parity Thesis

. . . Perhaps the strongest reason to hold that the parity thesis is true is something like the following:

1. Homosexual acts between consenting adults harm no one. And,
2. respecting persons' privacy and choices in harmless sexual matters maximizes individual freedom. And,
3. individual freedom should be maximized. But,
4. discrimination against homosexuals, because of their homosexuality, diminishes individual freedom since it ignores personal choice and privacy. So,
5. the toleration of homosexuality rather than discriminating against homosexuals is the preferable option since it would maximize individual freedom. Therefore,
6. the parity thesis is more plausible than the difference thesis.

Premise (2) is unimpeachable: if an act is harmless and if there are persons who want to do it and who choose to do it, then it seems clear that respecting the choices of those people would tend to maximize their freedom.[2] Step (3) is also beyond reproach: since freedom is arguably a great good and since there does not appear to be any ceiling on the amount of individual freedom—no "too much of a good thing"— (3) appears to be true.

At first glance, premise (1) seems true enough as long as we recognize that if there is any harm involved in the homosexual acts of consenting adults, it would be harm absorbed by the freely consenting participants. This is true, however, only if the acts in question are done in private. Public acts may involve more than just the willing participants. Persons who have no desire to participate, even if only as spectators, may have no choice if the acts are done in public. A real probability of there being unwilling participants is indicative of the public realm and not the private. However, where one draws the line between private acts and public acts is not always easy to discern; it is clear that different moral standards apply to public acts than to private acts.[3]

If premise (1) is understood to apply only to acts done in private, then it would appear to be true. The same goes for (4): discrimination against homosexuals for acts done in private would result in a diminishing of freedom. So (1)–(4) would lend support to (5) only if we understand (1)–(4) to refer to acts done in private. Hence, (5) must be understood as referring to private acts; and, as a consequence, (6) also must be read as referring only to acts done in private.

With regard to acts which involve only willing adult participants, there may be no morally relevant difference between homosexuality and heterosexuality. In other words, acts done in private. However, acts done in public add a new ingredient to the mix; an ingredient which has moral consequence. Consequently, the argument (1)–(6) fails in supporting the parity thesis. The argument (1)–(6) may show that there are some circumstances in which the moral status of homosexuality and heterosexuality are the same, but it gives us no reason for thinking that this result holds for all circumstances.[4]

Moral Impasses and Public Dilemmas

Suppose one person believes that X is morally wrong, while another believes that X is morally permissible. The two people, let's stipulate, are not involved in a semantical quibble; they hold genuinely conflicting beliefs regarding the moral status of X. If the first person is correct, then the second person is wrong; and, of course, if the second person is right, then the first must be wrong. This situation of conflicting claims is what we will call an "impasse." Impasses arise out moral disputes. Since the conflicting parties in an impasse take contrary views, the conflicting views cannot all be true, nor can they all be false.[5] Moral impasses may concern matters only of a personal nature, but moral impasses can involve public policy. An impasse is likely to have public policy ramifications if large numbers of people hold the conflicting views, and the conflict involves matters which are fundamental to a person's moral identity (and, hence, from a practical point of view, are probably irresolvable)

and it involves acts done in public. Since not every impasse has public policy ramifications, one can mark off "public dilemma" as a special case of moral impasses: those moral impasses that have public policy consequences. Public dilemmas, then, are impasses located in the public square. Since they have public policy ramifications and since they arise from impasses, one side or another of the dispute will have its views implemented as public policy. Because of the public policy ramifications and also because social order is sometimes threatened by the parties involved in the impasse, the state has a role to play in resolving a public dilemma.

A public dilemma can be actively resolved in two ways.[6] The first is when the government allies itself with one side of the impasse and, by state coercion and sanction, declares that side of the impasse the correct side. The American Civil War was an example of this: the federal government forcibly ended slavery by aligning itself with the Abolitionist side of the impasse.[7] Prohibition is another example. The Eighteenth Amendment and the Volstead Act allied the state with the Temperance side of the impasse. State mandated affirmative action programs provide a modem example of this. This kind of resolution of a public dilemma we can call a "resolution by declaration." The first of the examples cited above indicates that declarations can be morally proper, the right thing to do. The second example, however, indicates that declarations are not always morally proper. The state does not always take the side of the morally correct; nor is it always clear which side is the correct one.

The second way of actively resolving a public dilemma is that of accommodation. An accommodation in this context means resolving the public dilemma in a way that gives as much as possible to all sides of the impasse. A resolution by accommodation involves staking out some middle ground in a dispute and placing public policy in that location. The middle ground location of a resolution via accommodation is a virtue since it entails that there are no absolute victors and no absolute losers. The middle ground is reached in order to resolve the public dilemma in a way which respects the relevant views of the conflicting parties and which maintains social order. The Federal Fair Housing Act and, perhaps, the current status of abortion (legal but with restrictions) provide examples of actual resolutions via accommodation.[8]

In general, governments should be, at least as far as possible, neutral with regard to the disputing parties in a public dilemma. Unless there is some overriding reason why the state should take sides in a public dilemma—the protection of innocent life, or abolishing slavery, for instance—the state should be neutral, because no matter which side of the public dilemma the state takes, the other side will be the recipient of unequal treatment by the state. A state which is partial and takes sides in moral disputes via declaration, when there is no overriding reason why it should, is tyrannical. Overriding reasons involve, typically, the protection of generally recognized rights.[9] In the case of slavery, the right to liberty; in the case of protecting innocent life, the right involved is the negative right to life. If a public dilemma must be actively resolved, the state should do so (in the absence of an overriding reason) via accommodation and not declaration since the latter entails that a sizable number of people would be forced to live under a government which "legitimizes" and does not just tolerate activities which they find, immoral. Resolution via

declaration is appropriate only if there is an overriding reason for the state to throw its weight behind one side in a public dilemma.

Is moral rightness an overriding reason for a resolution via declaration? What better reason might there be for a resolution by declaration than that it is the right thing to do? Unless one is prepared to endorse a view that is called "legal moralism"—that immorality alone is a sufficient reason for the state to curtail individual liberty—then one had best hold that moral rightness alone is not an overriding reason. Since some immoral acts neither harm nor offend nor violate another's rights, it seems clear enough that too much liberty would be lost if legal moralism were adopted as public policy.[10]

Though we do not have a definite rule for determining a priori which moral impasses genuinely constitute public dilemmas, we can proceed via a case by case method. For example, many people hold that cigarette smoking is harmful and, on that basis, is properly suppressible. Others disagree. Is this a public dilemma? Probably not. Whether someone engages in an imprudent action is, as long as it involves no unwilling participants, a private matter and does not, on that account, constitute a public dilemma.[11] What about abortion? Is abortion a public dilemma? Unlike cigarette smoking, abortion is a public dilemma. This is clear from the adamant and even violent contrary positions involved in the impasse: Abortion is an issue which forces itself into the public square. So, it is clear that, even though we lack a rule which filters through moral impasses designating some as public dilemmas, not every impasse constitutes a public dilemma.

Conflicting Claims on Homosexuality

The theistic tradition, Judaism and Christianity and Islam, has a clear and deeply entrenched position on homosexual acts: they are prohibited. . . . As a consequence, many contemporary theistic adherents of theistic tradition . . ., hold that homosexual behavior is sinful. Though God loves the homosexual, these folk say, God hates the sinful behavior. To say that act X is a sin entails that X is morally wrong, not necessarily because it is harmful or offensive, but because X violates God's will. So, the claim that homosexuality is sinful entails the claim that it is also morally wrong. And, it is clear, many people adopt the difference thesis just because of their religious views: because the Bible or the Koran holds that homosexuality is wrong, they too hold that view.

Well, what should we make of these observations? We do not, for one thing, have to base our moral conclusions on those views, if for no other reason than not every one is a theist. If one does not adopt the religion-based, moral view, one must still respect those who do; they cannot just be dismissed out of hand.[12] And, significantly, this situation yields a reason for thinking that the difference thesis is probably true. Because many religious people sincerely believe homosexual acts to be morally wrong and many others believe that homosexual acts are not morally wrong, there results a public dilemma.[13]

The existence of this public dilemma gives us reason for thinking that the difference thesis is true. It is only via the difference thesis and not the parity thesis, that an accommodation can be reached. Here again, the private/public distinction will come into play.

To see this, take as an example the issue of homosexual marriages. A same-sex marriage would be a public matter. For the government to sanction same-sex marriage to grant the recognition and reciprocal benefits which attach to marriage would ally the government with one side of the public dilemma and against the adherents of religion-based moralities. . . .

Of course, some would respond here that by not sanctioning same-sex marriages the state is, and historically has been, taking sides to the detriment of homosexuals. There is some truth in this claim. But one must be careful here. The respective resolutions of this issue whether the state should recognized and sanction same-sex marriages do not have symmetrical implications. The asymmetry of this issue is a function of the private/public distinction and the fact that marriage is a public matter. If the state sanctions same-sex marriages, then there is no accommodation available. In that event, the religion-based morality proponents are faced with a public, state-sanctioned matter which they find seriously immoral. This would be an example of a resolution via declaration. On the other hand, if the state does not sanction same-sex marriages, there is an accommodation available: in the public realm the state sides with the religion-based moral view, but the state can tolerate private homosexual acts. That is since homosexual acts are not essentially public acts; they can be, and historically have been, performed in private. The state, by not sanctioning same-sex marriages is acting in the public realm, but it can leave the private realm to personal choice.[14]

The Argument from Conflicting Claims

It was suggested in the previous section that the public dilemma concerning homosexuality, and in particular whether states should sanction same-sex marriages, generates an argument in support the difference thesis. The argument, again using same-sex marriages as the particular case is as follows:

7. There are conflicting claims regarding whether the state should sanction same-sex marriages. And,
8. this controversy constitutes a public dilemma. And,
9. there is an accommodation possible if the state does not recognize same-sex marriages. And,
10. there is no accommodation possible if the state does sanction same sex marriages. And,
11. there is no overriding reason for a resolution via declaration. Hence,
12. the state ought not sanction same-sex marriages. And,
13. the state ought to sanction heterosexual marriages. So,
14. there is at least one morally relevant case in which discrimination against homosexuals, because of their homosexuality, is morally permissible. Therefore,
15. the difference thesis is true.

Since proposition (14) is logically equivalent to the difference thesis then, if (7)–(14) sound, proposition (15) certainly follows.

Premises (7) and (8) are uncontroversial. Premises (9) and (10) are based on the asymmetry that results from the public nature of marriage.

Since the strongest argument in support of the parity thesis fails, we have reason to think that there is no overriding reason why the state ought to resolve the public dilemma via declaration in favor of same-sex marriages. We have reason, in other words, to think that (11) is true.

Proposition (12) is based on the conjunction of (7)–(11) and the principle that, in the absence of an overriding reason for

state intervention via declaration, resolution by accommodation is the preferable route. Proposition (13) is just trivially true. So, given the moral difference mentioned in (12) and (13), proposition (14) logically follows.

Two Objections Considered

The first objection to the argument from conflicting claims would contend that it is unsound because a similar sort of argument would permit discrimination against some practice which, though perhaps controversial at some earlier time, is now widely thought to be morally permissible. Take mixed-race marriages, for example. The opponent of the argument from conflicting claims could argue that a similar argument would warrant prohibition against mixed-race marriages. If it does, we would have good reason to reject (7)–(14) as unsound.

There are three responses to this objection. The first response denies that the issue of mixed-race marriages is in fact a public dilemma. It may have been so at one time, but it does not seem to generate much, if any, controversy today. Hence, the objection is based upon a faulty analogy.

The second response grants for the sake of the argument that the issue of mixed-race marriages generates a public dilemma. But the second response points out that there is a relevant difference between mixed-race marriages and same-sex marriages that allows for a resolution by declaration in the one case but not the other. As evident from the earlier analysis of the argument in support of (1)–(6), there is reason to think that there is no overriding reason for a resolution by declaration in support of the parity thesis. On the other hand, it is a settled matter that state protection from racial discrimination is a reason sufficient for a resolution via declaration. Hence, the two cases are only apparently similar, and, in reality, they are crucially different. They are quite different because, clearly enough, if mixed-race marriages do generate a public dilemma, the state should use resolution by declaration in support of such marriages. The same cannot be said for same-sex marriages.

One should note that the second response to the objection does not beg the question against the proponent of the parity thesis. Though the second response denies that race and sexuality are strict analogues, it does so for a defensible and independent reason: it is a settled matter that race is not a sufficient reason for disparate treatment; but, as we have seen from the analysis of (1)–(6), there is no overriding reason to think the same about sexuality.[15]

The third response to the first objection is that the grounds of objection differ in the respective cases: one concerns racial identity; the other concerns behavior thought to be morally problematic. A same-sex marriage would involve behavior which many people find morally objectionable; a mixed-race marriage is objectionable to some, not because of the participants' behavior, but because of the racial identity of the participants. It is the race of the marriage partners which some find of primary complaint concerning mixed-race marriages. With same-sex marriages however, it is the behavior which is primarily objectionable. To see this latter point, one should note that, though promiscuously Puritan in tone the kind of sexual acts that are likely involved in a same-sex marriage are objectionable to some, regardless of whether done by homosexuals or heterosexuals.[16] So again, there is reason to reject the analogy between same-sex marriages and mixed-race marriages. Racial identity is an immutable trait and a complaint about mixed-race marriages

necessarily involves, then, a complaint about an immutable trait. Sexual behavior is not an immutable trait and it is possible to object to same-sex marriages based on the behavior which would be involved in such marriages. Put succinctly, the third response could be formulated as follows: objections to mixed-race marriages necessarily involve objections over status, while objections to same-sex marriages could involve objections over behavior. Therefore, the two cases are not strict analogues. . . .

The second objection to the argument from conflicting claims can be stated so: if homosexuality is biologically based—if it is inborn[17]—then how can discrimination ever be justified? If it is not a matter of choice homosexuality is an immutable trait which is, as a consequence, morally permissible. Just as it would be absurd to hold someone morally culpable for being of a certain race, likewise it would be absurd to hold someone morally culpable for being a homosexual. Consequently, according to this objection, the argument from conflicting claims "legitimizes" unjustifiable discrimination.

But this second objection is not cogent, primarily because it ignores an important distinction. No one could plausibly hold that homosexuals act by some sort of biological compulsion. If there is a biological component involved in sexual identity, it would incline but it would not compel. Just because one naturally (without any choice) has certain dispositions is not in itself a morally cogent reason for acting upon that disposition. Most people are naturally selfish, but it clearly does not follow that selfishness is in any way permissible on that account. Even if it is true that one has a predisposition to do X as a matter of biology and not as a matter of choice, it does not follow that doing X is morally permissible. For example, suppose that pyromania is an inborn predisposition.

Just because one has an inborn and, in that sense, natural desire to set fires, one still has to decide whether or not to act on that desire.[18] The reason that the appeal to biology is specious is that it ignores the important distinction between being a homosexual and homosexual acts. One is status; the other is behavior. Even if one has the status naturally, it does not follow that the behavior is morally permissible, nor that others have a duty to tolerate the behavior.[19]

But, while moral permissibility does not necessarily follow if homosexuality should turn out to be biologically based, what does follow is this: in the absence of a good reason to discriminate between homosexuals and heterosexuals, then, assuming that homosexuality is inborn, one ought not discriminate between them. If a certain phenomenon X is natural in the sense of being involuntary and non-pathological, and if there is no good reason to hold that X is morally problematic, then that is reason enough to think that X is morally permissible. In the absence of a good reason to repress X, one should tolerate it since, as per supposition, it is involuntary. The argument from conflicting claims, however, provides a good reason which overrides this presumption.

A Second Argument for the Difference Thesis

A second argument for the difference thesis, similar to the argument from conflicting claims, is what might be called the "no-exit argument." This argument is based on the principle that:

A. no just government can coerce a citizen into violating a deeply held moral belief or religious belief.

Is (A) plausible? It seems to be since the prospect of a citizen being coerced by the state into a practice which she finds profoundly immoral appears to be a clear example of an injustice. Principle (A), conjoined with there being a public dilemma arising over the issue of same-sex marriages, leads to the observation that if the state were to sanction same-sex marriages, then persons who have profound religious or moral objections to such unions would be legally mandated to violate their beliefs since there does not appear to be any feasible "exit right" possible with regard to state sanctioned marriage. An exit right is an exemption from some legally mandated practice, granted to a person or group, the purpose of which is to protect the religious or moral integrity of that person or group. Prominent examples of exit rights include conscientious objection and military service, home-schooling of the young because of some religious concern, and property used for religious purposes being free from taxation.

It is important to note that marriage is a public matter in the sense that, for instance, if one is an employer who provides health care benefits to the spouses of employees, one must provide those benefits to any employee who is married. Since there is no exit right possible in this case, one would be coerced, by force of law, into subsidizing a practice one finds morally or religiously objectionable.[20]

In the absence of an exit right, and if (A) is plausible, then the state cannot morally force persons to violate deeply held beliefs that are moral or religious in nature. In particular, the state morally could not sanction same-sex marriages since this would result in coercing some into violating a deeply held religious conviction.

Conclusion

It is important to note that neither the argument from conflicting claims nor the no-exit argument licenses wholesale discrimination against homosexuals. What they do show is that some discrimination against homosexuals, in this case the refusal to sanction same-sex marriages, is not only legally permissible but also morally permissible. The discrimination is a way of resolving a public policy dilemma that accommodates, to an extent, each side of the impasse and, further, protects the religious and moral integrity of a good number of people. In short, the arguments show us that there are occasions in which it is morally permissible to discriminate on the basis of homosexuality.

Notes

1. The terms "homosexuality" and "heterosexuality" are defined as follows. The former is defined as sexual feelings or behavior directed toward individuals of the same sex. The latter, naturally enough, is defined as sexual feelings or behavior directed toward individuals of the opposite sex.

   Sometimes the term "gay" is offered as an alternative to "homosexual." Ordinary use of "gay" has it as a synonym of a male homosexual (hence, the common expression, "gays and lesbians"). Given this ordinary usage, the substitution would lead to a confusing equivocation. Since there are female homosexuals, it is best to use "homosexual" to refer to both male and female homosexuals, and reserve "gay" to signify male homosexuals, and "lesbian" for female homosexuals in order to avoid the equivocation.

2. This would be true even if the act in question is immoral.

3. The standard answer is, of course, that the line between public and private is based on the notion of harm. Acts which carry a real probability of harming third parties are public acts.

4. For other arguments supporting the moral parity of homosexuality and heterosexuality, see Richard Mohr, *Gays/Justice: A Study of Ethics, Society and Law* (New York: Columbia, 1988); and see Michael Ruse, "The Morality of Homosexuality" in *Philosophy and Sex*, eds. R. Baker and F. Elliston (Buffalo, NY: Prometheus Books, 1984), pp. 370–390.

5. Perhaps it would be better to term the disputing positions "contradictory" views rather than "contrary" views.

6. Resolutions can also be passive in the sense of the state doing nothing. If the state does nothing to resolve the public dilemma, it stands pat with the status quo, and the public dilemma is resolved gradually by sociological changes (changes in mores and in beliefs).

7. Assuming plausibly enough, that the disputes over the sovereignty of the Union and concerning states' rights were at bottom disputes about slavery.

8. The Federal Fair Housing Act prohibits discrimination in housing on the basis of race, religion, and sex. But it does not apply to the rental of rooms in single-family houses, or to a building of five units or less if the owner lives in one of the units. See 42 U. S. C. Section 3603.

9. Note that overriding reasons involve generally recognized right. If a right is not widely recognized and the state nonetheless uses coercion to enforce it, there is a considerable risk that the state will be seen by many or even most people as tyrannical.

10. This claim is, perhaps, controversial. For a contrary view see Richard George, *Making Men Moral* (Oxford: Clarendon Press, 1993).

11. This claim holds only for smoking which does not affect other persons—smoking done in private. Smoking which affects others, second-hand smoke, is a different matter, of course, and may well constitute a public dilemma.

12. For an argument that religiously-based moral views should not be dismissed out of hand, see Stephen Carter, *The Culture of Disbelief: How American Law and Politics Trivialize Religious Devotion* (New York: Basic Books, 1993).

13. Two assumptions are these: that the prohibitions against homosexuality activity are part of the religious doctrine and not just an extraneous addition; second, that if X is part of one's religious belief or religious doctrine, then it is morally permissible to hold X. Though this latter principle is vague, it is, I think, clear enough for our purposes here (I ignore here any points concerning the rationality of religious belief in general, or in particular cases).

14. This point has implications for the moral legitimacy of sodomy laws. One implication would be this: the private acts of consenting adults should not be criminalized.

15. An *ad hominem* point: If this response begs the question against the proponent of the parity thesis, it does not beg the question any more than the original objection does by presupposing that sexuality is analogous with race.

16. Think of the sodomy laws found in some states which criminalize certain sexual acts, whether performed by heterosexuals or homosexuals.

17. There is some interesting recent research which, though still tentative, strongly suggests that homosexuality is, at least in part, biologically based. See Simon LeVay, *The Sexual Brain* (Cambridge, MA: MIT Press, 1993), pp. 120–122; and J. M. Bailey and R. C. Pillard, "A Genetic Study of Male Sexual Orientation," *Archives of General Psychiatry* 48 (1991): 1089–1096; and C. Burr, "Homosexuality and Biology," *The Atlantic* 271/3 (March 1993): 64; and D. Hamer, S. Hu, V. Magnuson, N. Hu, A. Pattatucci, "A Linkage Between DNA Markers on the X Chromosome and Male Sexual Orientation," *Science* 261 (16 July 1993): 321–327; and see the summary of this article by Robert Pool, "Evidence for Homosexuality Gene," *Science* 261 (16 July 1993): 291–292.

18. I do not mean to suggest that homosexuality is morally equivalent or even comparable to pyromania.

19. Even if one were biologically or innately impelled to do X, it clearly does not follow that one is thereby impelled to do X *in public*. Again, the public/private distinction is morally relevant.

20. Is the use of subsidy here inappropriate? It does not seem so since providing health care to spouses, in a society where this is not legally mandatory, seems to be more than part of a salary and is a case of providing supporting funds for certain end.

Study Questions for Section 4

1. What is marriage? Does it have an essentially religious feature?

2. Does a law that permits a particular act express social approval of that act? Does Jordan's view of "exit rights" help clarify the matter?

3. How should we understand the relation between morality and legality? Does the issue of whether the state should permit same-sex marriage turn on whether same-sex relationships are morally permissible?

SECTION 5

DRUG LEGALIZATION

9

LIBERAL NEUTRALITY AND DRUG PROHIBITIONS

Douglas N. Husak

Introduction

The most significant trend in the last decade that reflects a shift in the delicate balance between state power and individual liberty is the tremendous increase in the rate of incarceration. The total number of Americans jailed or imprisoned has recently exceeded 2 million, more than triple the rate of 1980. The incarceration ratio of 645 persons per 100,000 is perhaps the highest in the world, and almost certainly will rise in the foreseeable future.[1]

The single most important factor that has led to this remarkable increase in the prison population is the imposition of increasingly severe punishments for drug offenders. A few statistics tell the story. Since 1980, the incarceration rate for drug offenders has grown by over 1,000 percent. Each year, more persons are jailed or imprisoned for drug offenses than were jailed or imprisoned for all other crimes combined in any year from 1920 to 1970. More than a quarter of all new inmates are sentenced for "drug-only" offenses, without any other violent or criminal

behavior. On any given day, more than 400,000 persons are incarcerated for drug offenses in the United States—more than a third of whom have been convicted of simple possession.[2] Minorities have borne the brunt of this trend. Although minorities are about as likely as whites to use illicit drugs, their rate of imprisonment is grossly disproportionate to their representation in the drug-using population.[3]

Various strategies have been proposed to retard our excessive reliance on incarceration. Commentators have begun to explore imaginative modes of punishment that do not involve imprisonment.[4] Many of their recommendations are welcome. But there is little reason to anticipate a reversal of this trend without revisions in the substantive criminal law itself. Citizens in a democratic state must debate whether the conduct for which persons are punished should remain subject to the criminal sanction.

I doubt that criminal punishment for recreational drug use can be justified on grounds that liberals should accept.[5] My belief is hard to support in light of the enormous number and variety of liberal theories. I will be forced to limit my argument in two important respects. I will confine most of my attention to that class of liberal theories which require the state to remain *neutral* with respect to reasonable conceptions of the good life.[6] Still, theorists offer distinct interpretations of what neutrality requires, largely because they construct different defenses of why the state should maintain neutrality.[7] Therefore, I will focus on a particular rationale for neutrality. I will restrict most of my attention to attempts to defend neutrality as necessary to protect the *autonomy* of persons. I will tentatively conclude that this rationale fails to provide a justification for the criminalization of drug use that is acceptable to neutralist liberals. Anyone who shares my starting points has reason to worry that a significant number of persons are being imprisoned unjustly.

For two reasons, I describe my neutralist case against drug prohibitions as tentative. First, the failure of the rationales I will examine hardly proves that no alternative rationale can succeed; in addition, the arguments I will offer are inconclusive. I will suggest that the more respectable reasons for punishing drug users on grounds of liberal neutrality tend to gain their apparent plausibility by making unwarranted generalizations from worst-case scenarios that distort the more typical reality of drug use. Although my case is only presumptive, I hope to take a step toward undermining the justifiability of drug proscriptions generally.

Even though I intend to presuppose rather than to defend the neutrality constraint,[8] the issue of drug proscriptions provides an opportunity to comment on an argument sometimes advanced in its favor. John Rawls refers to the Inquisition in the course of contending that the imposition of a single conception of the good throughout society would require an oppressive use of state power.[9] This allegation about perfectionist states has been challenged. George Sher replies that "our government has long been nonneutral; yet we manage to live in comparative harmony."[10] Of course, Sher is able to select a number of examples to support his point. But the "we" in his rejoinder could hardly refer to the hundreds of thousands of Americans who have been imprisoned for drug offenses—or to the approximately 80 million Americans who have used illegal drugs at some time in their lives but have managed to evade prosecution and conviction. Rawls's warning seems vindicated by the sheer number of casualties of the drug war.

Whether drug proscriptions are defensible on liberal grounds depends largely on what liberalism is taken to be. . . . I will present the neutralist liberal case for permitting recreational drug use and discuss its most vulnerable presuppositions and commitments. . . . I will tentatively conclude that proscriptions of drug use are unjustifiable on neutralist liberal grounds. Although I hope to erode confidence in the justifiability of drug proscriptions generally, I am aware that some philosophers will construe my arguments as providing an embarrassment or even a counterexample to neutralist liberalism. Indeed, the specter of recreational drug use has figured far more prominently in attacks on liberalism than in defenses of it.[11]

Drug Proscription and Liberal Neutrality

In this section I will present and critically examine what I call the *affirmative case* for permitting drug use on grounds of liberal neutrality. The argument itself is deceptively simple and can be expressed in as few as three premises. In most of this section, I will discuss the possible grounds on which neutralist liberals might resist this argument. This discussion will help to identify what a (real or imaginary) drug would have to be like before neutralist liberals might proscribe its use. The issues I will address here do not depend on any particular justification a liberal might provide for adopting a principle of neutrality. . . . Although I do not pretend to resolve any of the controversies I will raise, I will provide reason to conclude that the affirmative case should be persuasive to neutralist liberals.

The affirmative case is as follows:

1. The state should be neutral with respect to reasonable conceptions of the good life.
2. Some of these reasonable conceptions of the good life include the recreational use of drugs. Therefore;
   The state should be neutral with respect to the recreational use of drugs.
3. Neutrality toward given conduct is violated by criminal prohibitions of that conduct. Therefore;
   The state should not criminally prohibit recreational drug use.

The first two premises in this affirmative case state, respectively, that reasonable conceptions of the good life are the objects of state neutrality, and that some of these conceptions include the recreational use of drugs. Are these statements acceptable? For present purposes, the controversies raised by these two premises are hard to disentangle. As I have indicated, I intend to assume rather than to defend a principle of state neutrality toward reasonable conceptions of the good life. Still, this assumption does not end all debate surrounding my use of premise (1). Theorists disagree about what a reasonable conception of the good life *is*. In particular, they disagree about whether and to what extent the satisfaction of tastes and preferences should be included in a reasonable conception of the

good life. Unless the satisfaction of some tastes and preferences is included in such a conception, however, there is little basis for believing premise (2)—that some of these reasonable conceptions include the recreational use of drugs. Thus, in the present context, a discussion of premise (1) is inextricably tied to a discussion of premise (2).

What exactly is a conception of the good life (reasonable or otherwise)? Those liberals who identify conceptions of the good life as the object of state neutrality seldom provide a detailed account of what this phrase is designed to encompass. Rawls does not elaborate on his description of a conception of the good as "the ends and purposes worthy of our devoted pursuit."[12] Perhaps his reluctance to offer a wide range of examples of worthy ends and purposes is designed to help support his point: Neutralist liberals allow persons to decide such matters for themselves.

Less reticence is found in Ronald Dworkin. He construes a "conception of the good life" as a view about "what gives value to life."[13] In addition to the philosopher's staple of "contemplation," Dworkin's examples of activities that might give value to life include "television-watching" and "beer-drinking."[14] These examples are instructive, as they indicate that even the most mundane activities can form part of a person's conception of the good. Thus, Dworkin includes the satisfaction of at least some tastes and preferences. If so, there is good reason to conclude that he would allow recreational drug use to be included in a conception of the good life. In fact, Dworkin *does* include recreational drug use, since the alcohol in his example of beer is a drug.[15]

Apart from the position of leading liberals on this issue, what general reason can be given to include the satisfaction of at least some tastes and preferences within a conception of the good life?[16] The best answer, I think, is that to exclude the satisfaction of *all* tastes and preferences would lead to counterintuitive results by exempting from the neutrality constraint much of what we value and believe should be protected by a theory with genuinely liberal credentials. My decision to eat pizza rather than fruit, to wear a blue shirt rather than a green sweater, to drink red wine rather than white, or to grow a mustache rather than shave, are typically based solely on my tastes and preferences. Neutralist liberalism would look extraordinarily illiberal if these sorts of decisions were unprotected and thus became eligible for criminalization.

And many of these activities almost certainly *would* become eligible for criminalization if they were unprotected by the neutrality constraint. I want to pause to consider why this is so. Neutralist liberals have tended to say little about the conditions that must be satisfied in order to criminalize those activities to which the neutrality constraint does not apply. In all likelihood, however, these conditions are minimal. Suppose that the state were not required to remain neutral about the satisfaction of any tastes or preferences. Suppose further that the only reason persons eat pepperoni rather than broccoli is because they prefer its taste. On this assumption, what conditions would have to be met in order to criminalize and thus imprison persons for eating pepperoni?

Different answers could be given. One answer is utilitarian; the state would be justified in criminalizing any activity (to which the neutrality constraint did not apply) that creates a net balance of disutility over utility. This constraint on criminalization may seem substantial. The main difficulty, however, is that no one has the slightest idea whether more utility than disutility would be promoted by proscribing pepperoni.[17] A case can be made in favor of the proscription; after all, not much can be said on behalf of pepperoni except that many people enjoy its taste. But this is mere conjecture about the utilitarian scales.

A second answer—the answer actually given in our legal system—is to defer to the democratic process. A legislature should be allowed to criminalize the act of eating pepperoni in the unlikely event that it actually decided to do so. Of course, majorities are subject to constitutional limitations. Inasmuch as no "fundamental rights" are burdened and no "suspect class" is targeted, however, the only constitutional constraint that would have to be satisfied by this hypothetical proscription is the "rational basis" test.[18] Very few statutes fail this test. Since the judgment that pepperoni is unhealthy to eat is rational, and the state has an interest in protecting health, it is clear that this hypothetical proscription has a rational basis. Thus, the state would be free to imprison persons for eating pepperoni.

Each of the foregoing answers is remarkably illiberal. When a criminal statute is enacted, conduct is *proscribed*, but not always *prevented*. Inevitably, some persons will violate that statute. Pepperoni will still be consumed—albeit illegally—whatever the legislature may say. When violations result in imprisonment, a fundamental right—freedom from incarceration—is infringed. More than a utilitarian gain or a mere "rational basis" should be required to enact and enforce such a law. Each criminal law that deprives persons of their fundamental right to be free from incarceration should meet more exacting standards than the foregoing answers provide.[19]

No political philosopher should acquiesce when hundreds of thousands of persons lose their right to be free from incarceration simply because a legislature has a utilitarian ground or a rational basis to imprison them. More specifically, no liberal should be happy if his version of liberalism allowed persons to be imprisoned for the crime of eating pepperoni. If liberalism is to be identified by the kinds of activities it protects, this hypothetical proscription serves as a better test case than pornography or abortion to decide whether a particular theory qualifies as liberal. Neutralist liberals have seemed not to worry, however, about how little protection is extended to the satisfaction of any tastes and preferences to which the neutrality constraint is thought not to apply. I suspect that this lack of concern is explained by the fact that contemporary Western states have shown virtually no inclination to criminalize such activities as the consumption of unhealthy foods.[20] Thus, persons tend to take such freedoms for granted, and there is no practical urgency to devise a rationale to protect them. By contrast, constant vigilance is needed to safeguard the particular freedoms (such as speech) that are threatened by the state. One can only imagine, however, the uproar from both political philosophers as well as the public that would greet proposals to put people in jail for eating unhealthy foods such as pepperoni. I am confident that liberals would scramble to find some basis within their theory to condemn such an outrageous law.

The most obvious such basis, of course, is to apply the neutrality constraint itself. That is, the conception of the good that persons are allowed to pursue under neutralist liberalism should include the freedom to eat whatever foods we like. This conclusion is crucial for my overall argument about drug use. Unless the satisfaction of some tastes and preferences is brought within the scope of conceptions of the good life, drug use for recreational purposes, like the consumption of food for the sake of its taste, is unlikely to receive any liberal protection. To be sure, some persons have sought to defend the use of given drugs by reference to their supposed positive contributions to such goods as spirituality and artistic creativity. Such defenses of drug use should not be rejected out of hand. At the very least, these efforts reveal the difficulty of categorizing any activity as purely recreational.[21] Still, I believe that such positive effects capture only a very small part of the explanation for why the use of many illicit drugs is so pervasive. The popularity of marijuana and cocaine is no more mysterious than the popularity of chocolate. Most persons use illicit drugs because they enjoy their effects, not because they hope to become more spiritual or creative. That is, most use of drugs such as marijuana and cocaine is recreational. In any event, this is the particular motivation to which my inquiry is directed; I ask whether the neutrality constraint offers any protection to the use of drugs for the purpose of gaining pleasure or euphoria.

The more difficult issue, I think, is not to decide whether the neutrality constraint applies to the satisfaction of any tastes and preferences, but to determine whether recreational drug use will qualify for liberal protection once the satisfaction of some tastes and preferences is included within the scope of conceptions of the good life. Admittedly, the good life does not require the satisfaction of *all* tastes and preferences. I make no effort to provide a comprehensive list of the various kinds of tastes and preferences that need not be satisfied with a conception of the good life.[22] Once we concede that the satisfaction of some tastes and preferences qualifies—such as a taste or preference for pepperoni—the more productive strategy is to search for possible reasons to *exclude* a taste or preference for drugs. I will briefly consider three such reasons, and argue that each fails to provide a persuasive basis for exempting all recreational drug use from a conception of the good to which the neutrality constraint applies. In general, these reasons provide no more justification (and frequently less justification) to exempt recreational drug use from the scope of liberal neutrality than any number of other tastes and preferences which, I have suggested, should receive protection from a theory with genuinely liberal credentials. Without a persuasive basis for disqualifying this particular taste or preference, I conclude that recreational drug use is entitled to protection from neutralist liberals.[23]

Consider some of the familiar reasons to exempt the satisfaction of a given taste or preference from a conception of the good life to which the neutrality constraint applies. Perhaps the best such reason is that some tastes and preferences are based on a material mistake of fact about the object of the preference. A mistake is material when the person would change his taste or preference if he came to learn the truth. Might recreational drug use be disqualified on this basis? This possibility cannot be dismissed. There are two grounds on which a taste or preference for, say, cocaine might be based on a factual error. First, the person may be mistaken about whether the use of cocaine will produce the desired psychological state of euphoria. Second, the person may be mistaken about the risks of cocaine—in particular, its health hazards or potential for addiction.

Prohibitionists have alleged that drug users are guilty of both kinds of mistakes. Those who characterize the pleasure of drugs as "deceptive" accuse users of the first kind of error.[24] Recreational drug users, according to this school of thought, do not *really* enjoy drugs. The motivation for drug use is rarely explained in the same terms as other recreational activities, but is widely attributed to peer pressure, boredom, alienation, immaturity, depression, or some other human pathology. Those who dissent, and publicly proclaim that drug use is run, are subjected to ridicule and denounced as irresponsible.

This strategy to exempt recreational drug use from the scope of liberal protection is highly implausible. Drug users are just as likely as users of any number of consumer items to enjoy the object of their preference. Of course, persons who admit to having lost all pleasure from the drug they consume can be identified. But there is no evidence that such persons represent a majority, or even a significant minority of the users of a given drug. The tendency to generalize from worst-case scenarios is prominent here. I suspect, however, that persons who describe the pleasures of drugs as deceptive do not really take themselves to be making an empirical claim. As C. L. Ten has warned, "where we disapprove of an activity, or cannot appreciate it, we tend to think that the agent himself derives little benefit from it."[25]

A second and more probable kind of material mistake of fact is that users are not adequately informed of the dangers of drugs.[26] But information about the hazards of illicit drugs is more widely disseminated than information about the risks of any number of foods, consumer items, dangerous recreational activities, and even drugs prescribed for medicinal purposes.[27] Illicit drug users are almost certainly *more* knowledgeable of the risks they take; few adolescents today are spared from drug education programs in schools. In any event, many prohibitionists have admitted that better drug education will not reduce the incidence of illicit drug use because ignorance does not cause such use.[28]

A second and very different reason to exempt the satisfaction of a given taste or preferences from a conception of the good life to which the neutrality constraint applies is that the taste or preference is somehow "unauthentic." Several possible grounds might be invoked to show that a taste or preference is unauthentic, and thus unprotected by liberal neutrality. The main difficulty, I think, is to avoid a model according to which preferences are authentic only when they are formed *ex nihilo*. For present purposes, the challenge is to explain why a taste or preference for a given drug might be less authentic than a taste or preference for any number of objects to which the liberal constraint applies. This challenge, I believe, cannot be overcome. To be sure, some preferences are created by conditioning or manipulation. These causal processes, however, are unlikely to play a substantial role in creating a preference for illicit drugs. After all, no advertising for marijuana or heroin has ever taken place. The fact that the pleasurable effects of drugs have a physiological basis,[29] coupled with the realization that drug use is prevalent in virtually all societies and even among animals,[30] help to establish these preferences as relatively authentic. In short, a taste for drugs, unlike, say, a taste for perfume, has a strong claim to authenticity.

Neither of the foregoing reasons provides a persuasive basis for denying that drug use can be included in a conception of the good life. I can think of only one plausible reason to disqualify such a preference. That is, I can think of only one plausible reason to include the satisfaction of a preference for pepperoni, but not the satisfaction of a preference for alcohol or cocaine, in a conception of the good life. The neutrality constraint does not apply to all conceptions of the good, but only to those that are *reasonable*.[31] Perhaps recreational drug use is unreasonable under some or all circumstances. No brief discussion can be expected to settle this issue. This challenge, like

others, is difficult to meet in the absence of a detailed argument designed to show that drug use is unreasonable.

What burden must such an argument satisfy? In order to begin to answer this question, one must understand the motivation for confining the neutrality constraint to only those conceptions of the good that are reasonable. This qualification is not intended to deny liberal protection to conceptions of the good that are silly, unhealthy, or wasteful. No neutralist liberal could approve of the use of the penal sanction to coerce persons to be nonfrivolous, healthy, or efficient. Instead, the motivation for this qualification is to distinguish neutralist liberals from anarchists. Liberals must impose *some* limitations on the conception of the good that persons are allowed to pursue; they are not resigned to impassivity when persons pursue a conception of the good that includes a preference for murder or rape. Why does the satisfaction of these victimizing preferences not qualify for liberal protection? Perhaps the best answer is that such conduct is unreasonable. Persons are reasonable, according to the conception I adopt here, when they "propose principles and standards as fair terms of cooperation and . . . abide by them willingly, given the assurance that others will likewise do so."[32] More succinctly, reasonable persons "cooperate with others on terms that all can accept."[33] On this account, drug use is reasonable if it is consistent with a commitment to abide by fair terms of cooperation.

I see no ground on which to condemn *all* recreational drug use—licit or illicit—as unreasonable. An adult who uses alcohol or cocaine in his home, for example, does not violate any principle that rational persons would accept as establishing fair terms of cooperation. What principle might he violate? Instances of his conduct need not harm anyone, victimize anyone, infringe anyone's rights, or undermine fair standards of interaction.[34] In these crucial respects, the conduct of the recreational drug user differs fundamentally from that of the murderer or rapist.

The only viable strategy to condemn the recreational use of a drug as unreasonable is to construe it as creating an unacceptable *risk* to fair terms of cooperation. In other words, drug offenses must be conceptualized and evaluated as instances of what are called inchoate, anticipatory, or nonconsummate offenses (such as attempt, conspiracy, and solicitation). According to this view, use *itself* is not the evil that drug proscriptions are designed to prevent. Instead, the evil to be prevented is some *further* harm that drug users are more likely to inflict on others. Undoubtedly, some recreational drug use in some circumstances—for example, substantial alcohol use while driving—would threaten fair terms of cooperation. Rational persons would demand assurance that others not subject them to this risk. But a categorical prohibition of alcohol is not needed to achieve this purpose. Fair terms of cooperation are preserved by regulating the time, place, and circumstances under which alcohol may be consumed. Similarly, a categorical prohibition of each of those drugs currently classified as illicit seems equally unnecessary for this purpose.

Of course, this conclusion is hard to demonstrate. The criteria by which a neutralist liberal should decide whether a given imposition of risk is reasonable are tremendously controversial.[35] Clearly, however, some such criteria are needed if liberalism is to remain liberal. After all, virtually any kind of conduct creates *some* level of risk. Moreover, evidence that the use of a drug would be likely to undermine a commitment to abide by fair terms of cooperation might be far more plausible for some drugs than for others. To this point,

my discussion has treated all drugs as relevantly similar for purposes of deciding whether their recreational use qualifies for protection under the neutrality constraint. But little imagination is needed to suppose that a given drug might be so detrimental to terms of cooperation that its use would be intolerable under any circumstances. Works of fiction describe such drugs vividly. No state should be required to bear the risk that a Dr. Jekyll might consume the potion that turned him into the homicidal Mr. Hyde. No drug literally turns users into monsters. But a plausible basis for claiming that a given drug is too risky to qualify for neutralist liberal protection is that persons who use it become significantly more likely to commit crimes that victimize and violate the rights of others.

It is impossible to do justice to the voluminous literature on the alleged link between drugs and crime. Since I have scrutinized this rationale for drug prohibitions elsewhere;[36] I will only summarize a few of my reservations here. In particular, it is important to remain clear about the data that are material in assessing the hypothesis that a given drug causes crime. The more telling statistic is not the percentage of criminals who use drugs, but the percentage of drug users who commit crimes. Theorists who contend that drug use should be punished because it causes crime must explain why relatively few of the approximately 80 million persons who have used illicit drugs in the United States have ever become criminals. Smokers of marijuana—the most frequently used illicit drug—may actually be underrepresented in the criminal population.[37] Moreover, an adequate understanding of the causal contribution of drugs to crime must exclude those economic and systemic offenses that would not have occurred were drugs not proscribed in the first place.[38] Even a number of influential prohibitionists have admitted that the enforcement of drug offenses may actually cause more crime than it prevents.[39] The hypothesis that drug use itself creates aggression and criminal activity—that drugs have a psychopharmacological link to crime—has little empirical support when researchers control for other variables such as the effects of culture.[40] Drug use in other countries is not nearly so closely correlated with violent criminal activity, undermining the hypothesis that drug use has a psychopharmacological link to crime.[41]

To my mind, however, the best reason to doubt that recreational drug users should be punished because of their tendencies to commit crimes is that the causal link between drugs and crime is too remote. As a general matter, conduct that creates a risk is more reasonable as it becomes increasingly remote from whatever harm it ultimately risks. The concept of remoteness, as used in causal contexts, is admittedly vague and imprecise. Still, once psychopharmacological accounts of the link between drugs and crime are set aside, one must be distressed at the degree of remoteness between drug use and the ultimate evil of crime that obtains in rationales for punishing typical drug users. Bennett, for example, contends that drug use must be prevented because, inter alia, it causes crime.[42] Why punish ordinary drug users who show no inclination toward criminal activity? Bennett answers that the "non-addicted casual" drug user "remains a grave issue of national concern," even though he "is likely to have a still-intact family, social and work life" and "to 'enjoy' his drug for the pleasure it offers." Nonetheless, he continues, this casual drug user should be punished severely, because he is "much more willing and able to proselytize his drug use—by action or example—among his remaining nonuser peers, friends, and acquaintances. A non-addict's drug use,

in other words, is *highly* contagious."[43] As I understand this rationale, problem-free drug users should be punished because they might be imitated by others who must be deterred because their experimentation may lead to an increase in the ultimate evil of crime. This causal link between casual drug use and crime, I submit, is too remote to justify the criminal sanction.

Unless some other basis can be found on which to condemn recreational drug use as unreasonable, I tentatively conclude that neutralist liberals should accept the first two premises in the affirmative case for permitting drug use. These liberals should believe that a reasonable conception of the good life to which the state should be neutral might include the recreational use of drugs.

Additional difficulties with the affirmative case arise with premise (3). According to this premise, the state is not neutral toward conduct that it criminalizes. On one level, this premise seems beyond controversy. Admittedly, liberals have quarreled about which means of promoting a conception of the good life are precluded by their commitment to neutrality. In particular, they have disagreed about whether the neutrality constraint disables the state from enacting taxes to discourage given conduct, from financing educational programs to teach persons the dangers of specified activities, or from offering various incentives, such as subsidized housing, on condition that recipients behave in approved ways.[44] In addition, they have divided over whether and to what extent neutrality constrains the private sector—to preclude drug testing as a condition for employment, for example. These questions are crucial for purposes of identifying the details of a drug policy that is optimal from the perspective of liberal justice. Fortunately, however, these difficult issues need not be resolved here. If neutrality creates any constraint on policy at all, it precludes the *state* from imposing the terrible power of the *criminal* sanction. In this respect, punishment has a unique and special status among all of the various devices a society may employ to discourage given kinds of behaviors. Or so I will suppose. Whatever else neutrality may require, I will assume that it limits the authority of the state to enact coercive legislation.

On another level, however, the third premise in the affirmative case is enormously controversial. For two distinct reasons, liberal neutrality may have *no* direct implications for the justifiability of particular instances of criminal legislation. First, liberals disagree about *what* features of a political system must conform to the neutrality constraint. Rawls, for example, applies neutrality to the basic structure of a modern constitutional democracy, and thus to the larger structure of social institutions within which laws are enacted.[45] This form of "structural liberalism" does not require that each particular criminal statute must satisfy the neutrality constraint in order to be justified.

Whether the application of neutrality to the basic structure of a constitutional democracy would offer any degree of protection to recreational drug use is complicated and unclear.[46] This question cannot be answered without identifying the content of the particular rights that would be included in a constitution that conformed to the neutrality constraint Of course, a right to use drugs is unlikely to be explicitly included in any such constitution. But this concession does not settle the matter; rights to marry or to use contraceptives are equally improbable candidates for explicit inclusion. A legal system might afford constitutional protection to such behaviors by broadly interpreting some other right.[47] Similarly, decisions about

what foods to eat or what clothes to wear, to return to my earlier examples, would only be protected by an expansive interpretation of some general constitutional right. Many questions about the scope of constitutional protection afforded to such conduct are unexplored in our legal system, mainly because contemporary liberal states have rarely sought to punish them. No case law exists about issues that have never been addressed.[48] Thus, the constitutional status of drug use cannot be resolved without a theory to interpret and apply the several rights that would be included in a constitution that satisfies the demands of neutrality.[49]

The third premise in the affirmative case—that liberal neutrality has direct implications for the justifiability of criminal prohibitions—is enormously controversial for a second reason. Even those who reject "structural liberalism" tend to apply the neutrality constraint not to particular laws, but to *rationales* for laws. This strategy is designed to avoid an objection that otherwise is devastating to liberal neutrality. According to this objection, virtually any action by the state has the *effect* of favoring some conceptions of the good over others. Liberals need not concede, however, that no state can be constrained by neutrality. Instead, this constraint should be construed to require *justificatory* rather than *consequential* neutrality. In other words, although the state may enact laws that have the *effect* of favoring some conceptions of the good over others, it may not enact laws *in order to* favor some such conceptions.[50]

Even though justificatory neutrality preserves the bare possibility of satisfying neutrality, it raises yet another host of difficulties. Most any law—certainly drug proscriptions—can be supported by a multiplicity of rationales. If state neutrality precludes only justifications for laws rather than laws themselves, one and the same statute might or might not conform to the neutrality constraint depending on the reasons that are advanced on its behalf. To make matters worse, the quest for the rationale of a law seems no less elusive than the quest for legislative intent. Different legislators may have a variety of reasons for voting in favor of a given statute. Some may support drug proscriptions for reasons that fail the test of liberal neutrality, while others may have reasons that pass that test. In light of these phenomena, how can anyone pretend to have identified *the* rationale of a law? Justificatory neutrality seems to impose no real limitation on the authority of the liberal state.

Jeremy Waldron has offered the most plausible response to this predicament. He proposes to understand the doctrine of liberal neutrality "as a basis for each lawmaker to evaluate his own intentions . . . rather than as a doctrine for evaluating legislation as such."[51] Alternatively, he suggests that liberal neutrality might "be seen as a constraint on the reasons *we* deploy in our reconstruction of the justification of some rule we support (whatever its original intention was)."[52] According to either of Waldron's helpful proposals, the neutrality constraint does not pass judgment on law per se, but only on the rationales that

legislators or citizens are permitted to employ in defense of a law.[53]

Suppose that Waldron's response is acceptable. Should liberals who subscribe to the neutrality constraint thus reject premise (3) in the affirmative case for permitting drug use? This conclusion, I think, would be hasty. Perhaps the gap between the evaluation of the rationale of a law and the evaluation of the law itself can be bridged. Liberals should struggle to decide whether *any* plausible rationale for drug proscriptions can satisfy the neutrality constraint. I have already responded to several such rationales. I invite liberal neutralists to defend some alternative basis for punishing persons whose conception of the good life includes the recreational use of drugs. Identifying and evaluating such rationales is the challenge that both friends and foes of liberal neutrality must undertake. Again, I cannot prove that we will never find a rationale for drug prohibitions that satisfies the test of justificatory neutrality. In the absence of such a rationale, however, liberals are entitled to make an inference about drug proscriptions themselves; they are warranted in believing that these laws reflect rationales that violate neutrality. I tentatively conclude that the affirmative case in favor of permitting recreational drug use on grounds of liberal neutrality is sound.

Notes

1. For a readable summary, see Elliott Gurrie, *Crime and Punishment in America* (New York: Henry Holt and Co., 1998).
2. See Ethan Nadelmann, "Commonsense Drug Policy," *Foreign Affairs* 77 (1998): 111, 112.
3. See Michael Tonry, *Malign Neglect: Race, Crime and Punishment in America* (New York: Oxford University Press, 1995), Chapter Three.
4. See, for example, Michael Tonry and Kathleen Hatlestad, *Sentencing Reform in*

Overcrowded Times (New York: Oxford University Press, 1997).
5. Three points are needed about my focus on the punishment of *recreational drug use*. First, I propose no precise criterion to identify when drug use is recreational. Roughly, use is recreational when it is intended to enhance the pleasure or euphoria of the user. Admittedly, the line between recreational and non-recreational activities is difficult to draw. See Note 21 *infra*. Second, most (but not all) persons punished for drug use are actually charged and convicted of drug *possession*. I assume that

states tend to punish possession rather than use for evidentiary reasons. Thus, I continue to refer to punishment for drug *use*. Finally, I do not discuss the justifiability of punishment for other drug offenses, most notably of drug sale.

6. There are, of course, many liberalisms. Admittedly, drug prohibitions are more likely to be acceptable on perfectionist than on neutralist modes of liberalism. Still, many of my arguments help to undermine the case for drug proscriptions on versions of liberalism that reject the neutrality constraint.

7. Leading liberals derive very different conclusions from their commitment to neutrality. These theorists include John Rawls, *A Theory of Justice* (Cambridge, MA: Harvard University Press, 1971); Robert Nozick, *Anarchy, State, and Utopia* (New York: Basic Books, 1974); Ronald Dworkin, "Liberalism," in Stuart Hampshire, ed., *Public & Private Morality* (Cambridge: Cambridge University Press, 1978), p. 113; Bruce Ackerman, *Social Justice in the Liberal State* (New Haven: Yale University Press, 1980); Charles Larmore, *Patterns of Moral Complexity* (Cambridge: Cambridge University Press, 1987); and Thomas Nagel, "Moral Conflict and Political Legitimacy," *Philosophy & Public Affairs* 16, no. 3 (Summer 1987): 215.

8. Of course, many philosophers reject the neutrality constraint. See, for example, Richard Kraut, "Politics, Neutrality, and the Good," *Social Philosophy & Policy* 16 (1999): 315. Since my project is to critique drug proscriptions on neutralist grounds rather than to defend neutrality, I make no effort to respond to such criticisms.

9. John Rawls, *Political Liberalism* (New York: Columbia University Press, 1993), p. 37.

10. George Sher, *Beyond Neutrality* (Cambridge: Cambridge University Press, 1997), pp. 118–19. Sher admits, however (at p. 121), that "the government acts that are most likely to engender discord ate heavy-handed applications of the criminal law."

11. See, for example, Ronald Beimer, *What's The Matter With Liberalism?* (Berkeley: University of California Press, 1992), pp. 67–68; and Harry Clor, *Public Morality and Liberal Society* (Notre Dame: University of Notre Dame Press, 1996), p. 104.

12. Rawls, *Political Liberalism*, p. 104.

13. Dworkin, "Liberalism," p. 127.

14. Ibid.

15. Although no entirely adequate definition of "drug" exists, any respectable candidate would include alcohol. Perhaps the most commonly cited definition is "any substance other than food which by its chemical nature affects the structure or function of the living organism." See Gerald Uelmen and Victor Haddox, eds., *Drug Abuse and the Law Sourcebook* (New York: Clark Boardman Co., 1988), p. 1-1.

16. In indicating that the satisfaction of some tastes and preferences should be included in a conception of the good life, I leave open the possibility that such satisfaction is valuable because of a psychological experience that is contingently produced. See Thomas Scanlon, "Value, Desire, and the Quality of Life," in Martha Nussbaum and Amartya Sen, eds., *The Quality of Life* (Oxford: Clarendon Press, 1993), p. 185.

17. Or by proscribing given drugs. Nonetheless, many people seem confident in their conjectures. According to one philosopher, "cocaine, heroin, marijuana, alcohol, peyote, LSD, amphetamines, barbiturates, and tobacco are *very likely* to result in a *clear* preponderance of pain over pleasure in the long run for users and/or for others." Rem Edwards, "Why We Should Not Use Some Drugs for Pleasure," in Steven Luper-Foy and Curtis Brown, eds., *Drugs, Morality and the Law* (New York: Garland Pub. Co., 1994), p. 183, 185 (emphasis added).

18. The constitutional limits on the authority of states to enact criminal legislation contained in the "fundamental rights," "suspect class," and "rational basis" doctrines are described in Lawrence Tribe, *American Constitutional Law*, 2nd ed. (Mineola, NY: Foundation Press, 1988).

19. For a defense of this position, see Sherry Colb. "Freedom from Incarceration: Why is This Right Different from All Other Rights?" *New York University Law Review* 69 (1994): 781.

20. States were not always so reluctant to proscribe foods. See Alan Hunt, *Governance of the Consuming Passion: A History of Sumptuary Law* (New York: St. Martin's Press, 1996).

21. Difficulties in distinguishing recreational from nonrecreational drug use make it easier rather than harder to argue that drug use qualifies for protection under the neutrality constraint. Protecting most other purposes for which drugs are used—medicinal or religious purposes, for example—should

prove less difficult for neutralist liberals. If marijuana has a medical use, the arguments for keeping it unavailable to patients are feeble. See George Annas, "Reefer Madness—The Federal Response to California's Marijuana Law," *New England Journal of Medicine* 337 (1997): 434.

22. For further discussion, see the collection in Christoph Fehige and Ulla Wessels, eds., *Preferences* (Berlin: Walter de Gruyter, 1998).

23. Joel Feinberg recounts a case in which a sane and informed adult decides to use a drug because "I'll get a lots of pleasure first, so much pleasure in fact, that it is well worth running the risk of physical harm." Feinberg describes this case as "easy"—as "the litmus test example for distinguishing the paternalist from the liberal." Joel Feinberg, *Harm to Self* (Oxford: Oxford University Press, 1986), p. 133.

24. William Bennett, *National Drug Control Strategy* (1989), p. 11.

25. C. L. Ten, *Mill on Liberty* (Oxford: Clarendon Press, 1980), p. 116.

26. Even if they are fully informed, some commentators have alleged that users do not really *appreciate* these risks; users often succumb to rationalizations and psychological fallacies to explain their behavior. See Robert Goodin, *No Smoking* (Chicago: University of Chicago Press, 1989), pp. 20–24.

27. For a discussion of the risks of prescription drugs, see Jason Latrou, et al., "Incidence of Adverse Drug Reactions in Hospitalized Patients," *Journal of the American Medical Association* 279 (1998): 1200.

28. "If ignorance is the problem, knowledge is the cure. I don't believe that for a large number of kids out there who use drugs, that ignorance is the problem." See Bennett "Doubts Value of Drug Education," *New York Times* (3 February 1990), p. AI:7.

29. See Alan Leshner, "Addiction is a Brain Disease, and It Matters," *Science* 278 (1997): 45.

30. See Ronald Siegel, *Intoxication: Life in Pursuit of Artificial Paradise* (New York: E. P. Dutton, 1989).

31. Many neutralist liberals exempt the distribution of "primary goods"—things persons want whatever else they may want—from the requirement of neutrality. Sometimes, liberals indicate that the neutrality constraint applies only "so far as is possible." See Dworkin, "Liberalism,"

p. 127. Or they restrict neutrality to *permissible* conceptions of the good—to "those that respect the principles of justice." See Rawls, *Theory of Justice*, p. 193.

32. Rawls, *Political Liberalism*, p. 49.

33. Ibid., p. 50.

34. Hence drugs consumed for recreational purposes differ importantly from drugs consumed to enhance performance. An athlete who breaks the rules by using a drug to improve his competitive abilities may undermine fair terms of cooperation.

35. For an argument that drug proscriptions falt the justificatory test that such offenses must satisfy, see Douglas Husak, "The Nature and Justifiability of Non-Consummate Offenses," *Arizona Law Review* 37 (1995): 151.

36. See Douglas Husak, *Drugs and Rights* (New York: Cambridge University Press, 1992), pp. 178—207.

37. See John Morgan and Lynn Zimmer, *Marijuana Myths, Marijuana Facts* (New York: Lindesmith Center, 1997), p. 90.

38. The most useful framework in which to understand the connection between drugs and crime is presented in Paul Goldstein, "The Drugs/Violence Nexus: A Tripartite Conceptual Framework," *Journal of Drug Issues* 15 (1985): 493.

39. James Q. Wilson, for example, writes, "It is not clear that enforcing the laws against drug use would reduce crime. On the contrary, crime may be caused by such enforcement." See his "Drugs and Crime" in Michael Tonry and James Q. Wilson, eds., *Drugs and Crime* (Chicago: Chicago University Press. 1990), p. 522.

40. See, for example, Jeffrey Fagan, "Intoxication and Aggression," in Tonry and Wilson, eds., *Drugs and Crime*, p. 241.

41. Cross-national data about illicit drug use and violent crime are examined in Franklin Zimring and Cordon Hawkins, *Crime Is Not the Problem* (New York: Oxford University Press, 1997), pp. 138–53.

42. Bennett, *National Drug Control Strategy*, p. 7.

43. Ibid., p. 11 (emphasis in original).

44. For a basis to differentiate some of these forms of state action, see Colin Macleod, "Liberal Neutrality or Liberal Tolerance?" *Law and Philosophy* 16 (1997): 529.

45. Rawls, *Theory of Justice*, p. 7. He later came to regard the term "neutrality" to be "unfortunate." See Rawls, *Political Liberalism*, p. 191.

46. See Peter de Marneffe, "Liberalism, Liberty, and Neutrality," *Philosophy & Public Affairs* 19, no. 3 (Summer 1990): 253. He suggests that constitutional neutrality is compatible with drug proscriptions, but legislative neutrality is not. He may be correct, but neither claim is as clear as he supposes.

47. The best candidate, of course, is the right to privacy—even though privacy itself may not be an enumerated right.

48. According to Laurence Tribe, it seems "preposterous" that courts would not apply a heightened level of scrutiny to assess the constitutionality of laws that burdened the ways in which the mind processes the sensory data it receives from the world. See Tribe, *American Constitutional Law,* p. 1324.

49. Recent efforts to extend constitutional protection to drug use are undertaken by Robert Sweet and Edward Harris, "Moral and Constitutional Considerations in Support of the Decriminalization of Drugs," in Jefferson Fish, ed., *How to Legalize Drugs* (Northvale: Jason Arenson, 1998), p. 430. For an earlier attempt, see David Richards, *Sex, Drugs, Death, and the Law* (Totowa: Rowman and Littlefield, 1982).

50. See Will Kymlicka, "Liberal Individualism and Liberal Neutrality," *Ethics* 99 (1989): 884.

51. Jeremy Waldron, "Legislation and Moral Neutrality," in his *Liberal Rights: Collected Papers* (Cambridge: Cambridge University Press, 1993), p. 151.

52. Ibid., p. 151 (emphasis in original).

53. Some theorists claim that justificatory neutrality is satisfied "if some significant number of the citizens initiating, framing, and pressing the policy are sincerely moved by neutral justifications." Harry Brighouse, "Neutrality, Publicity, and State Funding of the Arts," *Philosophy & Public Affairs* 24, no. 1 (Winter 1995): 35, 39.

LIBERALISM AND RIGHTS OF DRUG USE

Samuel Freeman

In recent years the criminal justice system in the United States has oriented itself toward waging a politically popular "war on drugs." It is a war that many will say is hopelessly lost, in the same way that Prohibition's war on alcohol was lost. Some argue that the war on drugs is self-defeating. No doubt, as a result of the criminalization of most psychoactive drugs (beginning with the Harrison Act of 1914), fewer people use them than would if such drugs were legalized.[1] But, as in the case of Prohibition under the 18th Amendment, this does not mean that less damage is done to individuals or to society as a whole. The criminalization of psychoactive drugs has, it is argued, grossly aggravated the incidence of violence and poverty in society and has even stimulated greater drug abuse and addiction. Having made opiates, depressants (except for alcohol), stimulants (except for nicotine), and hallucinogens illegal and attached severe penalties not only to their distribution but also to the individuals who use them, we have created a class of criminals whose size some analysts estimate to be as large as 30 to 40 million people. Less

than 3 percent of those who use drugs are apprehended and punished each year, and this comes at extraordinary costs to the legal system.[2] Most of those punished are African Americans, even though as a group they consume far fewer illicit drugs than middle-class Caucasians. This can only have damaging effects on many people's attitudes toward the fairness and efficiency of the criminal justice system and only increase African Americans' sense of social alienation and injustice.

Moreover, given the severe penalties attending drug distribution, the war on drugs has caused the distribution of narcotics to be placed, not in the hands of pharmacists or ordinary business people, but rather in the hands of violent gangs who reap monopoly profits and terrorize portions of our inner cities. These gangs (with names like the Jamaican posse, the Bloods, and the Crips) would not exist, it is argued, were it not for the fact that such severe penalties are attached to the use of psychoactive drugs and that, therefore, such enormous profits can be derived from their sale. Moreover, because legislatures assign severe penalties for use of even mild drugs such as marijuana, it is claimed that the war on drugs has caused drug dealers to create and dispense far more dangerous and addictive narcotics like crack cocaine. Many people believe that crack would not exist were it not for the illegality of drug use. As a general rule, "Where drugs are illegal, more damaging drugs drive out less damaging drugs."[3] Heroin and, now, crack cocaine have come to replace marijuana as the drug of choice, since they are far more profitable and easily transportable by drug dealers.[4]

Our court system has become clogged with the prosecution of drug dealers and users. Because of the war on drugs, criminal prosecutions against the drug trade and drug use have been assigned legislative priority in the judicial system to the degree that civil actions in federal and state courts often take at least two years. (In some federal districts, 70 percent of trial time is devoted to criminal drug cases.[5]) Moreover, enormous policing efforts are devoted to the war on drugs, at immense expense, thereby draining police resources from surveillance of other illegal activities. In addition the illegality of drugs has a corrupting influence on law enforcement itself when police accept bribes from drug dealers, confiscate for themselves illegal profits, or become actively involved in the drug trade itself.[6] And even without these problems, the overzealous police methods utilized during narcotics raids often lead to violation of the rights of many innocent persons, to illegal police searches and subsequent perjured testimony in the courts by police officers, and to a casual attitude toward the rights of the innocent as well as the guilty.[7] The dignity of many people is compromised by such tactics, and serious questions are raised regarding the role of the police in a free democratic society. For these and other reasons, some argue that

the war on drugs, by increasingly occupying the criminal justice system, is gradually undermining it.

Given these substantially adverse social, economic, and political consequences of the war on drugs at the federal and state level, plus the fact that the demonstrable benefits are so minimal, many people argue that a rational social policy calls for the decriminalization of drug use and its replacement with a regulatory scheme only somewhat more rigid than those programs that now regulate alcohol and nicotine. This suggested policy is based in the recognition that it is practically impossible to fully eradicate the use of opiates and stimulants in the absence of autocratic power that would undermine liberal and democratic society itself. The social costs of prohibition will always far exceed whatever benefits result from interdiction, particularly when increasingly stringent methods of interdiction violate so many people's rights and come to undermine confidence in the legal system.

If these claims and arguments regarding the adverse social costs of drug interdiction are correct (I do not say that they are) then it becomes difficult to mount a good case for the system of prohibition of psychoactive drugs that we now have in place. A convincing reply would need to show that even worse consequences would attend drug legalization. In the absence of these adverse consequences, the war on drugs should go the way of Prohibition. This is the best liberal argument for the decriminalization of psychoactive drugs. It is an argument that focuses on experience of the adverse consequences of criminalization as weighed against the adverse consequences of noncriminalization.

What I primarily want to address and draw into question, however, is a different liberal argument for legalization of psychoactive drugs. It is a purely philosophical argument, one that proceeds, not from pragmatic considerations of the adverse consequences of drug interdiction, but from the contention that in a liberal society citizens have a right to indulge in drugs, whatever the adverse consequences for themselves, so long as use is voluntary and informed and does not cause harm to the rights and interests of others. My sense is that this argument is overstated. It works from the premise that liberalism excludes all prohibitions on self-destructive conduct, a premise that I seriously question. Below, I show that there are certain kinds of purely self-destructive conduct that a liberal society can legitimately prohibit, and I consider the implications of this for use of psychoactive drugs. Finally, I return to the question raised in this introduction regarding the adverse social consequences of criminalization of drugs. Here I raise certain considerations about the effects of noninterdiction for the institutions of a liberal society, considerations which are often neglected in arguments for decriminalization.

The Issue

It is commonly recognized that a liberal society can and should regulate drugs to insure that users are apprised of the consequences of drug use, that use is voluntary, and that harmful substances do not fall into the hands of minors and incompetents. These so-called soft paternalistic measures are not such a difficult issue for liberals. Many liberals, however, do not concede that the outright prohibition of narcotics or even the regulation of drug use is legitimate when it can be shown that users, without endangering others, willingly and wittingly take drugs and are aware of their likely harmful consequences for their future well-being. Such prohibitions are seen as paternalistic (in the negative sense), and liberalism, it is claimed, is

incompatible with this kind of paternalism. That being the case, some people have argued that there is an unqualified right to use drugs regardless of the consequences of such use for the user.

I find the charge of paternalism in these contexts to be unhelpful at best, and for the most part misleading. It makes sense to speak of whole political systems as being paternalistic when they manage or govern individuals in the manner that fathers (or parents) traditionally have governed their children. Paternalism implies systematically restricting and regulating another's conduct and, at the limit, doing this in such a way as to instill in that person not just particular values but a general morality and complete conception of the good. As applied to political systems, paternalism is a charge that individuals are treated as mere subjects, benignly perhaps, but not as free citizens who are capable of taking responsibility for their lives. Clearly no liberal democratic system of laws is paternalistic in the sense that it denies individuals the complex scheme of rights that enables them to determine their own lives within the restrictions allowed by justice. So the charge of paternalism, when it is leveled in the context of a liberal democratic regime, can be one that only applies to particular laws and not to the political system as a whole. But when applied to laws, it is an obscure claim. For the fact is that most so-called paternalistic laws (such as seatbelt and motorcycle helmet laws, laws against suicide and gambling, and many laws against drugs) in no way enforce a particular conception of the good; rather they restrict or require specific actions, while leaving open the range of conceptions of the good that one may choose from. What more is being said, then, when a law is called paternalistic, than that this law prohibits some kind of self-destructive conduct? Some claim that the law also denies individuals the rights of self-determination and autonomy upon which liberalism is based. But (assuming that this is an accurate account of liberalism's basis) the issue then becomes whether liberal autonomy and self-determination require that there be no restrictions whatsoever on self-destructive conduct. I take this to be the really interesting issue in the debate over paternalistic laws, and it is not a debate that can be won by simply stipulating that part of the true meaning of autonomy is a complete absence of laws against self-destructive conduct.

My position is that liberalism is not incompatible with certain restrictions on self-destructive conduct, even if such conduct is informed, voluntary, and rational in the ordinary sense. When the aim and effect of restrictions against self-destructive conduct is to maintain the moral and rational integrity of the person—in the sense of the capacities for rational agency and moral responsibility upon which liberalism and liberal autonomy are based—then there is nothing illiberal about imposing restrictions on conduct that is harmful only to the agent concerned. By implication, citizens in a constitutional democracy have a duty to maintain the degree of competence necessary to exercise the capacities of agency that enable them to reflect on their good and observe the moral requirements of social life.

My argument does not imply that liberalism allows for the restriction of all psychoactive drugs. Such mildly intoxicating substances as marijuana, for example, cannot be prohibitable on the grounds I set forth. It may even be that most currently available drugs are not prohibitable on these grounds, including heroin and cocaine. This is an empirical issue. But there is, at least potentially, a class of drugs so intrinsically debilitating of one's capacities, that their prohibition is justified on liberal grounds.

What, then, is the point of this exercise? The point is to locate one of the parameters of liberalism: the extent to which individuals can go in exercising their freedom. My primary aim in this paper is to challenge the common idea that liberalism in some way requires that individuals be permitted to engage in any self-regarding conduct, no matter how detrimental its consequences may be for the agent. If nothing else, this exercise should help us gain a clearer insight into the scope and limits of a right to use drugs, if indeed such a right does exist in a liberal system. . . .

Most any liberal view must provide for a plurality of goods and worthwhile ways of life that are permissible for citizens to freely pursue. The capacities for moral and rational agency enable the pursuit of the wide range of opportunities and permissible conceptions of the good that a liberal society provides for and sanctions. To see exercise of these powers as a good that is to be maximized would deprive them of their point. So, rather than conceiving of development of the capacities for rational and moral agency as an incremental good (or even as intrinsic goods for each agent), they are more correctly seen as *essential conditions* for liberal citizens, allowing them to have a conception of the good and to comply with the norms of justice of a liberal society.[8]

While it is not the role of a constitutional democracy to fix any particular conception of the good for all its citizens, it is an appropriate, and indeed necessary, role of a constitutional democracy to maintain the conditions for citizens' free pursuit of their good in society. Exercising the capacities for moral and rational agency is fundamental among these conditions. One role of a liberal constitution is to specify the basic rights and duties that are required for this purpose. By so doing, it sets limits on the domain of conceptions of the good that are permissible to pursue. A conception of the good that requires violation of others' basic rights is clearly not within this domain. . . . Our question is whether recreational drug use is among the permissible activities or ways of life in a liberal society. . . .

A distinction can be drawn between normal risk-taking for the sake of valued activities (such as mountain climbing, motorcycle riding, parachuting, or eating fatty foods), as opposed to activities which, by their nature, destroy or permanently undermine a person's capacities for engaging in rationally chosen valued activities. Let us call this latter class "intrinsically debilitating activities." Among this class are such things as committing suicide, enlisting another to kill you, or permanently mutilating one's cognitive or conative capacities (such as through a frontal lobotomy). A liberal society can, I believe, legitimately prohibit these kinds of activities, except when there are special reasons. Special reasons might then justify assisted suicide—perhaps even active consensual euthanasia—when one is suffering from an incurable condition and death is imminent or one's capacities for agency are degenerating. Under conditions where the capacities for agency are no longer functional, the usual liberal reasons for asserting non-destructibility of one's own life no longer obtain. But one cannot voluntarily kill oneself for just any reason (on a bet, say, or because one has been jilted, or because one just likes the idea). The same is true of self-mutilation of one's cognitive and conative capacities.

On this line of reasoning, alcohol and smoking cigarettes would seem to be permissible activities. For drinking alcohol is clearly compatible with the full exercise of powers of rational and moral agency (indeed, in due proportion, an occasional drink can even help some of us along the way). There is nothing intrinsically debilitating about alcohol. Granted it can be abused, as can many other things (including exercise or dieting). But the activity itself is not such that, by its nature, it destroys one's capacities for agency. And the same is true of cigarettes. Though they may shorten one's life, they do not necessarily, if at all, debilitate one's capacities while one is living.

But alcohol is an intoxicating substance, and cigarettes are physically addictive. If these substances are permissible in a liberal society, then so too must be certain other presently illegal drugs (other things being equal). There is nothing intrinsically debilitating about marijuana or hashish, and the same may well be true about mescaline and LSD. Granted, taking these substances can temporarily suspend one's exercise of the capacities for agency, but then so too can overconsumption of alcohol and many other permitted activities. On the standard I have proposed, a substance must be such that by its nature it permanently undermines or at least indefinitely suspends ones capacities for rational and moral agency. None of these drugs meet that condition.

What about heroin and cocaine? These drugs are on most accounts physiologically addictive, but addiction by itself does not permanently undermine the exercise of one's capacities—compare them with nicotine. Many people function fairly normally while using cocaine recreationally, and perhaps the same is even true of heroin.[9] Douglas Husak has argued that, while breaking one's addiction to these substances may be painful and require strong acts of will, still it is doable and has been done by the majority of addicts.[10] On the other hand, for many addicts readdiction is a common phenomenon, largely for psychological and social reasons.[11] I am not in a position to judge whether heroin, cocaine, or crack cocaine can be classified as intrinsically debilitating drugs. It is an empirical issue, to be decided upon with advice from pharmacologists, psychologists, and other professionals.

In any case, it is highly likely that there is a large class of drugs currently prohibited which are not prohibitable on the grounds I have considered. (I assume, however, that even these drugs are legally regulable to varying degrees for other reasons, certainly to protect others from harm, and also for the reasons Feinberg mentions, namely, to insure that usage is voluntary and informed, and that minors are not allowed access.) Nonetheless, there also is a class of drugs which can be described as intrinsically debilitating of one's capacities—even if no such substance actually exist, then there is at least the potential of one.[12] Of the substances in this class, it can legitimately be claimed that a liberal government has the authority to prohibit their use for no other reason than that they permanently or indefinitely impair our capacities for rational and moral agency.

This argument does nothing to rule out activities which temporally make it difficult to exercise the powers of agency. People have the political right to be temporally intoxicated (as they have the right to mesmerize themselves before the TV). Doing that does not continuously deprive them of their faculties for practical reasoning so that they can no longer function as self-governing agents. After they sober up, they can continue their lives in a normal way. But where normalcy is permanent suspension of one's capacities, or deprivation to the degree that one is indefinitely incapacitated, a liberal system can legitimately prohibit such activities. The right to become intoxicated does not imply a right to make a zombie of oneself.

A liberal constitution has the authority to require that people develop their capacities for agency. This is one justification for mandatory education in a liberal society.

Mandatory education seeks to insure that children become capable of developing their faculties, forming a conception of their good, and understanding and taking advantage of the opportunities that are open to them; moreover, liberal education aims to guarantee that individuals can understand and comply with their public duties to respect the laws and the rights of others, and that they develop an interest in maintaining the continuation of liberal institutions.[13] For many of the same reasons, a liberal constitutional democracy has the legitimate authority to proscribe self-regarding conduct that by its nature permanently impairs the exercise or development of the capacities for agency that are part of the ideal of liberal sovereignty. One is free in a liberal society to choose whether or not to take advantage of the basic rights and opportunities it affords; one is not free to engage in activities designed to permanently impair one's capacities to exercise these rights, any more than one is free to alienate them.

On this principle, admittedly not everything will be clear cut; there are going to be many hard cases, as there will with most any principle. But even where a principle cannot resolve all ambiguities, still it helps us to understand why certain cases are hard to resolve. In so doing, it points us toward the kinds of considerations that are relevant to finally deciding the issue. If at the end of the day all of these considerations still do not suffice to resolve all ambiguities, then in a constitutional democracy the question can be left to majority decision as a means of political settlement. This may seem unsatisfactory to those who have a desire for clear lines of demarcation and systemization. But determinacy of outcome is not the first virtue of moral principles. It is more important that principles be capable of serving as a basis for public justification and fit with our most firmly considered moral convictions, inducting the ideal of the person that is implicit in our moral judgments of justice in a constitutional democracy.

Social Considerations

I have advanced one argument for limiting free availability of certain psychoactive drugs in response to the common contention that liberal autonomy is incompatible with restrictions on drug use no matter how self-destructive these drugs may be. My argument, however, agrees with the position of proponents of decriminalization to the extent that it implies that many (perhaps even most) currently interdicted drugs should be legalized. But there are considerations other than the nature and requirements of liberal autonomy that need be taken into account before a complete liberal drug policy can be formulated. The argument from autonomy addresses what may well be highly artificial circumstances, namely, where use of drugs does not substantially and adversely affect the interests of others. At the beginning of this essay, I recounted the social consequences of criminalization that lead many to argue for decriminalization. Here I conclude with some considerations regarding the potentially adverse social consequences of drug use, which need to be considered before this complicated issue can be resolved.

Suppose that free availability of a drug left people capable of exercising their capacities for agency to the minimum requisite degree. At the same time, it deprived them of the motivation or ability to do productive work and destabilized family life.[14] Suppose, too, that legalization and unrestricted availability of the drug had the effect of promoting widespread use on a scale larger than currently obtains. Consequently, living standards and familial stability decline considerably for many

people. Large numbers of children are left impoverished and neglected, and their education and socialization is impaired. Many are abandoned or abused, and consequently come to lead lives destructive not only of themselves, but also of others. These are legitimate grounds for restricting such a drug in a liberal constitutional democracy (assuming such measures effectively mitigate these adverse consequences). While it is not the function of a liberal government to inquire into the social productivity of its citizens and require them to perform work that a majority regards as useful, still it is legitimate for a liberal government to take necessary measures to maintain and reproduce liberal society so that it can insure the conditions of its continued stability.

To elaborate, one important role of a liberal government is to secure conditions for the production of adequate material resources that are needed to maintain a just society and the dignity of each of its members. This is not at all to say a liberal government's role is to encourage maximum productive output (certainly not without regard to distribution, as many classical liberals maintain). Economic efficiency is subordinate as a liberal end; it should be regulated and directed toward maintaining a society in which each person is enabled to effectively exercise basic rights and liberties, take advantage of fair opportunities, and achieve individual independence. But given this more basic distributive end, liberal society has a legitimate interest in providing and maintaining conditions under which people can be productive and self-supporting. This does not mean the able-bodied must labor to avoid sacrificing a government-sponsored basic income.[15] It means rather that government has the responsibility to maintain a setting in which they can develop their capacities and be productive. When a subculture of addiction becomes so severe and wide-spread that it affects individuals' opportunities to develop their abilities and engage in production, they are in effect denied fair opportunities, and liberal institutions themselves are undermined.

Another important role of a liberal government is to secure conditions necessary for the reproduction of liberal culture and the continuation of liberal society across generations. Herein lies government's interest in maintaining the integrity of family life (in some form), and seeing to it that parents and guardians protect, support, and educate children under their care. The reproduction of liberal institutions and culture also plays a significant role in justifying and defining the purposes of a mandatory educational system (discussed above). When the family and the system of education are undermined by adverse effects of free availability of drugs, liberal society's ongoing need to perpetuate itself is endangered.

So, if the consequences of free availability of a drug substantially impair the ability of a liberal society to produce adequate sustaining resources or to reproduce liberal culture and institutions from one generation to the next, then there are legitimate liberal reasons for restricting that drug, in order to protect the interests of current and future generations. As individuals cannot exercise liberal rights in a way that is calculated to destroy their capacities for agency, so they cannot exercise these rights in a way that destroys or undermines the conditions of liberal culture needed to sustain the free exercise of these capacities. Liberalism is not committed to standing by and passively witnessing the destruction of its culture and institutions to the point where society itself can only be sustained by illiberal and autocratic measures. These considerations need to be weighed in the balance, along with the arguments against drug interdiction recited at the outset of this paper, in finally coming to a decision about the permissibility of psychoactive drugs in a liberal constitutional democracy.

Notes

1. The difference is 30% fewer on some accounts. See Daniel Benjamin and Roger L. Miller, *Undoing Drugs* (New York: Basic Books, 1991). Others contend that there is no reliable way of predicting such figures. See John Kaplan, *The Hardest Drug: Heroin and Public Policy* (Chicago: University of Chicago Press, 1983), pp. 111ff.
2. Benjamin and Miller, *Undoing Drugs*, p. 85.
3. Ibid., p. 129.
4. Ibid. See also Kaplan, *The Hardest Drug*, pp. 64–65.
5. Benjamin and Miller, *Undoing Drugs*, p. 82.
6. Kaplan, *The Hardest Drug*, pp. 90, 97–98.
7. Ibid., pp. 95–96.
8. According to Rawls's political liberalism, Kantian liberalism of the kind here argued for need not make the working assumption that autonomy is an intrinsic good for each person, in other words, that autonomy is among the final ends about which it is rational for all people to structure their lives and which, therefore, provides a fundamental basis for laws and political institutions. This is one respect in which a Kantian politically liberal view differs from the perfectionist liberalism argued for by Michael Moore in this volume. I make a weaker claim: that autonomy, in the sense of the exercise and development of the powers of moral and rational agency, is essential to each person's good within the confines of a liberal and democratic society. This leaves open the more controversial claim that autonomy is an intrinsic good for each person. This may be true, but it is not necessary for the argument over what basic rights individuals have.
9. See Kaplan, *The Hardest Drug*, p. 33, on "chippers," long-term occasional users of heroin who do not become addicted.
10. As is evidenced by the majority of servicemen who gave up heroin, without

subsequent readdiction, upon return from the Vietnam War. See Kaplan, *The Hardest Drug*, p. 37. Kaplan says, "heroin withdrawal is not *that* serious. Pharmacologists compare it to a bad case of the one-week flu—a considerable degree of pain and discomfort, but not so serious that it cannot be borne by someone with considerable determination" (p. 35).

11. See Kaplan, *The Hardest Drug*, pp. 45–46.

12. Angel Dust may be in this category. There also exists a form of heroin called China White that matches the description of intrinsically debilitating drugs.

13. For a thorough account of the ends of education in a constitutional democracy, see Amy Gutmann, *Democratic Education* (Princeton, NJ: Princeton University Press, 1987).

14. Heroin may be such a drug. See Kaplan, *The Hardest Drug*, pp. 133–136.

15. Still it remains the case that those who are unable to work because of drug addiction have assumed ways of life that require other people's labor to support them. This is likely to cause resentment among those who labor on their behalf, and a diminished sense of self-respect among those who are unable to labor because of addiction. I do not mean to take a position here in the complicated debate on whether those who choose a life of leisure without labor should be entitled to do so without affecting their share of government benefits or an insured basic income. See the criticisms of Rawls in Phillippe Van Parijs, "Why Surfers Should be Fed: The Liberal Case for an Unconditional Basic Income," *Philosophy and Public Affairs* 20 (1991): 101–131, and his *Real Freedom for All* (Oxford: Oxford University Press, 1995), Chap. 4.

Study Questions for Section 5

1. What does it mean for a state to be neutral with respect to reasonable conceptions of the good life? What does it mean for a conception of the good life to be reasonable?

2. Freeman draws a distinction between "normal" risk-taking activities and activities that are by their very nature self-destructive. Is this distinction defensible?

3. Freeman maintains that the state has the authority to require citizens to develop their rational abilities. How would Husak respond to this claim?

SECTION 6

GUN CONTROL

THE LIBERAL BASIS OF THE RIGHT TO BEAR ARMS

Todd C. Hughes and Lester H. Hunt

Introduction

Bans on guns are typically considered a "liberal" policy, if only because those who support them generally consider themselves to be politically liberal in some sense or other.[1] We will argue, however, that broad bans on firearms are in fact not liberal policies at all. The policy of a state that disarms its citizenry conflicts with more than one of the fundamental principles of liberalism.

The degree and nature of the conflict between liberalism and gun bans depends, however, on how one conceives of liberalism. In this regard, gun bans serve as a means of illustrating the disparity between two fundamentally different versions of liberalism, which we shall call *wide* and *narrow* liberalism. We shall try to show that a complete ban on the private possession of firearms is impermissible on either view; in fact *any* meaningful restriction is difficult to justify in the context of wide liberalism. Narrow liberalism, on the other hand, permits more restriction, but, if applied consistently, is unlikely to allow

ones that will result in a significant decrease in violent crime.

Some Liberal Constraints

The assumption motivating most calls for bans on private possession of guns is that a causal relationship exists between the number of guns in the private sector and the number of victims of violent crime: an increase in the number of guns (in some sense) *causes* an increase in violent crime. This view has a special sort of plausibility in the United States, where violent crime has (or at least seems to have) escalated in tandem with gun ownership.[2] Of course, the government has a legitimate interest in protecting the health and safety of its citizens, and reducing crime is necessary to that end. Surely, one might conclude, the government ought to take measures to take firearms out of private circulation if that will curb criminal activity and foster the health and safety of the population.[3]

To date, nearly the whole of the controversy about bans on firearms has centered on this argument and on the causal connection it alleges. On the one hand, common sense and a good deal of scholarly research seems to support the idea that increases and decreases in gun ownership, respectively, cause increases and decreases in lethal crime.[4] On the other hand, criminologists have amassed a considerable amount of statistical evidence suggesting the relationship is weak or nonexistent. Perhaps their most impressive arguments so far rest on evidence that possession of guns by law-abiding citizens, the potential victims of crime, has the same effect that possession of guns by the police has: that of deterring crime.[5]

The empirical literature on this issue is baffling, at least to those not trained in mathematics and social science. Let us assume, for the sake of the argument, that the alleged causal relationship between guns and crime really exists. Is this sufficient to justify a government ban on firearms? In a liberal state, the answer is simple: it is *no*. In a consistently liberal system, it is considered highly problematic to dispose of the rights and liberties of citizens—where these rights and liberties are believed by their owners to be important—simply and solely because the community can extract a benefit from doing so.

Perhaps a few examples will serve to make this claim more vivid and persuasive. It is very obvious that we could prevent a great many deaths from AIDS by enacting a policy reputedly followed in Cuba: that of simply rounding up everyone known to have the disease and isolating them in special camps until they no longer carry the disease (presumably, because they are dead). We do not have such a policy, though we know perfectly well that thousands of people will die because we do not have it. The reason we do not have it is that we, or most of us, think that incarceration is a bad way to treat sick people. It violates their rights. Of course, there are many ways to explain why we tend to think this, and why we tend to find this thought so decisive. One perfectly good way to explain it, however, is to say that this country, unlike Cuba, is a liberal democracy: from a liberal point of view, the mere fact that a policy could save lives is not a sufficient reason for adopting it. The policy itself must be morally permissible. In a consistently liberal polity, the pursuit of all social goals, including the goal of saving thousands from dying horribly and pointlessly, is *constrained*.

There are many other examples of this feature of liberalism, including ones that are closer to the issues we are treating here. For instance: it is often pointed out that the U.S. has more homicide than any other industrialized nation. It is plausible to suppose that at least part of the cause of this phenomenon is to be found in the extensive safeguards the U.S. has in place that tend to protect those suspected of crime from being unjustly convicted.[6] The U.S. has far more such safeguards than any other modern industrialized nation, including even the Western European democracies whose institutions have been shaped by the political unrest and violence they have experienced over the past 80 years. Imagine, for a moment, that American liberals were to become convinced that they could diminish violent crime by giving up many of these safeguards. Precisely because they are liberals, they would be very resistant to doing so. This is not because, as anti-liberals sometimes say, they make an irrational "fetish" of such safeguards, but because they perceive them as procedural *rights*. This means that they think of them as constraints on the pursuit of all social goals, including the reduction of violent crime.[7]

As a matter of fact, liberalism is distinguished not merely by the fact that its pursuit of the good is constrained, but by the particular set of constraints it recognizes: an action, including a government policy, is considered unjust, and consequently unacceptable, if it violates one or more of these liberal constraints. There are a number of principles that could be included in this set, but our focus here will be on three of them—autonomy, neutrality, and equality— and most importantly on autonomy and equality.

The concept of *autonomy* can be formulated in many different ways, with many different degrees of stringency, but what the formulations have in common is the general notion that individuals should control their own lives and be the instruments of their own acts of will. The individual has certain fundamental rights against interference by others.[8] One way to formulate a usable version of the autonomy principle is to define a part of the individual's life as "private," in virtue of the fact that it includes behavior that has no significant effects on others without their consent, and to declare that, within this private domain, individuals may do whatever they wish. This is the method used by Mill and many others after him.[9] This way of interpreting the idea of autonomy can be called "minimal," in that it constrains government policy less than the other interpretations do. Probably the most "maximal" interpretation is the one associated with the Lockean notion of self-ownership.[10] On this view, a person owns his or her self and, by the same token, the product of the labor of that self.

Partly because it includes various sorts of physical property in the realm protected by the autonomy principle, the latter, most maximal interpretation gives the individual a wider immunity against interference than the minimalist interpretation does. This is an important factor in distinguishing different sorts of liberalism. All liberals, however, accept some form or other of this principle.

This principle is a major source of the familiar liberal animus against paternalism. Government acts paternalistically when it makes or restricts important choices for individuals in order to do those same individuals some good. Such a policy involves interfering with individual conduct even when it affects no one but the individual agent and, consequently, tends to run afoul of even the most minimal version of the autonomy constraint. Liberals have at times carved out exceptions to the autonomy principle, formulating "soft" forms of paternalism that allow interference when the individual conduct involved is seriously nonvoluntary, or when the rights and liberties disposed of are trivial.[11] Because liberalism rests on the principle of autonomy, however, it cannot go very far in justifying policies that are paternalistic.

The second liberal constraint is the principle of *neutrality*. It holds that the justification for state action must be neutral between particular conceptions of the good life. It is an indirect constraint on government action, in that what it constrains in the first instance is not the actions but the reasons that are given for them. The policies of liberal states have many side effects and, no doubt, some of them create conditions in which certain conceptions of the good can no longer be pursued. For instance, there may be values that can be achieved only by pursuing the way of life of a samurai warrior, an eighteenth-century aristocrat, or a medieval knight— ways of life that were extinguished by liberal institutions. From a liberal point of view, this effect can be just, but only if these policies can be defended on other grounds, apart from the fact that they tend to "stamp out" ways of life that liberals do not appreciate.

As was the case with the principle of autonomy, the *equality* constraint is open to widely different formulations, and substantially different ones tend to mark the differences between different sorts of liberalism. Common to all the versions of this principle is the idea that the state should treat its subjects as equals. At a minimum, it means that governments must respect equally the rights of its citizens. They must not discriminate against some citizens in favor of others. No one is to be either above or below the law. It also means that government must not function as an instrument by which the strong take advantage of the weak.

This idea—that governments must take the rights of citizens equally seriously—can be called the minimal interpretation of the equality constraint. It states something that all liberals believe. For instance, if it could be shown that state lotteries tend to take money from the relatively poor and uneducated (perhaps because such people tend to have a comparatively shaky grasp of probability theory) and tend to put this money into the hands of the relatively rich and educated, all liberals would feel that this is a weighty argument against state lotteries. They would all see such an arrangement as unjust because of the way in which it arbitrarily discriminates against people who are less well endowed in favor of those who already enjoy advantages.

It is possible, however, to interpret the principle of equality in ways that go beyond this minimal version of it: one can interpret it, as we shall say, *extraminimally*. There are many ways to do this, but all tend, to one degree or other, to claim that the liberal state is committed, not merely to respecting equally the rights of its citizens, but to equalizing the value of the rights that each person has. The forms that this idea takes range from the idea that inequalities in the distribution of goods, though allowable, are subject to egalitarian constraints,[12] to the idea that resources available in a society should be divided equally among its members through some scheme of redistribution.[13]

As we have already suggested, one can envision quite different varieties of liberalism depending on how one interprets the principles of autonomy and equality.[14] On the one hand, one could adopt an extremely extraminimal interpretation of the principle of equality, which would allow extensive state efforts to equalize the conditions of its citizens. Expecting this state activity to cut into the liberties of the individual, one might then adopt a relatively minimal interpretation of the autonomy constraint. On the other hand, one might adopt an extremely extraminimal interpretation of the principle of autonomy and, expecting this to limit aggressive redistribution policies, one could adopt a relatively minimal interpretation of the principle of equality. Because it allows wider liberty of action, we call the latter sort of position "wide liberalism." The former, for analogous reasons, we will call "narrow liberalism."[15]

As we shall see, it makes a difference, as far as the issue of bans on firearms is concerned, whether one is a wide or a narrow liberal. But we will also argue that it does not make as much difference as one might think. No position could be called liberal that did not accept, in one form or other, all three of the principles we have discussed. From a liberal point of view, a policy cannot be just if it is unduly paternalistic and neglectful of autonomy, fails to respect a particular conception of the good life, and treats a certain group of people unequally. We will argue that all three of these areas of concern tend to militate, though in different degrees and in different ways, against bans on firearms.

Firearms and Autonomy

Today, the very idea that the possession of a gun—a mere technological device prized by hobbyists and lunatics—is a right, like freedom of speech, freedom of religion, and the right against self-incrimination, strikes many people as silly.[16] Nonetheless, such a conclusion is more or less forced on us by a range of interpretations of the autonomy constraint, including some very plausible ones. To begin with the obvious: since this constraint is a guarantee against interference, all versions of it create a certain presumption in favor of liberty, and bans on firearms place limits on liberty. If a gun ban were to be enacted in a wide liberal state, responsible citizens who use their firearms for legitimate purposes would accuse the government of violating their autonomy, and their accusation would carry weight.

Admittedly, and again obviously, their accusation might carry little or no weight under a minimal interpretation of the autonomy constraint. Guns, being instruments of lethal force, can have important effects on people other than their owners, and thus might not seem to belong in the purely private domain protected by the minimal interpretation. We maintain, however, that a right to possess just the sort of lethal force that guns represent will follow from *any* plausible extraminimal version of the autonomy constraint, including even the mildest of them.

This may sound like a strange claim, but it becomes much less so when we clearly understand certain of its concrete implications. To this end, consider the case of Ms. Jackson of Atlanta, Georgia:

A College Park woman shot and killed an armed man she says was trying to carjack her van with her and her 1-year-old daughter inside, police said Monday. . . .

Jackson told police that the gunman accosted her as she drove into the parking lot of an apartment complex on Camp Creek Parkway. She had planned to watch a broadcast of the Evander

Holyfield-Mike Tyson fight with friends at the complex.

She fired after the man pointed a revolver at her and ordered her to "move over," she told the police. She offered to take her daughter and give up the van, but the man refused, police said.

"She was pleading with the guy to let her take the baby and leave the van, but he blocked the door," said College Park Detective Reed Pollard. "She was protecting herself and the baby."

Jackson, who told the police she bought the .44 caliber handgun in September after her home was burglarized, said she fired a shot from the gun, which she kept concealed in a canvas bag beside her car seat. "She didn't try to remove it," Pollard said. "She just fired."[17]

Considering the fact that Ms. Jackson's would-be abductor was threatening her with lethal force at the time she killed him, and considering also what his most likely motive was for refusing to simply steal her car and let her go free, it seems obvious that she had a right to do what she did. She has a right to self-defense.

Though this right is not protected by the minimal interpretation of the autonomy constraint (since the effect her act has on her assailant puts it well outside the domain of privacy) the reasons for adding it to the rights that are protected by this constraint seem to be as great as any could be. To take, for instance, one particularly plausible criterion for deciding whether a particular claim should have this status or not: suppose that the strength of the grounds for recognizing a right are proportionate to the importance of the human interests protected by it, so that the grounds are strongest if the interests involved are the most important. If the interests protected by the right to free speech are more important than the interests protected by the right to sell junk bonds, then the grounds for recognizing it are likewise stronger. The interest that is protected by Ms. Jackson's right to defend herself is life itself. The interests protected by other rights recognized by liberals—including not only freedom of speech, but also freedom of religion, the right against self-incrimination, and many others—are no more important than this one. In many cases, they are a good deal less important.

Of course, Ms. Jackson's action has an effect on her assailant, and effects on others can give rise to powerful claims from those others that their rights have been violated. Such claims are potential reasons for *not* adding the act to the list of rights that are protected by a fundamental principle. Here, however, the strength of such reasons are as low as they can be. Though the effect suffered by her assailant is a powerfully negative one, his attack on her clearly cancels any claims he might have had against her use of force against him.

If we suppose, then, that Ms. Jackson has *any* rights to act on her own volition, outside the domain of privacy, then she must have this right, a right of self-defense. Further, if this supposition settles the question of her right of self-defense, it also settles the question of whether she has a right to use her gun to shoot her assailant. Imagine that, as she raises her concealed gun to fire it at her assailant, someone else (perhaps a confederate of the assailant) reaches over and grasps it in such a way as to prevent the hammer from raising, thus rendering the weapon inoperative. Clearly, they would be violating (probably intentionally) her right of self-defense. Again, imagine that, shortly before the attack occurs, someone were coercively to take her gun away from her, knowing that she was vulnerable to attacks of just this sort. This would also be a clear violation of her right of self defense.

If, in either of these imaginary scenarios, Ms. Jackson's assailant killed her, the person who had effectively disarmed her would be partly responsible for her death. Coercively preventing her from using her gun, in such a case, would not only violate her rights, it would seem to be a very serious violation, similar to that involved in being complicit in a murder.[18]

So far, then, it would seem that even a very modestly extraminimal interpretation of the autonomy constraint would have to imply that Ms. Jackson has a right to use her weapon to defend herself, a right of non-interference that would be violated by having her weapon confiscated. The case we have made for this claim does make a certain assumption. Though it may require a lengthy inquiry to determine precisely what form the assumption should be given, it clearly must include the idea that one violates a right (in this case, Ms. Jackson's right of self-defense) if one coercively prevents them from using the only, or the best, means to exercising that right (here, Ms. Jackson's handgun). It would be interesting to discuss whether (or why) such a principle is true, but it is not necessary to do so here, since the same principle is recognized by liberals in other contexts. Most of them would agree, for instance, that the government would be violating our rights to freedom of expression if it made possessing a computer modem a crime punishable by a term in prison. The same would be true if the law allowed the police to give out modem permits in the event that they decide an individual citizen has a "valid" reason to possess one. On the face of it, the same principle would seem to apply to an agent, including a representative of the state, who takes Ms. Jackson's gun from her.

Liberals who support gun bans would actually be very unlikely to try to disagree with this principle, nor would they be likely to opt for a version of the autonomy constraint that is so minimal that it contains no right of self-defense. Rather, they would probably claim that the weakness in our argument rests on a fact to which we have not referred at all: that there is an obvious difference between a modem and a gun. A gun, unlike a modem, is a weapon, and advocates of gun bans argue that guns are substantially more dangerous than other weapons.[19] One very influential line of reasoning is based on what one research team calls the "instrumentality hypothesis," which states that a weapon's degree of dangerousness, as a factor "independent of any other factors," has "a substantial impact on the death rate from attack.[20] Firearms allow people to commit offenses they could not commit with other weapons, such as knives, clubs, and fists. They enable persons normally in a position of weakness to use the threat of harm to take the money, possessions, and even lives of their victims.

If the presence of guns in one's environment does indeed increase such dangers, and it is at least *prima facie* plausible to say that it does, the liberal autonomy constraint itself seems to support banning some or all of them. All liberals agree that the principle of autonomy, unlike the principle of equality, applies fully to individuals as well as to states. It is permissible for individuals to treat others in substantially unequal ways, but serious violations of the autonomy of others (at least of sane, innocent adults) is not permissible. Obviously, killing or maiming others is ordinarily such an impermissible violation. Consequently, the conclusion, which we tentatively suggested a moment ago, that even a modest autonomy constraint would imply that Ms. Jackson has a right against having her weapon confiscated, stands in need of further support. More needs to be said before we can draw such a conclusion.

Risk

No one would deny that a liberal state, even the relatively constrained state of wide liberalism, may prohibit activities that kill or maim others. Of course, a state that bans firearms like the one used by Ms. Jackson would not merely be prohibiting actions that *actually* do that sort of harm: they would rather be prohibiting an activity (owning a gun, or a gun of a certain sort) on the grounds that it creates a *risk* that such harm will be done. However, prohibiting activities that create such risks is itself something that a wide liberal state may do. Such a state may prohibit me from storing dynamite in my basement or driving while intoxicated, even when (luckily) these activities do not kill or maim anyone. One reason for this, and a sufficient one for our purposes, is that such risky activities are themselves violations of the autonomy of others.

Having admitted this, however, we claim that the mere fact of owning a gun, at least a gun like Ms. Jackson's .44, does not belong in this category: it does not create the *sort* of risk that justifies prohibition in the context of wide liberalism. In particular, it is starkly different from the two examples of risky activities that we just mentioned.

First, just as a gun is obviously different from a modem, it is also, though perhaps less obviously, different from dynamite. Dynamite is an unstable substance, which can be detonated, under some circumstances, by a mere tap. Its unpredictability, together with the sheer scale of the destruction caused when it does explode, justifies us in classifying dynamite as a substance that cannot be handled entirely safely.

In the relevant respect, guns are as different from dynamite as can be imagined. Like clocks, guns are (ignoring an exception that we will discuss shortly) precision instruments: they are designed to function precisely, and for more or less the same reasons that clocks are. People have clocks so that they will know exactly what time it is, and not approximately what time it is. Similarly, they have guns so they will be able to hit a target, and not nearby objects. The function of a gun is not simply to provide lethal force, but to provide precisely controlled lethal force. Partly because of this fact, it is a surprisingly simple matter to handle a gun safely. As millions of Americans know from their firearms safety training, there are a few easy-to-follow rules that, if they are followed, will guarantee that unplanned detonations will not occur.[21]

The same sorts of considerations suffice to show that possessing a gun is utterly different from drunk driving. Unlike drunk driving, gun ownership is not behavior that creates a significant likelihood of accidental injury. In 1993 there were 0.656 accidental deaths due to firearms per 100,000 firearms in the United States: far less than the more than 21 accidental deaths attributable to motor vehicles for that year, per 100,000 motor vehicles.[22] According to one report, the total number of accidental gun deaths due to guns is smaller than the number attributable to medical error.[23]

However, there is a sense in which the rate of accidental deaths from guns is actually a minor issue: the alleged risk involved in gun ownership that most often inspires proposals to ban guns probably has little or nothing to do with accidental death. The most important problem raised in the scholarly debate concerning bans on guns is *intentional* death: most of the anti-gun literature is sharply focused on the idea that guns make deliberate acts of violence more likely. This is the sort of risk that makes them especially dangerous

objects, allegedly justifying placing them under a ban of some sort.

We maintain, however, that, within the limits of wide liberalism, even of a very moderate conception of those limits, this sort of risk is not a legitimate reason for banning guns. To return to the case of Ms. Jackson: the notion that she might use her gun to attack someone impermissibly might conceivably justify confiscating her gun, but only if there is reason to think she will actually do so. It is very unlikely that such reasons exist. The overwhelming majority of gun owners—a group that, in the United States, comprises about 46 percent of all households[24]—are honest citizens who never use their weapons to commit crimes. Obviously, ownership of a gun does not destroy one's ability to make choices, turning gun owners into people who are likely to become violent criminals.

Some people would say that whether a gun is dangerous or not depends entirely on who is in control of it. A gun in the holster of an honest and competent security guard can make people much safer from intentional violence than they would be in its absence. At the moment she was under attack, Ms. Jackson's gun actually enhanced her safety and that of her daughter. There is, however, another way to understand the dangerousness of guns; one that has nothing to do with whether Ms. Jackson or any other individual gun owner will use their weapon for an impermissible act of violence. On this view, the risk of violence that belongs to guns is not a characteristic that attaches to particular guns. Rather, the idea is that guns in general, as a class, are dangerous, because of what *some* people can and will do with objects that are members of that class. Guns, as a class, can be dangerous on balance and on the whole, though individual guns may indeed be safety-enhancing.

Given this conception of the dangerousness of guns, the danger of intentional death and injury can furnish a reason for taking Ms. Jackson's gun away from her that actually has nothing to do with the idea that she will use it to do something wrong. It rests in part on the obvious fact that a liberal state, because it must treat individuals equally, can permit her to keep her gun only if it permits many other people to have guns as well. In consequence of this, one might argue, we ought to ban guns in general, as a class, on the grounds that they (again, as a class) are simply too dangerous to allow in a society like ours. The same argument can, with even greater plausibility, be made concerning some sub-class of guns that are thought to be especially dangerous in this way, such as handguns.

Some people might find the conception of danger on which this argument rests— what might be called type-danger, as opposed to token-danger—problematic. We assume, for the sake of the argument, that it is not. We maintain, however, that a very serious difficulty stands in the way of using this conception to justify state action under the liberal autonomy constraint. While, as we have noted, liberalism allows us to force individuals, as well as states, to conform to this constraint, there has always been in the liberal tradition a very powerful tendency to interpret this constraint individualistically. That is, the harm or risk that justifies us in using force against an individual is generally limited to harm or risk that is *caused* by the individual. In other words, only token danger will do.

Consider, for instance, the case of AIDS. AIDS is a disease with an extremely high degree of type-danger. It may nonetheless be true that an individual AIDS victim who adheres to a few simple rules poses no known danger to others. If this is actually the case—as, in fact, it seems very likely that it is—then the type-dangerousness of AIDS does not, on an individualist interpretation of the autonomy constraint, justify coercively interfering, to their detriment, with such harmless victims of the disease.

Part of the reason why this sort of thinking is part of political liberalism is the traditional liberal concern with fair play. To round up and incarcerate all members of a group, including those who are quite harmless, because other individual members of the group are dangerous, is from a liberal point of view grossly unfair to the harmless ones. We suggest that, from the same point of view, the same sort of reasoning must apply to Ms. Jackson. To disarm her, exposing her to mortal danger, because of behavior for which she apparently bears no causal responsibility at all, is grossly unfair to her. For a liberal, it is quite possible that we may sometimes have to live with a preventable epidemic, an epidemic of disease or of violence, because the only ways we have to prevent it involve state action that violates liberal constraints.

The autonomy constraint, we might say, prohibits us from inflicting harm, at least certain sorts of harm, but it does not in general prohibit possession of the *means* of harming others. The one possible exception to this can be founded on the claim that some guns simply cannot be used in ways that, under the autonomy constraint, are permissible. Arguably, the only relevant actions that a ban on these firearms would prevent would be violations of the autonomy constraint. Supposing such an argument can be made, then, even in the context of a fairly robust wide liberalism, it might serve as a justification for banning such weapons.

However, we would in that case need to take care to determine precisely what kinds of firearms this ban would affect.

The criterion for deciding whether a certain firearm is eligible for government restriction would seem to be something like this: the government may permissibly ban a type of gun if it has impermissible uses but has no permissible uses. Perhaps one sort of gun that would be eligible is the sawed-off shotgun. This is the weapon that seems to be the exception to the generalization we made earlier, that guns are precision instruments. Except at fairly close range, it cannot be aimed at all, only pointed: it sprays destruction over a vaguely defined area. It seems to have no value for purposes of target shooting and, because it would often be impossible to fire such a weapon without harming the innocent, it would in those cases be irresponsible to use it (where there is any alternative) for self-defense.

Nonetheless, even supposing such an argument can be rigorously made regarding short-barreled shotguns, very few types of guns seem to be like this: nearly all have permissible as well as impermissible uses.[25] We suspect that even military-style assault weapons would fail to be eligible for banning under this criterion. There are many people—private militia groups, for instance—whose conception of the good life involves owning, shooting, and training with automatic weapons. Of course, liberals hold notions about the good that are deeply different from those pursued by members of such groups. Liberals do not believe that proficiency in the use of deadly force is part of good citizenship or true "manhood," and they do not think it is healthy to view the world as full of menacing threats. It is probably difficult for them to see those who hold contrary views as pursuing a conception of the good at all, the conception involved is so deeply alien to their own. However, they clearly are, and, because of the neutrality constraint, liberals cannot raise such errors about the good as justifications for coercion. As long as these people are peacefully pursuing their strange activities, harming no one, a wide-liberal state cannot coercively deprive them of the means of pursuing them.[26] In view of this, we find that the set of guns it is permissible to ban using the aforementioned criterion is likely to be a very small one.

Before leaving the subject of risk, we need to comment briefly on one more risk commonly attributed to firearms: this is the alleged fact that possessing a gun makes it more likely that the possessor will commit suicide.[27]

The most obvious problem confronting liberals who might want to justify gun bans on the basis of this sort of reasoning lies in the fact that such reasoning is clearly paternalistic. Suicide belongs, if anything does, to the private domain that is protected even by the minimal interpretation of the autonomy constraint. Nonetheless, one might hope to justify some sort of ban by suitably extending the "soft paternalism" by which liberals sometimes justify measures like mandatory life jackets, seat belts, and motorcycle helmets.[28] The prospects of doing so, however, do not seem good. Requiring boaters to wear life jackets and drivers to wear seat belts does not prevent them from living lives in which boating and driving are important elements: it does not limit the liberty of individuals to choose activities that are really important to them. Boaters who are forced to use a life jacket might desire to go without it, but this desire is not crucial to their conception of the good life, in the way that their desire to go boating is. On the other hand, requiring gun owners to give up their guns does preclude the pursuit of various activities—namely, those that include using guns—that in many cases are very important to them and crucial to their notions of the good life.

More importantly, the desire to commit suicide is deeply felt and as important to those who experience it as any desire they could have. Further, supposing that they have carefully considered their decision to die, it is literally true that death is now part of their conception of the good, inasmuch as they have decided that being dead is (for them) better than being alive.

Perhaps there is some way to patch up an argument for gun bans that is based on reducing suicide rates, of repairing it in a way that avoids liberal qualms about paternalism.[29] Such an argument would still face another problem, one that is less obvious than its apparent paternalism, but potentially more serious. This is the fact that such arguments, like the other risk-based arguments we have considered, violate liberal individualism, and do so in a way that cannot be patched up. What these arguments, however they are modified, propose to do is to take guns (or some class of guns, such as handguns) away from everyone who possesses them, and not simply from those who would use them to take their own lives. The overwhelming majority of the individuals who own any particular sort of gun will never use their weapons to kill themselves. To deprive them of the meaningful activities that require guns (including the vitally important activity in which Ms. Jackson is engaged: self-defense) so that we can interfere with the private behavior of others seems grossly unfair.

The autonomy constraint is a formidable obstacle to justifying a ban on firearms. To the extent that a particular variety of liberalism relies on this constraint—to the extent, in other words, that it is an instance of wide liberalism—we can expect it to be inhospitable to arguments for bans on firearms. If people own guns and use them in permissible ways, there seems to be no reason for limiting their liberty to own them. The government should, of course, legitimately restrict what people may use firearms *for*, but that is quite a different matter. The adage "Guns don't kill people, people kill people," while hackneyed, is appropriate here. For wide liberalism, it is important what people do, not who they are or what they own.

Firearms and Equality

As we have said, though, wide liberalism is not the only form that liberalism takes. Narrow liberalism, which places less stress on the principle of autonomy, assumes a greater license to interfere with individual freedom of choice than wide liberalism does. The emphasis that wide liberalism places on the autonomy principle creates a strong presumption in favor of liberty that makes it extremely difficult to justify almost any sort of ban on firearms, since such a ban would be an infringement on liberty. In its many varieties, however, narrow liberalism tends to accept no more than the minimal interpretation of the autonomy constraint. Accordingly, narrow liberalism is probably unable to make a case for the right to bear arms that is based on notions of individual liberty.

We claim, however, that the narrow liberal commitment to equality, together with the neutrality constraint it shares with all forms of liberalism, strongly support the idea that gun ownership is a right that citizens must have. As was the case with the autonomy principle, it makes a difference whether one interprets the principle of equality minimally or extraminimally. Unlike the autonomy principle, however, equality can justify a substantial right to bear arms even under its minimal interpretations.

Recall that the minimal interpretation of the equality principle requires the state to respect equally the rights of its citizens.

This means, broadly speaking, that it must not discriminate against some of its citizens and in favor of others and, in particular, it must not function as a means by which the strong take advantage of the weak. So construed, the equality constraint has immediate implications for the right to own guns. To see this, consider the case of Ms. Johnson, a composite drawn from several news stories of a certain, far-too-familiar sort.

After enduring several years of increasingly severe physical abuse at his hands, Ms. Johnson divorced her husband, Mr. Johnson. Unfortunately, this was not enough to free her from him. After the divorce, he stalked her and beat her severely, for which he was sentenced to a term in prison. The punishment only seemed to make him more angry, and he repeatedly sent her death threats from prison. When his release was imminent, she called the police, but they had to tell her that, unfortunately, they cannot act as bodyguards for citizens in danger. Their role, they explained, is to help ensure that people are punished for crimes they have already committed and, if possible, to interrupt crimes in progress. "Call us right away if he comes to your apartment," was the best advice they could give her. When Mr. Johnson did come for her, he quickly beat down her door, shouting all the while that he has come to kill her. Fortunately, she owned a handgun and, before he had a chance to begin his attack in deadly earnest, she shot and killed him.

Suppose that, just before Mr. Johnson came to Ms. Johnson's apartment, someone (perhaps a confederate of his) interfered by disabling or taking away her gun. It would be obvious that they were acting as a means by which the strong take terrible advantage of the weak.[30] Another way to put the same argument is this. At the moment that Ms. Johnson's former husband broke down her door, it became very likely that one of them would die violently. The question was, which one should it be? As long as Ms. Johnson was able to use her handgun, it was very likely that the death would be Mr. Johnson's. If she were unable to use it, the death would very likely be hers. A government that disarms her is shifting the great burden of premature, violent death from the strong to the weak. According to the principle of equality, this shift is being made in the wrong direction.

This conclusion can easily be generalized. As one study has shown, men who batter their wives "average 45 pounds heavier and 4 to 5 inches taller" than their victims.[31] Such men do not need weapons to kill their wives. They can strangle them or simply beat them to death. If these women are disarmed by the government, relations between them and their batterers are made unequal in a way that any liberal would find extremely objectionable.

More generally still: The capacity of firearms to be a tool for self-defense promotes equality in general, and not merely between battered women and their male batterers. People in general can differ substantially in size, strength, and coordination. People who possess greater physical prowess have an advantage over others. Most especially, bigger people are more capable of harming others than smaller people are. The force of non-gun weapons such as knives and clubs is, like the force of bare hands, strongly contingent on the size, strength, and skill of their users: the weaker of two people equally armed with a non-gun weapon is still at a potentially fatal disadvantage. In typical self-defense situations, however, firearms are equally harmful in anyone's hands, provided the individuals handling them have the capacity to fire them and reasonably good aim at close range. Two people equally armed with guns, then, are very likely to have equal harming and coercive power, regardless of their physical disparities.[32] Firearms actually *equalize* the balance of power between persons who are naturally unequal.[33]

The minimal interpretation of the equality principle, then, is a very formidable obstacle to the banning of at least some sorts of firearms. If we interpret it extraminimally, this obstacle only becomes more formidable. In its various different guises, extraminimal equality imposes on the state an even stronger commitment to equality than the minimal variety does. As the strength of this commitment increases, so does the stringency of the constraint against disarming the weak and exposing them to attack by the strong.

Clearly, then, a narrow liberal state ought to grant the liberty to own firearms. However, there remains the problem of specifying the *extent* of that liberty: which sorts of firearms should citizens have a right to own? The answer to this question is not as straightforward as it is in wide liberalism. As we have said, narrow liberalism typically includes no strong presumption in favor of freedom of choice outside the private domain. Outside that realm, there is considerable room in narrow liberalism for curtailing the scope of liberty, as long as this is done for neutral reasons, and as long as the principle of equality (whichever formulation might apply) is observed.

Partly for this reason, narrow liberalism does seem to allow for limitations on the ownership of firearms. One available reason for adopting such limitations, within narrow liberalism, is the supposed causal relationship between the number of guns in private hands and the quantity of violent crime. If the justification for a ban on some types of firearms is that it will reduce the rates of violent crime, then it certainly meets the neutrality constraint. This justification, after all, has no

necessary connection with disapproval of someone's conception of the good.

The question, then, is whether a ban satisfies the autonomy and equality constraints: is it permissible to prohibit the ownership of significant classes of firearms without violating the minimal interpretation of the autonomy constraint, and without violating narrow liberalism's commitment to equality? The answer clearly seems to be *yes*. For example, consider a ban on the private possession of all firearms capable of killing several people in rapid succession or simultaneously, an extremely large category of firearms that includes automatic rifles, semi-automatic rifles, extremely high-powered handguns, grenade launchers, anti-tank weapons, and so on. Supposing that such weapons do increase the crime rate, the minimal version of the autonomy principle would not be violated by banning them. Further, it would not seem to violate the equality-based considerations we raised in defending Ms. Johnson's right to possess her handgun. These extremely advanced weapons are not practical for self-defense. Other firearms are much more useful for these purposes, and in many cases are less expensive and wasteful of ammunition. Banning them would not expose the weak to the doubtful mercies of the strong.

Of course, there are people, including members of private militia groups, whose conception of the good life includes training with and using these advanced firearms. They may find that marching about in the forest with mere facsimiles of military assault rifles does not fit their notions of what citizenship and manhood require of them. Their capacity to pursue their conception of the good, accordingly, will be diminished by banning such weapons. This fact, however, does not violate the neutrality constraint, which does not constrain the actions of the state directly, but only the reasons that are given for them. The reasons we are currently entertaining for banning these weapons do not rely on the idea that the conception of the good these people are pursuing must be fought, but only on the idea that violent crime must be fought: it is, in the requisite sense, quite neutral.[34]

It would seem, then, that we can have a ban on a substantial range of firearms that is consistent with narrow liberalism. However, it is important to consider the kinds of guns the ban would *not* include, for the results are bound to disappoint some people. As mentioned, firearms that are useful for self-defense are not subject to the ban.[35] There is a serious difficulty here for narrow liberals who would like to use gun bans to significantly reduce crime: the guns that are most useful for self-defense are handguns, which are also most useful for committing crimes. If gun bans are to be an important tool in fighting crime, handguns are the most rational targets of such bans, perhaps the only sort of firearm in common use that is really worth banning.[36] Certainly, the number of crimes committed with assault rifles is, by comparison, extremely small.[37] Thus, even though the narrow liberal state may permissibly restrict a large number of guns, the advocates of gun bans probably would not predict that these sorts of bans would actually bring about the state of affairs they want to produce: a major reduction in violent crime. Those who believe the causal theory that closely links the number of guns in civilian hands with the level of violent crime would expect to reduce such crime significantly only by banning the sorts of weapons that are most often involved in the commission of crimes. Narrow liberalism cannot approve such bans without betraying its commitment to equality.

It is clear that narrow liberalism enjoys a greater license than wide liberalism does to ban firearms: the narrow liberal state can legitimately control a greater number of guns than the wide liberal state. However, the prospects are very poor that this distinction would make a great difference in the rates of violent crime.

Conclusion

The issue of bans on firearms brings to the surface the fundamental ideological differences between wide and narrow liberalism. Wide liberalism, having a stronger presumption in favor of liberty, is less receptive to bans than narrow liberalism is. Wide liberalism must allow a weapon if it has permissible uses to which it *can* be put, while narrow liberalism must allow it only if it is *necessary* for the permissible activity of self-defense, or if it has no effect on others. On the other hand, rather surprisingly, the fundamental principle of narrow liberalism is more immediately inimical to bans than that of wide liberalism, since it implies a serious right to bear arms even in its minimal form, while that does not seem to be true of the principle that is fundamental to wide liberalism. Autonomy is inimical to bans only if it is interpreted extraminimally. In addition, the possible risks associated with guns raised the issue of whether the banned behavior might itself have some general tendency to violate the principle of autonomy, which in turn raised the issue of whether the principle might actually *require* some sort of ban. We found no analogous sort of issue in the case of the principle of equality.

Passionate defenders of gun control may well be tempted to say that, if our argument is cogent, it is simply a *reductio ad absurdum* of liberalism. It certainly does bring into sharp relief the fact that liberalism is, unlike some competing ideologies, a *constrained* view of the political realm. As we have already suggested, to be a liberal is to decide, in advance, that there may be epidemics, whether of the moral or the physical realms, for which there are no permissible remedies.

This can be a distressing thing to hear. One can hope to reduce this distress by searching further for remedies that *are* permissible. One might wonder about the permissibility of other gun control measures, such as mandatory waiting periods, background checks, gun buy-backs, licensing laws, and mandatory gun safety training. Most of these kinds of regulations may be more nearly compatible with either wide or narrow liberalism than actual prohibitions of firearms. This seems to be likely, in fact. However, one must be careful not simply to assume that other gun control policies are permissible alternatives to gun bans without first subjecting them to the sort of scrutiny we have carried out here.

One should also be willing to entertain the possibility that, if guns are a major part of the problem of crime, they may also be part of the solution. Non-discretionary "right to carry" laws, which permit the laws-abiding to carry concealed weapons, seem to be, if what we have said is correct, compatible with both wide and narrow liberalism. They are also worth considering as ways to reduce crime: a world in which a significant number of the potential victims of crime are armed may well be a world with less crime.

Epilogue: Liberal Neutrality

We have argued that the fundamental principle of narrow liberalism is more immediately inimical to bans than that of wide liberalism. If this is so, however, it seems odd that so many narrow liberals are so well disposed toward confiscatory firearms policies, including, in many cases, bans on handguns. Indeed, to many who

adhere to that sort of liberalism, certain aspects of the argument we have presented must have seemed not merely theoretically inadequate but personally offensive. Many would probably find it more or less horrifying that two academics would calmly suggest that wives should shoot and kill their husbands, or, more generally, that lethal force is part of the solution to pressing social problems. The fact that we suggest taking this position in the name of equality probably only compounds the horror.

This reaction to the position we have taken, a reaction of horror and not mere disagreement, suggests a possible explanation for the ease with which narrow liberals tend to support handgun confiscation. According to this explanation, this tendency has nothing to do with the principles of autonomy, neutrality, or equality, nor with the notion of individualism, nor any other part of the liberal conception of justice. It rests, rather, on the notion that such obviously personal and deep-seated reactions often arise from broad notions of what life is and should be like. As we suggested earlier, liberals tend to have a certain distinctive conception of the good. They believe in being reasonable and humane. To them, shooting people seems neither reasonable nor humane. They tend to view violence between human beings, especially lethal violence, as intrinsically bad. Even when it is necessary, it is always, due to the quality of evil that still clings to it, deeply regrettable.

From this point of view, a gun cannot be seen simply as a device for perforating objects, a sort of long-distance drill. A gun is made for the purpose of killing and maiming, and this fact alone makes guns intrinsically bad. This is especially true of the handgun, which is uniquely suited, and in fact intended, for the activity of killing and maiming *people*. To this technological device is transferred some of the horror that belongs to that horrifying activity. The thought of coercively stamping out this thing of horror is consequently deeply attractive.

We are suggesting that an important part of the reason why so many liberals favor the suppression of the private possession of hand-guns, despite the potential of the handgun for enhancing equality in situations were equality is desperately important, may well be a certain tension within the liberal view of the world. On the one hand, liberals have principles that constrain them from using certain methods in achieving their goals. On the other hand, like everyone else, they have their own

conception of the good.[38] In principle, this conception might, like any other, be promoted by violating those constraints. However, as we have said repeatedly, to interfere coercively with others because of preferences of one's own, preferences based solely on one's conception of the good, violates the principle of neutrality, and this is as true of the liberal conception of the good as it is of any other. If the tendency that we see in some parts of the liberal community to ban guns is indeed based on such preferences, it is actually illiberal. In that case, it represents a sort of illiberalism of which only liberals can be guilty: the urge to force *liberal* values on those who do not accept them.

Notes

1. Another possible reason for this characterization might lie in the fact that the legal argument for gun bans often rests on a "liberal" (as opposed to strict) interpretation of the Second Amendment. We will not discuss the Second Amendment in this essay. We wish to focus on the broad theoretical issue of the right to bear firearms in a liberal state, an issue that applies to any liberal state, and not merely the United States. For whatever it might be worth, our suspicion is that a Constitutional ban on firearms would require a *very* "liberal" interpretation of the Second Amendment. See Sanford Levinson, "The Embarrassing Second Amendment," *The Yale Law Journal* 99 (December 1989): 637–659.

2. See, however, Daniel Polsby and Don B. Kates, "American Homicide Exceptionalism," *University of Colorado law Review* 69 (1998): 94 and Table 1. The authors argue that, while handgun ownership more than doubled in the 20-year period 1975–94, homicide rates actually declined, and that the addition of more than 3 million additional handguns in the years 1995 and 1996 coincided with further declines in the homicide rate. See also Gary Kleck, *Targeting Guns: Firearms and Their Control* (New York: Aldine De Gruyter, 1997), p. 18.

3. The argument assumes, of course, that the crimes committed with guns will not be committed with some other weapon if guns are not available. This is a debatable assumption, but not without foundation. See Franklin E. Zimring and Gordon Hawkins, "Firearms and Assault: 'Guns Don't Kill People, People Kill People,'" in *The Gun Control Debate: You Decide*, ed. Lee Nisbet (Buffalo, NY: Prometheus Books, 1990), pp. 170–176.

4. See G. L. Carter, *The Gun Control Movement* (New York: Twayne, 1997).

5. The premier criminological study defending this position is Gary Kleck's *Targeting Guns*, cited in fn. 2 above, especially chap. 5. More recently, John Lott has collected information on changes in gun ownership rates and changes in crime rates in all 3,054 U.S. counties over eighteen years, and he appears to establish that concealed carry laws, which allow private citizens without criminal records to carry weapons, are highly cost-effective ways to *reduce* levels of violent crime. *More Guns, Less Crime* (Chicago: University of Chicago Press, 1998).

6. It is sometimes suggested that this phenomenon is *entirely* due to the availability of guns in the United States. This cannot be true. As Israeli Judge Abraham Tennenbaum has

noted, murder rates in his country are "much lower than in the United States . . . despite the greater availability of guns to law-abiding [Israeli] civilians." Abraham Tennenbaum, "Israel Has A Successful Gun Control Policy," in Charles P. Cozic, *Gun Control: Current Controversies* (San Diego: Greenhaven Press, 1992), p. 250.

7. We are indebted for this point to Don B. Kates.

8. A classic statement of this idea is Isaiah Berlin, "Two Concepts of Liberty," in *Liberalism and Its Critics*, ed. M. Sandel (New York: New York University Press, 1987), pp. 15–36.

9. John Stuart Mill, *On Liberty*, ed. David Spitz (New York: Norton, 1976), p. 13.

10. John Locke, *Second Treatise of Government* (New York: Bobbs-Merrill, 1965), chaps. 2 and 5.

11. Joel Feinberg, "Legal Paternalism," *Canadian Journal of Philosophy* 1, no. 1 (1971): 106–124. Gerald Dworkin, "Paternalism," *The Monist* 56, no. 1 (January 1972): 64–84. See also Dworkin's "Paternalism: Some Second Thoughts," in *Paternalism*, ed. R. Sartorius (Minneapolis: University of Minnesota Press, 1983), pp. 105–111.

12. John Rawls, "Social Utility and Primary Goods," in *Utilitarianism and Beyond*, ed. A. Sen and B. Williams (Cambridge: Cambridge University Press, 1982), pp. 159–186.

13. Ronald Dworkin, "What Is Equality? Part 1: Equality of Welfare," *Philosophy and Public Affairs* 10 (1981): 185–246; and "What Is Equality? Part 2: Equality of Resources," *Philosophy and Public Affairs* 10 (1981): 283–345.

14. One could introduce more complexity by entertaining different interpretations of the neutrality principle as well. It will turn out, however, that this principle is less directly related to our main area of concern, so we believe we can safely ignore this complication.

15. When its distinctive features are sufficiently pronounced, wide liberalism becomes what is sometimes called "classical" liberalism. Narrow liberalism, in its more fully developed forms, becomes what is sometimes called "left" liberalism.

16. We stress that this is true *today*. In the past, things seem to have been different. A long and prominent tradition held that civilian possession of effective arms for purposes of defense was an important part of citizenship, and that bans on such arms are an essential ingredient in tyranny. On the history of this tradition, see Joyce Lee Malcolm, *To Keep and Bear Arms: The Origins of an Anglo-American Right* (Cambridge: Harvard University Press, 1994).

17. "Mom Saves Self and Child with Handgun," *Atlanta Constitution*, November 12, 1996, p. E2. Quoted in Lott, *More Guns, Less Crime*, p. 3.

18. We assume, in what follows, that the question of whether Ms. Jackson's rights are violated by the act of coercively preventing her from using her gun is independent of the coercer's motives. For instance, if her gun were forcibly taken from her by a group of well-meaning pacifists who know that she is vulnerable to attacks such as the one that eventually happens, then the issue of whether she has a right against being treated that way is unaffected by their good intentions. Of course, the moral status of what they would be doing would be in other respects quite different from the status the same act would have if committed by a confederate of her attacker, but we are not concerned here with those other respects.

19. See Franklin Zimring and Gordon Hawkins, "Firearms and Assault," pp. 170–176.

20. Ibid., p. 173.

21. These include, most importantly: assume that every gun is loaded; keep the safety on until ready to shoot; keep your finger off the trigger until your sights are on the target; never let the muzzle cover anything you are not willing to destroy. *Source:* National Rifle Association leaflets.

22. Gary Kleck, *Targeting Guns*, p. 323. The number of handgun deaths per 100,000 guns was 1.087. Kleck also points out (p. 296) that, while about forty children under the age of five die every year in gun accidents, about five hundred drown in residential swimming pools. For small children, he says, the risk of fatal accidents from swimming pools is over one hundred times as great as from guns.

23. Morgan Reynolds and H. Sterling Burnett, "No Smoking Guns: Answering Objections to Right-to-Carry Laws," *National Policy Center Brief Analysis*, No. 246, Nov. 17, 1997. The authors also point out that, although gun ownership has increased dramatically

in recent decades, accidental deaths from guns have decreased. In the decade before their article, such deaths decreased by 19 percent Kleck reports that, in the two decades 1974–94, the all-time low in fatal accidents among children was 1994. *Targeting Guns*, p. 324.

24. Kleck, *Targeting Guns*, p. 64.

25. We should emphasize, however, that it is quite conceivable that, within the constraints of wide liberalism, it may be impossible for the state to ban any types of guns at all. If a convincing case should be made that all guns have uses that are permissible under the principle of autonomy, the only proper wide liberal response might be to ban the impermissible *uses* of a given weapon while allowing the permissible ones. For example, someone might make a convincing case that it is perfectly permissible for an elderly man, living alone in an urban apartment, to defend his home with a short-barrelled shotgun. In these circumstances, it could even be argued that this weapon has an ethical advantage, in that its low-velocity pellets are very unlikely to penetrate an apartment wall and hurt innocents on the other side. Perhaps, then, a wide liberal state would best conform to its constraints by allowing this use of this type of weapon but prohibiting others. We owe this example to Samuel C. Wheeler.

26. One might be tempted to argue at this point that people whose conception of the good life entails using certain weapons would be just as happy if they did not. Perhaps people who enjoy private military training with guns would enjoy just as much playing paintball if they desired that instead, and perhaps a system in which guns are unavailable would *cause* them to desire such substitute activities. After all, *we* do not need guns to have a good life, so it is unlikely that people currently using guns would fail to have a good life if their weapons were confiscated and their desires were suitably changed by the resulting new environment. This may be a powerful argument if one assumes some sort of unconstrained utilitarianism, but it is inconsistent with the principles of liberalism. It assumes one conception of the good—in which the good is simply desire-satisfaction—and uses it to justify coercing

people who may or may not share this conception. That, of course, violates the neutrality constraint.

27. See D. Hemenway, "Guns, Public Health, and Public Safety," in *Guns and the Constitution*, ed. D. A. Henigan, E. B. Nicholson, and D. Hemenway (Northampton, MA: Althei Press, 1995). For evidence on the other side of this empirical issue, to the effect that the causal relationship between suicide and gun availability is weak or nonexistent, see Kleck, *Targeting Guns*, pp. 286–288, and Don B. Kates et al., "Guns and Public Health: Epidemic of Violence or Pandemic of Propaganda?" *Tennessee Law Review* 62, no. 3 (Spring 1995): 561–566.

28. See fn. 11, above.

29. One attempt to do so might go like this: although suicide is not per se seriously non-voluntary, it is often impulsive and poorly thought out. By banning guns (or handguns, etc.) we are getting rid of the easiest and most efficient means of killing oneself. People who have to use one of the remaining means (automobile exhaust, cutting one's wrists, and so forth) will give the matter more careful consideration. The ban, therefore, would actually increase truly autonomous choice. Supposing that the factual assumptions in this argument can be supported, and supposing that its rather manipulative approach toward individual choice really does avoid the liberal animus against paternalism, it nonetheless falls before the difficulty we set out in the following text below.

30. If a government were to do the same thing, as part of a general policy of gun control, the motives might be entirely different from those that would drive Mr. Johnson's confederate but, on the basis of the assumptions we are making here, that does not affect the justice or injustice of what is being done. The principle such a policy violates is a constraint, and good intentions alone cannot justify such a violation.

31. D. G. Saunders, "When Battered Women Use Violence: Husband Abuse or Self-Defense," *Violence and Victims* 47, no. 1 (1986): 49. Cited in Don Kates, "Defensive Gun Ownership as a Response to Crime," in *Crime and Punishment: Philosophic Explorations*, ed. Michael Gorr and Sterling Harwood (Boston and London: Jones and Bartlett, 1995), p. 237.

32. Note that this fact will increase in importance to the extent that criminals will tend to *select* victims who, if unarmed, are physically weaker than themselves. This will be the case if, for instance, able-bodied male criminals have a preference for attacking women and the elderly.

33. Interestingly, the feature of guns that seems bad when we are thinking in terms of the autonomy principle—namely, the fact that they enable those who are normally in a position of weakness to commit successful acts of violence—actually speaks in their favor when we apply the principle of equality.

34. In some versions of narrow liberalism, such bans would, however, be in some danger of violating the principle of equality. These versions are ones in which the principle of equality requires that all citizens be given an equal chance of obtaining what they consider good if they pursue it. See Richard Arneson, "Equality and Equal Opportunity for Welfare," *Philosophical Studies* 56 (1989): 77–93. The sort of ban we are contemplating here burdens some citizens with an obstacle to achieving their conception of the good that others do not have to overcome. Proponents of this interpretation of equality might nonetheless believe that the public safety reasons for banning these weapons is so strong, and the number of people burdened is so small, that the ban is justified.

35. The fate of hunting rifles and other commonly used long guns is less clear. Such guns are not extremely serviceable for self-defense, though many of them are more practical for that purpose than assault rifles. On the other hand, a substantial ban on long guns would hinder millions of hunting enthusiasts from effectively pursuing the good life as they see it, placing a burden on them that is not shouldered by other citizens. This raises the sort of egalitarian worry we mentioned in the case of assault rifles in fn. 34, but in a more severe form, since the public safety considerations may be less strong in this case, while the number of people burdened is far greater, Consequently, a general ban on such weapons *might* be difficult to mount on the basis of narrow liberalism.

36. See Nicholas Dixon, "Why We Should Ban Handguns in the United States," in *Crime and Punishment: Philosophic Explorations*, pp. 205–232.

37. Nationwide figures on this subject do not seem to be available, but such local statistics as are available certainly bear out the claim we have just made. For instance, in Massachusetts from 1985 to 1991 assault weapons accounted for only 0.7 percent of shootings. In New Jersey in 1991 they were involved in 0.16 percent of murders, armed robberies, and aggravated assaults. In the state of New York during 1992 they were involved in 0.8 percent of murders. For the sources of these figures, and for a great deal more information that tends to support the same conclusions, see Kleck, *Targeting Guns*, pp. 141–142.

38. Perhaps we should say, in case we have created any doubt about this, that we have a great deal of sympathy with this conception. This may, in fact be a good part of the reason why neither of us has ever owned a gun.

GUN CONTROL

Hugh LaFollette

Many of us assume that we must either oppose or support gun control. Not so. We have a range of alternatives. Even this way of speaking oversimplifies our choices since there are two distinct scales on which to place alternatives. One scale concerns the degree (if at all) to which guns should be abolished. This scale moves from those who want no abolition (NA) of any guns, through those who want moderate abolition (MA)—that is, to forbid access to some subclasses of guns—to those who want absolute abolition (AA). The second scale concerns the restrictions (if any) on those guns that are available to private citizens. This scale moves from those who want absolute restrictions (AR) through those who want moderate restrictions (MR) to those who want no restrictions (NR) at all. Restrictions vary not only in strength but also in content. We could restrict who owns guns, how they obtain them, where and how they store them, and where and how they carry them.

Our options are further complicated by the union of these scales. On one extreme no private citizen can own any guns (AA, which is functionally equivalent to AR), while at the other extreme, every private citizen can own any gun with no restrictions (NA + NR). But once we leave those extremes, which few people hold, the options are defined by a pair of coordinates along these distinct scales. While most people embrace positions on the "same" end of both scales, others embrace more exotic mixtures: some will want few weapons available to private citizens but virtually no restrictions on those guns that are available (MA + NR), while others may prefer making most guns available but want to seriously restrict them (NA + MR).

So our choice is not merely to support or oppose gun control but to decide *who* can own *which* guns under *what conditions*. Although I cannot pretend to provide a definitive account here, I can isolate the central issues and offer the broad outline of an appropriate solution. To simplify discussion, I adopt the following locutions: those opposed to most abolition and most restrictions advocate a "serious right to bear arms," while those supporting more widespread abolition and more substantial restrictions are "gun control advocates." This simplification, of course, masks significant disagreements among advocates of each position.

Justifying Private Ownership of Guns

A Moral Question

Do citizens have a "serious right to bear arms"? This is a moral question, not a constitutional one. For even if the Constitution did grant this right, we should determine if there are sufficiently compelling arguments against private gun ownership to warrant changing the Constitution. By contrast, if this were not a constitutional right, we should determine if there are strong reasons why the state should not ban or control guns and if these reasons are sufficiently compelling to make this a constitutional right. Most defenders of private gun ownership claim we do have a moral right—as well as a constitutional one—and that this right is not an ordinary right but a fundamental one.

1. *A fundamental right*. If they are correct, they would have the justificatory upper hand. Were this a fundamental right, it would not be enough to show that society would benefit from controlling access to guns.[1] The arguments for gun control would have to be overwhelming. Yet there is also a hefty cost in claiming that this is a fundamental right: the evidence for the right must meet especially rigorous standards. . . .

Advocates must show that and how granting the right protects individuals' fundamental interests, and they must be prepared to respond to objections that granting that right type will harm society. These are serious obstacles for gun advocates. It is difficult to see that a serious right to bear arms satisfies either of these requirements, let alone both.

First, I see no compelling reason to think that owning a gun is a fundamental interest. Other fundamental interests are necessary to one's flourishing no matter what her particular desires, interests, and beliefs. It is difficult to see how this is true of guns. Moreover, the interests protected by paradigmatic fundamental rights—our interests in unfettered speech, freedom of religion, and freedom of association—are not merely means to my flourishing, they are elements constituting it. By contrast, having a gun in my bed stand, in my closet, or on my person might be a means for me to achieve my ends, but they are not constitutive elements of my flourishing. Hence, owning guns is not a fundamental interest. . . .

2. *A derivative right*. Suppose we determined that the right to bear arms is not a fundamental right but a derivative right. This would still be a significant finding since derivative rights, like fundamental ones, cannot be restricted without good evidence. Prima facie, I think we have such a derivative right. Each of us has a fundamental right of noninterference: we should be allowed to live our lives as we wish so long as we do not thereby harm others. This is a right each of us needs no matter what our particular interests. That general right derivatively protects personally important activities.

For instance, I would be furious if the state forbade me from sharing a pint with a friend. Nonetheless, although consuming alcohol is a particular interest and enjoyment I have, it is not a constitutive element of the good life in the way that the freedoms of speech, religion, and association are. That is why I do not have a fundamental right to consume alcohol. Consequently, the conditions under which my consumption of alcohol can be legitimately restricted are more lax than they would be if the activity were a fundamental interest.

Nonetheless, since I have a prima facie derivative right to consume alcohol, the state can legitimately abolish or restrict alcohol consumption only if it can show that doing so is an effective means of protecting the public from harm. They can do that in some cases: people who consume substantial amounts of alcohol are dangerous drivers. Since this behavior is unacceptably risky to others, the state can legitimately restrict drinking while driving. Whether privately owning guns is similarly risky is something we must discover.

Bad Public Policy

If private gun ownership were not a derivative right, it might still be bad policy to substantially restrict or abolish guns. There are always costs of enforcing a law. Sometimes these costs are prohibitive, especially when the public does not support that law. If the public will not voluntarily comply with the law, then the state must try to force compliance. In their efforts to do so, they invariably employ excessively intrusive methods. Such methods never entirely succeed, and, to the extent that they do, they undermine public confidence in and support for all law. Consider America's experience with Prohibition. Although one of Prohibition's aims—to protect innocents from harm caused by those under the influence—was laudable, the law was unenforceable and excessively costly. Consequently, less than two decades after Prohibition was passed via constitutional amendment, it was repealed.

The cost of enforcing any law—and especially an unpopular law—weighs against making any behavior illegal unless we have solid evidence that the behavior is seriously harmful. If we adopt a weaker standard—if we criminalize every action type whose tokens occasionally lead to some harm—then we would criminalize most behavior. As a result, even if there were no right to bear arms, we should still not seek to substantially limit private ownership of guns unless we had good reason to think that would prevent serious harm.

Summing Up: Justifying the Private Ownership of Guns

The preceding analysis isolates three questions we must answer in deciding whether people should be permitted to own guns: (1) How important is owning a gun to some people? (2) What are the consequences of private gun ownership? and (3) Is abolishing or restricting private ownership of guns bad policy? Although gun ownership is not a fundamental interest, many people want to own guns and think they have good reason to do so. That is sufficient to show that serious gun control would undermine gun owners' interests. Moreover, there is some reason to think that serious gun control in countries with a strong tradition of gun ownership would be bad policy. Therefore, we should certainly not abolish, and arguably should not restrict, private ownership of guns without good reason. Are there good reasons? To answer this question, we must determine the effects of private gun ownership: (a) How likely is it that private gun ownership seriously harms others? and (b) Are there substantial benefits of gun ownership that might counterbalance any harm?

Harm, Danger, and Risk

We must be careful when we say that guns cause harm. Guns kill people because agents use them to kill people (or misuse them in ways that cause people to be killed). As the National Rifle Association (NRA) puts it: "Guns don't kill people, people do." In one sense their claim is uncontroversial: murder is the act of an agent, and guns are not agents. In another way, their claim is irrelevant. No gun control advocate claims, hints, or suggests that guns are moral agents. Guns are objects, and objects do no evil. But not all objects are created equal. Imagine the NNWA (National Nuclear Weapons Association) claiming that "tactical nuclear weapons don't kill people, people do." While in one sense their claim would be true, in a more profound way, it would be ludicrous.

Of course guns are not nuclear weapons. Guns are not as dangerous as nuclear weapons, and some guns have seemingly legitimate uses. The question is whether the character of guns makes them especially harmful. We know that some objects—tactical nuclear weapons, biochemical weapons, live grenades, and so forth, are much more dangerous than feathers, ice cream, and butter knives. Where do guns fall along this continuum?

There are two distinct but related questions: (1) Are guns inherently dangerous? and (2) What is the empirical probability that guns cause serious harm? "Inherently dangerous" objects are those whose nature or design is sufficient to justify our prediction that they will cause harm independent of any empirical evidence. We do not need double-blind empirical studies to know that nuclear weapons are inherently dangerous: they were designed to cause harm, and their nature is such that we can confidently predict they will cause harm. The two questions are intricately related since inherently dangerous objects are more likely to cause serious harm. Yet they are separable because some dangerous objects are not inherently so. Automobiles, alcohol, and cigarettes were not designed to cause harm, but all are causally implicated in many people's deaths. Other things being equal, we are more prone to control inherently dangerous objects than objects that merely have harm as an unwanted side effect.

Guns, unlike autos, are inherently dangerous. Guns were invented for the military; they were designed to cause (and threaten) harm.[2] The same aims determine the ways in which guns are redesigned: they are changed to make them more efficient at causing harm. In contrast, a significant aim of redesigning automobiles is to make them less dangerous. To some extent these efforts have succeeded. Although the absolute number of annual traffic fatalities has not noticeably declined, the number of fatalities

per mile traveled has declined 75 percent since the 1950s.[3] We have enhanced the auto's original aim of efficient transportation while lessening harmful side effects. That is why we can sensibly say that the automobile is not inherently dangerous despite the fact that it causes harm. We cannot say the same for guns.

The literature of gun advocates supports my contention that guns are inherently dangerous. They advocate the private ownership of guns to prevent crime and to arm the militia. Guns can serve these purposes only because they are an effective means of inflicting and threatening harm. Even guns normally not used to harm humans have purposes that ride piggyback on this fundamental purpose. Shotguns are used to kill animals, and target guns are designed to be especially accurate. Taken together, this evidence supports the common view that guns are inherently dangerous. That is why we have special reasons to regulate them.

Although inherently dangerous, guns are far less dangerous than weapons of mass destruction, and they do have seemingly legitimate uses. That is why we must show just how risky they are before we can legitimately abolish or seriously restrict them. We must also determine if they have sufficient benefits such that we should permit them, even if risky.

An Intermediate Conclusion

We have shown that owning guns is not a fundamental interest and that guns are inherently dangerous. That is why we cannot categorically dismiss all forms of gun control. However, this is a weak conclusion. For although guns are inherently dangerous, they may not be so dangerous as to justify more than a system of minimal registration. What seems clear is that their inherent dangerousness precludes the idea that guns cannot be subject to governmental control. Some form of gun control cannot be categorically dismissed. Before determining the actual danger that guns present, we should first determine how risky an action must be before we can justifiably restrict it.

Risk

Humans are notoriously bad at judging risk. Often we are unaware of, or are inattentive to, the seriousness of risks. For instance, we may drive while inebriated. At other times we overestimate the risks. For instance, we may refuse to fly because we think it is too dangerous. A proper determination of risk would be based on a careful accounting of the action's costs and benefits. We should determine (1) the probability of harm, (2) the seriousness of harm (the product of the gravity and extent of the harm), (3) the probability of achieving the benefits, (4) the significance of the benefits (the product of the importance and extent of the benefit), and then act accordingly. Of course even if we reach the same determination to the above questions, we might still disagree about whether to act: we might disagree about what risks are worth which benefits. Nonetheless, we can all agree that (*a*) as the likelihood and seriousness of harm increase, we have increased reason to refrain from acting, while (*b*) as the likelihood and importance of the benefits increase, we have increased reasons to act. We can import these lessons into the law.

Legal Rules

But not straightforwardly. The issue is not whether we should own guns if they are legal, although that is a fascinating question. The question is whether the state should curtail private gun ownership. The foregoing considerations are relevant but not decisive. The decision to permit private ownership of guns is shaped by two factors pulling in opposite directions. First, even if we think Roger (an adult) stupidly engages in a dangerous activity (sky diving or boxing or racing), we might think Roger's autonomy requires that we permit it. Our commitment to individual liberty weighs against the government's abolishing or restricting the private ownership of guns as a way of limiting harm.[4] Second, some actions (smoking in public places) that are acceptably risky to Roger might be unacceptably risky to others. Are guns also unacceptably risky to others?

Put differently, gun control does not concern what private individuals should do but what governments should allow private individuals to do. We must determine the risk of permitting the private ownership of guns, constrained by these complicating considerations. To illustrate how this might work, consider the following example. We have evidence that a number of wrecks are caused by drivers using cellular phones. Roger wants to use his cellular phone while commuting to work. He decides the inconvenience of not using the cellular phone is worse than the small probability of personal harm. He might overestimate the inconvenience of not being able to use his cellular phone or insufficiently appreciate the seriousness of the risk. However, since he is an adult, we might think we should not interfere with his decision to use a cellular phone while driving. That is what autonomy requires. Yet Roger is not the only person at risk. Passengers in his or other cars may also be harmed. The seriousness of harm to them must also be considered in deciding to permit or restrict drivers' use of cellular phones.

These judgments of risk must be further tempered by the costs of enforcement mentioned earlier. Although we know that using cellular phones while driving may lead to accidents, we also know other activities may do the same—drinking coffee while driving, eating a donut, looking at a map, talking to a passenger, driving more than two hours without stopping, driving on less than six hours of sleep, driving home after a bad day at the office, and so forth. We can reasonably presume that we should not make all these activities illegal. The probabilities of serious harm are small, and enforcing such laws would require far-reaching intrusions into everyone's life. When the risks of an activity's causing grave harm to many others are small and the costs of interference are significant, then we should not criminalize the action. But as the probability of grave and widespread harm increases, then, other things being equal, we should criminalize the action.

For instance, when people are released from prison (and not just on parole) they have "paid their debt to society." Yet we do not permit them to own a gun. We judge that they are more likely to harm others. Of course not all of them—and likely not a majority of them—would harm others if they were permitted to own a gun. They are prevented from owning guns because they are members of a group statistically more likely to cause harm: we judge that allowing former felons to own guns is unacceptably risky. The NRA and most other gun advocates agree. . . .

This is our rationale for all laws proscribing risky actions. Every drunk driver does not cause an accident. Most do not. Yet we do not flinch at laws forbidding drunk driving. For it is not merely that drunk drivers are statistically more likely to cause harm; they are more likely to cause harm *because* they are inebriated. We can arguably use the same rationale to justify restricting access to guns. We restrict access not only because guns are inherently dangerous but because—if gun-control advocates are right—permitting private ownership of guns is very risky.

What We Need to Know

We can now specify what we must know in order to intelligently decide whether to prohibit or restrict gun ownership (or any other risky action): (1) Is there a statistically significant correlation between the action (private ownership of guns) and harm (homicides, accidental deaths, suicides, armed robbery, etc.)? (2) Do we have good reason to think this correlation indicates that the purportedly risky action causes the harm? (3) How serious are these resultant harms? and (4) How important is the activity that the state wishes to control (*a*) to the individual agent and (*b*) to the society?

In deciding whether to restrict the behavior, we must balance these considerations using the following general guidelines: (1) If we have evidence that the behavior causes harm, then we have some reason to limit the behavior. As the evidence increases, the reasons for prohibiting the behavior increase. As the probability that the behavior will lead to *serious* harm (the product of the gravity and extent of the harm) approaches certainty, then the reasons for forbidding the behavior become very strong. (2) The more grave and widespread the potential harm, the more reason we have to constrain the behavior. If the gravity and extent of the harm are substantial, we might constrain the behavior even if our evidence that the behavior causes the harm is moderate. (3) The higher the probability that allowing the action will have important benefits, the stronger the reason to permit it. The greater the benefits, the greater the reason to permit it.

Libertarians might claim that individuals' rights are so strong that the state cannot justifiably intervene even to constrain those who put others at extreme risk. The state should not proscribe risky actions, although they can intervene after harm has occurred.

This use of "risk" is misleading. If on one occasion I drive while inebriated, I engage in a risky action: there is some probability that I and others will be harmed. However, permitting people to drive while inebriated will definitely cause harm, although we cannot specify in advance who will be harmed. A personal decision to own a gun is risky in the former sense. A decision to permit citizens to privately own guns is— depending on the evidence— risky in the latter sense. If gun control advocates are right about the evidence, then we have good grounds to constrain private gun use. The question is, are they right?

Assessing the Evidence

Armchair Arguments

Debates over gun control typically begin, and sometimes end, with armchair arguments. Both sides offer armchair explanations of why (and how) the presence (or absence) of guns will increase (or decrease) violent crime. It is tempting to categorically dismiss armchair arguments since they seem to be poor substitutes for empirical evidence. However, it would be a mistake to assume we could devise sound empirical studies or understand their results without armchair arguments. In a study to discover if widespread availability of guns increases the number of homicides or decreases crime, we need armchair arguments to tell us which variables we should control.[5] Without them we would not know that we should control for the extent of poverty, the incidence of drug use, increases in the number of police officers, or the introduction of tougher (or more lax) penalties. Without them we would not know that we do not need to control for the price of mayonnaise, the criminal's eye color, or who won the World Series.

Armchair arguments also take center stage in evaluating empirical studies, in criticizing experimental design, and in reinterpreting the reported findings.[6] So before I discuss the empirical evidence, I summarize some significant armchair arguments employed by gun advocates and gun-control advocates.

1. *More weapons, more violence.* Gun control supporters offer empirical evidence of a positive correlation between murder rates and the availability of guns (especially handguns). Availability of guns is also positively correlated with suicide and accident rates. This empirical evidence is best understood against the background of the following armchair arguments. (1) Guns (and especially handguns) are the easiest way to kill others or oneself. People can stand at a relatively safe distance and pull the trigger. (2) When people are angry, they can act in ways they would not act normally. They may strike out at others. If they had a gun close to hand, they would be more likely to use that gun. Although they could resort to a knife or a baseball bat, they would be less likely to do so, and, even if they did, those weapons are less likely to cause a serious or fatal injury. (3) When people are depressed, they can act in ways they would not act normally. If they had a gun close to hand, they would be more likely to kill themselves. Although they might slit their wrists or take pills, they would be less likely to do so, and, even if they did, they would be less likely to kill themselves. (4) When people handle guns, even for a legitimate purpose, the probability of serious or fatal injury to themselves or others increases. When children have access to guns, the likelihood of an accident increases still more.

The conclusion of the armchair argument is clear: the more widely available guns are, the more people will be murdered, will commit suicide, and will die of accidents. This is a plausible armchair prediction. Perhaps it is wrong. Maybe it is reasonable but overinflated. Or it might be that the prediction is well founded but that the widespread availability of guns is nonetheless justified. What is apparent is that the claim that widespread availability of guns increases the number of homicides, suicides, and accidental deaths is highly plausible, it is difficult to imagine that it is false.

2. *Availability of guns prevents or stops crimes.* Gun advocates offer empirical evidence supporting the claim that guns prevent crime; their armchair arguments undergird and explain those studies. The motivating idea is simple: most criminals want to minimize their risks when committing a crime. If they know that someone in a house is armed, they will be less likely to enter that house, at least when the person is home and awake. Potential criminals are also less likely to assault or rob someone whom they believe is carrying a weapon. Finally, when criminals try to rob or assault an armed person, the person is more likely to foil the crime. This, too, is a plausible armchair prediction. Perhaps it is wrong. Maybe the claim is overinflated. Perhaps guns have these benefits, but there are other effects of owning guns—for example, those mentioned above—which outweigh them. What is apparent is that the claim that the widespread availability of guns would prevent or thwart some crimes is highly plausible. It is difficult to imagine that it is false. Of course we cannot stop with these armchair arguments. We must assess the empirical evidence.

The Data

The empirical evidence is difficult to assess, and, to the extent that we can, it does not univocally support either side. You might not know this from listening to the public policy debate. Some gun-control advocates imply that strict gun laws would all but eliminate murder, while some gun advocates imply that having a gun in every home would virtually end crime. Both claims are unfounded. Gun control will not virtually eliminate murder. Arming all citizens will not virtually eliminate crime. About that we can be confident. The problem is determining the precise effects of permitting or restricting guns. The available evidence is less than compelling. But we must make a judgment based on the best evidence we have.

1. *The connection between availability of guns and murder.* Perhaps the most well-established statistic is this: the more widely available guns (especially handguns) are, the more people are murdered. The figures are duplicated time and again in country after country. Here is the bottom line: "The correlation between any gun-prevalence and the overall murder rate is .67, while it is .84 between handgun prevalence and overall murder rate."[7] These figures are significant to the .01 level; that is, the chance that these correlations could occur merely by chance is less than one out of 100. This correlation meets the statisticians' gold standard.

But this does not resolve the issue, for it does not establish what gun control advocates claim it shows, namely, that gun control is an effective way of substantially lessening the murder rate. First, a statistical correlation shows that two things are linked, but it does not tell us if the first caused the second, the second caused the first, or if there is some third factor which caused both. Second, even if the items are causally related, we do not know that changing the cause will straightforwardly change the effect since another factor might intervene to sustain the effect.

Gun advocates proffer their own armchair explanation for the correlations: these correlations reflect the character of the respective social and political systems. The European countries where murder rates are lower have more social solidarity and are more heterogeneous than the United States. Whether these social factors explain all of the correlation is debatable, but I am confident they explain some of it. Were the United States to regulate guns as tightly as most European countries, our murder rates arguably would fall, but they would not plummet immediately to European levels.

We might settle the issue if we could conduct controlled experiments, randomly dividing our population in half, giving half of them guns, removing all the guns from the other half, and then monitoring the murder rate. Of course, that would be morally unacceptable, politically unrealistic, and probably even scientifically unachievable. Before we had enough time to exclude all possible intervening causes, sufficient time might have elapsed so that new intervening causes could have emerged. But we are not left in the dark. We have empirical evidence that helps adjudicate between competing explanations of the correlation.

First, we have empirical evidence, bolstered by armchair arguments, that guns are more lethal than other weapons. Some claim the ratio is 5:1; no estimates are lower than 2:1.[8] This partly explains the strong correlation between guns and homicides. If people get angry the same number of times, those using the most lethal weapons are more likely to kill their victims.

Second, the nature of secondary gun markets helps explain how the widespread availability of guns increases crime in general and homicides in particular. Various opponents of gun control claim that "If we outlaw guns, only outlaws will have guns." Armchair arguments suggest why this is a silly claim. Where, one might ask, do criminals get their guns? They often steal them or buy them from those who purchased them legally. Even guns obtained from other criminals are usually traceable to people who purchased them legally. Empirical evidence supports this armchair supposition. Most criminals report having stolen their guns, received them from a friend or family member, or purchased them from someone who had stolen it. At least half a million guns are stolen each year, and these swell the numbers of guns available illegally.[9]

Not only does the primary (legal) market affect the availability of guns on secondary markets, it also affects the price of guns on those markets, much "like the analogous markets for motor vehicles or prescription drugs."[10] As we restrict the availability of guns in the primary market, the supply of guns in the secondary markets decreases and their cost increases.[11] This increase in cost will diminish teenagers' ability to obtain guns since they are least able to afford hefty prices. Since teenagers commit most deadly crimes, decreasing the availability of legal guns will thereby decrease the number of homicides. The converse is true as well: having huge numbers of legally available guns

increases the number of guns on secondary markets and typically lowers their price. This makes it easier for prospective criminals, including teenagers, to obtain guns.

Third, having a gun around the house (or on the person)—even for self-protection—apparently increases the chance that someone in the family will kill themselves with the gun or will be the victim of a homicide or an accident. One study found that "for every time a gun in the home was involved in a self-protection homicide, they noted 1.3 unintentional deaths, 4.5 criminal homicides, and 37 firearm suicides."[12] This implies that for every case where someone in a gun-owning household uses a gun to successfully stop a life-threatening attack, nearly forty-three people in similar households will die from a gunshot. Taken together the evidence does not prove that widespread availability of guns increases the number of homicides. However, that empirical evidence, bolstered by earlier armchair arguments, makes the claim highly plausible.

2. The use of guns to prevent crime. The biggest "gun" in the anti-gun-control lobby is the claim that having (and perhaps carrying) a gun prevents crime. As I noted earlier, this is a sensible armchair claim. Someone contemplating a robbery is more likely to proceed if they think they can succeed with little risk to themselves. So if a prospective robber believes the tenants are at home and have a gun they know how to use, then he likely will seek another target. Two surveys support this belief. According to one survey, 4 percent of all Americans have used a handgun in the past five years to avert a crime. Given those figures, researchers estimate that there are at least 600,000 defensive uses of guns per year. Kleck uses these results, in conjunction with another survey, to claim that the number might be as high as 2.5 million.[13] Given the number of violent crimes using guns, "the best evidence indicates that guns are used about as often for defensive purposes as for criminal purposes."[14] If true, that is a powerful reason to resist attempts to limit availability of guns.[15] Such statistics, particularly when bolstered by moving anecdotes of those who have saved their lives by having a gun, cannot be cavalierly dismissed by gun control advocates.

However, these figures are inflated, likely dramatically so. First, Kleck's methodology is flawed. Surveys have an inherent tendency to overestimate rare events. Kleck made his estimates based on phone interviews with people in 5,000 dwelling units. One percent of those units claimed to have used a gun defensively in the past year. Kleck inferred from these responses that there are 2.5 million defensive handgun uses per year. However, since this inference is based on an affirmative answer by one person out of a hundred, that means that for every chance for a false negative (someone who falsely denies using a gun defensively) there are ninety-nine chances for a false positive (someone who falsely claims to have used a gun defensively).[16] The probability that this or some other bias skews the findings is substantial.

Second, Kleck's findings are inconsistent with findings by the National Crime Victimization Survey (NCVS), which interviewed far more people and interviewed them more regularly.[17] Kleck's estimates even clash with the findings of the NCVS on the incidence and circumstances of robberies (which seems less subject to reporting bias). If Kleck's figures were correct, then "Kleck asks us to believe that burglary victims in gun-owning households use their guns in self-defense more than 100% of the time, even though most were initially asleep."[18]

Finally, if there were 2.5 million defensive gun uses each year, how many of those were necessary? Given the negative results of private gun ownership, gun advocates should show not only that guns deter crime but that they are the best way of doing so. Some people plausibly claim that owning a dog is an effective deterrent. If true, then a not insignificant percentage of those who used a gun defensively could have achieved the same results without the accompanying danger. In summary, there is no doubt that guns deter some crime and stop the completion of other crimes, just not in the numbers that Kleck claims.

John Lott supplements Kleck's argument by claiming that the wide-spread use of concealed weapons would decrease the annual number of homicides by 1,400; rapes by 4,200; aggravated assaults by 60,000; and robberies by 12,000.[19] If true, and if there were no countervailing costs, this would be a powerful reason not only to permit guns but to encourage people to have and carry them. However, Lott's conclusions have also come under severe criticism: "The central problem is that crime moves in waves, yet Lott's analysis does not include variables that can explain these cycles. For example, he used no variables on gangs, on drug consumption, or community policing. As a result, many of Lott's findings make no sense. He finds for instance, that both increasing the rate of unemployment and reducing income reduces the rate of violent crimes."[20] Perhaps the most compelling critique comes from Jens Ludwig, who compares the rate of violent crime toward youths and adults in states that passed shall-issue carrying permits. Most of these states issue gun permits only to people over twenty-one. Armchair considerations predict that younger people, who cannot legally carry, will not receive the full benefits from the purported deterrent effect of shall-issue laws. Thus, those under twenty-one years of age are a natural control group to track general swings in crime. Once we include this factor, we find that shall-issue laws lead to higher—not lower—homicide and robbery rates.[21]

I also have an overarching worry about Lott's conclusions. The one correlation in the gun control debate that seemingly is beyond dispute is the high correlation between the presence of guns—especially handguns—and homicide rates. Gun advocates offer explanations for the correlation, but no one I have seen seriously challenges it. I find it difficult to square this correlation with Kleck's and Lott's claims that having more guns—and toting them—will lower crime.

An Overall Assessment of the Empirical Evidence

The strong correlation between the presence of guns and a higher murder rate is compelling. Since the correlation is statistically significant to a .01 level, it is difficult to believe that limiting private gun ownership will not have a noticeable effect on the numbers of murders. Gun advocates disagree: they claim that cultural factors explain the correlation. Although I think they are partly correct, they draw the wrong inference. For one crucial difference between European and American cultures is the widespread presence of guns. Each culture is the way it is, at least in part, because of the role of guns (or their absence) played in its creation and maintenance. Therefore, curtailing the private possession of guns might well change the American culture so that it would be less violent. Consequently, it is not only that fewer guns would directly cause some decline in violent crimes—which it should. It is also likely to reshape the cultural values which, along with the ready availability of deadly weapons, led to such an extraordinarily high murder rate in America.

However, the statistical evidence that guns prevent or thwart crimes is suggestive and cannot be ignored despite its identified weaknesses. In summary, the overall statistical evidence tilts in favor of gun control advocates, although the evidence is disputable. But we should not expect nor do we need indisputable evidence. We can act on the best evidence we have while being open to new evidence. If widespread availability of guns were responsible for even one-fourth of the increase in the number of murders, that would be a significant harm that the state should prevent if it could do so in a relatively unintrusive and morally acceptable way.

There is little doubt that we could do that, at least to some degree. If nothing else, we could control some types of guns and ammunition. To take one obvious example, teflon-coated bullets are designed to pierce protective vests. People do not use these bullets to pierce the vests on a deer or a squirrel, on a target or a clay

pigeon. They use them to pierce the vests on people, usually law-enforcement officers. This ammunition has no purpose except to cause harm. Hence, we are justified in abolishing teflon bullets and in establishing severe criminal penalties for those possessing them. This would not save large numbers of lives. But, assuming the enforcement of this ban is not impractical, then, if it saved even a few lives, that would be a compelling reason to outlaw such bullets.

Some guns, however, have a much wider use, even if they occasionally are used for ill. People have seemingly legitimate uses for shotguns and single-shot rifles. Consequently, barring strong evidence to the contrary, we should not abolish them. We should, however, study their contributory role in causing harm and explore ways we might reduce this harm in a relatively unintrusive way.

The central debate concerns handguns. The evidence we have shows that handguns are disproportionately used in homicides and in robberies. Although "there are approximately three times as many long guns as handguns in the U.S., more than 80 percent of gun homicides and 90 percent of gun robberies involve handguns."[22] The experience in Canada suggests that criminals will not switch to long guns if handguns are unavailable. Given the special role handguns play in causing harm, we have compelling reasons to extensively control, or perhaps even abolish, handguns. But policy considerations, mentioned earlier, should give us pause.

A Third Way

In the past we not only assumed that we must either support or oppose gun control, we assumed that the only way to control guns is to legally proscribe access to them. We should consider other options. Although I find the idea of a world without handguns immensely appealing, there are reasons to seek alternatives, especially in countries like the United States with a deeply entrenched gun culture. In the present political climate, the abolition or serious control of guns in the United States is unlikely to work and unlikely to happen. There are far too many people who desperately want guns. There are far too many people who own guns. Any attempt to disarm the society would be beset with problems like those that plagued Prohibition. We have other possibilities.

We could employ elements of a policy that we use to control another inherently dangerous object: dynamite. Dynamite has many beneficial uses. That is why we permit people to own it under specifiable conditions, for example, to build a road. But it is also inherently dangerous. That is why we heavily restrict its purchase, storage, and use. I cannot own dynamite for recreation (I like the flash), for hunting (I am a lousy shot), or for protection (I would not hear an intruder). Owning dynamite is rarely a significant interest and never a fundamental one. More important to the present point, even when we do permit people to own dynamite, we subject them to strict legal liability. The owner is financially liable for any harm caused by his dynamite, even if he was not negligent.

I propose we make handgun owners (and perhaps ultimately all gun owners) strictly liable for harm caused by the use of their guns. If Jones's child takes his gun and kills someone while committing a crime, then Jones will be financially responsible to those harmed. If Jones's child accidentally kills a neighbor's child, Jones will be financially responsible to the child's family. If someone steals Jones's gun and kills someone while robbing them, then Jones will owe the victim compensatory damages. And if Jones were negligent in the storing of the gun, he could be subject to punitive damages as well. Perhaps if he were grossly negligent in storing the gun (he left it lying in his front yard, next to a school playground), we might even bring criminal charges against him.

This procedure is justified since guns are inherently dangerous, and it is only reasonable to expect people to take responsibility for their risky actions. The benefits are notable: many people would be disinclined to own guns, while those owning guns would likely take greater care in storing, handling, and using them. This arguably could achieve the central aims of gun control without direct government intervention. Doubtless that means that some people will be forced to pay for the misdeeds or mistakes of others in ways we might dislike. However, that is a more attractive policy than continuing the current scheme in which guns are easily obtained in the United States or than in completely denying individuals' interest in owning guns.

To make this option more palatable, we could let gun owners purchase liability insurance to cover potential losses. We might even require them to purchase insurance. After all, most states require drivers to have automobile insurance. This insurance-based system of strict liability would make people take more care with any guns they own while providing financial remuneration to those harmed by the use of those guns.

Perhaps this will not work. Other proposals might work better. What seems clear to me is that we need to do something: we cannot continue with the status quo.

Notes

1. Todd C. Hughes and Lester H. Hunt, "The Liberal Basis of the Right to Bear Arms," *Public Affairs Quarterly* 14, No. 1 (2000): pp. 1–25.
2. Charles Singer, E. J. Holmyard, A. R. Hall, and Treavor Williams, *A History of Technology*, 7 vols. (Oxford: Oxford University Press, 1956), vol. 2, p. 367.
3. David Hemenway, "Guns, Public Health, and Public Safety," in *Guns and the Constitution*, ed. Dennis A. Henigan, F. Bruce Nicholson, and David Hemenway (Northampton, MA: Aletheia Press, 1995), pp. 49–82, p. 52.
4. Hughes and Hunt.
5. John R. Lott, *More Guns, Less Crime: Understanding Crime and Gun-Control Laws* (Chicago: University of Chicago Press, 1998), pp. 21–24.
6. Dan Black and Daniel Nagin, "Do Right-to-Carry Laws Deter Violent Crime?" *Journal of Legal Studies* 27 (1998): 209–20; Philip J. Cook, Stephanie Mollinoni, and Thomas B. Cole, "Regulating Gun Markets," *Journal of Criminal Law and Criminology* 86 (1995): 59–92; Phillip J. Cook, Jens Ludwig, and David Hemenway, "The Gun Debate's New Mythical Number: How Many Defensive Uses Per Year?" *Journal of Policy Analysis and Management* 16 (1997): 463–69; David Hemenway, "The Myth of Millions of Annual Self-Defense Gun Uses: A Case Study of Survey Overestimates of Rare Events," *Chance* 10 (1997): 6–10; "Review of *More Guns, Less Crime*," *New England Journal of Medicine* 339 (1998): 2029–30; Lott; Wheeler.
7. Gregg Lee Carter, *The Gun Control Movement* (New York: Twayne Publishers, 1997), p. 3.
8. Albert J. Reiss, Jr., and Jeffrey A. Roth, eds., *Understanding and Preventing Violence* (Washington, DC: National Academy Press, 1993), p. 260.
9. Cook, Mollinoni, and Cole, p. 81.
10. Ibid., p. 71.
11. Ibid., p. 73.
12. Reiss and Roth, eds., p. 267.
13. Gary Kleck, *Point Blank: Guns and Violence in America* (New York: Aldine De Gruyter, 1991), pp. 105–6.
14. Ibid., p. 107.
15. Gary Kleck, *Targeting Guns: Firearms and Their Control* (New York: Aldine de Gruyter, 1997).
16. David Hemenway, "Survey Research and Self-Defense Gun Use: An Explanation of Extreme Overestimates," *Journal of Criminal Law and Criminology* 87 (1997): 1430–45.
17. U.S. Department of Justice, *Criminal Victimization in the United States, 1993: A National Crime Victimization Survey* (Washington, DC: Government Printing Office, 1996).
18. Hemenway, "Survey Research and Self-Defense Gun Use: An Explanation of Extreme Overestimates," p. 1442.
19. Lott, p. 54.
20. Hemenway, "Review of *More Guns, Less Crime*," p. 2029.
21. Jens Ludwig, "Concealed Gun-Carrying Laws and Violent Crime: Evidence from State Panel Data," *International Review of Law and Economics* 18 (1998): 239–54.
22. Hemenway, "Guns, Public Health, and Public Safety," p. 60.

Study Questions for Section 6

1. Hughes and Hunt argue that gun ownership can promote equality. What do they mean by "equality," and is their argument persuasive?

2. Evidence suggests that a ban on guns would significantly reduce the number of homicides. Is this evidence relevant to the question of gun control?

3. Liberalism is committed to a range of values, such as liberty, autonomy, equality, and civic peace. Do these come into conflict in the gun-control debate? If so, how should the matter be resolved?

SECTION 7

TERRORISM

TERRORISM: A CRITIQUE OF EXCUSES

Michael Walzer

The word "terrorism" is used most often to describe revolutionary violence. That is a small victory for the champions of order, among whom the uses of terror are by no means unknown. The systematic terrorizing of whole populations is a strategy of both conventional and guerrilla war, and of established governments as well as radical movements. Its purpose is to destroy the morale of a nation or a class, to undercut its solidarity; its method is the random murder of innocent people. Randomness is the crucial feature of terrorist activity. If one wishes fear to spread and intensify over time, it is not desirable to kill specific people identified in some particular way with a regime, a party, or a policy. Death must come by chance to individual Frenchmen, or Germans, to Irish Protestants, or Jews, simply because they are Frenchmen or Germans, Protestants or Jews, or until they feel themselves fatally exposed and

demand that their governments negotiate for their safety.

In war, terrorism is a way of avoiding engagement with the enemy army. It represents an extreme form of the strategy of the "indirect approach."[1] It is so indirect that many soldiers have refused to call it war at all. This is a matter as much of professional pride as of moral judgment. Consider the Statement of a British admiral in World War II, protesting the terror bombing of German cities: "We are a hopelessly unmilitary nation to imagine that we [can] win the war by bombing German women and children instead of defeating their army and navy."[2] The key word here is unmilitary. The admiral rightly sees terrorism as a civilian strategy. One might say that it represents the continuation of war by political means. Terrorizing ordinary men and women is first of all the work of domestic tyranny, as Aristotle wrote: "The first aim and end [of tyrants] is to break the spirit of their subjects."[3] The British described the "aim and end" of terror bombing in the same way: what they sought was the destruction of civilian morale.

From Michael Walzer, *Terrorism: A Critique of Excuses*, Steven Luper-Foy, ed., Problems of International Justice (Westview Press, 1988). Reprinted by permission.

Tyrants taught the method to soldiers, and soldiers to modern revolutionaries. That is a crude history; I offer it only in order to make a more precise historical point: that terrorism in the strict sense, the random murder of innocent people, emerged as a strategy of revolutionary struggle only in the period after World War II, that is, only after it had become a feature of conventional war. In both cases, in war and revolution, a kind of warrior honor stood in the way of this development, especially among professional officers and "professional revolutionaries." The increasing use of terror by far left and ultranationalist movements represents the breakdown of a political code first worked out in the second half of the nineteenth century and roughly analogous to the laws of war worked out at the same time. Adherence to this code did not prevent revolutionary militants from being called terrorists, but in fact the violence they committed bore little resemblance to contemporary terrorism. It was not random murder but assassination, and it involved the drawing of a line that we will have little difficulty recognizing as the political parallel of the line that marks off combatants from noncombatants.

The Russian Populists, the IRA, and the Stern Gang

I can best describe the revolutionary "code of honor" by giving some examples of so-called terrorists who acted or tried to act in accordance with its norms. I have chosen three historical cases. The first will be readily recognizable, for Albert Camus made it the basis of his play *The Just Assassins*.

1. In the early twentieth century, a group of Russian revolutionaries decided to kill a Tsarist official, the Grand Duke Sergei, a man personally involved in the repression of radical activity. They planned to blow him up in his carriage, and on the

appointed day one of their number was in place along the Grand Duke's usual route. As the carriage drew near, the young revolutionary, a bomb hidden under his coat, noticed that his victim was not alone; on his lap he held two small children. The would-be assassin looked, hesitated, then walked quickly away. He would wait for another occasion. Camus has one of his comrades say, accepting this decision. "Even in destruction, there's a right way and a wrong way—and there are limits."[4]

2. During the years 1938–39, the Irish Republican Army waged a bombing campaign in Britain. In the course of this campaign, a republican militant was ordered to carry a pre-set time bomb to a Coventry power station. He traveled by bicycle, the bomb in his basket, took a wrong turn, and got lost in a maze of streets. As the time for the explosion drew near, he panicked, dropped his bike, and ran off. The bomb exploded, killing five passersby. No one in the IRA (as it was then) thought this a victory for the cause; the men immediately involved were horrified. The campaign had been carefully planned, according to a recent historian, so as to avoid the killing of innocent bystanders.[5]

3. In November 1944, Lord Moyne, British Minister of State in the Middle East, was assassinated in Cairo by two members of the Stern Gang, a right-wing Zionist group. The two assassins were caught, minutes later, by an Egyptian policeman. One of them described the capture at his trial: "We were being followed by the constable on his motorcycle. My comrade was behind me. I saw the constable approach him . . . I would have been able to kill the constable easily, but I contented myself with . . . shooting several times into the air. I saw my comrade fall off his bicycle. The constable was almost upon him. Again, I could have eliminated the constable with a single bullet, but I did not. Then I was caught."[6]

What is common to these cases is a moral distinction, drawn by the "terrorists," between people who can and people who cannot be killed. The first category is not composed of men and women bearing arms, immediately threatening by virtue of their military training and commitment. It is composed instead of officials, the political agents of regimes thought to be oppressive. Such people, of course, are protected by the war convention and by positive international law. Characteristically (and not foolishly), lawyers have frowned on assassination, and political officials have been assigned to the class of nonmilitary persons, who are never the legitimate objects of attack.[7] But this assignment only partially represents our common moral judgments. For we judge the assassin by his victim, and when the victim is Hitler-like in character, we are likely to praise the assassin's work, though we still do not call him a soldier. The second category is less problematic: ordinary citizens, not engaged in political harming—that is, in administering or enforcing laws thought to be unjust—are immune from attack whether or not they support those laws. Thus the aristocratic children, the Coventry pedestrians, even the Egyptian policeman (who had nothing to do with British imperialism in Palestine)—these people are like civilians in wartime. They are innocent politically as civilians are innocent militarily. It is precisely these people, however, that contemporary terrorists try to kill.

The war convention and the political code are structurally similar, and the distinction between officials and citizens parallels that between soldiers and civilians (though the two are not the same). What lies behind them both, I think, and lends them plausibility, is the moral difference between aiming and not aiming—or, more accurately, between aiming at particular people because of things they have done or are doing, and aiming at whole groups of people, indiscriminately, because of who they are. The first kind of aiming is appropriate to a limited struggle directed against regimes and policies. The second reaches beyond all limits; it is infinitely threatening to whole peoples, whose individual members are systematically exposed to violent death at any and every moment in the course of their (largely innocuous) lives. A bomb planted on a streetcorner, hidden in a bus station, thrown into a cafe or pub—this is aimless killing, except that the victims are likely to share what they cannot avoid, a collective identity. Since some of these victims must be immune from attack (unless liability follows from original sin), any code that directs and controls the fire of political militants is going to be at least minimally appealing. It is so much of an advance over the willful randomness of terrorist attacks. One might even feel easier about killing officials than about killing soldiers, since the state rarely conscripts its political, as it does its military agents; they have chosen officialdom as a career.

Soldiers and officials are, however, different in another respect. The threatening character of the soldier's activities is a matter of fact; the unjust or oppressive character of the official's activities is a matter of political judgment. For this reason, the political code has never attained the same status as the war convention. Nor can assassins claim any rights, even on the basis of the strictest adherence to its principles. In the eyes of those of us whose judgments of oppression and injustice differ from their own, political assassins are simply murderers, exactly like the killers of ordinary citizens. The case is not the same with soldiers, who are not judged politically at all and who are called murderers only when they kill noncombatants. Political killing imposes risks quite unlike those of combat, risks whose character is best revealed by the fact that there is no such thing as benevolent quarantine for the duration of the political struggle. Thus the young Russian revolutionary, who eventually killed the Grand Duke, was tried and executed for murder, as were the

Stern Gang assassins of Lord Moyne. All three were treated exactly like the IRA militants, also captured, who were held responsible for the deaths of ordinary citizens. That treatment seems to me appropriate, even if we share the political judgments of the men involved and defend their resort to violence. On the other hand, even if we do not share their judgments, these men are entitled to a kind of moral respect not due to terrorists, because they set limits to their actions.

The Vietcong Assassination Campaign

The precise limits are hard to define, as in the case of noncombatant immunity. But we can perhaps move toward a definition by looking at a guerrilla war in which officials were attacked on a large scale. Beginning at some point in the late 1950s, the NLF waged a campaign aimed at destroying the governmental structure of the South Vietnamese countryside. Between 1960 and 1965, some 7,500 village and district officials were assassinated by Vietcong militants. An American student of the Vietcong, describing these officials as the "natural leaders" of the Vietnamese society, argues that "by any definition this NLF action . . . amounts to genocide."[8] This assumes that all Vietnam's natural leaders were government officials (but then, who was leading the NLF?) and hence that government officials were literally indispensable to national existence. Since these assumptions are not remotely plausible, it has to be said that "by any definition" the killing of leaders is not the same as the destruction of entire peoples. Terrorism may foreshadow genocide, but assassination does not.

On the other hand, the NLF campaign did press against the limits of the notion of officialdom as I have been using it. The Front tended to include among officials

anyone who was paid by the government, even if the work he was doing—as a public health officer, for example—had nothing to do with the particular policies the NLF opposed.[9] And it tended to assimilate into officialdom people like priests and landowners who used their nongovernmental authority in specific ways on behalf of the government. They did not kill anyone, apparently, just because he was a priest or a landowner; the assassination campaign was planned with considerable attention to the details of individual action, and a concerted effort was made "to ensure that there were no unexplained killings."[10] Still, the range of vulnerability was widened in disturbing ways.

One might argue, I suppose, that any official is by definition engaged in the political efforts of the (putatively) unjust regime, just as any soldier, whether he is actually fighting or not, is engaged in the war effort. But the variety of activities sponsored and paid for by the modern state is extraordinary, and it seems intemperate and extravagant to make all such activities into occasions for assassination. Assuming that the regime is in fact oppressive, one should look for agents of oppression and not simply for government agents. As for private persons, they seem to me immune entirely. They are subject, of course, to the conventional forms of social and political pressure (which are conventionally intensified in guerrilla wars) but not to political violence. Here the case is the same with citizens as with civilians; if their support for the government or the war were allowable as a reason for killing them, the line that marks off immune from vulnerable persons would quickly disappear. It is worth stressing that political assassins generally don't want that line to disappear; they have reasons for taking careful aim and avoiding indiscriminate murder. "We were told," a Vietcong guerrilla reported to his American captors, "that in Singapore the rebels on certain days would dynamite every 67th streetcar . . . the next day it might be every 30th, and so on; but that this hardened the hearts of the people against the rebels because so many people died needlessly."[11]

I have avoided noticing until now that most political militants don't regard themselves as assassins at all but rather as executioners. They are engaged, or so they regularly claim, in a revolutionary version of vigilante justice. This suggests another reason for killing only some officials and not others, but it is entirely a self-description. Vigilantes in the usual sense apply conventional conceptions of criminality, though in a rough and ready way. Revolutionaries champion a new conception, about which there is unlikely to be wide agreement. They hold that officials are vulnerable because or insofar as they are actually guilty of "crimes against the people." The more impersonal truth is that they are vulnerable, or more vulnerable than ordinary citizens, simply because their activities are open to such descriptions. The exercise of political power is a dangerous business. Saying this, I do not mean to defend assassination. It is most often a vile politics, as vigilante justice is most often a bad kind of law enforcement; its agents are usually gangsters, and sometimes madmen, in political dress. And yet "just assassinations" are at least possible, and men and women who aim at that kind of killing and renounce every other kind need to be marked off from those who kill at random—not as doers of justice, necessarily, for one can disagree about that, but as revolutionaries with honor. They do not want the revolution, as one of Camus' characters says, "to be loathed by the whole human race."

However the political code is specified, terrorism is the deliberate violation of its norms, for ordinary citizens are killed and no defense is offered—none could be offered—in terms of their individual activities. The names and occupations of the dead are not known in advance; they are killed simply to deliver a message of fear to others like themselves. What is the content of the message? I suppose it could be anything at all; but in practice terrorism, because it is directed against entire peoples or classes, tends to communicate the most extreme and brutal intentions—above all, the tyrannical repression, removal, or mass murder of the population under attack. Hence contemporary terrorist campaigns are most often focused on people whose national existence has been radically devalued: the Protestants of Northern Ireland, the Jews of Israel, and so on. The campaign announces the devaluation. That is why the people under attack are so unlikely to believe that compromise is possible with their enemies. In war, terrorism is associated with the demand for unconditional surrender and, in similar fashion, tends to rule out any sort of compromise settlement.

In its modern manifestations, terror is the totalitarian form of war and politics. It shatters the war convention and the political code. It breaks across moral limits beyond which no further limitation seems possible, for within the categories of civilian and citizen, there isn't any smaller group for which immunity might be claimed (except children; but I don't think children can be called "immune" if their parents are attacked and killed). Terrorists anyway make no such claim; they kill anybody. Despite this, terrorism has been defended, not only by the terrorists themselves, but also by philosophical apologists writing on their behalf. The political defenses mostly parallel those that are offered whenever soldiers attack civilians. They represent one or another version of the argument from military necessity. It is said, for example, that there is no alternative to terrorist activity if oppressed peoples are to be liberated. And it is said, further, that this has always been so: terrorism is the only means and so it is the ordinary means of destroying oppressive regimes and founding new nations.[12] The cases I have already worked through suggest the falsity of these assertions. Those who make them, I think, have lost their grip on the historical past; they suffer from a malign forgetfulness, erasing all moral distinctions along with the men and women who painfully worked them out.

Notes

1. But Liddell Hart, the foremost strategist of the "indirect approach," has consistently opposed terrorist tactics: see, for example, *Strategy* (2nd rev. ed., New York, 1974), pp. 349–50 (on terror bombing).
2. Rear Admiral L. H. K. Hamilton, quoted in Irving, *Destruction of Convoy PQ 17*, p. 44.
3. *Politics,* trans. Ernest Barker (Oxford, 1948), p. 288 (1314a).
4. *The Just Assassins,* in *Caligula and Three Other Plays,* trans. Stuart Gilbert (New York, 1958), p. 258. The actual historical incident is described in Roland Gaucher, *The Terrorists; from Tsarist Russia to the OAS* (London, 1965), pp. 49, 50 n.
5. J. Bowyer Bell, *The Secret Army: A History of the IRA* (Cambridge, MA, 1974), pp. 161–62.
6. Gerold Frank, *The Deed* (New York, 1963), pp. 248–49.
7. James E. Bond, *The Rules of Riot; Internal Conflict and the Law of War* (Princeton, 1974), pp. 89–90.
8. Douglas Pike, *Viet Cong* (Cambridge, MA 1968), p. 248.
9. Jeffrey Race, *War Comes to Long An* (Berkeley, 1972), p. 83, which suggests that it was precisely the *best* public health officers, teachers, and so on who were attacked—because they constituted a possible anti-communist leadership.
10. Pike, p. 250.
11. Pike, p. 251.
12. The argument, I suppose, goes back to Machiavelli, though most of his descriptions of the necessary violence of founders and reformers have to do with the killing of particular people, members of the old ruling class: see *The Prince,* ch. VIII, and *Discourses,* 1:9, for examples.

IS TERRORISM DISTINCTIVELY WRONG?

Lionel K. McPherson

Many people, including philosophers, believe that terrorism is necessarily and egregiously wrong. I will call this "the dominant view." The dominant view maintains that terrorism is akin to murder. This forecloses the possibility that terrorism, under any circumstances, could be morally permissible—murder, by definition, is wrongful killing. The unqualified wrongness of terrorism is thus part of this understanding of terrorism.

I will criticize the dominant view. Some philosophers have argued that terrorism might not be impermissible on either a rights-based or a consequentialist analysis.[1] But I will not pursue the question of whether terrorism could ever be justifiable. Rather, I will argue that the dominant view's condemnatory attitude toward terrorism as compared to conventional war cannot be fully sustained. I propose that a version of the argument that terrorists do not have adequate authority to undertake political violence—and not the prominent argument that noncombatants should be immune from deliberate use of force against them—is the most plausible basis

for finding terrorism objectionable. While the argument from authority does not show that terrorism is necessarily wrong, the argument does show that there is a distinctive sense in which terrorism can be wrong when it is wrong. By "distinctive" I do not mean unique; acts of political violence that might not count as terrorism, such as rebellions, can also be carried out by groups that might lack adequate authority. Yet the distinctive sense in which terrorism as compared to conventional war can be wrong helps to draw a qualified moral boundary between terrorism and war.

Too often, criticism of the prevailing discourse has been dismissed as an attempt to excuse terrorism.[2] I seek to offer no excuse for terrorism, any more than I would for war as such. The principal challenge for those who believe that terrorism is distinctively wrong lies in morally accounting for noncombatant casualties of conventional war. This challenge holds even when wars are fought according to international law, for example, as codified in the 1977 Geneva Protocol I on International Armed Conflicts.[3] Terrorism might be morally objectionable for reasons that hardly apply less to conventional war, for the laws of war are not beyond moral scrutiny. A credible argument that would demonstrate the distinctive wrongness of terrorism is not as obvious as proponents of the dominant view believe.

Definitional Issues

The dominant view finds characteristic expression in the following definition: "Terrorism is a type of political violence that intentionally targets civilians (noncombatants) in a ruthlessly destructive, often unpredictable manner. . . . Essentially, terrorism employs horrific violence against unsuspecting civilians as well as combatants, in order to inspire fear and create panic, which in turn will advance the terrorists' political or religious agenda."[4] Much of this language is not helpful in morally distinguishing terrorism, since conventional war tends to be at least as "ruthlessly destructive," "unpredictable," and "horrific" for noncombatants and combatants.

I will define "terrorism" as the deliberate use of force against ordinary noncombatants, which can be expected to cause wider fear among them, for political ends. My definition focuses on the aspect of terrorism—namely, targeting of ordinary noncombatants—that commonly is thought to characterize its distinctive wrongness as compared to conventional war. Left out of the definition, for instance, is the claim that noncombatants are "innocent." The relevant understanding of innocence in war is a contested matter, and my argument will not depend on how this is settled.[5] I will assume provisionally that ordinary non-combatants in general are innocent.

There are sophisticated, more expansive definitions. David Rodin defines "terrorism" as "the deliberate, negligent, or reckless use of force against noncombatants, by state or nonstate actors for ideological ends and in the absence of a substantively just legal process."[6] While Rodin's fuller account of terrorism is compelling in significant respects, his definition of terrorism has difficulties that highlight advantages of adopting a less expansive definition. I will address these and related difficulties in the rest of this section. The discussion will help to set up my revisionist account of terrorism's distinctive wrongness.

The innocence of noncombatants underlies why Rodin considers his definition a "moral definition," that is, "an analysis of the features of acknowledged core instances of terrorism which merit and explain the moral reaction which most of us have toward them. These reactions are undeniably negative."[7] Actually, these reactions seem mixed. When we judge that certain political ends are just and urgent, many of us might concede that terrorism is not absolutely wrong or raise sudden doubts about whether the questionable acts constitute terrorism—if we also judge that the means are vital for success. Thus Michael Walzer, the influential just war theorist and ostensible proponent of the dominant view of terrorism, defends "overriding" the rules of war in a "supreme emergency," which is when "we are face-to-face not merely with defeat but with a defeat likely to bring disaster to a political community."[8] He admits that certain cases of terrorism could be (and have been) legitimate under such circumstances.[9] This lends credence to the saying "One man's terrorist is another man's freedom fighter." We have reason to be wary, then, about letting negative reactions to putative core instances of terrorism serve as our moral guide in analyzing terrorism.

More important now is to recognize that I am not working with a moral definition of terrorism. My nonmoral definition reflects common extension of the word to political violence that targets ordinary noncombatants, without carrying the connotation that this makes terrorism wrong. The motivation for my approach is to avoid philosophically unproductive and often politicized dispute over the definition. A familiar, nonmoral definition suits the purpose of addressing the substantive question of why terrorism might be distinctively wrong as compared to war. Given this purpose, it is not crucial which precise definition we adopt, among various alternatives, as long as the definition is nonmoral and provides a description of roughly the kind of conduct under consideration.

Acts of political violence that might not count as terrorism, for example, use of force that does not target noncombatants yet does not take due care to avoid harming them, could still be morally like terrorism. Acknowledging a non-morally descriptive difference between such acts and terrorism does not entail accepting that there is a deep moral difference in their character. For example, the September 11, 2001, attacks on the World Trade Center unambiguously count as terrorism, whereas the U.S. fire-bombing of Tokyo during World War II might count as, say, "quasi-terrorism" in its heavy and foreseeable, if technically collateral, infliction of noncombatant casualties. But my definition does not identify certain acts as terrorist on the basis of whether they are committed by nonstate actors. By contrast, the "political status" definition holds that only nonstate actors can commit terrorist acts.[10] When acts committed by states are otherwise indistinguishable from these nonstate acts, I see no reason to describe them differently, though nothing is morally at stake if we reserve a different label, such as "state terrorism," for them.

The fear-effects clause of my definition restricts what counts as terrorism to political violence that not only targets ordinary noncombatants but also can be expected to cause wider fear among them. This helps

descriptively to distinguish terrorism from other forms of political violence, such as assassination of political officials or police officers. In addition, while I have argued elsewhere that combatants on the unjust side of a war cannot legitimately attack just and thereby morally innocent combatants, not all political violence directed against the morally innocent need be thought to constitute terrorism.[11] We typically have in mind a more limited phenomenon: deliberate use of force against ordinary noncombatants where wider fear among them is warranted by the increased threat of harm to them.[12] Cases of violence against combatants, for example, the bombing of the U.S. Marine barracks in Lebanon in 1983, have been described as terrorism. Nevertheless, deliberate use of force against ordinary noncombatants is widely acknowledged as the paradigm case. Extension of the word to include some cases of violence against combatants seems parasitic; agents who employ such violence are seen as generally being in the business also of deliberately attacking noncombatants. If these agents do not target ordinary noncombatants, they would not be terrorists, strictly speaking on my definition.

It might turn out that deliberate use of force against noncombatants is wrong, in principle or practice. So why argue that terrorism is wrong by definition? Rodin anticipates this question when he claims that "the immunity of noncombatants is the foundational element in our moral thinking, and whether or not the just war theory is ultimately able to sustain the permissibility of killing combatants is irrelevant to this fact."[13] Yet noncombatant immunity is not unequivocally a foundational element in our moral thinking, for there is no consensus about how such a principle ought to be understood. A version of noncombatant immunity that prohibits deliberate use of force against noncombatants is part of the roughly standard theory of the just war.[14] This represents a limited prohibition on use of force against them. As we will see, the prohibition is highly controversial in its permissiveness.

My point has been to question the merits of building a definition of terrorism around a moral judgment. I will go on to argue that a moral definition of terrorism, in concentrating on deliberate use of force against noncombatants, can exaggerate the moral significance of a distinction between intending and not intending harm.[15] The usual emphasis on this distinction marks a basic weakness in standard just war theory and the dominant view of terrorism. In sum, a descriptive, nonmoral definition of terrorism is appropriate for thinking about the ethics of terrorism. It frees us for a levelheaded inquiry and has no real disadvantages. Our moral judgments about terrorism, as with conventional war, have to be substantiated through a fuller account.

Challenging the Dominant View

Moral evaluation of terrorism might begin with the question of what makes terrorism wrong. A better opening question, I believe, is whether use of force that leads to casualties among ordinary noncombatants is morally objectionable. The latter question prompts comparison of terrorism and conventional war. Judging by practice and common versions of just war theory, the answer is plainly no. The journalist Chris Hedges reports these facts: "Between 1900 and 1990, 43 million soldiers died in wars. During the same period, 62 million civilians were killed. . . . In the wars of the 1990s, civilian deaths constituted between 75 and 90 percent of all war deaths."[16] Such numbers may seem counterintuitive. More noncombatants than combatants have died in war, by

a sizable margin, and the margin has only grown in an era of the most advanced weapons technology. We must conclude that war generally is highly dangerous for noncombatants. I will characterize this as the brute reality of war for noncombatants. This reality cannot be attributed simply to the conduct of war departing from the laws of war.

There is an ambiguity in the data I have cited: they do not clearly support the claim that most noncombatants who died in these wars were killed by military actions, for example, through the use of bombs, artillery, and land mines. Many noncombatant deaths in war have been the result of displacement and the lack of shelter, inability to get food, and the spread of disease. At the same time, modern warfare is marked by a nontrivial number of noncombatant deaths that are the direct result of military actions. The ratio of war to "war-related" noncombatant casualties and the distribution of moral responsibility for these casualties will not be at issue here. I proceed on the assumption that evaluating the ethics of war involves recognizing that war, directly or indirectly, leads to a great many noncombatant casualties. Modern warfare and widespread harm to noncombatants are virtually inextricable. In fact, this motivates a strain of pacifist skepticism about the just war tradition.[17] Although I would defend a revisionist version of just war theory. I do not believe we can deny that modern warfare raises the moral stakes to a degree that calls for reevaluating the view that terrorism is intrinsically worse than war.

Immediately doubtful is the popular notion that terrorism is distinctively wrong because of the fear it usually spreads among ordinary noncombatants. Recall that my nonmoral definition of terrorism includes a fear-effects clause which descriptively distinguishes terrorism from other forms of political violence. However, this does not morally distinguish terrorism and conventional war. The brute reality of war for noncombatants indicates that in general they have more to fear from conventional war than (nonstate) terrorism, particularly since (nonstate) terrorists rarely have had the capacity to employ violence on a mass scale.[18] Noncombatants in states that are military powers might have more to fear from terrorism than conventional war, since these states are relatively unlikely to be conventionally attacked. But surely this situational advantage that does not extend more broadly to noncombatants cannot ground the claim that terrorism is distinctively wrong.

The laws of war recognize a principle that prohibits disproportionate or excessive use of force, with an emphasis on noncombatants. For example, Article 51 (5) (b) of the 1977 Geneva Protocol I rules out use of force "which may be expected to cause incidental loss of civilian life, injury to civilians, damage to civilian objects, or a combination thereof, which would be excessive in relation to the concrete and direct military advantage anticipated."[19] Standard just war theory considers this the proportionality principle. Proponents of the dominant view might take the proportionality principle to illuminate an essential moral difference between conventional war and terrorism. They might claim that, unlike proper combatants, terrorists do not care about disproportionate harm to noncombatants. But the full impact of this charge is not easily sustained for two reasons.

The first reason is that terrorists could have some concern about disproportionate harm to noncombatants. This point is most salient when proportionality is understood in instrumental terms of whether violence is gratuitous, namely, in exceeding what is minimally necessary to achieve particular military or political goals, despite the availability of an alternative course of action that would be less harmful and no less efficacious. Terrorists may possess a normative if flawed sensibility that disapproves of instrumentally gratuitous violence, for the harm done would serve no strategic purpose. So the plausible charge is that terrorists reject the proportionality principle as conventionally construed (since it implicitly rules out deliberate use of force against non-combatants), not that they lack all concern for disproportionate harm to noncombatants.

The second reason is that the proportionality principle requires rather modest due care for noncombatants. Force may be used against them, provided that the incidental, or collateral, harm to them is not excessive when measured against the expected military gains. According to one legal scholar, "the interpretation by the United States and its allies of their legal obligations concerning the prevention of collateral casualties and the concept of proportionality comprehends prohibiting only two types of attacks: first, those that intentionally target civilians; and second, those that involve negligent behavior in ascertaining the nature of a target or the conduct of the attack itself."[20] Such an interpretation seems accurately to reflect the principle's leniency. Indeed, the U.S. general and military theorist James M. Dubik argues that commanders have a special moral duty "not to waste lives of their soldiers" in balancing the responsibility to ensure that due care is afforded to noncombatants.[21] A commander may give priority to limiting risk of harm to his own combatants, for their sake, at the expense of noncombatants on the other side.

We find, then, that the proportionality principle does not express a commitment to minimizing noncombatant casualties. The principle more modestly would reduce noncombatant casualties in requiring that they be worth military interests. Perhaps my reading appears too narrow. A prominent reason for thinking that terrorism is distinctively wrong is that terrorists, unlike combatants who comply with the laws of war, do not acknowledge the moral significance of bearing burdens in order to reduce noncombatant casualties for the sake of noncombatants themselves. To reply that terrorists might well be motivated to reduce noncombatant casualties on strategic grounds, for example, to avoid eroding sympathy for their political goals, would miss the point. Basic respect for the lives of noncombatants seems evidenced instead by a willingness to bear burdens in order to reduce harm to them. Terrorists, the objection goes, do not have this respect for noncombatant lives, which is a major source of the sense that terrorism is distinctively wrong as compared to conventional war.

There are difficulties with this objection. It suggests that the laws of war are imbued with a certain moral character, namely, fundamental moral concern for noncombatants. These laws, though, are part of the war convention, adopted by states and codified in international law for reasons that seem largely to reflect their shared interests, at least in the long run.[22] We do not have to be political realists to see this. Given that noncombatants are vulnerable enough on all sides and no state generally has much to gain by harming them, states usually are prudent to accept mutually a principle that seeks to reduce noncombatant casualties. States usually are also prudent to comply with the laws of war, since this compliance is a benchmark of moral and political respectability on the world stage. Simply put, states, like terrorists, would seem contingently motivated to accept the proportionality principle on broadly strategic grounds.

Now the objection might go that, even if a realist analysis of the proportionality principle's place in the war convention is correct, this is no barrier to states' recognizing that the principle has independent, nonprudential moral standing. But the same can be true for terrorists. Familiar characterizations of them as "evil" or unconstrained by moral boundaries are an unreliable indication of moral indifference to harming noncombatants. As Virginia Held observes, "Terrorists often believe, whether mistakenly or not, that violence is the only course of action open to them that can advance their political objectives."[23] When terrorism is seen by its agents as a means of last resort, this provides some evidence that they acknowledge the moral significance of bearing burdens out of respect for the lives of noncombatants. Such agents will not have employed terrorism earlier, despite their grievances.

A model case is the African National Congress (ANC) in its struggle against apartheid in South Africa. Nelson Mandela, during the 1964 trial that produced his sentence of life imprisonment, summed up the ANC's position as follows:

a. It was a mass political organization with a political function to fulfill. Its members had joined on the express policy of nonviolence.

b. Because of all this, it could not and would not undertake violence. This must be stressed.

c. On the other hand, in view of this situation I have described, the ANC was prepared to depart from its fifty-year-old policy of nonviolence. . . . There is sabotage, there is guerrilla warfare, there is terrorism, and there is open revolution. We chose to adopt the first method and to exhaust it before taking any other decision.[24]

Mandela was implying that violence, including terrorism, became an option "only when all else had failed, when all channels of peaceful protest had been barred to us," which led the ANC to conclude that "to continue preaching peace and nonviolence at a time when the government met our peaceful demands with force" would be "unrealistic and wrong."[25] By the 1980s, at the height of government repression, the ANC did resort to acts of terrorism before reaffirming its earlier position on controlled violence that does not target civilians.[26] The case of the ANC demonstrates that those who employ terrorism can have and sometimes have had fundamental moral concern for noncombatants. Such moral concern, however, is overriding neither for terrorists nor for proper combatants.

Thus considerations other than proportionality and basic respect for the lives of noncombatants would have to show that terrorism is intrinsically worse than conventional war. Of course, a terrorist proportionality requirement would not exclude noncombatants as legitimate targets, whereas the standard proportionality principle prohibits deliberately attacking noncombatants. This prohibition, though, derives from another principle. Article 51 (2) of the 1977 Geneva Protocol I states: "The civilian population as such, as well as individual civilians, shall not be the object of attack. Acts or threats of violence the primary purpose of which is to spread terror among the civilian population are prohibited."[27] I will characterize this as the limited noncombatant immunity principle (LNI). Noncombatants, according to LNI, rightfully are immune from deliberate use of force against them. They are not broadly immune from use of force through legitimate acts of war that can be expected to harm them. That is, use of force against noncombatants—if they are not its intended targets—does not necessarily fail LNI.

Within the war convention, LNI is tied to a consequentialist aim to reduce noncombatant casualties. I have suggested that this reflects the shared, prudential interest that states have in avoiding gratuitous harm to noncombatants. While a commitment by states to LNI on this basis is presumably better for noncombatants than no commitment to LNI, the brute reality of war undermines the notion that the laws of war provide robust protection for noncombatants. Nor does the consequentialist orientation of LNI within the war convention fit well with the dominant view of terrorism, on which deliberate use of force against ordinary noncombatants appears to be intrinsically wrong—not wrong because this means of achieving political goals cannot be justified on strategic grounds. Within commonsense morality, LNI is tied to the nonconsequentialist Doctrine of Double Effect (DDE). The deontological orientation of this doctrine fits better with the dominant view of terrorism. So the question is whether intention is a cogent basis—as is widely believed—for morally distinguishing terrorism and conventional war.

Justice Beyond the DDE

Roughly, the Doctrine of Double Effect holds that one may never intend to cause an evil, even to achieve a greater good. One may pursue a good end through neutral means, even if foreseeing that this will have evil effects, provided that the evil is proportionate to the good and there is no better way of achieving the good.[28] On standard just war theory, the DDE rules out terrorism, since intending to harm ordinary noncombatants would be to aim at causing an evil. Arts of conventional war that unintentionally harm noncombatants are not necessarily ruled out, since such acts have only military targets. The DDE is applied in a manner internal to the standard theory's account of neutral means of fighting. Once a war is in progress, the issue of which side has a just cause would have virtually no bearing on the principles governing the conduct of combatants. The purpose of these principles is not to promote success on the side of a just cause for war. From this perspective, justice is irrelevant to the conception of a good end and neutral means: destruction of a military target is a good end, and conventionally legitimate acts of war are a neutral means of achieving the end, regardless of whether achieving the end would advance a just cause.[29] Justice in the most basic moral sense is left to fate, which makes justice hostage to the superior fighting force.

Purist advocates of the DDE could find this application of it dubious. They might object that the DDE is morally plausible to the extent that it considers only ends that truly are good. Suppose, for instance, that soldiers for Nazi Germany were acting within the rules of war in trying to repel Allied soldiers during the Normandy invasion. Nonetheless, the German use of force at Normandy did not have a morally good end: which combatants were killed made a moral difference, since justice clearly was on the side of the Allies. The notion that good ends in war must be understood solely in terms of the destruction of military targets is morally implausible, especially when the stakes for justice are high enough. In short, purist advocates of the DDE could argue that it is not a justice-independent test of the permissibility of acts. Hence the DDE would not operate squarey within the parameters of standard just war theory and rationalize its principles.

Rodin raises a different kind of root challenge to the DDE. He argues that the laws of war overemphasize the moral relevance of intention and underemphasize the moral relevance of recklessness and negligence. The concepts of recklessness and negligence refer to conduct that has or could have unintended evil effects due to the agent's culpable failure to avoid the risk of causing such effects. While the DDE prohibits conduct whose evil effects are unneccessary and disproportionate under the circumstances, Rodin believes that this is too weak. On his view, "Persons have rights against being harmed or used for the benefit of others. . . . Because of this there is an additional element to the reasonableness test which goes beyond the necessity and proportionality requirements, namely: is it justifiable to inflict such a risk upon this particular person?"[30] This emphasis on a fundamental right of individual noncombatants not to be harmed through use of force—whether deliberate, reckless, or negligent—represents a major revision of common versions of just war theory. Noncombatants would have almost absolute immunity from uses of force that could be expected to harm them.

The intention to harm noncombatants, then, might be only one manifestation of culpable failure to observe a reasonable standard of care in using force. This failure often is no less evident in acts of conventional war: the associated noncombatant casualties—being likely, foreseeable, and avoidable—cannot be construed merely as accidents. Rodin draws the conclusion that "the unintentional killing of some noncombatants in the course of military operations is morally culpable to the same degree and for the same reasons that typical acts of terrorism are culpable."[31] The DDE would be preempted by a more stringent standard of due care. Although I am sympathetic to this approach, I am skeptical of a fundamental right of noncombatants not to be harmed through foreseeable and avoidable use of force. Almost absolute noncombatant immunity is insufficiently responsive to the stakes for justice and to the available means of advancing a just cause.[32] I would argue for a less stringent view of what counts as reckless or negligent use of force, particularly when there is a just and urgent cause for resorting to violence.

Some philosophers directly challenge the DDE as a test of the permissibility of acts by challenging the relevance of intention. Judith Thomson presents the following case: A bomber pilot seeks advice from his superior officers about the permissibility of an attack that would destroy a munitions factory and an adjacent hospital in which noncombatants would be killed.[33] The superiors assure the pilot that the military gains would be necessary and proportionate in relation to the noncombatant casualties. Still, the superiors want to know whether the pilot intends to destroy the factory or intends to destroy the hospital. Thomson finds absurd the notion that their advice would turn on which intention the pilot has. The properties of the bombing are known in advance and seem on their own to render the act impermissible or not under the circumstances.[34] The pilot's moral character or his disposition to act on objectionable motives in other situations is not at issue.

Perhaps Thomson's charge of absurdity against the DDE is overstated. If the pilot intends to destroy the hospital and not the factory, it would be better for his superiors to send a different pilot on the mission to destroy the factory. But if no other pilot is available, the DDE might not prohibit sending the pilot who intends to destroy the hospital: his superiors might exploit his bad moral character and wrongful intention in order to fulfill their acceptable intention to destroy the factory.[35] The intention of the pilot would make a moral difference but need not make a decisive moral difference to what his superiors could permissibly have him do, which could save the DDE from absurdity. Yet the cost of this save is high. If the pilot's superiors know that he would be acting wrongly due to his

wrongful intention, it seems plausible to think that they would be acting wrongly in allowing him to act wrongly. Presumably, advocates of the DDE do not want to maintain that we can act permissibly regarding our own ultimate, acceptable intentions when the good ends would have to be brought about by exploiting the bad moral character and wrongful intentions of others. No less a friend of the importance of intention than Elizabeth Anscombe would scorn this as "double-think about double effect."[36] The proposed save looks like a moral responsibility shell game, marked by bad faith if not absurdity.

To clarify, I am not endorsing a sweeping rejection of the relevance of intention to permissibility. I am expressing doubt more specifically about the moral significance of intention in cases where use of force can be expected to lead to extensive casualties among noncombatants. There are deontological and virtue-based accounts of morality that deem intention relevant to permissibility. Intuition rooted in commonsense morality also lends support to the notion that intention can be morally significant. Our moral judgments are often guided by assessments of intention when conduct that results in unwarranted harm prompts us to ask whether the harm is accidental. The driver hit the pedestrian. The policeman shot the bystanders. The parent caused bodily harm to the child. How we assess the agent's intention seems to make a moral difference in such cases.

Acts of conventional war, however, are not as susceptible to evaluation through this feature of commonsense morality. The harm done to noncombatants through many of these acts is likely, foreseeable, avoidable, and extensive—which would appear largely to overshadow the relevance of the combatants' intentions to permissibility. Commonsense morality recognizes that agents might not be morally culpable when, despite what they reasonably could expect, they do unwarranted harm. But when the unwarranted harm can reasonably be expected, commonsense morality is not committed to recognizing that the agents' intentions make a moral difference, at least in the manner that the conventional interpretation of the DDE allows. Against this background, commonsense morality hardly seems unequivocal about the relevance of intention to permissibility in the context of conventional war.

Prospective noncombatant victims, of course, will care much less about the distinction between intended harm and foreseen unintended harm than about not being harmed at all. Yet their point of view may reflect more than sheer self-interest. While they might acknowledge that the distinction sometimes makes a moral difference, they might ask the following question: are there just and urgent goals, which could not otherwise be achieved, that would offset the harm to us? The question focuses attention on whether the distinction between intended harm and foreseen unintended harm morally comes into play under the circumstances. A plausible answer is that if likely, foreseeable, avoidable, and extensive harm to ordinary noncombatants can ever be justified, or even excused, this must be relative to the stakes for justice—and not merely to a standard of acceptable intention that is internal to the conventional interpretation of the DDE. This claim does not depend on noncombatants' having almost absolute immunity from use of force but, rather, on their presumptive right not to be harmed representing a fundamental moral interest. Their presumptive right must prevail at least in the absence of a competing, fundamental, justice-based interest. This is consistent with the purist interpretation of the DDE and does not seem inconsistent overall with commonsense morality.

Finally, the DDE is susceptible to yielding dubious results. Frances Kamm describes a threshold deontological point of view. Suppose that it would be permissible to kill a million noncombatants as an unintended effect of tactical bombing in a war of just cause; a permissible alternative might be to kill a few hundred different noncombatants as an intended effect of terror bombing.[37] The DDE would not be an overriding deontological constraint, since the cost of acting within the constraint exceeds any reasonable threshold. How could it be impermissible to kill through terrorism so many fewer persons of the same type, who otherwise would be killed through conventional war? We are not presupposing that the agent's intention makes an essential moral difference. A ready response comes from an objection to consequentialism: noncombatants have a right not to be harmed that cannot simply be traded off against the collectivized interests of a greater number of noncombatants or against some other greater good.[38]

Whether or not this is seen as a viable objection to consequentialism, it is much less compelling in support of the DDE. The threshold deontological argument can be reformulated. Suppose that the few hundred noncombatants who would be killed intentionally are among the million noncombatants who otherwise would be killed collaterally. The presumptive right not to be harmed that the prospective terror bombing victims have would be violated anyway, since they are a subset of the prospective tactical bombing victims who also have this right. There is no consequentialist sacrifice of the lives of noncombatants who would not be harmed, only minimization of the loss of life among noncombatants who would be killed through the alternative. Still, the DDE would prohibit the course of action through which fewer noncombatants would be killed, since the doctrine rules out intentionally killing them. Even proponents of agent-centered moral theories might balk at this conclusion. Christine Korsgaard, for example, defends a Kantian view on which "To treat someone as an end . . . is to respect his right to use his own reason to determine whether and how he will contribute to what happens [to him]."[39] The prospective terror bombing victims may well elect to be killed intentionally if confronted with the narrow choice, in order to minimize loss of life among the larger set of noncombatants that includes them. To deny them this measure of influence over their fate suggests a doctrinaire refusal to share their sensible perspective. The DDE's overwhelming emphasis on the intentions of the harm-doing agents would amount to indifference to the victims' choice and their concern for the good of their people.

Standard just war theory's application of the Doctrine of Double Effect is all too compatible with the brute reality of war for noncombatants. The conventional interpretation of the DDE permits use of force against noncombatants once its prohibition on intending to harm them and its requirements of necessity and proportionality have been satisfied. If we believe that fewer noncombatant casualties is a goal morally worth striving for, we are led to the discomfiting conclusion that terrorism in some situations might better achieve this goal than use of force that satisfies the limited noncombatant immunity principle. While this conclusion does not require accepting that terrorism can be justifiable, it does call into question the moral integrity of standard just war theory.

The Argument From Representative Authority

Earlier I was critical of the political status definition of terrorism, which maintains that terrorism can only be committed by nonstate actors. Acts of political violence committed by nonstate actors are not intrinsically worse than otherwise indistinguishable acts of political violence committed by states. Yet the political status definition does reflect that terrorism often is not backed by *representative authority*, by which I mean adequate license for acting on behalf of a people through their approval. The argument from representative authority that I will elaborate is related to a familiar argument from legitimate authority, while the latter is too restrictive, the former provides a qualified basis for the view that terrorism is a distinctively objectionable form of political violence.

The large and difficult topic of legitimate authority will have to be confined to a brief discussion for present purposes. One prominent approach draws from Hobbesian social contract theory: a state's authority depends on its ability to impose law and order on the persons within its domain.[40] They must fare better than they could expect to if left to their own devices. That is, the state would have legitimate authority by virtue of being able to mediate the aggressive pursuit of self-interest by individual members, who rationally would agree to be governed through coercive power for the sake of their mutual interest. Another prominent approach, which also utilizes a social contract model, regards members of a state as political constituents and moral agents, not mainly as subjects. This is exemplified when the members of a state are organized around a substantially just and democratic government. Rawls gives the following characterization: "The government is effectively under their political and electoral control, and . . . it answers to and protects their fundamental interests as specified in a written or unwritten constitution and in its interpretation. The regime is not an autonomous agency pursuing its own bureaucratic ambitions.

Moreover, it is not directed by the interests of large concentrations of private economic and corporate power veiled from public knowledge and almost entirely free from accountability."[41] The state's legitimate authority would derive from the people, whose government operates through and for them. At the same time, advancing their interests must be compatible with justice.

It might be thought, as the political status definition implies, that terrorism is distinctively wrong because terrorist groups by their nature lack legitimate authority. But this would presuppose that legitimate authority could be a decisive condition for permissible resort to political violence. A plausible argument for such a position is not obvious, especially on a view that grounds the state's authority merely on its ability to provide civil order. Indeed, authoritarian states are capable of achieving civil order. They do not thereby have moral standing, despite the claim they may have to political sovereignty under international law and custom. A decent state must do more than protect its members against internal anarchy and external threats: it also must protect their other fundamental interests and do so through acceptable means. That non-state terrorism would offend against a morally weak, Hobbesian account of legitimate authority hardly seems a compelling reason for judging that nonstate terrorism is wrong.

The appeal even to morally robust legitimate authority has limits. Walzer's influential version of just war theory, for example, supports a two-level account of moral responsibility: combatants bear no responsibility for fighting a war of unjust cause (the level of *jus ad bellum),* but they are responsible for how they fight (the level of *jus in bello).* Given a state's legitimate authority, Walzer believes, any choice combatants have about whether to fight "effectively disappears as soon as

fighting becomes a legal obligation and a patriotic duty."[42] Moral responsibility for their fighting would lie solely with the executives of the state, namely, its political leaders. The state's legitimate authority would be for combatants a decisive condition for the permissibility of their fighting. I have argued elsewhere for rejecting this two-level account of combatant moral responsibility.[43] Legal obligation and patriotic duty do not have moral weight that could permit or completely excuse fighting in the service of a war or unjust cause, no matter how outrageous, whenever the state sponsoring that war has legitimate authority. The dictates of law and morality can come apart.

Thus I contend that legitimate authority is not sufficient to permit combatants to fight at the state's behest. Two issues can be separated in order to avoid confusion. First, legitimate authority provides no justification for combatants for an unjust war to inflict casualties on bystanders to or just combatants against the unjust aggression.[44] Second legitimate authority does not best explain why combatants should not be punished for fighting in the service of an unjust war. A more plausible explanation is that punishing such combatants is generally not feasible or constructive *past bellum.*[45] The summary point is that appreciating the significance of a state's morally robust legitimate authority does not entail accepting the normative consequences found in common versions of just war theory.

A limited appeal to adequate license does help to draw a moral boundary between terrorism and conventional war. In the ideal scenario, a democratic state functions with a considerable degree of control by its people and transparency regarding political processes. This provides no guarantee that political decisions will be substantively just. Nor am I suggesting that the ideal scenario of decision making in democratic states is closely approximated in real-world scenarios. There are no official referenda about decisions to go to war, let alone about how a war is fought, and political leaders can shape public opinion through selective dissemination of information and appeals to national interest that have a chilling effect on public debate. Yet political representatives in a democracy are under pressure from their constituents to justify going to war and to maintain support for a war that is already under way. Reasonable institutional procedures can provide checks and balances on the exercise of political power, presumably with a tendency to yield political decisions that are not egregiously unjust. What about states that are not democratic? Consider Rawls's proposal that their regimes might have a "decent consultation hierarchy": although the citizens are not granted equal political representation as individuals, they could belong to groups represented in a consultation hierarchy, having by proxy "the right at some point in the procedure of consultation (often at the stage of selecting a group's representatives) to express political dissent."[46] Substantial political representation of a people and accountability to them are possible in the absence of democracy. Representative authority is not exclusive to democratic states.

The deeply distinctive problem for nonstate terrorists now emerges. That they lack legitimate authority is only a rough indication of the problem. Political violence by nonstate actors is objectionable when they employ it on their own initiative, so that their political goals, their violent methods, and, ultimately, their claim to rightful use of force do not go through any process of relevant public review and endorsement. Non-state terrorism's distinctive wrongness does not lie in the terrorism but rather in the resort to political

violence without adequate license from a people on whose behalf the violence is purportedly undertaken.

We must recognize a distinction here between legitimate authority and representative authority. For nonstate actors, representative authority is the crucial kind of authority. While states are usually treated as the entities that have legitimacy in international relations, lack of statehood does not strictly indicate the deeper problem with political violence by nonstate actors. A nonstate group may have representative authority: the group not only would take itself to act on behalf of a people but also would be acting on the people's behalf given credible measures of approval by that people. Such measures, for example, mass demonstrations, general strikes, and polling, might lie outside formal political procedures. This raises concerns about the reliability of the measures and their interpretation by actors unfettered by the responsibilities of formal political leadership. These concerns are less of an issue when the right to resort to political violence belongs only to the state, that is, when the state has morally robust legitimate authority. Viable states function with established lines of authority for political decision making, which undergirds domestic stability and practicable international relations. In addition, states are more susceptible than nonstate actors to inducements and deterrents (e.g., economic cooperation, political sanctions, the threat of military action) aimed at promoting justice at home and abroad. Considerations of this sort motivate the prevailing view that statehood is prerequisite to permissible resort to political violence.

But the argument from the importance of statehood seems mainly pragmatic. The tendency that a state monopoly of political violence has to yield morally salient advantages does not indicate that political violence by nonstate actors is always morally objectionable. That a nonstate group does not have control of a state, does not exercise the full functions of a government, and has not conducted elections or put into place a just consultation hierarchy is not a sufficient basis for denying that the group has representative authority as a condition for permissible resort to political violence. The representative authority that nonstate groups may have, if in fact they often lack it, can be morally analogous to the legitimate authority of states. For instance, the FLN (National Liberation Front) came to have representative authority in relation to the Algerian people during Algeria's fight for independence from France, whereas Al-Qaeda does not have representative authority in pursuing militant Islamist goals in the name of the Muslim people. Appropriate wariness about nonstate groups claiming to have representative authority does not warrant rejecting all such claims *tout court.*

There is an apparent difficulty with how to construe a people. Individuals may be thought of as a people when they collectively identify on the basis of their self-ascribed nationality, ethnicity, culture, or religion, or on the basis of being victims of common oppressors (e.g., members of non-Arab ethnic groups in the Darfur region of Sudan vis- à-vis the Janjaweed militia). This differs from an understanding on which "the concept of 'people' belongs to the same social category as 'family' or 'tribe,' that is, a people is one of those social units whose existence is independent of their members' consciousness."[47] The former, more expansive understanding is at work in my argument from representative authority, which leads to a worry. If individuals can collectively identify to comprise a people, there could be a proliferation of peoples, with the result that all kinds of groups could have

gerrymandered representative authority.[48] Al-Qaeda could have representative authority that derives from the support of militant, fundamentalist Muslims in particular rather than of Muslims generally.

While my account of representative authority seems open to such a possibility, the worry is not as pressing as it may seem. Nonstate actors usually purport to represent as broad a constituency as possible in undertaking political violence. The reason is clear: the broader and less gerrymandered the constituency, for example, "the Muslim people" or "the nation," the greater the appearance of representative authority that is morally compelling. "In a verse applicable to all Muslims," contends Zayn Kassam, "Quran 5:32 states, 'whosoever kills a human being for other than manslaughter or corruption in the earth, it shall be as if he had killed all human kind. . . .' Can the assertion of what constitutes 'manslaughter' or 'corruption' be left to the judgment of individuals not accountable to civic institutions? Surely not."[49] While I would substitute accountability to a people in place of accountability to civic institutions, Kassam's point is well taken. Any morally serious claim to having adequate license to employ political violence, namely, through having representative authority, will not come from a parochial source that answers only to the edicts of leaders who lack relevant public approval.

I have suggested that accountability through approval by a people is necessary for resorting to political violence on its behalf. This kind of license can be a practical means of keeping violence under control. But if political violence is objectively justifiable under the circumstances, perhaps concerned actors permissibly could employ it without being backed by either legitimate authority or representative authority.[50] When there is an indisputable humanitarian disaster,

for example, such as the Rwandan genocide, no appeal to the victimized people's
express approval seems necessary to permit violent intervention to protect its
members. My view can accommodate
such cases, since the victimized peoples
almost certainly would accept any helpful intervention. In cases where political
violence may seem objectively justifiable
but the humanitarian situation is not
as dire, we cannot be as confident about
the warrant to intervene. For instance,
Indians may well have had just cause for
resorting to violence in their anticolonial
struggle for independence from British
rule. It would have been objectionable,
though, to disregard the Indian people's
ethical and strategic commitment to pursuing independence through nonviolent
resistance under Gandhi. To recognize
that there is just cause for resorting to
political violence is not simply to permit
concerned actors to employ it without the
approval of the people on whose behalf
the violence would be undertaken.

All of this invites the basic question of
why representative authority is as important as I have claimed. On my view, a
people must have the opportunity to determine what its significant interests are and
how those interests are to be pursued
within the boundaries of justice. The value
of this kind of autonomy is partly instrumental. We should assume, analogously to
the case of individuals, that a people is
most motivated and best situated to evaluate its own interests. Further, we should
assume that a people has the capacity to
act accordingly, by enlisting its own members or seeking assistance from others,
unless there is strong evidence to the contrary. But the value of autonomy is not
merely instrumental: its value is fundamentally tied to treating individuals or a
people with respect that is due rational,

reasonable agents. In concrete terms,
autonomy means that a people must have
a substantial say over actions that would
be done in its name and for its sake. When
the matter is as serious as the resort to
political violence, whether this takes the
form of terrorism or conventional war,
the value of autonomy is heightened. False
or unfounded claims to representative
authority are especially objectionable in
this context.

The requirement of representative
authority as a condition for employing
political violence on behalf of a people
expresses the value of autonomy. Typically,
nonstate actors engaged in terrorism do not
meet this requirement, though there have
been notable exceptions that include the
ANC, the FLN, and the PLO (Palestinian
Liberation Organization) at some periods
in their histories. Tyrannical regimes,
despite having control of a state, never
meet this requirement, though dictatorial
regimes that have the majority support of
their people might. A state that lacks legitimate authority is also likely to lack representative authority to act on behalf of the
major substate groups or peoples within its
territory, such as Kurds, Shiites, and
Sunnis in Iraq. More precisely, then, my
claim that there is a distinctive sense in
which terrorism can be wrong holds with
regard to a defeasible perspective from
which nonstate actors lack representative
authority and states have it.

The ultimate source of the value of
autonomy as expressed by the requirement of representative authority is internal to a people on whose behalf political
violence would be undertaken. It is true
that, in order to meet this requirement,
the goals and methods of political violence must go through a process of relevant public review and endorsement—a
process that seems more likely than some

nonrepresentative route to yield courses of action that are, at least, less unjust. To this extent, outsiders to a people have moral reason to care about representative authority. But the requirement of representative authority is not driven by the interests of outsiders, even as prospective victims. The internal moral importance of representative authority might make no difference to them. If the cause for political violence is just, victims on the other side would not be wronged with respect to the fact that the violence does not meet the representative authority requirement. When the cause is unjust, the representative authority requirement is morally moot from any perspective.

Conclusion

Let there be no misunderstanding: nonstate groups that have representative authority do not thereby have carte blanche to employ political violence. The same is true for states that have legitimate authority. Representative authority for nonstate groups, like legitimate authority for states, is not sufficient to permit resorting to political violence without just cause. Also worth emphasizing is that the argument from representative authority belongs to my moral evaluation of terrorism. Political violence that has adequate license through relevant public approval may descriptively constitute terrorism, and I have not argued whether terrorism could ever be justifiable. However, when nonstate actors lack morally compelling representative authority, as is often the case, this preempts the possibility of their resort to political violence of any kind being justifiable, except in cases of in disputable humanitarian disaster. States that have morally robust legitimate authority do not face this hurdle—but adequate license is only one condition for

permissible resort to political violence. While nonstate groups often fail at the level of representative authority and often would subsequently fail at the level of just cause, states often directly fail at the level of just cause. The distinctive wrongness of much nonstate terrorism does not support the dominant view that terrorism is necessarily wrong and intrinsically worse than conventional war.

I have argued that terrorism is not distinctively wrong as compared to conventional war in the following respects. Both types of political violence may be waged for just or unjust causes. Both types employ use of force against noncombatants, with conventional war usually causing them many more casualties. War and terrorism hence can be expected to produce fear widely among noncombatants where force is used. Further, states do not necessarily have and nonstate groups do not necessarily lack an adequate kind of authority that is a condition for permissible resort to political violence.

If we believe that terrorism is an evil because of the harm it does to ordinary noncombatants, we should be prepared to accept that the brute reality of war for noncombatants is an evil that is at least on par. The notion that an essential moral difference lies in whether the agents using force intend to harm noncombatants is, in the context of political violence, misplaced. If we believe that war can be justifiable on grounds of just cause and the unavailability of less harmful means, despite the harm it does to noncombatants, we must take seriously whether these same grounds could ever justify terrorism. The failures of the dominant view of terrorism should lead us to adopt either a more critical attitude toward conventional war or a less condemnatory attitude toward terrorism.

Notes

1. See, most notably, Virginia Held, "Terrorism, Rights and Political Goals," in *Violence, Terrorism ans Justice*, ed., R. G. Frey and Christopher W. Morris (Cambridge: Cambridge University Press, 1991), 59–85.
2. See, e.g., Michael Walzer, "Terrorism: A Critique of Excuses," in *Arguing about War* (New Haven, CT: Yale University Press, 2004), 51–66.
3. See Adam Roberts and Richard Guelff, eds., *Documents on the Laws of War*, 3rd ed. (Oxford: Oxford University Press, 1982).
4. Louis P. Pojman, "The Moral Response to Terrorism and Cosmopolitanism," in *Terrorism and International Justice*, ed., James P. Sterba (New York: Oxford University Press, 2003), 135–57, 140.
5. For the revisionist view of the relevance of moral innocence and noninnocence, see Lionel K. McPherson, "Innocence and Responsibility in War," *Canadian Journal of Philosophy* 34 (2004): 485–506; and Jeff McMahan, "The Ethics of Killing in war," *Ethics* 114 (2004): 693–733.
6. David Rodin, "Terrorism without Intention," *Ethics* 114 (2004): 752–71, 755.
7. Ibid., 753.
8. Michael Walzer, *Just and Unjust Wars*, 3rd ed. (New York: Basic, 1977), 255, 268.
9. Walzer's account of "supreme emergency" is controversial. For criticism of this alleged exception to the laws of war, see, e.g., C. A. J. Goady, "Terrorism, Morality, and Supreme Emergency," *Ethics* 114 (2004): 772–89.
10. See C. A. J. Coady, "Terrorism and Innocence," *Journal of Ethics* 8 (2004): 37–58, 40.
11. See McPherson, "Innocence and Responsibility in War."
12. Since the fear-effects clause is not tied to the intentions of the agents using force, there is no issue about assesing an intention to cause fear. The intentions motivating use of force can be irrelevant to the production of fear.
13. Rodin, "Terrorism without Intention," 758.
14. For an account of the just war that is widely cited and accepted, see Walzer, *Just and Unjust Wars*.
15. See, e.g., Coady, "Terrorism and Innocence," 39. Coady's definition refers to "use of violence to attack non-combatants,"
where "attack" means that the violence against them is deliberate.
16. Chris Hedges, *What Every Person Should Know about War* (New York: Free Press, 2003), 7.
17. See, e.g., A. J. Coates, *The Ethics of War* (Manchester: Manchester University Press, 1997), 80.
18. I add the qualification "nonstate" since states have employed tactics (e.g., fire-bombing of cities) and weapons (e.g., chemical, biological, and nuclear) that could count as terrorist.
19. Roberts and Guelff, *Documents on the Laws of War*, 449.
20. Judith Gail Gardam, "Proportionality and Force in International Lar," *American Journal of International Law* 87 (1993): 391–413, 410. To be clear, Gardam is not endorsing this interpretation. For a critical assessmant of standard treatments of proportionality and an altrenative approach, see Lionel K. McPherson, "Excessive Force in War, A 'Golden Rule' Test," *Theoretical Inquiries on Law* 7 (2005): 81–95.
21. James M. Dubik, *Philosophy of Public Affairs* 11 (1982): 351–71, 368. Dubik is responding to Walzer's more demanding requirements that combatants must accept greater costs to themselves for the sake of minimizing harm to noncombatants. See Walzer, *Just and Unjust Wars*, 155.
22. For criticism of the war convention as a source of moral obligation, see Lionel K. McPherson, "The Limits of the War Convention," *Philisophy and Social Criticism* 31 (2005): 147–63.
23. Virginia Held, "Terrorism and War," *Journal of Ethics* 8 (2004): 59–75, 69.
24. Nelson Mandela, "I Am Prepared to Die," in *Mandela, Tambo, and the African National Congress: The Struggle against Apartheid, 1948–1990: A Documentary Survey*, ed. Sheridan Johns and R. Hunt Davis Jr. (New York: Oxford University Press 1991). 115–33, 121.
25. Ibid., 120.
26. Sheridan Johns and R. Hum Davis Jr., "Conclusion: Mandela, Tambo, and the ANC in the 1990s," in their *Mandela, Tambo, and the African National Congress*, 309–17, 312.
27. Roberts and Guelff, *Documents on the Lines of War*, 489. Also see, e.g., Walzer, *Just and Unjust Wars*, 145–46.

28. See, e.g., F. M. Kamm. "Failures of just War Theory: Terror, Harm, and Justice," *Ethics* 114 (2004): 650–92, 652–53.

29. See, e.g., Walzer, *Just and Unjust Wars*, 153.

30. Rodin, "Terrorism without Intention," 764.

31. Ibid., 769.

32. For arguments to a similar conclusion, see Kamm, "Failures of Just War Theory," 664.

33. Judith Jarvis Thomson, "Self-Defense," *Philosophy of Public Affairs* 20 (1991): 283–310. 293.

34. See also Kathrn, "Failures of Just War Theory," 667–68; and T. M. Scanlon, "Intention and Permissibility," *Proceedings of the Aristoledian Society* 74 (2000): S301–S317, S310–S312.

35. This response to Thomson was suggested to me by Jeff McMahan.

36. G. E. M. Anscombe "War and Murder," in her *Ethics, Religion and Politics* (Mineapolis: University of Minnesota Press, 1981), 51–61, 58. It is tempting to believe that Thompson-type cases are peculiarly unrepresentative and thus misleading about the DDE's application to conventional war. In typical cases, combatants do not harm to noncombatants. and even foreseeable high risk is not Knowledge. Yet the DDE, does not invoke a distinction between prior knowledge of evil effects and risk of evil effects. The agent's intention is supposed to make a moral difference in its own right.

37. Kamm, "Failures of Just War Theory," 664.

38. A similar point, albert against the DDE, and its requirements of necessity and proportionality, is made by Rodin, "Terrorism without Intention," 765.

39. Christine M. Korsgaard, "The Reasons We Can Share: An Attack on the Distinction between Agent-Relative and Agent-Neutral Values," *Social Philosophy and Policy* 10 (1993): 24–51, 46.

40. See Thomas Hobbes, *Leviathan* (1631), cd. G. B. Macpherson (Harmondsworth: Penquin, 1968), chaps. 13–14. Also see Charles R. Beitz, *Political Theory and International Relations* (Princeton, NJ: Princeton University Press, 1979), chaps. 1–2; and David Rochin, *War and Self-Defence* (New York: Oxford University Press, 2002), 144–18.

41. John Rawls, *The Law of Peoples* (Cambridge, MA: Harvard University Press, 1999), 24.

42. Walzer, *Just and Unjust Wars*, 28.

43. See McPherson, "Innocense and Responsibility in War," 494–97.

44. The fact that combatants for an unjust war fight under domestic legal and parriotie duress and in personal self-defense is immaterial to the permissibility of conduct that their conduct typically is excusable to some degree.

45. This is compatible with recognizing that punishment can be appropriately imposed on the political leaders, who, in administrating the state's authority and sending combatants to fight an unjust war, bear primary moral responsibility for the injustice done by the combatants on the battlefield.

46. Rawls, *The Law of Peoples*, 71–72.

47. Yael Tamir, *Liberal Nationalism* (Princeton, NJ: Princeton University Press, 1993), 65.

48. Sharon Street pressed me on this point.

49. Zayn Kassam, "Can a Muslim Be a Terrorist?" in Sterba, *Terrorism and International Justice*, 113–3–1, 130.

50. Jeff McMahan pressed me on this point.

Study Questions for Section 7

1. Walzer and McPherson work with somewhat different definitions of terrorism. How does this feature of their arguments affect their conclusions?

2. Do you agree with Walzer in finding a moral difference between attacking soldiers and attacking political officials?

3. McPherson argues that terrorism is not distinctively wrong as compared to war, and thus our moral attitudes toward war and terrorism should be roughly similar. Are his arguments compelling? How would Walzer respond?

SECTION 8

TORTURE

TORTURE

Henry Shue

But no one dies in the right place
Or in the right hour
And everyone dies sooner than his time
And before he reaches home.

—*Reza Baraheni*

Whatever one might have to say about torture, there appear to be moral reasons for not saying it. Obviously I am not persuaded by these reasons, but they deserve some mention. Mostly, they add up to a sort of Pandora's Box objection: if practically everyone is opposed to all torture, why bring it up, start people thinking about it, and risk weakening the inhibitions against what is clearly a terrible business?

Torture is indeed contrary to every relevant international law, including the laws of war. No other practice except slavery is so universally and unanimously condemned in law and human convention. Yet, unlike slavery, which is still most definitely practiced but affects relatively few

people, torture is widespread and growing. According to Amnesty International, scores of governments are now using some torture—including governments which are widely viewed as fairly civilized—and a number of governments are heavily dependent upon torture for their very survival.[1]

So, to cut discussion of this objection short, Pandora's Box is open. Although virtually everyone continues ritualistically to condemn all torture publicly, the deep conviction, as reflected in actual policy, is in many cases not behind the strong language. In addition, partial justifications for some of the torture continue to circulate.[2]

One of the general contentions that keeps coming to the surface is: since killing is worse than torture, and killing is sometimes permitted, especially in war, we ought sometimes to permit torture, especially when the situation consists of a protracted, if undeclared, war between a government and its enemies. I shall try first to show the weakness of this argument. To establish that one argument for permitting some torture is unsuccessful is, of course, not to establish that no torture is to be permitted. But in the

From Henry Shue, "Torture," *Philosophy & Public Affairs*, vol. 1, no. 2, (1978). Reprinted by permission of Blackwell Publishing.

remainder of the essay I shall also try to show, far more interestingly, that a comparison between some type of killing in combat and some types of torture actually provides an insight into an important respect in which much torture is morally worse. This respect is the degree of satisfaction of the primitive moral prohibition against assault upon the defenseless. Comprehending how torture violates this prohibition helps to explain—and justify—the peculiar disgust which torture normally arouses.

The general idea of the defense of at least some torture can be explained more fully, using "just-combat killing" to refer to killing done in accord with all relevant requirements for the conduct of warfare.[3] The defense has two stages:

> A since (1) just-combat killing is total destruc-
>   tion of a person.
>
>   (2) torture is—usually—only partial
>   destruction or temporary inca-
>   pacitation of a person, and
>
>   (3) the total destruction of a person is
>   a greater harm than the partial
>   destruction of a person is,
>
>   then (4) just-combat killing is a greater
>   harm than torture usually is.
>
> B since (4) just-combat killing is a greater
>   harm than torture usually is, and
>
>   (5) just-combat killing is sometimes
>   morally permissible,
>
>   then (6) torture is sometimes morally
>   permissible.

To state the argument one step at a time is to reveal its main weakness. Stage B tacitly assumes that if a greater harm is sometimes permissible, then a lesser harm is too, at least sometimes. The mistake is to assume that the only consideration relevant to moral permissibility is the amount of harm done. Even if one grants that killing someone in combat is doing him or her a greater harm than torturing him or her (Stage A), it by no means follows that there could not be a justification for the

greater harm that was not applicable to the lesser harm. Specifically, it would matter if some killing could satisfy other moral constraints (besides the constraint of minimizing harm) which no torture could satisfy.[4]

A defender of at least some torture could, however, readily modify the last step of the argument to deal with the point that one cannot simply weigh amounts of "harm" against each other but must consider other relevant standards as well by adding a final qualification:

> (6') torture is sometimes morally permissi-
> ble, provided that it meets whichever stan-
> dards are satisfied by just-combat killing.

If we do not challenge the judgment that just-combat killing is a greater harm than torture usually is, the question to raise is: Can torture meet the standards satisfied by just-combat killing? If so, that might be one reason in favor of allowing such torture. If not, torture will have been reaffirmed to be an activity of an extremely low moral order.

Assault upon the Defenseless

The laws of war include an elaborate, and for the most part long-established, code for what might be described as the proper conduct of the killing of other people. Like most codes, the laws of war have been constructed piecemeal and different bits of the code serve different functions.[5] It would almost certainly be impossible to specify any one unifying purpose served by the laws of warfare as a whole. Surely major portions of the law serve to keep warfare within one sort of principle of efficiency by requiring that the minimum destruction necessary to the attainment of legitimate objectives be used.

However, not all the basic principles incorporated in the laws of war could be justified as serving the purpose of minimizing destruction. One of the most basic principles for the conduct of war (*jus in bello*) rests on the distinction between combatants and noncombatants and requires that insofar as possible, violence not be directed at noncombatants.[6] Now, obviously, there are some conceptual difficulties in trying to separate combatants and noncombatants in some guerrilla warfare and even sometimes in modern conventional warfare among industrial societies. This difficulty is a two-edged sword, it can be used to argue that it is increasingly impossible for war to be fought justly as readily as it can be used to argue that the distinction between combatants and noncombatants is obsolete. In any case, I do not now want to defend or criticize the principle of avoiding attack upon noncombatants but to isolate one of the more general moral principles this specific principle of warfare serves.

It might be thought to serve, for example, a sort of efficiency principle in that it helps to minimize human casualties and suffering. Normally, the armed forces of the opposing nations constitute only a fraction of the respective total populations. If the casualties can be restricted to these official fighters, perhaps total casualties and suffering will be smaller than they would be if human targets were unrestricted.

But this justification for the principle of not attacking noncombatants does not ring true. Unless one is determined a priori to explain everything in terms of minimizing numbers of casualties, there is little reason to believe that this principle actually functions primarily to restrict the number of casualties rather than, as its own terms suggest, the *types* of casualties.[7] A more convincing suggestion about the best justification which could be given is that the principle goes some way toward keeping combat humane, by protecting those who are assumed to be incapable of defending themselves. The principle of warfare is an instance of a more general moral principle which prohibits assaults upon the defenseless.[8]

Nonpacifists who have refined the international code for the conduct of warfare have not necessarily viewed the killing involved in war as in itself any less terrible than pacifists view it. One fundamental function of the distinction between combatants and noncombatants is to try to make a terrible combat fair, and the killing involved can seem morally tolerable to nonpacifists in large part because it is the outcome of what is conceived as a fair procedure. To the extent that the distinction between combatants and noncombatants is observed, those who are killed will be those who were directly engaged in trying to kill their killers. The fairness may be perceived to lie in this fact: that those who are killed had a reasonable chance to survive by killing instead. It was kill or be killed for both parties, and each had his or her opportunity to survive. No doubt the opportunities may not have been anywhere near equal—it would be impossible to restrict wars to equally matched opponents. But at least none of the parties to the combat were defenseless.

Now this obviously invokes a simplified, if not romanticized, portrait of warfare. And at least some aspects of the laws of warfare can legitimately be criticized for relying too heavily for their justification on a core notion that modern warfare retains aspects of a knightly joust, or a duel, which have long since vanished, if ever they were present. But the point now is not to attack or defend the efficacy of the principle of warfare that combat is more acceptable morally if restricted to official combatants, but to notice one of its moral bases, which, I am suggesting, is that it allows for a "fair fight" by means of protecting the utterly defenseless from assault. The resulting picture of war—accurate or not—is not of victim and perpetrator (or, of mutual victims) but of a winner and a loser, each of whom might have enjoyed, or suffered, the fate of the other. Of course, the satisfaction of the requirement of providing for a "fair fight" would not by itself make a conflict morally acceptable overall. An unprovoked and otherwise unjustified invasion does not become morally acceptable just because attacks upon noncombatants, use of prohibited weapons, and so on are avoided.

At least part of the peculiar disgust which torture evokes may be derived from its apparent failure to satisfy even this weak constraint of being a "fair fight." The supreme reason, of course, is that torture begins only after the fight is—for the victim—finished. Only losers are tortured. A "fair fight" may even in fact already have occurred and led to the capture of the person who is to be tortured. But now that the torture victim has exhausted all means of defense and is powerless before the victors, a fresh assault begins. The surrender is followed by new attacks upon the defeated by the now unrestrained conquerors. In this respect torture is indeed not analogous to the killing in battle of a healthy and well-armed foe: it is a cruel assault upon the defenseless. In combat the other person one kills is still a threat when killed and is killed in part for the sake of one's own survival. The torturer inflicts pain and damage upon another person who, by virtue of now being within his or her power, is no longer a threat and is entirely at the torturer's mercy.

It is in this respect of violating the prohibition against assault upon the defenseless, then, that the manner in which torture is conducted is morally more reprehensible than the manner in which killing would occur if the laws of war were honored. In this respect torture sinks below even the well-regulated mutual slaughter of a justly fought war.

Torture within Constraints?

But is all torture indeed an assault upon the defenseless? For, it could be argued in support of some torture that in many cases there is something beyond the initial surrender which the torturer wants from the victim and that in such cases the victim could comply and provide the torturer with whatever is wanted. To refuse to comply with the further demand would then be to maintain a second line of defense. The victim would, in a sense, not have surrendered—at least not fully surrendered—but instead only retreated. The victim is not, on this view, utterly helpless in the face of unrestrainable assault as long as he or she holds in reserve an act of compliance which would satisfy the torturer and bring the torture to an end.

It might be proposed, then, that there could be at least one type of morally less unacceptable torture. Obviously the torture victim must remain defenseless in the literal sense, because it cannot be expected that his or her captors would provide means of defense against themselves. But an alternative to a capability for a literal defense is an effective capability for surrender, that is, a form of surrender which will in fact bring an end to attacks. In the case of torture the relevant form of surrender might seem to be a compliance with the wishes of the torturer that provides an escape from further torture.

Accordingly, the constraint on the torture that would, on this view, make it less objectionable would be this: the victim of torture must have available an act of compliance which, if performed, will end the torture. In other words, the purpose of the torture must be known to the victim, the purpose must be the performance of some action within the victim's power to perform, and the victim's performance of the desired action must produce the permanent cessation of the torture.

I shall refer to torture that provides for such an act of compliance as torture that satisfies the constraint of possible compliance. As soon becomes clear, it makes a great difference what kind of act is presented as the act of compliance. And a person with an iron will, a great sense of honor, or an overwhelming commitment to a cause may choose not to accept voluntarily cessation of the torture on the terms offered. But the basic point would be merely that there should be some terms understood so that the victim retains one last portion of control over his or her fate. Escape is not defense, but it is a manner of protecting oneself. A practice of torture that allows for escape through compliance might seem immune to the charge of engaging in assault upon the defenseless. Such is the proposal.

One type of contemporary torture, however, is clearly incapable of satisfying the constraint of possible compliance. The extraction of information from the victim, which perhaps—whatever the deepest motivations of torturers may have been— has historically been a dominant explicit purpose of torture is now, in world practice, overshadowed by the goal of the intimidation of people other than the victim.[9] Torture is in many countries used primarily to intimidate potential opponents of the government from actively expressing their opposition in any form considered objectionable by the regime. Prohibited forms of expression range, among various regimes, from participation in terroristic guerrilla movements to the publication of accurate news accounts. The extent of the suffering inflicted upon the victims of the torture is proportioned, not according to the responses of the victim, but according to the expected impact of news of the torture upon other people over whom the torture victim normally has no control. The function of general intimidation of others, or deterrence of dissent, is radically different from the function of extracting specific information under the control of the victim of torture, in respects which are central to the assessment of such torture. This is naturally not to deny that any given instance of torture may serve, to varying degrees, both purposes— and, indeed, other purposes still.

Terroristic torture, as we may call this dominant type, cannot satisfy the constraint of possible compliance, because its purpose (intimidation of persons other than the victim of the torture) cannot be accomplished and may not even be capable of being influenced by the victim of the torture. The victim's suffering—indeed, the victim—is being used entirely as a means to an end over which the victim has no control. Terroristic torture is a pure case—the purest possible case—of the violation of the Kantian principle that no person may be used *only* as a means. The victim is simply a site at which great pain occurs so that others may know about it and be frightened by the prospect. The torturers have no particular reason not to make the suffering as great and as extended as possible. Quite possibly the more terrible the torture, the more intimidating it will be—this is certainly likely to be believed to be so.

Accordingly, one ought to expect extensions into the sorts of "experimentation" and other barbarities documented recently in the cases of, for example, the Pinochet government in Chile and the Amin government in Uganda.[10] Terroristic torturers have no particular reason not to carry the torture through to the murder of the victim, provided the victim's family or friends can be expected to spread the word about the price of any conduct compatible with disloyalty. Therefore, terroristic torture clearly cannot satisfy even the extremely mild constraint of providing for the possibility of compliance by its victim.[11]

The degree of need for assaults upon the defenseless initially appears to be quite different in the case of torture for the purpose of extracting information, which we may call *interrogational torture*.[12] This type of torture needs separate examination because, however condemnable we ought in the end to consider it overall, its purpose of gaining information appears to be consistent with the observation of some constraint on the part of any torturer genuinely pursuing that purpose alone. Interrogational torture does have a built-in end-point: when the information has been obtained, the torture has accomplished its purpose and need not be continued. Thus, satisfaction of the constraint of possible compliance seems to be quite compatible with the explicit end of interrogational torture, which could be terminated upon the victim's compliance in providing the information sought. In a fairly obvious fashion the torturer could consider himself or herself to have completed the assigned task—or probably more hopefully, any superiors who were supervising the process at some emotional distance could consider the task to be finished and put a stop to it. A pure case of interrogational torture, then, appears able to satisfy the constraint of possible compliance, since it offers an escape, in the form of providing the information wanted by the torturers, which affords some protection against further assault.

Two kinds of difficulties arise for the suggestion that even largely interrogational torture could escape the charge that it includes assaults upon the defenseless. It is hardly necessary to point out that very few actual instances of torture are likely to fall entirely within the category of interrogational torture. Torture intended primarily to obtain information is by no means always in practice held to some minimum necessary amount. To the extent that the torturer's motivation is sadistic or otherwise brutal, he or she will be strongly inclined to exceed any rational calculations about what is sufficient for the stated purpose. In view of the strength and nature of a torturer's likely passions—of, for example, hate and self-hate, disgust and self-disgust, horror and fascination, subservience toward superiors and aggression toward victims—no constraint is to be counted upon in practice.

Still, it is of at least theoretical interest to ask whether torturers with a genuine will to do so could conduct interrogational torture in a manner which would satisfy the constraint of possible compliance. In order to tell, it is essential to grasp specifically what compliance would normally involve. Almost all torture is "political" in the sense that it is inflicted by the government in power upon people who are, seem to be, or might be opposed to the government. Some torture is also inflicted by opponents of a government upon people who are, seem to be, or might be supporting the government. Possible victims of torture fall into three broad categories: the ready collaborator, the innocent bystander, and the dedicated enemy.

First, the torturers may happen upon someone who is involved with the other side but is not dedicated to such a degree that cooperation with the torturers would, from the victim's perspective, constitute a betrayal of anything highly valued. For such a person a betrayal of cause and allies might indeed serve as a form of genuine escape.

The second possibility is the capture of someone who is passive toward both sides and essentially uninvolved. If such a bystander should happen to know the relevant information—which is very unlikely—and to be willing to provide it, no torture would be called for. But what if the victim would be perfectly willing to provide the information sought in order to escape the torture but does not have the information? Systems of torture are notoriously incompetent. The usual situation is captured with icy accuracy by the reputed informal motto of the Saigon police: "If they are not guilty, beat them until they are."[13] The victims of torture need an escape not only from beatings for what they know but also from beatings for what they do not know. In short, the victim has no convincing way of demonstrating that he or she cannot comply, even when compliance is impossible. (Compare the reputed dunking test for witches: if the woman sank, she was an ordinary mortal.)

Even a torturer who would be willing to stop after learning all that could be learned, which is nothing at all if the "wrong" person is being tortured, would have difficulty discriminating among pleas. Any keeping of the tacit bargain to stop when compliance has been as complete as possible would likely be undercut by uncertainty about when the fullest possible compliance had occurred. The difficulty of demonstrating that one had collaborated as much as one could might in fact haunt the collaborator as well as the innocent, especially if his or her collaboration had struck the torturers as being of little real value.

Finally, when the torturers succeed in torturing someone genuinely committed to the other side, compliance means, in a word, betrayal; betrayal of one's ideals and one's comrades. The possibility of betrayal cannot be counted as an escape. Undoubtedly some ideals are vicious and some friends are partners in crime—this can be true of either the government, the opposition, or both. Nevertheless, a betrayal is no escape for a dedicated member of either a government or its opposition, who cannot collaborate without denying his or her highest values.[14]

For any genuine escape must be something better than settling for the lesser of two evils. One can always try to minimize one's losses—even in dilemmas from which there is no real escape. But if accepting the lesser of two evils always counted as an escape, there would be no situations from which there was no escape, except perhaps those in which all alternatives happened to be equally evil. On such a loose notion of escape, all conscripts would become volunteers, since they could always desert. And all assaults containing any alternatives would then be acceptable. An alternative which is legitimately to count as an escape must not only be preferable but also itself satisfy some minimum standard of moral acceptability. A denial of one's self does not count.

Therefore, on the whole, the apparent possibility of escape through compliance tends to melt away upon examination. The ready collaborator and the innocent bystander have some hope of an acceptable escape, but only provided that the torturers both (a) are persuaded that the victim has kept his or her part of the bargain by telling all there is to tell and (b) choose to keep their side of the bargain in a situation in which agreements cannot be enforced upon them and they have nothing to lose by continuing the torture if they please. If one is treated as if one is a dedicated enemy, as seems likely to be the standard procedure, the fact that one actually belongs in another category has no effect. On the other hand, the dedicated enemies of the torturers, who presumably tend to know more and consequently are the primary intended targets of the torture, are provided with nothing which can be considered an escape and can only protect themselves, as torture victims always have, by pretending to be collaborators or innocents, and thereby imperiling the members of these two categories.

Morally Permissible Torture?

Still, it must reluctantly be admitted that the avoidance of assaults upon the defenseless is not the only, or even in all cases an overriding, moral consideration. And, therefore, even if terroristic and interrogational torture, each in its own way, is bound to involve attacks upon people unable to defend themselves or to escape, it is still not utterly inconceivable that instances of one or the other type of torture might sometimes, all things considered, be justified. Consequently, we must sketch the elements of an overall assessment of these two types of torture, beginning again with the dominant contemporary form: terroristic.

Anyone who thought an overall justification could be given for an episode of terroristic torture would at the least have to provide a clear statement of necessary conditions, all of which would have to be satisfied before any actions so extraordinarily cruel as terroristic torture could be morally acceptable. If the torture were actually to be justified, the conditions would, of course, have to be met in fact. An attempt to specify the necessary conditions for a morally permissible episode of terroristic torture might include conditions such as the following. A first necessary condition would be that the purpose actually being sought through the torture would need to be not only morally good but supremely important, and examples of such purposes would have to be selected by criteria of moral importance which would themselves need to be justified. Second, terroristic torture would presumably have to be the least harmful means of accomplishing the supremely important goal. Given how very harmful terroristic torture is, this could rarely be the case. And it would be unlikely unless the period of use of the torture in the society was limited in an enforceable manner. Third, it would have

to be absolutely clear for what purpose the terroristic torture was being used, what would constitute achievement of that purpose, and thus, when the torture would end. The torture could not become a standard practice of government for an indefinite duration. And so on.

But is there any supremely important end to which terroristic torture could be the least harmful means? Could terroristic torture be employed for a brief interlude and then outlawed? Consider what would be involved in answering the latter question. A government could, it might seem, terrorize until the terror had accomplished its purpose and then suspend the terror. There are few, if any, clear cases of a regime's voluntarily renouncing terror after having created, through terror, a situation in which terror was no longer needed. And there is considerable evidence of the improbability of this sequence. Terroristic torture tends to become, according to Amnesty International, "administrative practice": a routine procedure institutionalized into the method of governing.[15] Some bureaus collect taxes, other bureaus conduct torture. First a suspect is arrested, next he or she is tortured. Torture gains the momentum of an ingrained element of a standard operating procedure.

Several factors appear to point in the direction of permanence. From the perspective of the victims, even where the population does not initially feel exploited, terror is very unsuitable to the generation of loyalty. This would add to the difficulty of any transition away from reliance on terror. Where the population does feel exploited even before the torture begins, the sense of outrage (which is certainly rationally justified toward the choice of victims, as we have seen) could often prove stronger than the fear of suffering. Tragically, any unlikelihood that the terroristic torture would "work" would almost guarantee that it would continue to be used. From the perspective of the torturers, it is rare for any entrenched bureau to choose to eliminate itself rather than to try to prove its essential value and the need for its own expansion. This is especially likely if the members of the operation are either thoroughly cynical or thoroughly sincere in their conviction that they are protecting "national security" or some other value taken to be supremely important. The greater burden of proof rests. I would think, on anyone who believes that controllable terroristic torture is possible.

Rousseau says at one point that pure democracy is a system of government suitable only for angels—ordinary mortals cannot handle it. If Rousseau's assumption is that principles for human beings cannot ignore the limits of the capacity of human beings, he is surely right. (This would mean that political philosophy often cannot be entirely nonempirical.) As devilish as terroristic torture is, in a sense it too may be technique only for angels; perhaps only angels could use it within the only constraints which would make it permissible and, then, lay it aside. The partial list of criteria for the acceptable use of terroristic torture sketched above, in combination with strong evidence of the uncontrollability of terroristic torture, would come as close to a reductio ad absurdum as one could hope to produce in political philosophy. Observance of merely the constraints listed would require a degree of self-control and self-restraint, individual and bureaucratic, which might turn out to be saintly. If so, terroristic torture would have been shown to be justifiable only if it could be kept within constraints within which it could almost certainly not be kept.

But if the final objection against terroristic torture turned out to be empirical evidence that it is probably uncontrollable, would not the philosophical arguments themselves turn out to have been irrelevant? Why bother to show that terroristic torture assaults the defenseless, if in the end the case against it is going to rest on an empirical hypothesis about the improbability of keeping such torture within reasonable bounds?

The thesis about assault upon the defenseless matters, even though it is not in itself conclusive, because the uncontrollability thesis could only be probable and would also not be conclusive in itself. It could not be shown to be certain that terroristic torture will become entrenched, will be used for minor purposes, will be used when actually not necessary, and so on. And we sometimes go ahead and allow practices which might get out of hand. The relevance of showing the extent of the assault upon defenseless people is to establish how much is at stake if the practice is allowed and then runs amok. If the evidence for uncontrollability were strong, that fact plus the demonstration of extreme cruelty would constitute a decisive case against terroristic torture. It would, then, never be justified.

Much of what can be said about terroristic torture can also be said about instances involving interrogational torture. This is the case primarily because in practice there are evidently few pure cases of interrogational torture.[16] An instance of torture which is to any significant degree terroristic in purpose ought to be treated as terroristic. But if we keep in mind how far we are departing from most actual practice, we may, as before, consider instances in which the *sole* purpose of torture is to extract certain information and therefore the torturer is willing to stop as soon as he or she is sure that the victim has provided all the information which the victim has.

As argued in the preceding section, interrogational torture would in practice be difficult to make into less of an assault upon the defenseless. The supposed possibility of escape through compliance turns out to depend upon the keeping of a bargain which is entirely unenforceable within the torture situation and upon the making of discriminations among victims that would usually be difficult to make until after they no longer mattered. In fact, since any sensible willing collaborator will cooperate in a hurry, only the committed and the innocent are likely to be severely tortured. More important, in the case of someone being tortured because of profoundly held convictions, the "escape" would normally be a violation of integrity.

As with terroristic torture, any complete argument for permitting instances of interrogational torture would have to include a full specification of all necessary conditions of a permissible instance, such as its serving a supremely important purpose (with criteria of importance), its being the least harmful means to that goal, its having a clearly defined and reachable endpoint, and so on. This would not be a simple matter. Also as in the case of terroristic torture, a considerable danger exists that whatever necessary conditions were specified, any practice of torture once set in motion would gain enough momentum to burst any bonds and become a standard operating procedure. Torture is the ultimate shortcut. If it were ever permitted under any conditions, the temptation to use it increasingly would be very strong.

Nevertheless, it cannot be denied that there are imaginable cases in which the harm that could be prevented by a rare instance of pure interrogational torture would be so enormous as to outweigh the cruelty of the torture itself and, possibly, the enormous potential harm which would result if what was intended to be a rare instance was actually the breaching of the dam which would lead to a torrent of torture. There is a standard philosopher's

example which someone always invokes: suppose a fanatic, perfectly willing to die rather than collaborate in the thwarting of his own scheme, has set a hidden nuclear device to explode in the heart of Paris. There is no time to evacuate the innocent people or even the movable art treasures—the only hope of preventing tragedy is to torture the perpetrator, find the device, and deactivate it.

I can see no way to deny the permissibility of torture in a case *just like this*. To allow the destruction of much of a great city and many of its people would be almost as wicked as purposely to destroy it, as the Nazis did to London and Warsaw, and the Allies did to Dresden and Tokyo, during World War II. But there is a saying in jurisprudence that hard cases make bad law, and there might well be one in philosophy that artificial cases make bad ethics. If the example is made sufficiently extraordinary, the conclusion that the torture is permissible is secure. But one cannot easily draw conclusions for ordinary cases from extraordinary ones, and as the situations described become more likely, the conclusion that the torture is permissible becomes more debatable.

Notice how unlike the circumstances of an actual choice about torture the philosopher's example is. The proposed victim of our torture is not someone we suspect of planting the device: he *is* the perpetrator. He is not some pitiful psychotic making one last play for attention: he *did* plant the device. The wiring is not backwards, the mechanism is not jammed: the device *will* destroy the city if not deactivated.

Much more important from the perspective of whether general conclusions applicable to ordinary cases can be drawn are the background conditions that tend to be assumed. The torture will not be conducted in the basement of a small-town jail in the provinces by local thugs popping pills: the prime minister and chief justice are being kept informed; and a priest and a doctor are present. The victim will not be raped or forced to eat excrement and will not collapse with a heart attack or become deranged be fore talking: while avoiding irreparable damage, the antiseptic pain will carefully be increased only up to the point at which the necessary information is divulged, and the doctor will then immediately administer an antibiotic and a tranquilizer. The torture is purely interrogational.[17]

Most important, such incidents do not continue to happen. There are not so many people with grievances against this government that the torture is becoming necessary more often, and in the smaller cities, and for slightly lesser threats, and with a little less care, and so on. Any judgment that torture could be sanctioned in an isolated case without seriously weakening existing inhibitions against the more general use of torture rests on empirical hypotheses about the psychology and politics of torture. There *is* considerable evidence of all torture's metastatic tendency. If there is also evidence that interrogational torture can sometimes be used with the surgical precision which imagined justifiable cases always assume, such are uses would have to be considered.

Does the possibility that torture might be justifiable in some of the rarefied situations which can be imagined provide any reason to consider relaxing the legal prohibitions against it? Absolutely not. The distance between the situations which must be concocted in order to have a plausible case of morally permissible torture and the situations which actually occur is, if anything, further reason why the existing prohibitions against torture should remain and should be strengthened by making torture an international crime. An act of torture ought to remain illegal so that anyone who sincerely believes such an act to be the least available evil is placed in the position of needing to justify his or her act morally in order to defend himself or herself legally. The torturer should be in roughly the same position as someone who commits civil disobedience. Anyone who thinks an act of torture is justified should have no alternative but to convince a group of peers in a public trial that all necessary conditions for a morally permissible act were indeed satisfied. If it is reasonable to put someone through torture, it is reasonable to put someone else through a careful explanation of why. If the situation approximates those in the imaginary examples in which torture seems possible to justify, a judge can surely be expected to suspend the sentence. Meanwhile, there is little need to be concerned about possible injustice to justified torturers and great need to find means to restrain totally unjustified torture.

Notes

1. See Amnesty International, *Report on Torture* (New York: Farrar, Straus and Giroux, 1975), pp. 21–33.
2. I primarily have in mind conversations which cannot be cited, but for a written source see Roger Trinquier, *La Guerre Moderne* (Paris: La Table Ronde, 1961), pp. 39, 42, 187–191. Consider the following: "Et c'est tricher que d'admettre sereinement que l'artillerie ou l'aviation peuvent bombarder des villages où se trouvent des femmes et des enfants qui setont inutilement massacrés, alors que le plus souvent les ennemis visés auront pu s'enfuir. et refuser que des spécialistes en interrogeant un terroriste permettent de se saisir des vrais coupables et d'épargner les innocents" (p. 42).
3. By "just combat" I mean warfare which satisfies what has traditionally been called *jus in bello*, the law governing how war may be fought once underway, rather than *jus ad bellum*, the law governing when war may be undertaken.

4. Obviously one could also challenge other elements of the argument—most notably, perhaps, premise (3), Torture is usually humiliating and degrading—the pain is normally experienced naked and amidst filth. But while killing destroys life, it need not destroy dignity. Which is worse, an honorable death or a degraded existence? While I am not unsympathetic with this line of attack, I do not want to try to use it. It suffers from being an attempt somehow just to intuit the relative degrees of evil attached respectively to death and degradation. Such judgments should probably be the outcome, rather than the starting point, of an argument. The rest of the essay bears directly on them.

5. See James T. Johnson, *Ideology, Reason, and the Limitation of War: Religious and Secular Concepts 1200–1740* (Princeton: Princeton University Press, 1975). Johnson stresses the largely religious origins at *jus ad bellum* and the largely secular origins of *jus in bello*.

6. For the current law, see Geneva Convention Relative to the Protection of Civilian Persons in Time of War, 12 August 1949 [1955], 6 U.S.T. 3516; T.I.A.S. No. 3365; 75 U.N.T.S. 287. Also see United States, Department of the Army, *The Law of Land Warfare*, Field Manual 27–10 (Washington: Government Printing Office, 1956), Chap. 5, "Civilian Persons"; and United States, Department of the Air Force, *International Law—The Conduct of Armed Conflict and Air Operations*, Air Force Pamphlet 110–31 (Washington: Government Printing Office, 1976), Chap. 3, "Combatants, Noncombatants and Civilians." This Convention was to be revised at a Geneva Conference in 1977; of considerable interest are the recommendations for greater protection of civilians advanced in Subcomm. on International Organizations of the House Comm. on Foreign Affairs, 93d Cong., 2d Sess. (1974), *Human Rights in the World Community: A Call for U.S. Leader ship*, p. 38.

For the history, see Johnson, especially pp. 32–33 and 42–46, although I am interested here in the justification which could be given for the principle today, not the original justification (insofar as it was different).

The prohibition against attack upon noncombatants is considered by some authorities to be fundamental. See, for example, Jean Pictet. *The Principles of International Humanitarian Law* (Geneva: International Committee of the Red Cross, 1966), p. 53:

"This general immunity of the civilian population has not been clearly defined in positive law, but it remains, in spite of many distortions, the basis of the laws of war." It is often assumed by others that the exigencies of a stable form of mutual assured destruction (MAD) make unavoidable the targeting of a nuclear deterrent on the enemy's civilian population and that therefore priority on avoidance of civilian casualties is impossible in nuclear war. For a persuasive contrary view, see Bruce M. Russett, "Assured Destruction of What? A Counter-Combatant Alternative to Nuclear MADness," *Public Policy* 22 (1974): 121–138.

7. This judgment is supported by Stockholm International Peace Research Institute. *The Law of War and Dubious Weapons* (Stockholm: Almqvist & Wiksell, 1976), p. 9: "The prohibition on deliberately attacking the civilian population as such is not based exclusively on the principle of avoiding unnecessary suffering."

8. To defend the bombing of cities in World War II on the ground that *total* casualties (combatant and noncombatant) were thereby reduced is to miss, or ignore, the point.

9. See Amnesty International, 69.

10. See United Nations, General Assembly, Report of the Economic and Social Council. *Protection of Human Rights in Chile* (UN Document A/31/253, 8 October 1976, 31st Session), p. 97; and *Uganda and Human Rights: Reports to the UN Commission on Human Rights* (Geneva: International Commission of Jurists, 1977), p. 118.

11. A further source of arbitrariness is the fact that there is, in addition, no natural limit on the "appropriate" targets of terroristic torture, since the victim does not need to possess any specific information, or to have done anything in particular, except possibly to have acted "suspiciously." Even the latter is not necessary if the judgment is made, as it apparently was by the Nazis, that random terror will be the most effective.

It has been suggested that there might be a category of "deserved" terroristic torture, conducted only after a fair trial had established the guilt of the torture victim for some beinous crime. A fair procedure for determining who is to be tortured would transform the torture into a form of deterrent punishment—doubtless a cruel and unusual one.

Such torture would stand only with a general deterrent theory of punishment according to which *who* is punished depends upon guilt, but *how much* he or she is punished depends upon supposed, deterrent effects. I would think that any finding that terroristic torture could be fitted within a deterrent theory of punishment (provided the torture was preceded by a fair trial) could cut either way and would be at least as plausible a reason for rejecting the general theory as it would be for accepting the particular case of terroristic torture. But I will not pursue this because I am not aware of any current practice of reserving torture as the sentence for people after they are convicted by a trial with the usual safeguards. Torture customarily precedes any semblance of a trial. One can, of course, imagine various sorts of torture other than the two common kinds discussed here.

12. These two categories of torture are not intended to be, and are not, exhaustive. See previous note.
13. Amnesty International, 166.
14. Defenders of privilege customarily portray themselves as defenders of civilization against the vilest barbarians. Self-deception sometimes further smooths the way to treating whoever are the current enemies as beneath contempt and certainly unworthy of equal respect as human beings. Consequently, I am reluctant to concede, even as a limiting case, that there are probably rare individuals so wicked as to lack integrity, or anyway to lack any integrity worthy of respect. But, what sort of integrity could one have violated by torturing Hitler?

    Any very slight qualification here must not, however, be taken as a flinging wide open of the doors. To be beyond the pale in the relevant respect must involve far more than simply serving values which the torturers find abhorrent. Otherwise, license has been granted simply to torture whoever are one's greatest enemies—the only victims very many torturers would want in any case. Unfortunately, I cannot see a way to delimit those who are genuinely beyond the pale which does not beg for abuse.

15. I am assuming the unrestrained character of terroristic torture as it is actually practiced. Besides the general study by Amnesty International cited above and below,

Amnesty International regularly issues studies of individual countries. Of particular interest, perhaps, is: *Report on Allegations of Torture in Brazil,* 3d ed. (London: Amnesty International Publications, 1976). The Committee on International Relations of the United States House of Representatives has published during 1975–1977 extensive hearings on torture in dozens of countries. And other nongovernmental organizations, such as the International Commission of Jurists and the International League for Human Rights, have published careful accounts of the nature of the torture practiced in various particular countries. I believe that the category of terroristic torture used in this article is an accurate reflection of a very high proportion of the actual cases of contemporary torture. It would be tedious to document this here, but see, for example. Amnesty International, pp. 21, 26, 103, 199.

Nevertheless, it can be granted that terroristic torture is not necessarily unrestrained. It is conceivable for torture to fail to be constrained by the responses of its victim but to be subject to other constraints: to use brutality of only a certain degree, to conduct torture of unlimited (or limited) brutality but for only a limited time, to select victims who "deserve" it (compare note II), etc. I have not discussed such a category of "constrained terroristic torture" because I believe it to be empty—for very good psychological and political reasons. On the methodological question here, see the concluding paragraphs of this article.

16. Amnesty International, pp. 24–25, 114–242.
17. For a realistic account of the effects of torture, see *Evidence of Torture: Studies by the Amnesty International Danish Medical Group* (London: Amnesty International Publications, 1977). Note in particular "Undoubtedly the worst sequelae of torture were psychological and neurological" (p. 12). For suggestions about medical ethics for physicians attending persons being tortured, see "Declaration of Tokyo: Guidelines for Medical Doctors Concerning Torture," in United Nations. General Assembly, Note by the Secretary-General, *Torture and Other Cruel, Inhuman or Degrading Treatment or Punishment in Relation to Detention and Imprisonment* (UN Document A/31/234, 6 October 1976. 31st Session), Annex II.

Ticking Bombs, Torture, and the Analogy with Self-Defense

Daniel J. Hill

Introduction

One reads in the press that the agents of many countries, and, indeed, many private individuals, engage in torture to coerce others into performing certain actions, frequently the divulging of information ("interrogational torture"). Sometimes this is undertaken for a good end, such as the saving of lives by the disarming of a ticking time-bomb, or the rescue of a kidnap victim. It will be argued in this paper that such torture and, more generally, interrogational coercion are never morally permissible. This will be a specific application of a general moral principle that will be proposed:

> (P) It is never permissible intentionally to inflict severe pain or severe harm on someone unwiliing, unless the pain/harm is intended (i) for their benefit, or (ii) as a punishment, or (iii) as part of the pursuit of a legitimate war, or (iv) to prevent the individual from causing severe pain or severe harm to innocents.[1]

From Daniel J. Hill, "Ticking Bombs, Torture, and the Analogy with Self-Defense," *American Philosophical Quarterly*, vol. 44, no. 1, Copyright © 2007 by the journal and published with its permission.

Disagreement with this absolute rejection of interrogational torture could come from several directions. Act utilitarians would assert that it is fairly easy to imagine circumstances in which the ends would justify the means of torture: if it were known that many would be killed or suffer extreme pain as a result of a bomb's exploding it would surely be for the greatest happiness of the greatest number that one inflict some not-too-extreme pain on a single individual with the knowledge of the whereabouts of the bomb—provided, of course, that one knew there to be no danger of setting a precedent that would lead to abuses that would outweigh the happiness of the lives saved and pain averted. The key word here is "imagine": many of those that assert that it is possible to *imagine* circumstances in which torture would be justified also assert that *in real life* such circumstances will never obtain.[2] It should further be noted that many suggest that our intuitions concerning imaginary cases are not reliable.[3] This point will not be argued against here, however (even though the argument of this paper depends heavily on intuitions), since those opposed to the thesis of this paper—i.e., those that argue that interrogational torture *is* sometimes permissible—defend their position on the basis of intuition, so this is not a disputed point in this context.

On the other hand, some deontologists may object that principle (P) does not, despite its intended purpose, rule out interrogational torture, for interrogational torture is indeed intended to "prevent the individual from causing severe pain or severe harm to innocents." More generally, some deontologists argue that it is permissible to inflict severe pain or severe harm in self-defense or in defense of another, and that cases of interrogational torture are analogous to these in the relevant moral respects.[4] The bulk of this paper will be devoted to resisting these objections and arguments, and, therefore, to arguing that (P) does indeed absolutely prohibit interrogational torture. Because of the close connection between the objection to (P) and the analogy from self-defense this paper will often simply say "in self-defense" rather than "to prevent the individual from causing severe pain or severe harm to innocents": nevertheless it is the longer formulation that represents the precise position of this paper. This paper will deal only with cases of severe pain/harm, and will also use "torture" interchangeably with "inflict severe pain or severe harm," because the admitted differences in meaning between these two are not in view in this paper. The paper will also ignore, as not relevant to the project in hand, the differences in meaning between "torture" and "coerce."

The Intention to Cause Pain

Let us consider a couple of examples that might be cited to support the analogy between self-defense and interrogational torture.

> Defense Case: A police officer spots a known terrorist about to detonate a bomb, which, if it goes off, will illicitly inflict serious harm and serious pain on many innocents.[5] The officer fires a Taser at the terrorist, intending to cause no serious lasting harm but so much pain that the terrorist will be paralyzed and unable to detonate the bomb.[6]

Most deontologists (and consequentialists) would agree here that it is morally permissible for the police officer to Taser the terrorist in self-defense or defense of others. So far so good, but let us now consider the supposedly analogous case from the world of interrogation.

> Interrogation Case: A known terrorist is in the captivity of the security services of a certain country. He is known to have planted somewhere a ticking bomb, which, if it goes off, will illicitly inflict serious harm and serious pain on many innocents. The security services know that he knows where the bomb is, but he is refusing to divulge its whereabouts. In order to get him to talk they give him electric shocks, intending to cause no serious lasting harm but so much pain that he will say where the bomb is.[7]

The contention of this paper will be that the analogy between Defense and Interrogation is superficial. In fact, it will be contended that there is a fundamental difference between the two. There is a way, admittedly, in which they are similar: each case is a case of intent that pain/harm will be caused—in Defense the terrorist is trying there and then to cause severe pain and severe harm, and in Interrogation the terrorist is deliberately not cooperating in order that the earlier causal chain that he set in motion may reach the terminus he desires. There is also, however, a way in which they are different: Interrogation is not a case of aggression, unlike Defense. In Defense the terrorist is *doing* something—he is attempting to inflict severe pain or severe harm—and force is being used to prevent him from causing a tragedy to happen. In Interrogation, by contrast, the terrorist is powerless, in the custody of the security services, and is not *doing* anything—he has *already* set in motion a causal chain threatening a tragedy, and force is being used to cause him to perform the positive action of causing a tragedy not to happen.[8] It will be argued that this distinction is of crucial moral significance.

It is tempting to say that the reason why it is not permissible in Interrogation to inflict pain on the terrorist to get him to talk is that in this case one would be treating him as a mere means. This may well be correct, but this paper will not pursue that line as it is not wholly clear whether cases of self-defense count as treating aggressors as means. There will now be adumbrated a case to illustrate this point and to refute another possible objection.

The next possible objection to be considered states that the difference between Defense and Interrogation is merely that in Defense the terrorist is not being caused to perform any action, whereas in Interrogation he is. To show that this is too simple, an example of a *permissible* case in which one *does cause* the terrorist to perform an action will now be presented. This case is a slight variation on Defense above:

> Reflex Case: A police officer spots a known terrorist about to detonate a bomb, which, if it goes off, will illicitly inflict serious harm and serious pain on many innocents. The officer sprays the terrorist with a pepper spray, intending to cause on serious lasting harm but so much pain in his eyes that he will instinctively start rubbing his eyes in an effort to relieve the pain, and so won't be able to press the detonator.

Is it permissible to cause the terrorist this pain in order to cause him to rub his eyes and thereby not be able to detonate the bomb? Intuitively, it is, even though here the terrorist is being prevented from detonating

the bomb by being caused to perform an action, unlike in Defense in which the terrorist had been prevented from performing an action (the action of detonation) without being caused to *do* anything.

Is the terrorist being used as a mere means in Reflex? This is not clear, and so this paper will not press the line that this is why it is impermissible to inflict pain in Defense.

Causing a Conscious Action

It might yet be pressed, however, that Reflex was not analogous to Interrogation, because the action was a mere reflex action rather than a consciously chosen one. Once more this does not seem a sound objection. For one thing, it might well be that when in great pain some individuals would "break" and instinctively shout out the answers to questions without consciously choosing to do so. But in any case Reflex can itself be adapted, as is demonstrated by the following case:

> Holding Case: A police officer spots a known terrorist about to detonate a bomb, which, if it goes off, will illicitly inflict serious harm and serious pain on many innocents. The detonator button needs to be held down for ten seconds for the bomb to go off. The only way the terrorist can be prevented from holding down the detonator button for ten seconds is if he is caused such pain that he will choose to take his finger off the detonator button in order to get the pain to stop. The officer shoots the terrorist in the foot, intending to cause no serious lasting harm but so much pain that he will make a conscious decision to stop priming the bomb and turn his attention to nursing his foot.[9]

Intuitively, in Holding the police officer is justified in inflicting pain on the terrorist in order to cause him to choose not to detonate the bomb by choosing to take his finger off the detonation button.

Compare this with the following case:

Withholding Case: A police officer spots a known terrorist about to detonate a bomb, which, if it goes off, will illicitly inflict serious harm and serious pain on many innocents. The detonator button needs to be in the down position for ten seconds for the bomb to go off. The device works in such a way, however, that once pressed the button will remain depressed unless pulled up by someone with the terrorist's fingerprint. The only way the detonator button can be prevented from remaining depressed for ten seconds is if the terrorist is caused such pain that he will choose to pull the detonator button up in order to get the pain to stop. The officer shoots the terrorist in the foot, telling the terrorist that he can expect more pain in the other foot unless he pulls up the detonator button.[10]

Withholding and Holding are superficially very similar, but there is one crucial difference: in Holding the terrorist is prevented from performing an action (holding the button down) and in Withholding the terrorist is not preventing from doing anything—instead he is (just) caused to perform an action, the action of pulling the button up.[11] It would seem that this makes a moral difference. Intuitively, it is not permissible to inflict pain in Withholding in order to compel the terrorist to pull the button up, but intuitively it *is* permissible (as previously stated) for pain to be inflicted in Holding in order that the terrorist might be prevented from pushing the button down.

A Possible Reply: Loss of Human Rights

It might be replied that it is permissible for pain to be inflicted on the terrorist in Withholding and similar cases because the terrorist is guilty of attempting a terrorist atrocity and, as a result of this, has lost his right not to have pain inflicted on him, just as those guilty of crimes lose their right to freedom for a certain time.[12] This means, so the objection goes, that it is morally permissible for pain to be inflicted on him in order that he might be compelled to pull up the detonator button.

It is curious that, while most of those that advance this argument believe that the removal of freedom is a standard punishment for the guilty, relatively few of them believe that the infliction of pain is a standard punishment for the guilty, Yet the removal of freedom is inflicted as a punishment precisely because (at least on a deontological understanding) it is judged that the guilty party has lost the right to freedom: why then do not the proponents of the objection suggest the infliction of pain as a routine punishment? Furthermore, even the proponents of this objection would still think it morally unacceptable if terrorists were tortured for fun, or if the torturers continued to torture even after the terrorists had aborted the ticking bomb. Of course, it could be replied that the terrorists have lost the right against the infliction of less than a certain amount of pain, such as the amount of pain that they themselves were prepared to inflict. This, however, is in marked contrast to the "I'll do whatever it takes to break you" attitude that is usually associated with the torture of terrorist suspects. It also does not accommodate the intuition accepted by proponents of the objection that it is morally obligatory to try to prevent the torture from passing the minimum level necessary to get the terrorist to abort the tragedy. Finally, the supposition that all terrorists lose their right not to have pain inflicted on them has the counter-intuitive consequence of legitimizing the infliction of pain in the following example:

Fellow Case: A terrorist from a large terrorist organization has just been captured. The terrorist has planted a ticking bomb somewhere and it is imperative that its whereabouts be discovered. The terrorist refuses to talk, however. Also in custody is one of his fellow terrorists, from the same terrorist organization, who was captured some time ago, and does not know the whereabouts of the ticking bomb, nor was he involved in this particular attack. The psychologist suggests that the quickest way to get the information out of the newly captured terrorist would be to torture his fellow terrorist in front of him. He says that since both are terrorists, both have lost their right not to have pain inflicted on them.

Surely the psychiatrist would be wrong to suggest the torturing of the fellow, uninvolved, terrorist to get the newly captured one to talk, despite the fact that the fellow terrorist is himself guilty of serious terrorist offences. This seems to show that committing a terrorist outrage does not remove one's right not to be tortured, i.e., to have serious pain or serious harm inflicted on one without one's consent when it is not for one's benefit.

Another Possible Reply: Still Causing the Atrocity

It might be responded that the terrorist in Interrogation and Withholding and similar cases *is* still performing an evil action, viz., the causation of the terrorist atrocity, and that, therefore, the torturer *is* preventing the terrorist from performing an action, and so there is, after all, a similarity with Defense and Holding and similar cases. Miller (2006) puts it thus:

> [T]he terrorist is in the process of completing his (jointly undertaken) action of murdering thousands of innocent people. He has already undertaken his individual actions of, say, transporting and arming the nuclear device; he has performed these individual actions (in the context of other individual actions performed by the other members of the terrorist cell) in

order to realise the end (shared by the other members of the cell) of murdering thousands of Londoners. In refusing to disclose the location of the device the terrorist is preventing the police from preventing him from completing his (joint) action of murdering thousands of innocent people.

Sussman (2005, p. 16) also defends this line:

> Consider again the captured terrorist who we know to have planted a powerful bomb in some crowded civilian area. Although the terrorist is in our power, he refuses to reveal the bomb's location, hoping to strike one last blow against us by allowing a train of events that he has set in motion to come to its intended conclusion. In one sense, the terrorist is indeed defenseless. We can do anything we like to him, and there is nothing he can do to resist or shield himself against us. But such helplessness means neither that the terrorist has ceased to engage in hostilities against us, nor that he is no longer an active military threat. His placing of the bomb was the beginning of an attack on us; his silence, although not any kind of further overt act, is nevertheless voluntary behavior undertaken for the sake of bringing that act to completion. His continued silence thus might well be considered a part of his attack, understood as a temporally extended action.

This raises the big metaphysical question of when one completes an action, (a) when its effects come about, or (b) when one finishes the *basic* actions (i.e., the bodily movements[13]) that ultimately lead to the effects. Intuitively only (b) is tenable as if (a) were correct one would continue performing lots of actions long after one's death. Admittedly, (b) does have the counter-intuitive consequence that a killer kills the victim before the victim dies, but this is less counter-intuitive than the view that one might kill someone after one's death.[14] It follows from (b) that facts about one's actions are "soft facts,"[15] i.e., facts that obtain at least partly in virtue of later events, so, for example, A's killing B on Monday obtains partly in virtue of B's dying on the following Wednesday, as well as partly in virtue of A's leaving slow-acting poison in B's glass on Monday, and B's drinking the poison on Tuesday. It follows, further, that the torturer in Interrogation and Withholding etc. is not preventing the terrorist from performing an action of terror but preventing him from *having performed* an action of terror, and this difference between such cases as Interrogation and Withholding on the one hand, and Defense and Holding on the other hand, seems to make the difference between the licensing of the intentional infliction of severe pain or severe harm in Defense and Holding, but not in Interrogation and Withholding.

Another Possible Reply: Prevention of Non-Cooperation

It might be responded that the terrorist that refuses to abort the bomb or refuses to divulge its whereabouts still uncontroversially intends to perform a different morally evil action, viz., refusing to co-operate with the authorities, and that it is morally permissible to inflict severe pain or severe harm on him to prevent him from fulfilling this intention. The first part of this is quite correct, but not every morally evil action licenses the infliction of severe pain, even in self-defense, as should be made clear by the following example:

> Non-Cooperation Case: Suppose the terrorist has been killed but his wife has been detained alive. She didn't know that her husband was a terrorist, but she does know where he's been spending a lot of time lately. She won't, however, say where until a lawyer skilled in the law of her native land and religion arrives to witness her statement. There is no time to wait for this lawyer, however, but the psychologist suggests that if she were tortured she'd divulge the information in a couple of minutes.

Surely it is not morally permissible to torture the terrorist's innocent wife in Non-cooperation. A historically important case of innocent motives behind non-cooperation is that of the "seal of confession": if a terrorist confesses to a Roman Catholic priest the priest is not allowed to reveal the location of the ticking bomb to the authorities. And we might imagine that even those that are not Roman Catholic priests could promise not to reveal what someone was about to tell them and regard themselves, rightly or wrongly, as absolutely bound by their promise. It would surely be unacceptable to torture them to get the information out of them.[16] This would seem to show that the infliction of pain in Withholding and the like cannot be defended on the grounds that it is designed to prevent the terrorist committing the evil of non-cooperation.

Finally, it may be argued that, although the terrorist in cases of torture such as Withholding and the like doesn't have the intention to perform an action evil enough to justify the infliction of pain to prevent him from performing this action, he does have another intention, which *is* evil enough to warrant torture; he intends that the planned atrocity should happen after all, and this is why he refuses to cooperate. But clearly the fact that he has this intention does not license him to be tortured; there are many terrorist sympathizers throughout the world that have this evil intention, and yet it would be wrong to inflict pain on them unless it were to prevent them from performing an evil action themselves. It may be objected that the terrorist and the sympathizers do not have the *intention* that the atrocity occur: they merely have the *desire* that it occur. It is unclear that this is correct, but if it is permissible to speak of the terrorist's having the intention surely it is also permissible to speak of the sympathizers' having it, at least if they intend to aid and abet it in a certain minor way such as by funding it or praying for its success. It is implausible to maintain that funding a terrorist atrocity is an offence that licenses torture; surely it is even less plausible to maintain that praying for the success of a terrorist atrocity is an offence that licenses torture.

Positive and Negative Duties

What is the basis of this moral difference between preventing someone from performing an action that will cause a tragedy and causing someone to cause a tragedy not to occur? It is an instance of the distinction between our duties to perform certain acts of causation on the one hand, our "positive" duties, and our duties not to perform certain different acts of causation on the other hand, our "negative" duties. Although both the distinction itself and its moral significance have been much attacked in the literature, they do seem to have intuitive support:[17]

> Drowning Case: Suppose A's father and spouse have been deliberately pushed by B into a lake and are drowning; A can rescue one, but only one, of them. A chooses to swim past his father to save his spouse.

Intuitively, in Drowning, A has not caused the death of his father; that was caused by B. And intuitively there is a moral difference between A's choosing to refrain from saving his father in order to save his spouse on the one hand, and the deliberate pushing in by B of A's father on the other hand. Even if A's action of refraining from saving his father is morally bad, it surely isn't as morally bad as that of B. Finally, intuitively there is a distinction between the negative duty not deliberately to push the unwilling non-swimmer into a lake—a duty flouted by B—and the positive duty to save one's father from drowning if one can—a duty not satisfied by A, who could have saved his father, but saved his spouse instead.

It seems permissible, then, in some circumstances to inflict pain to force people to comply with their negative duties, but it does not seem permissible to inflict pain in order to force people to comply with their positive duties, even extremely important positive duties, such as the duty to avert an atrocity that the people in question have set in motion. In this sense negative duties are more important than positive duties, and the infliction of pain to force some-one to comply with a positive duty would *itself* be a breach of a negative duty. On the other hand, failure to inflict pain to enforce a positive duty would not itself be a breach of a positive duty, though failure to inflict pain to enforce a negative duty in certain circumstances *would* be a breach of a positive duty: if a police officer refuses to shoot a terrorist in the foot when that is the only way to prevent him from detonating a devastating bomb then he or she is in breach of his or her duty to defend innocent citizens. On the other hand, as has been argued, the officer's duty to defend innocent citizens does not extend to a duty to shoot a captured terrorist in the foot to force him to divulge the whereabouts of a ticking bomb, as this would be a breach of a negative duty.

One can see that it is not the case that positive duties should be enforced by the infliction of pain by considering the following case:

> Expert Case: A ticking bomb has been located, and the only person that can defuse it is a retired bomb-disposal expert. He, however, doesn't want to come to defuse the bomb because he

doesn't want to leave the bedside of his dying wife.

It would clearly be wrong on the deontological scheme to torture the bomb-disposal expert in Expert to get him to defuse the bomb, even if he has a duty to help. Moreover, intuitively it would still be wrong to torture him even if he was "on duty" and not retired, but was being insubordinate.

Conclusion

It appears that what underlies the cases that have been discussed in this paper is the principle mentioned earlier:

(P) It is never permissible intentionally to inflict severe pain or severe harm on someone unwilling, unless the pain/harm is intended (i) for their benefit, or (ii) as a punishment, or (iii) as part of the pursuit of a legitimate war, or (iv) to prevent the individual from causing severe pain or severe harm to innocents.

(P) implies that it is impermissible to act in standard torture cases (such as Interrogation). It does not imply that it is impermissible to act in standard cases of self-defense and defense of others (such as Defense). This is as it should be, for it is intuitively permissible to inflict severe pain or severe harm in Defense and similar cases to prevent the aggressor from causing severe pain or severe harm to innocents, but intuitively impermissible to inflict severe pain or severe harm in cases such as Interrogation and standard torture cases.

In this paper it has been argued that there is no inconsistency in giving different moral opinions on the different cases: Defense and similar cases on the one hand, and Interrogation and similar cases on the other hand. An attempt has been made to identify the relevant difference in these cases: the fact that in Defense and similar cases pain is being inflicted in order to enforce a negative duty, i.e., to prevent the individual from causing severe pain or severe harm to innocents, whereas in Interrogation and similar cases it is not. It has been conceded that it is not true that it is never permissible to inflict severe pain or severe harm with the intention of causing the aggressor to perform an action—some cases of the infliction of pain in self-defense are counter-examples. A suggestion has been made that it was permissible for a police officer to inflict pain to cause a terrorist to choose to, perform the action of nursing his foot (thereby preventing him from holding down the detonator button) in Holding. But it was maintained that this was permissible only as a means to the intended end of enforcing a negative duty, i.e., preventing that same person from causing severe pain or severe harm to innocents. It follows that the common practice of torture cannot successfully be justified on grounds of a supposed similarity to self-defense, for, in the common practice as opposed to cases of self-defense pain is not being inflicted in order to enforce a negative duty, but rather to enforce a positive one.

Notes

1. Note that "innocents" here has a technical meaning, intended to exclude material or formal aggressors. It is not intended in a kind of theological sense to exclude all that have ever done wrong. Of course, it is not being suggested that if one of the conditions mentioned (the pain or harm is intended for the individual's benefit, as a punishment, as part of the pursuit of a legitimate war, or to prevent the individual from causing severe pain or harm to innocents) is present that automatically makes the action permissible. Rather, it is being asserted that if none of the conditions mentioned is present that automatically makes the action impermissible.
2. Cf. Davis 2005, p. 174 and Shue 1978, pp. 141–142.

3. Cf. Davis 2005, p. 172.
4. Cf. Kershnar 2005, pp. 228–234.
5. The innocents may or may not include the police officer. Since the police officer is charged by the state with the defense of others, this makes no difference.
6. A Taser is a kind of gun that fires projectiles that administer an electric shock.
7. Note that the political elements of terrorism are not essential to the examples.The examples could be reworked to feature kidnappers instead of terrorists.
8. This point will be defended later.
9. This case is analogous to the case of the fatman's sitting on an innocent discussed in Sussman 2005 (pp. 16–17).
10. This case was suggested by Dr. James Heather. Dr. Heather intended this example as a *reductio ad absurdum* of the view of this paper, however. The reader may judge for him- or herself whether he was right.
11. Of course, in causing him to pull the button up one is thereby preventing him from performing incompatible actions, but this is not to the point, as these preventions are not part of the plan to stop the terrorist outrage.
12. Cf. Kershnar 2005, pp. 228–234.
13. The terms "basic action" and "non-basic action" are due to Danto 1963. Davidson 1971 identifies these with bodily movements.
14. An anonymous referee proposed the following objection in defense of the view that one can perform actions after one's death: "Now, if Stonewall Jackson, the general, ceased to exist when he died, how is it possible to remember his exploits? Surely, they were done by a being of whom it is still possible to predicate them truthfully or untruthfully (unlike the present King of France)." Against this, surely it is possible to remember the general's exploits and the general himself, and to make true statements about them, because they once existed. Memory is a present mental state whose object is in the past. One cannot remember things that never happened, but one can remember things that no longer obtain. (Indeed, it's even possible to see things that no longer exist, as when one looks up at the night sky and sees a far-off star that has exploded since it sent out its light.) But the fact that one can now remember the general as he was then doesn't imply that the general is *now* doing something. The view here defended is, of course, philosophically controversial: it supposes that the past in some sense exists. The view also supposes that the future in some sense exists: it is possible for A to kill B today even if B doesn't die till tomorrow. It would take too long to defend these views in detail here; suffice it to say that an argument that torture is permissible that rests on the philosophical view that the future or past does not exist looks self-defeating: *ex hypothesi* the terrorist's setting of the ticking bomb is in the past and the bomb's detonation is in the (potential) future.
15. For a detailed definition and discussion of "hard facts" and "soft facts" see Hill, 2005, p. 95. The terms seem to have been introduced into the literature by Pike, 1966.
16. There have been prosecutions in the past of Roman Catholic priests for not revealing information told to them under the seal of confession. The most famous concerned that early act of terrorism, the gunpowder plot: see http://www.newadvent.org/cathen/l3649b.htm, accessed on 7 June 2006.
17. The distinction seems first to have been brought to prominence in contemporary moral philosophy by Foot, 1967. It is criticized in. e.g., Glover, 1977 (p. 97).

References

Danto, Arthur, 1963. "What We Can Do." *Journal of philosophy*, vol. 60, pp. 434–445.

Davidson, Donald, 1971. "Agency," in *Agent, Action, and Reason*, cd. R. Binkley, R. Bronaugh, and A. Marras. Toronto: University of Toronto Press.

Davis, Michael, 2005. "The Moral Justification of Torture and Other Cruel, Inhuman, or Degrading Treatment." *International Journal of Applied Philosophy*, vol. 19, no. 2, pp. 161–178; http://www.pdcnet.org/pdf/ijap192-Davis.pdf, accessed on 19 June 2007.

Foot, Philippa, 1967. "The Problem of Abortion and the Doctrine of Double Effect." *Oxford Review*, vol. 5, pp. 5–15.

Glover, Jonathan, 1977. *Causing Death and Saving Lives*. London: Penguin.

Hill, Daniel J, 2005. *Divinity and Maximal Greatness*. London: Routledge.

Kershnar, Stephen, 2005. "For Interrogational Torture." *International Journal of Applied Philosophy,* vol. 19, no. 2, pp. 223–241; http://www.pdcnet.org/pdf/ijap192-Kershnar.pdf, accessed on 16 June 2007.

Miller, Seumas, 2006. "Torture." *The Stanford Encyclopedia of Philosophy* (Spring 2006 Edition), ed., Edward N. Zalta; http://plato.stanford.edu/archives/spr2006/entries/torture/, accessed on 15 July 2006.

Pike, Nelson, 1966. "Of God and Freedom: A Rejoinder." *The Philosophical Review,* vol. 74, pp. 27–46.

Shue, Henry, 1978. "Torture." *Philosophy & Public Affairs,* vol. 7, pp. 124–143.

Sussman, David, 2005. "What's Wrong With Torture?" *Philosophy & Public Affairs,* vol. 33, no. 1, pp. 1–33.

Study Questions for Section 8

1. Is killing worse than torture?

2. What is the difference between a negative and a positive duty? How does this distinction work in Hill's arguments against torture?

3. Is the morality of torture affected by how often it yields reliable information?

SECTION 9

CAPITAL PUNISHMENT

IN DEFENSE OF THE DEATH PENALTY

Ernest van den Haag

Is the death penalty morally just and/or useful? This is the essential moral, as distinguished from the constitutional, question. Discrimination is irrelevant to this moral question. If the death penalty were distributed equally and uncapriciously and with superhuman perfection to all the guilty, but were morally unjust, it would be unjust in each case. Contrariwise, if the death penalty is morally just, however discriminatorily applied to only some of the guilty, it remains just in each case in which it is applied.

The utilitarian (political) effects of unequal justice may well be detrimental to the social fabric because they outrage our passion for equality before the law. Unequal justice also is morally repellent. Nonetheless unequal justice is still justice. The guilty do not become innocent or less deserving of punishment because others escaped it. Nor does any innocent deserve

punishment because others suffer it. Justice remains just, however unequal, while injustice remains unjust, however equal. While both are desired, justice and equality are not identical. Equality before the law should be extended and enforced—but not at the expense of justice.

Capriciousness, at any rate, is used as a sham argument against capital punishment by abolitionists. They would oppose the death penalty if it could be meted out without any discretion. They would oppose the death penalty in a homogeneous country without racial discrimination. And they would oppose the death penalty if the incomes of those executed and of those spared were the same. Actually, abolitionists oppose the death penalty, not its possible maldistribution.

What about persons executed in error? The objection here is not that some of the guilty escape, but that some of the innocent do not—a matter far more serious than discrimination among the guilty. Yet, when urged by abolitionists, this, along with all distributional arguments, is a sham. Why? Abolitionists are opposed to

From Ernest van den Haag, "In Defense of the Death Penalty: A Practical and Moral Analysis," in *Criminal Law Bulletin*, Vol. 14. Copyright © 1978, Reprinted by permission of the journal.

the death penalty for the guilty as much as for the innocent. Hence, the question of guilt, if at all relevant to their position, cannot be decisive for them. Guilt is decisive only to those who urge the death penalty for the guilty. They must worry about distributions—part of the justice they seek.

The execution of innocents believed guilty is a miscarriage of justice that must be opposed whenever detected. But such miscarriages of justice do not warrant abolition of the death penalty. Unless the moral drawbacks of an activity or practice, which include the possible death of innocent bystanders, outweigh the moral advantages, which include the innocent lives that might be saved by it, the activity is warranted. Most human activities—medicine, manufacturing, automobile and air traffic, sports, not to speak of wars and revolutions—cause the death of innocent bystanders. Nevertheless, if the advantages sufficiently outweigh the disadvantages, human activities, including those of the penal system with all its punishments, are morally justified.

Is there evidence supporting the usefulness of the death penalty in securing the life of the citizens? Researchers in the past found no statistical evidence for the effects sought, marginal deterrent effects, or deterrent effects over and above those of alternative sanctions. However, in the last few years new and more sophisticated studies have led Professor Isaac Ehrlich to conclude that over the period 1933–1969, "an additional execution per year . . . may have resulted (on the average) in 7 or 8 fewer murders."[1] Other investigators have confirmed Ehrlich's tentative results. Not surprisingly, refutations have been attempted, and Professor Ehrlich has offered his rebuttals.[2] The matter will remain controversial for some time. However, two tentative conclusions can be drawn with some confidence. First, Ehrlich has shown that previous investigations, that did not find deterrent effects of the death penalty, suffered from fatal defects. Second, there is now some likelihood—much more than hitherto—of statistically demonstrating marginal deterrent effects.

Thus, with respect to deterrence, we must now choose

1. To trade the certain shortening of the life of a convicted murderer against the survival of between seven and eight innocent victims whose future murder by others becomes more probable, unless the convicted murderer is executed.
2. To trade the certain survival of the convicted murderer against the loss of the lives of between seven and eight innocent victims, who are more likely to be murdered by others if the convicted murderer is allowed to survive.

Prudence as well as morality command us to choose the first alternative.[3]

If executions had a zero marginal effect, they could not be justified in deterrent terms. But even the pre-Ehrlich investigations did not demonstrate this. They merely found that an above-zero effect could not be demonstrated statistically. While we do not know at present the degree of confidence with which we can assign an above marginal deterrent effect to executions, we can be more confident than in the past. I should now regard it as irresponsible not to shorten the lives of convicted murderers simply because we cannot be altogether sure that their execution will lengthen the lives of innocent victims: It seems immoral to let convicted murderers survive at the probable—or even at the merely possible—expense of the lives of innocent victims who might have been spared had the murderers been executed.

In principle, one could experiment to test the hypothesis of zero marginal effect. The most direct way would be to legislate the death penalty for certain kinds of murder if committed, say, on weekdays, but never on Sunday. Or, on Monday, Wednesday, and Friday, and not on other days. (The days could be changed around every few years to avoid possible bias.) I am convinced there would be fewer murders on death penalty than on life imprisonment days. Unfortunately, the experiment faces formidable obstacles.[4]

Our penal system rests on the proposition that more severe penalties are more deterrent than less severe penalties. We assume, rightly, I believe, that a $5 fine deters rape less than a $500 fine, and that the threat of five years in prison will deter more than either fine.[5] This assumption of the penal system rests on the common experience that, once aware of them, people learn to avoid natural dangers the more likely these are to be injurious and the more severe the likely injuries. People endowed with ordinary common sense (a class which includes some sociologists) have found no reason why behavior with respect to legal dangers should differ from behavior with respect to natural dangers. Indeed, it does not. Hence, the legal system proportions threatened penalties to the gravity of crimes, both to do justice and to achieve deterrence in proportion to that gravity.

Thus, if it is true that the more severe the penalty the greater the deterrent effect, then the most severe penalty—the death penalty—would have the greatest deterrent effect. Arguments to the contrary assume either that capital crimes never are deterrable (sometimes merely because not all capital crimes have been deterred), or that, beyond some point, the deterrent effect of added severity is necessarily zero. Perhaps. But the burden of proof must be borne by those who presume to have located the point of zero marginal returns before the death penalty.

As an additional commonsense observation, I should add that without the death penalty, we necessarily confer immunity on just those persons most likely to be in need of deterrent threats. Thus, prisoners serving life sentences can kill fellow prisoners or guards with impunity. Prison wardens are unlikely to prevent violence in prisons as long as they give humane treatment to inmates and have no threats of additional punishment available for the murderers among them who are already serving life sentences. I cannot see the moral or utilitarian reasons for giving permanent immunity to homicidal life prisoners, thereby endangering the other prisoners and the guards, and in effect preferring the life prisoners to their victims.

Outside the prison context, an offender who expects a life sentence for his offense may murder his victim, or witnesses, or the arresting officer, to improve his chances of escaping. He could not be threatened with an additional penalty for his additional crime—an open invitation. Only the death penalty could deter in such cases. If there is but a possibility—and I believe there is a probability—that it will, we should retain it.

However, deterrence requires that the threat of the ultimate penalty be reserved for the ultimate crime. It may be prevented by that threat. Hence, the extreme punishment should never be prescribed when the offender, because already threatened by it, might add to his crimes with impunity. Thus, rape, or kidnapping, should not incur the death penalty, while killing the victim of either crime should. This may not stop an Eichman after his first murder, but it will stop most people before. The range of punishments is not infinite: it is necessarily more restricted than the range of crimes. Since death is the ultimate penalty, it must be reserved for the ultimate crime.

Consider now some popular arguments against capital punishment.

According to Beccaria, with the death penalty the "laws which punish homicide . . . themselves commit it," thus giving "an example of barbarity." Those who speak of "legalized murder" use an oxymoronic phrase to echo this allegation. Legally imposed punishments such as fines, incarcerations, or executions, although often physically identical to the crimes punished, are not crimes or their moral equivalent. The difference between crimes and lawful acts is not physical, but legal. Driving a stolen car is a crime, although not physically different from driving a car you own. Unlawful imprisonment and kidnapping need not differ physically from the lawful arrest and incarceration used to punish unlawful imprisonment and kidnapping. Finally, whether a lawful punishment gives an "example of barbarity" depends on how the moral difference between crime and punishment is perceived. To suggest that its physical quality, ipso facto, morally disqualifies the punishment, is to assume what is to be shown.

It is possible that all displays of violence, criminal or punitive, influence people to engage in unlawful imitations. This seems one good reason not to have public executions. But it does not argue against executions. Objections to displaying on television the process of violently subduing a resistant offender do not argue against actually engaging in the process.[6] Arguments against the public display of vivisections, or of painful medications, do not argue against either. Arguments against the public display of sexual activity do not argue against sexual activity. Arguments against public executions, then, do not argue against executions.[7] While the deterrent effect of punishments depends on their being known, the deterrent effect does not depend on punishment being carried out publicly. For example, the threat of imprisonment deters, but incarcerated persons are not on public display.

Abolitionists often maintain that most capital crimes are "acts of passion" that (1) could not be restrained by the threat of the death penalty, and (2) do not deserve it morally even if other crimes might. It is not clear to me why a crime motivated by, say, sexual passion, is morally less deserving of punishment than one motivated by passion for money. Is the sexual passion morally more respectable than others? More gripping? More popular? Generally, is violence in personal conflicts morally more excusable than violence among people who do not know each other? A precarious case might be made for such a view, but I shall not attempt to make it.

Perhaps it is true, however, that many murders are irrational "acts of passion" that cannot be deterred by the threat of the death penalty. Either for this reason or because "crimes of passion" are thought less blameworthy than other homicides, most "crimes of passion" are not punishable by death now.[8]

But if most murders are irrational acts, it would seem that the traditional threat of the death penalty has succeeded in deterring most rational people, or most people when rational, from committing the threatened act, and that the fear of the penalty continues to deter all but those who cannot be deterred by any penalty. Hardly a reason for abolishing the death penalty. Indeed, that capital crimes are committed mostly by irrational persons and only by some rational ones would suggest that more might commit these crimes if the penalty were lower. This hardly argues against capital punishment. Else, we would have to abolish penalties whenever they succeed in deterring people. Yet, abolitionists urge that capital punishment be abolished because capital crimes are often committed by the irrational—as though deterring the rational is not quite enough.

Finally, some observations on an anecdote reported by Boswell and repeated ad nauseam. Dr. Johnson found pickpockets active in a crowd assembled to see one of their number hanged. He concluded that executions do not deter. His conclusion does not follow from his observation.

1. Since the penalty Johnson witnessed was what pickpockets had expected all along, they had no reason to reduce their activities. Deterrence is expected to increase only when penalties do.

2. At most, a public execution could have had the deterrent effect Dr. Johnson expected because of its visibility. But it may have had a contrary effect: the spectacle of execution was probably more fascinating to the crowd than other spectacles; public executions thus might distract attention from the activities of pickpockets and thereby increase their opportunities more than other spectacles would. Hence, an execution crowd might have been more inviting to pickpockets than other crowds. (As mentioned before, deterrence depends on knowledge, but does not require visibility.)

3. Even when the penalty is greatly increased, let alone when it is unchanged, the deterrent effect of penalties is usually slight with respect to those already committed to criminal activities.[9] Deterrence is effective by restraining people as yet not committed to a criminal occupation from entering it.

    The risk of a penalty is the cost of crime offenders must expect. When this cost is high enough, relative to the expected benefit, it will deter a considerable number of people who would have entered an occupation—criminal or otherwise—had the cost been lower. In this respect, the effects of the costs of crime are not different from the effects of the cost of automobiles or movie tickets, or from the effects of the cost of any occupation relative to its benefits. When (comparative) net benefits decrease because of cost increases, the flow of new entrants does. But those already in the occupation usually continue.

4. Finally, Dr. Johnson did not actually address the question of the deterrent effect of execution in any respect whatever. To do so, he would have had to compare the number of pocket-picking episodes in the crowd assembled to witness the execution with the number of such episodes in a similar crowd assembled for some other purpose. He did not do so, probably because he thought that a deterrent effect occurs only if the crime is altogether eliminated. That is a common misunderstanding. Crime can only be reduced, not eliminated. However harsh the penalties, there are always nondeterrables. Thus, most people can be deterred, but never all.

One popular moral objection to capital punishment is that it gratifies the desire for revenge, regarded as unworthy. The Bible quotes the Lord declaring, "Vengeance is mine" (Romans 12:19). He thus legitimized vengeance and reserved it to Himself. However, the Bible also enjoins, "the murderer shall surely be put to death" (Numbers 35:16–18), recognizing that the death penalty can be warranted—whatever the motive. Religious tradition certainly suggests no less.[10]

The motives for the death penalty may indeed include vengeance. Vengeance as a compensatory and psychologically reparatory satisfaction for an injured party, group, or society may be a legitimate human motive—despite the biblical injunction. I do not see wherein that motive is morally blameworthy. When regulated and directed by law, vengeance also is socially useful: legal vengeance solidifies social solidarity against lawbreakers and is the alternative to the private revenge of those who feel harmed.

However, vengeance is irrelevant to the death penalty, which must be justified by its purpose, whatever the motive. An action, or rule, or penalty is neither justified nor discredited by the motive for it. No rule should be discarded or regarded as morally wrong because of the motive of those who support it. Actions, or rules, or penalties, are justified by their intent and by their effectiveness in achieving it, not by the motives of supporters.[11] Capital punishment is warranted if it achieves its purpose; doing justice and deterring crime, regardless of whether it gratifies vengeful feelings.

We must examine now the specific characteristics of capital punishment before turning to its purely moral aspects. Capital punishment is feared above all punishments because (1) it is not merely irreversible as most other penalties are, but also irrevocable; (2) it hastens an event, which unlike pain, deprivation, or injury, is unique in every life and never has been reported on by anyone. Death is an experience that cannot actually be experienced and ends all experience.[12] Because it is as unknown as it is certain, death is universally feared. The fear of death is often attached to the penalty that hastens it—as though, without the penalty, death would not come. (3) When death is imposed as a deliberate punishment by one's fellow men, it signifies a complete severing of human solidarity. The convict is rejected by human society, found unworthy of sharing life with it. This total rejection exacerbates the natural separation anxiety and fear of annihilation. The marginal deterrent effect of executions depends on these characteristics, and the moral justification of the death penalty, above and beyond the deterrent effect, does no less.

Hitherto I have relied on logic and fact. Without relinquishing either, I must appeal to plausibility as well, as I turn to questions of morality unalloyed to other issues. For, whatever ancillary service facts and logic can render, what one is persuaded to accept as morally right or wrong ultimately depends on what seems to be plausible.

If there is nothing for the sake of which one may be put to death, can there be anything worth dying for? If there is nothing worth dying for, is there any moral value worth living for? Is a life that cannot be transcended by anything beyond itself more valuable than one that can be transcended? Is existence, life itself, a moral value never to be given up for the sake of anything? Does a value system in which any life, however it is lived, becomes the highest of goods, enhance the value of human life or cheapen it? I shall content myself here with raising the questions.[13]

"The life of each man should be sacred to each other man," the ancients tell us. They unflinchingly executed murderers.[14] They realized it is not enough to proclaim the sacredness and inviolability of human life. It must be secured as well, by threatening with the loss of their own life those who violate what has been proclaimed as inviolable—the right of innocents to live. Else, the inviolability of human life is neither credibly proclaimed nor actually protected. No society can profess that the lives of its members are secure if those who did not allow innocent others to continue living are themselves allowed to continue living—at the expense of the community. Does it not cheapen human life to punish the murderer by incarcerating him as one does a pickpocket? Murder differs in quality from other crimes and deserves, therefore, a punishment that differs in quality for other punishments.

If it were shown that no punishment is more deterrent than a trivial fine, capital punishment for murder would remain just, even if not useful. For murder is not a trifling offense. Punishment must be proportioned to the gravity of the crime, if only to denounce it and to vindicate the importance of the norm violated. Thus, all penal systems proportion punishments to crimes. The worse the crime the higher the penalty deserved. Why not the highest penalty—death—for the worst crime—wanton murder? Those rejecting the death penalty have the burden of showing that no crime deserves capital punishment[15]—a burden which they have not so far been willing to bear.

Abolitionists are wrong when they insist that we all have an equally inalienable right to live to our natural terms—that if the victim deserved to live, so does the murderer. That takes egalitarianism too far for my taste: the crime sets victim and murderer apart; if the victim died, the murderer does not deserve to live. The thought that there are some who think that murderers have as much right to live as their victims oppresses me. So does the thought that a Stalin or a Hitler should have the right to go on living.

Never to execute a wrongdoer, regardless of how depraved his acts, is to proclaim that no act can be so irredeemably vicious as to deserve death—that no human being can be wicked enough to be deprived of life. Who actually believes that? I find it easier to believe that those who affect such a view do so because of a failure of nerve. They do not think themselves—and therefore anyone else—competent to decide questions of life and death. Aware of human frailty they shudder at the gravity of the decision and refuse to make it. The irrevocability of a verdict of death is contrary to the modern spirit that likes to pretend that nothing ever is definitive, that everything is open-ended, that doubts must always be entertained and revisions made. Such an attitude may be proper for inquiring philosophers and scientists. But not for courts. They can evade decisions on life and death only by giving up their paramount duties: to do justice, to secure the lives of the citizens, and to vindicate the norms society holds inviolable.

One may object that the death penalty either cannot actually achieve the vindication of violated norms, or is not needed for it. If so, failure to inflict death does not belittle the crime, nor imply that the life of the criminal is of greater importance than the moral value he violated, or the harm he did to his victim. But it is not so. In all societies, the degree of social disapproval of wicked acts is expressed in the degree of punishment threatened.[16] Thus, punishments both proclaim and enforce social values according to the importance given to them. There is no other way for society to affirm its values. To refuse to punish any crime with death, then, is to avow that the negative weight of a crime can never exceed the positive value of the life of the person who committed it. I find that proposition implausible.

Notes

1. Ehrlich, "The Deterrent Effect of Capital Punishment: A Question of Life and Death," *American Economic Review* (June 1975). In the period studied, capital punishment was already infrequent and uncertain. Its deterrent effect might be greater when more frequently imposed for capital crimes, so that a prospective offender would feel more certain of it.

2. See *Journal of Legal Studies* (January 1977); *Journal of Political Economy* (June 1977); and *American Economic Review* (June 1977).

3. I thought so even when I believed that the probability of deterrent effects might remain unknown. (See van den Haag, "On Deterrence and the Death Penalty," *Journal of Criminal Law, Criminology, and Political Science* [June 1969].) That probability is now more likely to become known and to be greater than was apparent a few years ago.

4. It would, however, isolate deterrent effects of the punishment from incapacitating ones, and also from the effect of Durkheimian "normative validation" where it does not depend on threats.

5. As indicated before, demonstrations are not available for the exact addition to deterrence of each added degree of severity in various circumstances, and with respect to various acts. We have so far coasted on a sea of plausible assumptions.

6. There is a good argument against unnecessary public displays of violence here. See van den Haag, "What to Do About TV Violence," *The Alternative* (August–September 1976).

7. It may be noted that in Beccaria's time, executions were regarded as public entertainments. . . .

8. I have reservations on both these counts, being convinced that many crimes among relatives and friends are as blameworthy and as deterrable as crimes among strangers. Thus, major heroin dealers in New York are threatened with life imprisonment. In the absence of the death penalty, they find it advantageous to have witnesses killed. Such murders surely are not acts of passion in the classical sense, although they occur among associates. They are in practice encouraged by the penal law.

9. The high degree of uncertainty and arbitrariness of penalization in Johnson's time may also have weakened deterrent effects. Witnessing an execution cannot correct this defect.

10. Since religion expects both justice and vengeance in the world to come, the faithful may dispense with either in this world, and with any particular penalties, although they seldom have. But a secular state must do justice here now, it cannot assume that another power, elsewhere, will do justice where its courts did not.

For that matter, Romans 12:19 barely precedes Romans 13:4, which tells us [the ruler] "beareth not the sword in vain for he is the minister of God, a revenger to execute wrath upon him that doeth evil." It is not unreasonable to interpret Romans 12:19 to mean that revenge is to be delegated by the injured to the authorities.

11. Different motives (the reasons why something is done) may generate the same action (what is done), purpose, or intent, just as the same motive may lead to different actions.

12. Actually, being dead is no different from not being born, a (non) experience we all had before being born. But death is not so perceived. The process of dying, a quite different matter, is confused with it. In turn, dying is feared mainly because death is anticipated, even though death is feared because it is confused with dying.

13. Insofar as these questions are psychological, empirical evidence would not be irrelevant. But it is likely to be evaluated in terms depending on moral views.

14. Not always. On the disastrous consequences of periodic failure to do so. Sir Henry Maine waxes with eloquent sorrow in his *Ancient Law,* 408–409.

15. One may argue that some crimes deserve more than execution, and that on the above reasoning, torture may be justified. But penalties have already been reduced to a few kinds—fines, confinement, and execution—so the issue is academic. Unlike the death penalty, torture also has become repulsive to us. Some reasons for this public revulsion are listed in Chapter X. van den Haag, *Punishing Criminals: Concerning a Very Old and Painful Question* (1975).

16. Social approval is usually less unanimous, and the system of rewards reflects it less.

CAPTIAL PUNISHMENT

Hugo Adam Bedau

The Analogy with Self-Defense

Capital punishment, it is sometimes said, is to the body politic what self-defense is to the individual. If the latter is not morally wrong, how can the former be morally wrong? In order to assess the strength of this analogy, we need to inspect rather closely the morality of self-defense.

Except for the absolute pacifists, who believe it is morally wrong to use violence even to defend themselves or others from unprovoked and undeserved aggression, most of us believe that it is not morally wrong and may even be our moral duty to use violence to prevent aggression. The law has long granted persons the right to defend themselves against the unjust aggressions of others, even to the extent of killing a would-be assailant. It is very difficult to think of any convincing argument that would show it is never rational to risk

the death of another in order to prevent death or grave injury to oneself or to others. Certainly self-interest dictates the legitimacy of self-defense. So does concern for the well-being of others. So also does justice. If it is unfair for one person to attempt violence on another, then it is hard to see why morality compels the victim to acquiesce in the attempt by another to hurt him or her, rather than to resist it, even if that resistance may involve injury to the assailant.

The foregoing account assumes that the person acting in self-defense is innocent of any provocation of the assailant. It also assumes that there is no alternative to victimization except resistance. In actual life, both assumptions—especially the second—are often false, because there may be a third alternative: escape, or removing oneself from the scene of danger and imminent aggression. Hence, the law imposes on us the so-called "duty to retreat." Before we use violence to resist aggression, we must try to get out of the way, lest unnecessary violence be used to resist aggression. Now suppose that unjust aggression is imminent, and there is no path open for escape. How much violence may justifiably be used to ward off aggression? The answer is no more violence than is necessary to prevent the aggressive assault. Violence beyond that is unnecessary and therefore unjustified. We may restate the principle governing the use of violence in self-defense in terms of the use of "deadly force" by the police in the discharge of their duties. The rule is this: use of deadly force is justified only to prevent loss of life in immediate jeopardy where a lesser use of force cannot reasonably be expected to save the life that is threatened.

In real life, violence in self-defense in excess of the minimum necessary to prevent aggression is often excusable. One cannot always tell what will suffice to deter or prevent becoming a victim, and the law looks with a certain tolerance upon the frightened and innocent would-be victim who turns upon a vicious assailant and inflicts a fatal injury even though a lesser injury would have been sufficient. What is not justified is deliberately using far more violence than is necessary to prevent becoming a victim. It is the deliberate, not the impulsive, use of violence that is relevant to the death penalty controversy, since the death penalty is enacted into law and carried out in each case only after ample time to weigh alternatives. Notice that we are assuming that the act of self-defense is to protect one's person or that of a third party. The reasoning outlined here does not extend to the defense of one's property. Shooting a thief to prevent one's automobile from being stolen cannot be excused or justified in the way that shooting an assailant charging with a knife pointed at one's face can be. In terms of the concept of "deadly force," our criterion is that deadly force is never justified to prevent crimes against property or other violent crimes not immediately threatening the life of a person.

The rationale for self-defense as set out above illustrates two moral principles of great importance to our discussion . . . One is that if a life is to be risked, then it is better that it be the life of someone who is guilty (in our context, the initial assailant) rather than the life of someone who is not (the innocent potential victim). It is not fair to expect the innocent prospective victim to run the added risk of severe injury or death in order to avoid using violence in self-defense to the extent of possibly killing his assailant. It is only fair that the guilty aggressor run the risk.

The other principle is that taking life deliberately is not justified so long as there is any feasible alternative. One does not expect miracles, of course, but in theory, if shooting a burglar through the foot will stop the burglary and enable one to call the police for help, then there is no reason to shoot to kill. Likewise, if the burglar is unarmed, there is no reason to shoot at all. In actual life, of course, burglars are likely to be shot at by aroused householders because one does not know whether they are armed, and prudence may dictate the assumption that they are. Even so, although the burglar has no right to commit a felony against a person or a person's property, the attempt to do so does not give the chosen victim the right to respond in whatever way he or she pleases in retaliation, and then to excuse or justify such conduct on the ground that he or she was "only acting in self-defense." In these ways the law shows a tacit regard for the life of even a felon and discourages the use of unnecessary violence even by the innocent; morality can hardly do less.

Preventing Crime Versus Deterring Crime

The analogy between capital punishment and self-defense requires us to face squarely the empirical questions surrounding the preventive and deterrent effects of the death penalty. Let us distinguish first between preventing and deterring crime. Executing a murderer in the name of punishment can be seen as a crime-*preventive* measure just to the extent it is reasonable to believe that if the murderer had not been executed he or she would have committed other crimes (including, but not necessarily confined to, murder). Executing a murderer can be seen as a crime *deterrent* just to the extent it is reasonable to believe that by the example of the execution other persons are frightened off from committing murder. Any punishment can be a crime preventive without being a crime deterrent, and it can be a deterrent without being a preventive. It can also be both or neither. Prevention and deterrence are theoretically independent because they operate by different methods. Crimes can be prevented by taking guns out of the hands of criminals, by putting criminals behind bars, by alerting the public to be less careless and less prone to victimization, and so forth. Crimes can be deterred only by making would-be criminals frightened of being arrested, convicted, and punished for crimes—that is, making persons overcome their desire to commit crimes by a stronger desire to avoid the risk of being caught and punished.

The Death Penalty as a Crime Preventive

Capital punishment is unusual among penalties because its preventive effects limit its deterrent effects. The death penalty can never deter the executed person from further crimes. At most, it can prevent him or her from committing them. Popular discussions of the death penalty are frequently confused and misleading because they so often involve the assumption that the death penalty is a perfect and infallible deterrent so far as the executed criminal is concerned, whereas nothing of the sort is true.

It is even an exaggeration to think that in any given case of execution the death penalty has proved to be an infallible crime preventive. What is obviously true is that once a person has been executed, it is physically impossible for him or her to commit any further crimes. But this does not prove that by executing a murderer society has in fact prevented any crimes. To prove this, one would need to know what crimes the executed criminal would have committed if he or she had not been executed and had been punished only in some less severe way (e.g., by imprisonment).

What is the evidence that the death penalty is an effective crime preventive? From the study of imprisonment, and parole and release records, it is clear that in general, if the murderers and other criminals who have been executed are like the murderers who were convicted but not executed, then (a) executing all convicted murderers would have prevented few crimes, but not many murders (less than one convicted murderer in a hundred commits another murder); and (b) convicted murderers, whether inside prison or outside after release, have at least as good a record of no further criminal activity as does any other class of convicted felon.

These facts show that the general public tends to overrate the danger and threat to public safety constituted by the failure to execute every murderer who is caught and convicted. While one would be in error to say that there is no risk such criminals will repeat their crimes—or similar ones—if they are not executed, one would be equally in error to say that by executing every convicted murderer we know that many horrible crimes will never be committed. All we know is that a few such crimes will never be committed; we do not know how many or by whom they would have been committed. (Obviously, if we did we could have prevented them.) This is the nub of the problem. There is no way to know in advance which if any of the incarcerated or released murderers will kill again. It is useful in this connection to remember that the only way to guarantee that no horrible crimes ever occur is to execute *everyone* who might conceivably commit such a crime. Similarly, the only way to guarantee that no convicted murderer ever commits another murder is to execute them all. No society has ever done this, and for 200 years our society has been moving steadily in the opposite direction.

These considerations show that our society has implicitly adopted an attitude toward the risk of murder rather like the attitude it has adopted toward the risk of fatality from other sources, such as automobile accidents, lung cancer, or drowning. Since no one knows when or where or upon whom any of these lethal events will befall, it would be too great an invasion of freedom to undertake the severe restrictions that alone would suffice to prevent any of them from occurring. It is better to take the risks and keep our freedom than to try to eliminate the risks altogether and lose our freedom in the process. Hence, we have lifeguards at the beach, but swimming is not totally prohibited; smokers are warned, but cigarettes are still legally sold; pedestrians may be given the right of way in a crosswalk, but marginally competent drivers are still allowed to operate motor vehicles. Some risk is therefore imposed on the innocent; in the name of our right to freedom, our other rights are not protected by society at all costs.

The Death Penalty as a Crime Deterrent

Determining whether the death penalty is an effective deterrent is even more difficult than determining its effectiveness as a crime preventive. In general, our knowledge about how penalties deter crimes and

whether in fact they do—whom they deter, from which crimes, and under what conditions—is distressingly inexact. Most people nevertheless are convinced that punishments do deter, and that the more severe a punishment is the better it will deter. For more than a generation, social scientists have studied the question of whether the death penalty is a deterrent and of whether it is a better deterrent than the alternative of imprisonment. Their verdict, while not unanimous, is fairly clear. Whatever may be true about the deterrence of lesser crimes by other penalties, the deterrence achieved by the death penalty for murder is not measurably greater than the deterrence achieved by long-term imprisonment. In the nature of the case, the evidence is quite indirect. No one can identify for certain any crimes that did not occur because the would-be offender was deterred by the threat of the death penalty and that would not have been deterred by a lesser threat. Likewise, no one can identify any crimes that did occur because the offender was not deterred by the threat of prison even though he would have been deterred by the threat of death. Nevertheless, such evidence as we have fails to show that the more severe penalty (death) is really a better deterrent than the less severe penalty (imprisonment) for such crimes as murder.

If the conclusion stated above is correct, and the death penalty and long-term imprisonment are equally effective (or ineffective) as deterrents to murder, then the argument for the death penalty on grounds of deterrence is seriously weakened. One of the moral principles identified earlier comes into play and requires us to reject the death penalty on moral grounds. This is the principle that unless there is a good reason for choosing a more rather than a less severe punishment for a crime, the less severe penalty is to be preferred. This principle obviously commends itself to anyone who values human life and who concedes that, all other things being equal, less pain and suffering is always better than more. Human life is valued in part to the degree that it is free of pain, suffering, misery, and frustration, and in particular that it is free of such experiences when they serve no purpose. If the death penalty is not a more effective deterrent than imprisonment, then its greater severity than imprisonment is gratuitous, purposeless suffering and deprivation.

A Cost-Benefit Analysis of the Death Penalty

A full study of the costs and benefits involved in the practice of capital punishment would not be confined solely to the question of whether it is a better deterrent or preventive of murder than imprisonment. Any thoroughgoing utilitarian approach to the death penalty controversy would need to examine carefully other costs and benefits as well, because maximizing the balance of social benefits over social costs is the sole criterion of right and wrong according to utilitarianism. Let us consider, therefore, some of the other costs and benefits to be calculated. Clinical psychologists have presented evidence to suggest that the death penalty actually incites some persons of unstable mind to murder others, either because they are afraid to take their own lives and hope that society will punish them for murder by putting them to death, or because they fancy that they, too, are killing with justification analogously to the justified killing involved in capital punishment. If such evidence is sound, capital punishment can serve as a counterpreventive or an incitement to murder, and these incited murders become part of its social cost. Imprisonment, however, has not been known to incite any murders or other crimes of violence in a

comparable fashion. (A possible exception might be found in the imprisonment of terrorists, which has inspired other terrorists to take hostages as part of a scheme to force the authorities to release their imprisoned comrades.) The risks of executing the innocent are also part of the social cost. The historical record is replete with innocent persons indicted, convicted, sentenced, and occasionally legally executed for crimes they did not commit, not to mention the guilty persons unfairly convicted, sentenced to death, and executed on the strength of perjured testimony, fraudulent evidence, subornation of jurors, and other violations of the civil rights and liberties of the accused. Nor is this all. The high costs of a capital trial, of the inevitable appeals, the costly methods of custody most prisons adopt for convicts on "death row," are among the straightforward economic costs that the death penalty incurs. No scientifically valid cost-benefit analysis of capital punishment has ever been conducted, and it is impossible to predict exactly what such a study would show. Nevertheless, based on such evidence as we do have, it is quite possible that a study of this sort would favor abolition of all death penalties rather than their retention.

What If Executions Did Deter?

From the moral point of view, it is quite important to determine what one should think about capital punishment if the evidence clearly showed that the death penalty is a distinctly superior method of social defense by comparison with less severe alternatives . . . To oppose the death penalty in the face of incontestable evidence that it is an effective method of social defense seems to violate the moral principle that where grave risks are to be run, it is better that they be run by the guilty than by the innocent. Consider in this connection an imaginary world in which by executing a murderer the victim is invariably restored to life, whole and intact, as though the murder had never occurred. In such a miraculous world, it is hard to see how anyone could oppose the death penalty on moral grounds. Why shouldn't a murderer die if that will infallibly bring the victim back to life? What could possibly be morally wrong with taking the murderer's life under such conditions? It would turn the death penalty into an instrument of perfect restitution, and it would give a new and better meaning to *lex talionis*, "a life for a life." The whole idea is fanciful, of course, but it shows better than anything else how opposition to the death penalty cannot be both moral and wholly unconditional. If opposition to the death penalty is to be morally responsible, then it must be conceded that there are conditions (however unlikely) under which that opposition should cease.

But even if the death penalty were known to be a uniquely effective social defense, we could still imagine conditions under which it would be reasonable to oppose it. Suppose that in addition to being a slightly better preventive and deterrent than imprisonment, executions also have a slight incitive effect (so that for every ten murders an execution prevents or deters, it also incites another murder). Suppose also that the administration of criminal justice in capital cases is inefficient, unequal, and tends to secure convictions of murderers who least "deserve" to be sentenced to death (including some death sentences and a few executions of the innocent). Under such conditions, it would still be reasonable to oppose the death penalty, because on the facts supposed more (or not fewer) innocent lives are being threatened and lost by using the death penalty than would be risked by abolishing it. It is important to remember throughout our evaluation of the deterrence

controversy that we cannot ever apply the principle . . . that advises us to risk the lives of the guilty in order to save the lives of the innocent. Instead, the most we can do is weigh the risk for the general public against the execution of those who are *found* guilty by an imperfect system of criminal justice. These hypothetical factual assumptions illustrate the contingencies upon which the morality of opposition to the death penalty rests. And not only the morality of opposition: the morality of any defense of the death penalty rests on the same contingencies. This should help us understand why, in resolving the morality of capital punishment one way or the other, it is so important to know, as well as we can, whether the death penalty really does deter, prevent, or incite crime, whether the innocent really are ever executed, and whether any of these things are likely to occur in the future.

How Many Guilty Lives Is One Innocent Life Worth?

The great unanswered question that utilitarians must face concerns the level of social defense that executions should be expected to achieve before it is justifiable to carry them out. Consider three possible situations. (1) At the level of a hundred executions per year, each additional execution of a convicted murderer reduces the number of murder victims by ten. (2) Executing every convicted murderer reduces the number of murders to 5,000 victims annually, whereas executing only one out of ten reduces the number to 5,001. (3) Executing every convicted murderer reduces the murder rate no more than does executing one in a hundred and no more than a random pattern of executions does.

Many people contemplating situation (1) would regard this as a reasonable trade-off: the execution of each further guilty person saves the lives of ten innocent ones. (In fact, situation (1) or something like it may be taken as a description of what most of those who defend the death penalty on grounds of social defense believe is true.) But suppose that, instead of saving 10 lives, the number dropped to 0.5, i.e., one victim avoided for each two additional executions. Would that be a reasonable price to pay? We are on the road toward the situation described in situation (2), where a drastic 90 percent reduction in the number of persons executed causes the level of social defense to drop by only 0.0002 percent. Would it be worth it to execute so many more murderers at the cost of such a slight decrease in social defense? How many guilty lives is one innocent life worth? In situation (3), of course, there is no basis for executing all convicted murderers, since there is no gain in social defense to show for each additional murderer executed after the first out of each hundred murderers has been executed. How, then, should we determine which out of each hundred convicted murderers is the unlucky one to be put to death?

It may be possible, under a complete and thoroughgoing cost-benefit analysis of the death penalty, to answer such questions. But an appeal merely to the moral principle that if lives are to be risked then let it be the lives of the guilty rather than the lives of the innocent will not suffice. (We have already noticed . . . that this abstract principle is of little use in the actual administration of criminal justice, because the police and the courts do not deal with the guilty as such but only with those *judged* guilty.) Nor will it suffice to agree that society deserves all the crime prevention and deterrence it can get by inflicting severe punishments. These principles are consistent with too many different policies. They are too vague by themselves to resolve the choice on grounds of social defense when confronted with hypothetical situations like those proposed above.

Since no adequate cost-benefit analysis of the death penalty exists, there is no way to resolve these questions from this standpoint at the present time. Moreover, it can be argued that we cannot have such an analysis without already establishing in some way or other the relative value of innocent lives versus guilty lives. Far from being a product of a cost-benefit analysis this comparative evaluation of lives would have to be brought into any such analysis. Without it, no cost-benefit analysis can get off the ground. Finally, it must be noted that we have no knowledge at present that begins to approximate anything like the situation described above in (1), whereas it appears from the evidence we do have that we achieve about the same deterrent and preventive effects whether we punish murder by death or by imprisonment. Therefore, something like the situation in (2) or in (3) may be correct. If so, this shows that the choice between the two policies of capital punishment and life imprisonment for murder will probably have to be made on some basis other than social defense; on that basis the two policies are equivalent and therefore equally acceptable.

Crime Must Be Punished

[T]here cannot be any dispute over this principle. In embracing it, of course, we are not automatically making a fetish of "law and order," in the sense that we would be if we thought that the most important single thing society can do with its resources is to punish crimes. In addition, this principle is not likely to be in dispute between proponents and opponents of the death penalty. Only those who completely oppose punishment for murder and other erstwhile capital crimes would appear to disregard this principle. Even defenders of the death penalty must admit that putting a convicted murderer in prison for years is a punishment of that criminal. The principle that crime must be punished is neutral to our controversy, because both sides acknowledge it and comply with it.

It is the other principle of retributive justice that seems to be a decisive one. Under the principle of retaliation, *lex talionis*, it must always have seemed that murderers ought to be put to death. Proponents of the death penalty, with rare exceptions, have insisted on this point, and it seems that even opponents of the death penalty must give it grudging assent. The strategy for opponents of the death penalty is to show either (a) that this principle is not really a principle of justice after all, or (b) that although it is, other principles outweigh or cancel its dictates. As we shall see, both these objections have merit.

Is Murder Alone to Be
Punished by Death?

Let us recall, first, that not even the Biblical world limited the death penalty to the punishment of murder. Many other non-homicidal crimes also carried this penalty (e.g., kidnapping, witchcraft, cursing one's parents). In our own recent history, persons have been executed for aggravated assault, rape, kidnapping, armed robbery, sabotage, and espionage. It is not possible to defend any of these executions (not to mention some of the more bizarre capital statutes, like the one in Georgia that used to provide an optional death penalty for desecration of a grave) on grounds of just retribution. This entails that either such executions are not justified or that they are justified on some ground other than retribution. In actual practice, few if any defenders of the death penalty have ever been willing to rest their case entirely on the moral principle of just retribution as formulated in terms of "a life for a life." Kant seems to have been a conspicuous exception. Most defenders of the death penalty have implied by their willingness

to use executions to defend limb and property, as well as life, that they did not place much value on the lives of criminals when compared to the value of both lives and things belonging to innocent citizens.

Are All Murders to Be Punished
by Death?

Our society for several centuries has endeavored to continue the death penalty to some criminal homicides. Even Kant took a casual attitude toward a mother's killing of her illegitimate child. ("A child born into the world outside marriage is outside the law . . . and consequently it is also outside the protection of the law."[1]) In our society, the development nearly 200 years ago of the distinction between first- and second-degree murder was an attempt to narrow the class of criminal homicides deserving of the death penalty. Yet those dead owing to manslaughter, or to any kind of unintentional, accidental, unpremeditated, unavoidable, unmalicious killing are just as dead as the victims of the most ghastly murder. Both the law in practice and moral reflection show how difficult it is to identify all and only the criminal homicides that are appropriately punished by death (assuming that any are). Individual judges and juries differ in the conclusions they reach. The history of capital punishment for homicides reveals continual efforts, uniformly unsuccessful, to identify before the fact those homicides for which the slayer should die. Benjamin Cardozo, a justice of the United States Supreme Court fifty years ago, said of the distinction between degrees of murder that it was

> . . . so obscure that no jury hearing it for the first time can fairly be expected to assimilate and understand it. I am not at all sure that I understand it myself after trying to apply it for many years and after diligent study of what has been written in the books. Upon the basis of this fine

distinction with its obscure and mystifying psychology, scores of men have gone to their death.[2]

Similar skepticism has been registered on the reliability and rationality of death penalty statutes that give the trial court the discretion to sentence to prison or to death. As Justice John Marshall Harlan of the Supreme Court observed a decade ago:

> Those who have come to grips with the hard task of actually attempting to draft means of channeling capital sentencing discretion have confined the lesson taught by history . . . To identify before the fact those characteristics of criminal homicide and their perpetrators which call for the death penalty, and to express these characteristics in language which can be fairly understood and applied by the sentencing authority, appear to be tasks which are beyond present human ability.[3]

The abstract principle that the punishment of death best fits the crime of murder turns out to be extremely difficult to interpret and apply. If we look at the matter from the standpoint of the actual practice of criminal justice, we can only conclude that "a life for a life" plays little or no role whatever. Plea bargaining (by means of which one of the persons involved in a crime agrees to accept a lesser sentence in exchange for testifying against the others to enable the prosecutor to get them all convicted), even where murder is concerned, is widespread. Studies of criminal justice reveal that what the courts (trial or appellate) decide on a given day is first-degree murder suitably punished by death in a given jurisdiction could just as well be decided in a neighboring jurisdiction on another day either as second-degree murder or as first-degree murder but without the death penalty. The factors that influence prosecutors in determining the charge under which they will prosecute go far beyond the simple principle of "a life for a

life." Nor can it be objected that these facts show that our society does not care about justice. To put it succinctly, either justice in punishment does not consist of retribution, because there are other principles of justice; or there are other moral considerations besides justice that must be honored; or retributive justice is not adequately expressed in the idea of "a life for a life."

Is Death Sufficiently Retributive?

Given the reality of horrible and vicious crimes, one must consider whether there is not a quality of unthinking arbitrariness in advocating capital punishment for murder as the retributively just punishment. Why does death in the electric chair or the gas chamber or before a firing squad or on a gallows meet the requirements of retributive justice? When one thinks of the savage, brutal, wanton character of so many murders, how can retributive justice be served by anything less than equally savage methods of execution for the murderer? From a retributive point of view, the often-heard exclamation, "Death is too good for him!" has a certain truth. Yet few defenders of the death penalty are willing to embrace this consequence of their own doctrine.

The reason they do not and should not is that, if they did, they would be stooping to the methods and thus to the squalor of the murderer. Where criminals set the limits of just methods of punishment, as they will do if we attempt to give exact and literal implementation to *lex talionis*, society will find itself descending to the cruelties and savagery that criminals employ. But society would be deliberately authorizing such acts, in the cool light of reason, and not (as is often true of vicious criminals) impulsively or in hatred and anger or with an insane or unbalanced mind. Moral restraints, in short, prohibit us from trying to make executions perfectly retributive.

Once we grant the role of these restraints, the principle of "a life for a life" itself has been qualified and no longer suffices to justify the execution of murderers.

Other considerations take us in a different direction. Few murders, outside television and movie scripts, involve anything like an execution. An execution, after all, begins with a solemn pronouncement of the death sentence from a judge, is followed by long detention in maximum security awaiting the date of execution, various appeals, perhaps a final sanity hearing, and then "the last mile" to the execution chamber itself. As the French writer Albert Camus remarked,

> For there to be an equivalence, the death penalty would have to punish a criminal who had warned his victim of the date at which he would inflict a horrible death on him and who, from that moment onward, had confined him at his mercy for months. Such a monster is not encountered in private life.[4]

Differential Severity Does Not Require Executions

What, then, emerges from our examination of retributive justice and the death penalty? If retributive justice is thought to consist in *lex talionis*, all one can say is that this principle has never exercised more than a crude and indirect effect on the actual punishments meted out. Other principles interfere with a literal and single-minded application of this one. Some murders seem improperly punished by death at all; other murders would require methods of execution too horrible to inflict; in still other cases any possible execution is too deliberate and monstrous given the nature of the motivation culminating in the murder. Proponents of the death penalty rarely confine themselves to reliance on this principle of just retribution and nothing else, since they rarely confine

themselves to supporting the death penalty only for all murders.

But retributive justice need not be thought to consist of *lex talionis*. One may reject that principle as too crude and still embrace the retributive principle that the severity of punishments should be graded according to the gravity of the offense. Even though one need not claim that life imprisonment (or any kind of punishment other than death) "fits" the crime of murder, one can claim that this punishment is the proper one for murder. To do this, the schedule of punishments accepted by society must be arranged so that this mode of imprisonment is the most severe penalty used. Opponents of the death penalty need not reject this principle of retributive justice, even though they must reject a literal *lex talionis*.

Equal Justice and Capital Punishment

During the past generation, the strongest practical objection to the death penalty has been the inequities with which it has been applied. As Supreme Court Justice William O. Douglas once observed, "One searches our chronicles in vain for the execution of any member of the affluent strata of this society."[5] One does not search our chronicles in vain for the crime of murder committed by the affluent. Every study of the death penalty for rape has confirmed that black male rapists (especially where the victim is a white female) are far more likely to be sentenced to death (and executed) than white male rapists. Half of all those under death sentence during 1976 and 1977 were black, and nearly half of all those executed since 1930 were black. All the sociological evidence points to the conclusion that the death penalty is the poor man's justice; as the current street saying has it, "Those without the capital get the punishment."

Let us suppose that the factual basis for such a criticism is sound. What follows for the morality of capital punishment? Many defenders of the death penalty have been quick to point out that since there is nothing intrinsic about the crime of murder or rape that dictates that only the poor or racial-minority males will commit it, and since there is nothing overtly racist about the statutes that authorize the death penalty for murder or rape, it is hardly a fault in the idea of capital punishment if in practice it falls with unfair impact on the poor and the black. There is, in short, nothing in the death penalty that requires it to be applied unfairly and with arbitrary or discriminatory results. It is at worst a fault in the system of administering criminal justice (and some, who dispute the facts cited above, would deny even this).

Presumably, both proponents and opponents of capital punishment would concede that it is a fundamental dictate of justice that a punishment should not be unfairly—inequitably or unevenly—enforced and applied. They should also be able to agree that when the punishment in question is the extremely severe one of death, then the requirement to be fair in using such a punishment becomes even more stringent. Thus, there should be no dispute in the death penalty controversy over these principles of justice. The dispute begins as soon as one attempts to connect these principles with the actual use of this punishment.

In this country, many critics of the death penalty have argued, we would long ago have got rid of it entirely if it had been a condition of its use that it be applied equally and fairly. In the words of the attorneys who argued against the death penalty in the Supreme Court during 1972, "It is a freakish aberration, a random extreme act of violence, visibly arbitrary and discriminatory—a penalty reserved for unusual application because, if it were usually used, it would affront universally shared standards of public decency."[6] It is difficult to dispute this judgment, when

one considers that there have been in the United States during the past fifty years about half a million criminal homicides but only about 4,000 executions (all but 50 of which were of men).

We can look at these statistics in another way to illustrate the same point. If we could be assured that the 4,000 persons executed were the worst of the worst, repeated offenders without exception, the most dangerous murderers in captivity—the ones who had killed more than once and were likely to kill again, and the least likely to be confined in prison without imminent danger to other inmates and the staff—then one might accept half a million murders and a few thousand executions with a sense that rough justice had been done. But the truth is otherwise. Persons are sentenced to death and executed not because they have been found to be uncontrollably violent, hopelessly poor parole and release risks, or for other reasons. Instead, they are executed for entirely different reasons. They have a poor defense at trial; they have no funds to bring sympathetic witnesses to court; they are immigrants or strangers in the community where they were tried; the prosecuting attorney wants the publicity that goes with "sending a killer to the chair"; they have inexperienced or overworked counsel at trial; there are no funds for an appeal or for a transcript of the trial record; they are members of a despised racial minority. In short, the actual study of why particular persons have been sentenced to death and executed does not show any careful winnowing of the worst from the bad. It shows that the executed were usually the unlucky victims of prejudice and discrimination, the losers in an arbitrary lottery that could just as well have spared them as killed them, the victims of the disadvantages that almost always go with poverty. A system like this does not enhance respect for human life; it cheapens and degrades it. However heinous murder and other crimes are, the system of capital punishment does not compensate for or erase those crimes. It only tends to add new injuries of its own to the catalogue of our inhumanity to each other.

Conclusion

Our discussion of the death penalty from the moral point of view shows that there is no one moral principle the validity of which is paramount and that decisively favors one side to the controversy. Rather, we have seen how it is possible to argue either for or against the death penalty, and in each case to be appealing to moral principles that derive from the worth, value, or dignity of human life. We have also seen how it is impossible to connect any of these abstract principles with the actual practice of capital punishment without a close study of sociological, psychological, and economic factors. By themselves, the moral principles that are relevant are too abstract and uncertain in application to be of much help. Without the guidance of such principles, of course, the facts (who gets executed, and why) are of little use, either.

My own view of the controversy is that on balance, given the moral principles we have identified in the course of our discussion (including the overriding value of human life), and given the facts about capital punishment and crimes against the person, the side favoring abolition of the death penalty has the better of the argument. And there *is* an alternative to capital punishment: long-term imprisonment. Such a punishment is retributive and can be made appropriately severe to reflect the gravity of the crime for which it is the punishment. It gives adequate (though hardly perfect) protection to the public. It is free of the worst defect to which the death penalty is liable: execution of the innocent. It tacitly acknowledges that there is no way for a criminal, alive or dead, to make amends for murder or other grave crimes against the person. Finally, it has symbolic significance. The death penalty, more than any other kind of killing, is done in the name of society and on its behalf. Each of us has a hand in such a killing, and unless such killings are absolutely necessary they cannot really be justified.

Notes

1. Immanuel Kant, *The Metaphysical elements of Justice* (1797), trans. John Ladd, p. 106.
2. Benjamin Gardozo, "What Medicine Can Do for Law" (1928), reprinted in Margaret E. Hall, ed., *Selected Writings of Benjamin Nathan Cardozo* (1047), p. 204.
3. *McGautha v California*, 402 U.S. 183 (1971), at p. 204.
4. Albert Gamus, *Resistance, Rebellion, and Death* (1961), p. 199.
5. *Furman v. Georgia,* 408 U.S 238 (1972), at pp. 251–52.
6. NAACP Legal Defense and Educational Fund Brief for Petitioner in *Aikens v. California*, O.T. 1971. No. 68-5027, reprinted in Philip English Mackey, ed., *Voices Against Death: American Opposition to Capital Punishment, 1787–1975* (1975), p. 288.

Study Questions for Section 9

1. Van den Haag claims that "even if it were shown that no punishment is more deterrent than a trivial fine, capital punishment for murder would remain just, even if not useful." Why does he hold this view? Is his argument persuasive?

2. Is long-term imprisonment a punishment that is, as Bedau contends, proportional to the crime of murder?

3. Might some punishments be deserved but inappropriate for the state to impose?

SECTION 10

AFFIRMATIVE ACTION

TWO CONCEPTS OF AFFIRMATIVE ACTION

Steven M. Cahn

In March 1961, less than two months after assuming office, President John F. Kennedy issued Executive Order 10925, establishing the President's Committee on Equal Employment Opportunity. Its mission was to end discrimination in employment by the government and its contractors. The order required every federal contract to include the pledge that "The contractor will not discriminate against any employe[e] or applicant for employment because of race, creed, color, or national origin. The contractor will take affirmative action to ensure that applicants are employed, and that employe[e]s are treated during employment, without regard to their race, creed, color, or national origin."

Here, for the first time in the context of civil rights, the government called for "affirmative action." The term meant taking appropriate steps to eradicate the then widespread practices of racial, religious, and ethnic discrimination.[1] The goal, as the president stated, was "equal opportunity in employment."

In other words, *procedural* affirmative action, as I shall call it, was instituted to ensure that applicants for positions would be judged without any consideration of their race, religion, or national origin. These criteria were declared irrelevant. Taking them into account was forbidden.

The Civil Rights Act of 1964 restated and broadened the application of this principle. Title VI declared that "No person in the United States shall, on the ground of race, color or national origin, be excluded from participation in, be denied the benefits of, or be subjected to discrimination under any program or activity receiving Federal financial assistance."

But before one year had passed, President Lyndon B. Johnson argued that fairness required more than a commitment to such procedural affirmative action. In his 1965 commencement address at Howard University, he said, "You do not take a person who for years has been hobbled by chains and liberate him, bring him up to the starting line of a race and then say, 'you're free to compete with all the others,' and still justly believe that you have been completely fair."

And so several months later Johnson issued Executive Order 11246, stating that

"It is the policy of the Government of the United States to provide equal opportunity in Federal employment for all qualified persons, to prohibit discrimination in employment because of race, creed, color, or national origin, and to promote the full realization of equal employment opportunity through a positive, continuing program in each department and agency." Two years later the order was amended to prohibit discrimination on the basis of sex.

While the aim of Johnson's order is stated in language similar to that of Kennedy's, Johnson's abolished the Committee on Equal Employment Opportunity, transferred its responsibilities to the Secretary of Labor, and authorized the secretary to "adopt such rules and regulations and issue such orders as he deems necessary and appropriate to achieve the purposes thereof."

Acting on this mandate, the Department of Labor in December 1971, during the Nixon administration, issued Revised Order No. 4, requiring all federal contractors to develop "an acceptable affirmative action program," including "an analysis of areas within which the contractor is deficient in the utilization of minority groups and women, and further, goals and timetables to which the contractor's good faith efforts must be directed to correct the deficiencies." Contractors were instructed to take the term "minority groups" to refer to "Negroes, American Indians, Orientals, and Spanish Surnamed Americans." (No guidance was given as to whether having only one parent, grandparent, or great-grandparent from a group would suffice to establish group membership.) The concept of "underutilization," according to the Revised Order, meant "having fewer minorities or women in a particular job classification than would reasonably be expected by their availability." "Goals" were not to be "rigid and inflexible quotas," but "targets reasonably attainable by

means of applying every good faith effort to make all aspects of the entire affirmative action program work."[2]

Such *preferential* affirmative action, as I shall call it, requires that attention be paid to the same criteria of race, sex, and ethnicity that procedural affirmative action deems irrelevant. Is such use of these criteria justifiable in employment decisions?[3]

Return to President Johnson's claim that a person hobbled by discrimination cannot in fairness be expected to be competitive. How is it to be determined which specific individuals are entitled to a compensatory advantage? To decide each case on its own merits would be possible, but this approach would undermine the argument for instituting preferential affirmative action on a group basis. For if some members of a group are able to compete, why not others? Thus, defenders of preferential affirmative action maintain that the group, not the individual, is to be judged. If the group has suffered discrimination, then all its members are to be treated as hobbled runners.

But note that while a hobbled runner, provided with a sufficient lead in a race, may cross the finish line first, giving that person an edge prevents the individual from being considered as fast a runner as others. An equally fast runner does not need an advantage to be competitive.

This entire racing analogy thus encourages stereotypical thinking. For example, recall those men who played in baseball's Negro Leagues. That these athletes were barred from competing in the Major Leagues is the greatest stain on the history of the sport. But while they suffered discrimination, they were as proficient as their counterparts in the Major Leagues. They needed only to be judged by the same criteria as all others, and ensuring such equality of consideration is the essence of procedural affirmative action.

Granted, if individuals are unprepared or ill-equipped to compete, then they ought to be helped to try to achieve their goals. But such aid is appropriate for all who need it, not merely for members of particular racial, sexual, or ethnic groups.

Victims of discrimination deserve compensation. Former players in the Negro Leagues ought to receive special consideration in the arrangement of pension plans and any other benefits formerly denied them due to unfair treatment. The case for such compensation, however, does not imply that present black players vying for jobs in the Major Leagues should be evaluated in any other way than their performance on the field. To assume their inability to compete is derogatory and erroneous.

Such considerations have led recent defenders of preferential affirmative action to rely less heavily on any argument that implies the attribution of noncompetitiveness to an entire population.[4] Instead the emphasis has been placed on recognizing the benefits society is said to derive from encouraging expression of the varied experiences, outlooks, and values of members of different groups.

This approach makes a virtue of what has come to be called diversity.[5] As a defense of preferential affirmative action, it has at least two advantages. First, those previously excluded are now included not as a favor to them but as a means of enriching all. Second, no one is viewed as hobbled; each competes on a par, although with varied strengths.

Note that diversity requires preferential hiring. Those who enhance diversity are to be preferred to those who do not. But those preferred are not being chosen because of their deficiency; the larger group is deficient, lacking diversity. By including those who embody it, the group is enhanced.

But what does it mean to say that a group lacks diversity? Or to put the question another way, would it be possible to decide which member of a ten-person group to eliminate in order to decrease most markedly its diversity?

So stated, the question is reminiscent of a provocative puzzle in *The Tyranny of Testing*, a 1962 book by the scientist Banesh Hoffman. In this attack on the importance placed on multiple-choice tests, he quotes the following letter to the editor of the *Times* of London:

> Sir.—Among the "odd one out" type of questions which my son had to answer for a school entrance examination was: "Which is the odd one out among cricket, football, billiards, and hockey?" [In England "football" refers to the game Americans call "soccer," and "hockey" here refers to "field hockey."]

The letter continued:

> I said billiards because it is the only one played indoors. A colleague says football because it is the only one in which the ball is not struck by an implement. A neighbour says cricket because in all the other games the object is to put the ball into a net. . . . Could any of your readers put me out of my misery by stating what is the correct answer. . .?

A day later the *Times* printed the following two letters:

> Sir.—"Billiards" is the obvious answer . . . because it is the only one of the games listed which is not a team game.

> Sir.—. . . football is the odd one out because. . . it is played with an inflated ball as compared with the solid ball used in each of the other three.

Hoffman then continued his own discussion:

> When I had read these three letters it seemed to me that good cases had been made for football and billiards, and that the case for cricket was particularly clever. . . . At first I thought this made hockey easily the worst of the four choices and, in effect, ruled it out. But

then I realized that the very fact that hockey was the only one that could be thus ruled out gave it so striking a quality of separateness as to make it an excellent answer after all—perhaps the best.

Fortunately for my piece of mind, it soon occurred to me that hockey is the only one of the four games that is played with a curved implement.

The following day the *Times* published yet another letter, this from a philosophically sophisticated thinker:

Sir.—[The author of the original letter] . . . has put his finger on what has long been a matter of great amusement to me. Of the four—cricket, football, billiards, hockey—each is unique in a multitude of respects. For example, billiards is the only one in which the colour of the balls matters, the only one played with more than one ball at once, the only one played on a green cloth and not on a field. . . .

It seems to me that those who have been responsible for inventing this kind of brain teaser have been ignorant of the elementary philosophical fact that every thing is at once unique and a member of a wider class.

With this sound principle in mind, return to the problem of deciding which member of a ten-person group to eliminate in order to decrease most markedly its diversity. Unless the sort of diversity is specified, the question has no rational answer.

In searches for college and university faculty members, we know what sorts of diversity are typically of present concern: race, sex, and certain ethnicities. Why should these characteristics be given special consideration?

Consider, for example, other nonacademic respects in which prospective faculty appointees can differ: age, religion, nationality, regional background, economic class, social stratum, military experience, bodily appearance, physical soundness, sexual orientation, marital status, ethical standards, political commitments, and cultural values. Why should we not seek diversity of these sorts?

To some extent schools do. Many colleges and universities indicate in advertisements for faculty positions that they seek persons with disabilities or Vietnam War veterans. The City University of New York requires all searches to give preference to individuals of Italian-American descent.

The crucial point is that the appeal to diversity never favors any particular candidate. Each one adds to some sort of diversity but not another. In a department of ten, one individual might be the only black, another the only woman, another the only bachelor, another the only veteran, another the only one over 50, another the only Catholic, another the only Republican, another the only Scandinavian, another the only socialist, and the tenth the only Southerner.

Suppose the suggestion is made that the sorts of diversity to be sought are those of groups that have suffered discrimination. This approach leads to another problem, clearly put by the philosopher John Kekes:

It is true that American blacks, Native Americans, Hispanics, and women have suffered injustice as a group. But so have homosexuals, epileptics, the urban and the rural poor, the physically ugly, those whose careers were ruined by McCarthyism, prostitutes, the obese, and so forth. . . .

There have been some attempts to deny that there is an analogy between these two classes of victims. It has been said that the first were unjustly discriminated against due to racial or sexual prejudice and that this is not true of the second. This is indeed so. But why should we accept the suggestion . . . that the only form of injustice relevant to preferential treatment is that which is due to racial or sexual prejudice? Injustice occurs in many forms, and those who value justice will surely object to all of them.[6]

Kekes's reasoning is cogent. But another difficulty looms for the proposal to seek diversity only of groups that have suffered discrimination. For diversity is supposed to be valued not as compensation to the disadvantaged, but as a means of enriching all.

Consider, for example, a department in which most of the faculty members are women. In certain fields such as nursing and elementary education, such departments are common. If diversity by sex is of value, then such a department, when making its next appointment, should prefer a man. But men as a group have not been victims of discrimination. So, to achieve valued sorts of diversity, the question is not which groups have been discriminated against, but which valued groups are not represented. The question thus reappears as to which sorts of diversity are to be most highly valued. I know of no compelling answer.

Seeking to justify preferential affirmative action in terms of its contribution to diversity raises yet another difficulty. For preferential affirmative action is commonly defended as a temporary rather than a permanent measure.[7] Yet preferential affirmative action to achieve diversity is not temporary.

Suppose it were. Then once an institution had appointed an appropriate number of members of a particular group, preferential affirmative action would no longer be in effect. Yet the institution may later find that it has too few members of that group. Since lack of valuable diversity is presumably no more acceptable at one time than another, preferential affirmative action would have to be reinstituted. Thereby it would in effect become a permanent policy.

Why do so many of its defenders wish it to be only transitional? They believe the policy was instituted in response to irrelevant criteria for appointment having been mistakenly treated as relevant. To adopt any policy that continues to treat essentially irrelevant criteria as relevant is to share the guilt of those who discriminated originally. Irrelevant criteria should be recognized as such and abandoned as soon as feasible.

Some defenders of preferential affirmative action argue, however, that an individual's race, sex, or ethnicity is germane to fulfilling the responsibilities of a faculty member. They believe, therefore, that preferential affirmative action should be a permanent feature of search processes, since it takes account of criteria that should be considered in every appointment.

At least three reasons have been offered to justify the claim that those of a particular race, sex, or ethnicity are particularly well-suited to be faculty members. First, it has been argued that they would be especially effective teachers of any student who shares their race, sex, or ethnicity.[8] Second, they have been supposed to be particularly insightful researchers due to their experiencing the world from distinctive standpoints.[9] Third, they have been taken to be role models, demonstrating that those of a particular race, sex, or ethnicity can perform effectively as faculty members.[10]

Consider each of these claims in turn. As to the presumed teaching effectiveness of the individuals in question, no empirical study supports the claim.[11] But assume compelling evidence were presented. It would have no implications for individual cases. A particular person who does not share race, sex, or ethnicity with students might teach them superbly. An individual of the students' own race, sex, or ethnicity might be ineffective. Regardless of statistical correlations, what is crucial is that individuals be able to teach effectively all sorts of students, and it is entirely consistent with procedural affirmative action to seek individuals who give evidence of satisfying this criterion. But knowing an individual's race, sex, or ethnicity does not reveal whether that person will be effective in the classroom.

Do members of a particular race, sex, or ethnicity share a distinctive intellectual perspective that enhances their scholarship? The philosopher Celia Wolf-Devine has aptly described this claim as a form of "stereotyping" that is "demeaning." As she puts it, "A Hispanic who is a Republican is no less a Hispanic, and a woman who is not a feminist is no less a woman."[12] Furthermore, are Hispanic men and women supposed to have the same point of view in virtue of their common ethnicity, or are they supposed to have different points of view in virtue of their different sexes?

If our standpoints are thought to be determined by our race, sex, and ethnicity, why not also by the numerous other significant respects in which people differ, such as age, religion, sexual orientation, and so on? Since each of us is unique, can anyone else share my point of view?

That my own experience is my own is a tautology that does not imply the keenness of my insight into my experience. The victim of a crime may as a result embrace an outlandish theory of racism. But neither who you are nor what you experience guarantees the truth of your theories.

To be an effective researcher calls for discernment, imagination, and perseverance. These attributes are not tied to one's race, sex, ethnicity, age, or religion. Black scholars, for example, may be more inclined to study black literature than are non-black scholars. But some non-black literary critics are more interested in and more knowledgeable about black literature than are some black literary critics. Why make decisions based on fallible racial generalizations when judgments of individual merit are obtainable and more reliable?

Perhaps the answer lies in the claim that only those of a particular race, sex, or ethnicity can serve as role models, exemplifying to members of a particular group the possibility of their success. Again, no empirical study supports the claim, but in this case it has often been taken as self-evident that, for instance, only a woman can be a role model for a woman, only a black for a black, only a Catholic for a Catholic. In other words, the crucial feature of a person is supposed to be not what the person does but who the person is.

The logic of the situation, however, is not so clear. Consider, for example, a black man who is a Catholic. Presumably he serves as a role model for blacks, men, and Catholics. Does he serve as a role model for black women, or can only a black woman serve that purpose? Does he serve as a role model for all Catholics or only for those who are black? Can I serve as a role model for anyone else, since no one else shares all my characteristics? Or perhaps I can serve as a role model for everyone else, since everyone else belongs to at least one group to which I belong.

Putting aside these conundrums, the critical point is supposed to be that in a field in which discrimination has been rife, a successful individual who belongs to the discriminated group demonstrates that members of the group can succeed in that field. Obviously success is possible without a role model, for the first successful individual had none. But suppose persuasive evidence were offered that a role model, while not necessary, sometimes is helpful, not only to those who belong to the group in question, but also to those prone to believe that no members of the group can perform effectively within the field. Role models would then both encourage members of a group that had suffered discrimination and discourage further discrimination against the group.

To serve these purposes, however, the person chosen would need to be viewed as having been selected by the same criteria as all others. If not, members of the group that has suffered discrimination as well as those prone to discriminate would be confirmed in their common view that members of the group never would have been chosen unless membership in the group had been taken into account. Those who suffered discrimination would conclude that it still exists, while those prone to discriminate would conclude that members of the group lack the necessary attributes to compete equally.

How can we ensure that a person chosen for a position has been selected by the same criteria as all others? Preferential affirmative action fails to serve the purpose, since by definition it differentiates among people on the basis of criteria other than performance. The approach that ensures merit selection is procedural affirmative action.

By its demand for vigilance against every form of discrimination, it maximizes equal opportunity for all.

The policy of appointing others than the best qualified has not produced a harmonious society in which prejudice is transcended and all enjoy the benefits of self-esteem. Rather, the practice has bred doubts about the abilities of those chosen while generating resentment in those passed over.

Procedural affirmative action had barely begun before it was replaced by preferential affirmative action. The difficulties with the latter are now clear. Before deeming them necessary evils in the struggle to overcome pervasive prejudice, why not try scrupulous enforcement of procedural affirmative action? We might thereby most directly achieve that equitable society so ardently desired by every person of good will.

Notes

1. A comprehensive history of one well-documented case of such discrimination is Dan A. Oren, *Joining the Club: A History of Jews and Yale* (New Haven and London: Yale University Press, 1985). Prior to the end of World War II, no Jew had ever been appointed to the rank of full professor in Yale College.

2. 41 C.F.R. 60-2.12. The Order provides no suggestion as to whether a "good faith effort" implies only showing preference among equally qualified candidates (the "tie-breaking" model), preferring a strong candidate to an even stronger one (the "plus factor" model), preferring a merely qualified candidate to a strongly qualified candidate (the "trumping" model), or cancelling a search unless a qualified candidate of the preferred sort is available (the "quota" model).

   A significant source of misunderstanding about affirmative action results from both the government's failure to clarify which type of preference is called for by a "good faith effort" and the failure on the part of those conducting searches to inform applicants

which type of preference is in use. Regarding the latter issue, see my "Colleges Should Be Explicit About Who Will Be Considered for Jobs," *The Chronicle of Higher Education,* XXXV (30), 1989, reprinted in *Affirmative Action and the University: A Philosophical Inquiry,* Steven M. Cahn (ed.) (Philadelphia: Temple University Press, 1993), pp. 3–4.

3. Whether their use is appropriate in a school's admission and scholarship decisions is a different issue, involving other considerations, and I shall not explore that subject in this article.

4. See, for example, Leslie Pickering Francis, "In Defense of Affirmative Action," in Cahn, *op. cit.,* especially pp. 24–26. She raises concerns about unfairness to those individuals forced by circumstances not of their own making to bear all the costs of compensation, as well as injustices to those who have been equally victimized but are not members of specified groups.

5. The term gained currency when Justice Lewis Powell, in his pivotal opinion in the Supreme Court's 1978 *Bakke* decision, found "the attainment of a diverse student body" to be a goal that might justify the use of race in student admissions. An incisive analysis

of that decision is Carl Cohen, *Naked Racial Preference* (Lanham, MD: Madison Books, 1995), pp. 55–80.

6. Cahn, *op. cit.*, p. 151.

7. Consider Michael Rosenfeld, *Affirmative Action and Justice: A Philosophical and Constitutional Inquiry* (New Haven and London: Yale University Press, 1991), p. 336: "Ironically, the sooner affirmative action is allowed to complete its mission, the sooner the need for it will altogether disappear."

8. See, for example, Francis, *op. cit.*, p. 31.

9. See, for example, Richard Wasserstrom, "The University and the Case for Preferential Treatment," *American Philosophical Quarterly*, 13 (4), 1976, pp. 165–170.

10. See, for example, Joel J. Kupperman, "Affirmative Action: Relevant Knowledge and Relevant Ignorance," in Cahn, *op. cit.*, pp. 181–188.

11. Consider Judith Jarvis Thomson, "Preferential Hiring," *Philosophy and Public Affairs*, 2 (4), 1973, p. 368: "I do not think that as a student I learned any better, or any more, from the women who taught me than from the men, and I do not think that my own women students now learn any better or any more from me than they do from my male colleagues."

12. Cahn, *op. cit.*, p. 230.

IN FAVOR OF AFFIRMATIVE ACTION

Tom L. Beauchamp

Affirmative action policies have had their strongest appeal when discrimination that barred groups from desirable institutions persisted although forbidden by law. Policies that establish target goals, timetables, and quotas were initiated to ensure more equitable opportunities by counterbalancing apparently intractable prejudice and systemic favoritism. The policies that were initiated with such lofty ambitions are now commonly criticized on grounds that they establish quotas that unjustifiably elevate the opportunities of members of targeted groups, discriminate against equally qualified or even more qualified members of majorities, and perpetuate racial and sexual paternalism.

Affirmative action policies favoring *groups* have been controversial since President Lyndon Johnson's 1965 executive order that required federal contractors to develop affirmative action policies.[1] Everyone now agrees that *individuals* who have been injured by past discrimination should be made whole for the injury, but it remains controversial whether and how past discrimination against groups justifies preferential treatment for the group's *current* members. Critics of group preferential policies hold that compensating individuals for unfair discrimination can alone be justified, but it is controversial whether individuals can be harmed merely by virtue of a group membership.[2]

Those who support affirmative action and those who oppose it both seek the best means to the same end, a color-blind, sex-blind society. Their goals do not differ. Nor do they entirely disagree over the means. If a color-blind, sex-blind society can be achieved and maintained by legal guarantees of equal opportunities to all, both parties agree that social policies should be restricted to this means. Here agreement ends. Those who support affirmative action do not believe such guarantees can be fairly and efficiently achieved other than by affirmative action policies. Those who seek an end to affirmative action believe that the goals can be achieved in other ways and that affirmative action policies themselves unjustifiably discriminate. I will be supporting affirmative action policies against this counterposition.

Two Pivotal Concepts

Like virtually all problems in practical ethics, the meaning of a few central terms can powerfully affect one's moral viewpoint. The terms "affirmative action" and "quotas" have proved particularly troublesome, because they have been defined in both minimal and maximal ways. The original meaning of "affirmative action" was minimalist. It referred to plans to safeguard equal opportunity, to protect against discrimination, to advertise positions openly, and to create scholarship programs to ensure recruitment from specific groups.[3] Few now oppose open advertisement and the like, and if this were all that were meant by "affirmative action," few would oppose it. However, "affirmative action" has assumed new and expanded meanings. Today it is typically associated with quotas and preferential policies that target specific groups, especially women or minority members.

I will not favor either the minimalist or the maximalist sense of "affirmative action." I will use the term to refer to positive steps taken to hire persons from groups previously and presently discriminated against, leaving open what will count as a "positive step" to remove discrimination. I thus adopt a broad meaning.

A number of controversies have also centered on the language of *quotas*.[4] A "quota," as I use the term, does not mean that fixed numbers of a group must be admitted, hired, or promoted—even to the point of including less-qualified persons if they are the only available members of a targeted group. Quotas are target numbers or percentages that an employer, admissions office, recruitment committee, and the like sincerely attempt to meet. Less-qualified persons are occasionally hired or promoted under a policy that incorporates quotas; but it is no part of affirmative action or the meaning of "quotas" to hire persons who lack basic qualifications. Quotas are numerically expressible goals pursued in good faith and with due diligence.

The language of "quotas" can be toned down by speaking of hopes, objectives, and guidelines; but cosmetic changes of wording only thinly obscure a policy established to recruit from groups in which the goals are made explicit by numbers. Thus when John Sununu—presumably a strong opponent of quotas—told Secretary of Defense Richard Cheney that he, Sununu, "wanted 30 percent of the remaining 42 top jobs in the Defense Department to be filled by women and minorities,"[5] he was using a quota. Likewise, universities sometimes use quotas when the subtleties of faculty and staff hiring and promotion and student admission make no mention of them. For example, if the chair of a department says the department should hire two to three women in the next five available positions, the formula constitutes a quota, or at least a numerical target.

Reasons typically offered in defense of targeted affirmative action, with or without quotas, are the following: "We have many women students who need and do not have an ample number of role models and mentors." "The provost has offered a group of special fellowships to bring more minorities to the university." "More diversity is much needed in this department." "The goals and mission of this university strongly suggest a need for increased representation of women and minorities." In pursuing these objectives, members of departments and committees commonly act in ways that suggest they willingly endorse what either is or has a strong family resemblance to a specific target.

The Prevalence of Discrimination as the Rationale for Affirmative Action

The moral problem of affirmative action is primarily whether specific targets, including quotas in the broad sense, can legitimately be used. To support affirmative action as a weapon against discrimination is not necessarily to endorse it in all institutions. Racial, sexual, and religious forms of discrimination affecting admission, hiring, and promotion have been substantially reduced in various sectors of American society, and perhaps even completely eliminated in some. The problem is that in other social sectors it is common to encounter discrimination in favor of a favored group or discrimination against disliked, distrusted, unattractive, or neglected groups. The pervasive attitudes underlying these phenomena are the most important background conditions of the debate over affirmative action, and we need to understand these pockets of discrimination in order to appreciate the attractions of affirmative action.

Statistics Statistics constituting at least prima facie evidence of discrimination in society are readily available. These data indicate that in sizable parts of American society white males continue to receive the highest entry-level salaries when compared to all other social groups; that women with similar credentials and experience to those of men are commonly hired at lower positions or earn lower starting salaries than men and are promoted at one-half the rate of their male counterparts, with the consequence that the gap between salaries and promotion rates is still growing at an increasing rate; that 70 percent or more of white-collar positions are held by women, although they hold only about 10 percent of management positions; that three out of seven U.S. employees occupy white-collar positions, whereas the ratio is but one of seven for African Americans; and, finally, that a significant racial gap in unemployment statistics is a consistent pattern in the United States, with the gap now greatest for college-educated, African-American males.[6] Whether these statistics

demonstrate invidious discrimination is controversial, but additional data drawn from empirical studies reinforce the judgment that racial and sexual discrimination are reasons for and perhaps the best explanation of these statistics.

Housing For example, studies of real estate rentals, housing sales, and home mortgage lending show a disparity in rejection rates—for example, loan rejection rates between white applicants and minority applicants. Wide disparities exist even after statistics are adjusted for economic differences; minority applicants are over 50 percent more likely to be denied a loan than white applicants of equivalent economic status. Other studies indicate that discrimination in sales of houses is prevalent in the United States. Race appears to be as important as socioeconomic status in failing to secure both houses and loans, and studies also show that the approval rate for African Americans increases in lending institutions with an increase in the proportion of minority employees in that institution.[7]

Jobs A similar pattern is found in employment. In 1935 the Grier Partnership and the Urban League produced independent studies that reveal striking disparities in the employment levels of college-trained African Americans and whites in Washington, DC, one of the best markets for African Americans. Both studies found that college-trained African Americans have much more difficulty than their white counterparts in securing employment. Both cite discrimination as the major underlying factor.[8]

In a 1991 study by the Urban Institute, employment practices in Washington, DC, and Chicago were examined. Equally qualified, identically dressed white and African-American applicants for jobs were used to test for bias in the job market, as presented by newspaper-advertised positions. Whites and African Americans were matched identically for speech patterns, age, work experience, personal characteristics, and physical build. Investigators found repeated discrimination against African-American male applicants. The higher the position, the higher the level of discrimination. The white men received job offers three times more often than the equally qualified African Americans who interviewed for the same position. The authors of the study concluded that discrimination against African-American men is "widespread and entrenched."[9]

These statistics and empirical studies help frame racial discrimination in the United States. Anyone who believes that only a narrow slice of surface discrimination exists will be unlikely to agree with what I have been and will be arguing, at least if my proposals entail strong affirmative action measures. By contrast, one who believes that discrimination is securely and almost invisibly entrenched in many sectors of society will be more likely to endorse or at least tolerate resolute affirmative action policies.

Although racism and sexism are commonly envisioned as intentional forms of favoritism and exclusion, intent to discriminate is not a necessary condition of discrimination. Institutional networks can unintentionally hold back or exclude persons. Hiring by personal friendships and word of mouth are common instances, as are seniority systems. Numerical targets are important remedies for these camouflaged areas, where it is particularly difficult to shatter patterns of discrimination and reconfigure the environment.[10]

The U.S. Supreme Court has rightly upheld affirmative action programs with numerically expressed hiring formulas when intended to quash the effects of both intentional and unintentional discrimination.[11] The Court has also maintained that such formulas have sometimes been structured so that they unjustifiably exceed proper limits.[12] The particulars of the cases will determine how we are to balance different interests and considerations.

The Justification of Affirmative Action

This balancing strategy is warranted. Numerical goals or quotas are justified if and only if they are necessary to overcome the discriminatory effects that could not otherwise be eliminated with reasonable efficiency. It is the intractable and often deeply hurtful character of racism and sexism that justifies aggressive policies to remove their damaging effects. The history of affirmative action, though short, is an impressive history of fulfilling once-failed promises, displacing disillusion, and protecting the most vulnerable members of society against demeaning abuse. It has delivered our country from what was little more than a caste system and a companion of apartheid.

We have learned in the process that numerical formulas are sometimes essential tools, sometimes excessive tools, and sometimes permissible but optional tools—depending on the subtleties of the case. We can expect each case to be different, and for this reason we should be cautious about general pronouncements regarding the justifiability of numerical formulas—as well as the merit of merit-based systems and blind systems. The better perspective is that until the facts of particular cases have been carefully assessed, we are not positioned to support or oppose any particular affirmative action policy or its abandonment.

The Supreme Court has allowed these numerical formulas in plans that are intended to combat a manifest imbalance in traditionally segregated job categories (even if the particular workers drawn from minorities were not victims of past discrimination). In *Local 28 v. Equal Employment Opportunity Commission,* a minority hiring goal of 29.23 percent had been established. The Court held that such specific numbers are justified when dealing with persistent or egregious discrimination. The Court found that the history of Local 28 was one of complete "foot-dragging resistance" to the idea of hiring without discrimination in its apprenticeship training programs from minority groups. The Court argued that "affirmative race-conscious relief" may be the only reasonable means to the end of assuring equality of employment opportunities and to eliminate deeply ingrained discriminatory practices.[13]

In a 1989 opinion, by contrast, the Supreme Court held in *City of Richmond v. J. A. Croson* that Richmond, Virginia, officials could not require contractors to set aside 30 percent of their budget for subcontractors who owned "minority business enterprises." This particular plan was not written to remedy the effects of prior or present discrimination. The Court found that *this way* of fixing a percentage based on race, in the absence of evidence of identified discrimination, denied citizens an equal opportunity to compete for subcontracts. Parts of the reasoning in this case were reaffirmed in the 1995 case of *Adarand Constructors Inc. v. Pena.*

Some writers have interpreted *Croson, Adarand,* and the 1997 decision of a three-judge panel of the 9th U.S. Circuit Court of Appeals to the effect that California's voter-approved ban on affirmative action (Proposition 209) is constitutional as the dismantling of affirmative action plans that use numerical goals. Perhaps this prediction will turn out to be correct, but the U.S. Supreme Court has consistently adhered to a balancing strategy that I believe captures the fitting way to frame issues of affirmative action.[14] It allows us to use race and sex as relevant bases of policies if and only if it is essential to do so in order to achieve a larger and justified social purpose.

These reasons for using race and sex in policies are far distant from the role of these properties in invidious discrimination. Racial discrimination and sexual discrimination typically spring from feelings of superiority and a sense that other groups deserve lower social status. Affirmative action entails no such attitude or intent. Its purpose is to restore to persons a status they have been unjustifiably denied, to help them escape stigmatization, and to foster relationships of interconnectedness in society.[15]

Affirmative action in pockets of the most vicious and visceral racism will likely be needed for another generation, after which we should have reached our goals of fair opportunity and equal consideration. Once these goals are achieved, affirmative action will no longer be justified and should be abandoned. The goal to be reached at that point is not proportional representation, which has occasionally been used as a basis for fixing target numbers in affirmative action policies, but as such is merely a means to the end of discrimination, not an end to be pursued for its own sake. The goal is simply fair opportunity and equal consideration.

Voluntary Affirmative Action Plans

Many affirmative action policies are voluntary plans, and these plans have often been more successful than government-mandated policies.[16] Numerous American institutions have learned that discrimination causes the institution to lose opportunities to make contact with the full range of qualified persons who might be contacted. Their competitive position is thereby weakened, just as a state university would be weakened if it hired faculty entirely from its own state. These institutions have found that promoting diversity in the workforce is correlated with high-quality employees, reductions in the costs of discrimination claims, a lowering of absenteeism, less turnover, and increased customer satisfaction.[17]

If we were now to abolish these established forms of affirmative action hiring, we would open old wounds in many institutions that have been developing plans through consent decree processes with courts as well as direct negotiations with minority groups and unions. Many corporations report that they have invested heavily in eliminating managerial biases and stereotypes while training managers to hire appropriately. They are concerned that without the pressure of an affirmative action plan, which they draft internally, managers will fail to recognize their own biases and stereotypes.[18]

Tolerating Reverse Discrimination

It has often been said that reverse discrimination is caused by affirmative action policies and that this discrimination is no better than the racial or sexual discrimination that affirmative action allegedly frustrates.[19] Some instances of such discriminatory exclusion do occur, of course, and compensation or rectification for an injured party is sometimes the appropriate response. However, some of these setbacks to the interests of those excluded by a policy may be no more objectionable than various burdens produced by social policies that advantage some members of society and disadvantage others. Inheritance laws, for example, favor certain members of society over others, whereas policies of eminent domain disadvantage persons who wish to retain what is legitimately their property in

order to advance the public good. Such laws and outcomes are warranted by a larger public benefit and by justice-based considerations that conflict with the interests of the disadvantaged parties. The point is that disadvantages to majorities produced by affirmative action may be warranted by the promotion of social ideals of equal treatment for groups that were severely mistreated in the past.

In assessing the disadvantages that might be caused to members of majorities (primarily white males), we should remember that there are disadvantages to other parties that operate in the current system, many of which will not be affected by affirmative action or by its absence. For example, just as young white males may now be paying a penalty for wrongs committed by older white males (who will likely never be penalized), so the older members of minority groups and older women who have been most disadvantaged in the past are the least likely to gain an advantage from affirmative action policies. Paradoxically, the younger minority members and women who have suffered least from discrimination now stand to gain the most from affirmative action. Despite these unfairnesses, there is no clear way to remedy them.

Policies of affirmative action may have many other shortcomings as well. For example, they confer economic advantages upon some who do not deserve them and generate court battles, jockeying for favored position by a multiple array of minorities, a lowering of admission and work standards in some institutions, heightened racial hostility, and continued suspicion that well-placed women and minority group members received their positions purely on the basis of quotas, thereby damaging their self-respect and the respect of their colleagues. Affirmative action is not a perfect social tool, but it is the best tool yet created as a way of preventing a recurrence of the far worse imperfections of our past policies of segregation and exclusion.

Judging the Past and the Present

Looking back at this deplorable history and at the unprecedented development of affirmative action policies over the past thirty years, what moral judgments can we reach about persons who either initiated these policies or those who failed to initiate such programs? Can we say that anyone has engaged in moral wrongdoing in implementing these policies, or exhibited moral failure in not implementing them? Addressing these questions should help us better judge the present in light of the past.

I will examine these questions through the classic AT&T affirmative action agreement in the 1970s. The salient facts of this case are as follows: The U.S. Equal Employment Opportunity Commission (EEOC) had investigated AT&T in the 1960s on grounds of alleged discriminatory practices in hiring and promotion. In 1970 the EEOC stated that the firm engaged in "pervasive, system-wide, and blatantly unlawful discrimination in employment against women, African-Americans, Spanish-surnamed Americans, and other minorities."[20] The EEOC argued that the employment practices of AT&T violated several civil rights laws and had excluded women from all job classifications except low-paying clerical and operator positions.

AT&T denied all charges and produced a massive array of statistics about women and minorities in the workforce. However, these statistics tended to undermine the corporation's own case. They showed that half the company's 700,000 employees were female, but that the women were all either secretaries or operators. It became apparent that the company categorized

virtually all of its jobs in terms of men's work and women's work. The federal government was determined to obliterate this aspect of corporate culture in the belief that no other strategy would break the grip of this form of sexism. Eventually AT&T threw in the towel and entered a consent decree, which was accepted by a court in Philadelphia in 1973. This agreement resulted in payments of $15 million in back wages to 13,000 women and 2,000 minority-group men and $23 million in raises to 36,000 employees who had been harmed by previous policies.

Out of this settlement came a company-wide "model affirmative action plan" that radically changed the character of AT&T hiring and its promotion practices. The company agreed to create an "employee profile" in its job classifications to be achieved faster than would normally occur. It established racial and gender goals and intermediate targets in fifteen job categories to be met in quarterly increments. The goals were determined by statistics regarding representative numbers of workers in the relevant labor market. The decree required that under conditions of a target failure, a less-qualified (but qualified) person could take precedence over a more-qualified person with greater seniority. This condition applied only to promotions, not to layoffs and rehiring, where seniority continued to prevail.

As was inevitable under this arrangement, reverse discrimination cases emerged. The well-known McAleer case came before Judge Gerhard A. Gesell, who held in 1976 that McAleer was a faultless employee who became an innocent victim through an unfortunate but justifiable use of the affirmative action a process.[21] Gesell ruled that McAleer was entitled to monetary compensation (as damages), but not entitled to the promotion to which he thought he was entitled because the discrimination the consent decree had been designed to eliminate might be perpetuated if a qualified woman were not given the promotion.[22]

This AT&T case history, like many affirmative action cases, is a story of changed expectations and changing moral viewpoints. At the core of any framework for the evaluation of such cases is a distinction between *wrongdoing* and *culpability*, which derives from the need to evaluate the moral quality of actions by contrast to agents. For example, we might want to say that AT&T hiring practices were wrong and that many employees were wronged by them, without judging anyone culpable for the wrongs done.

Virtually everyone is now agreed, including AT&T officials, that AT&T's hiring and promotion practices did involve unjustified discrimination and serious wrongdoing. Even basic moral principles were violated—for example, that one ought to treat persons with equal consideration and respect, that racial and sexual discrimination are impermissible, and the like. Less clear is whether the agents involved should be blamed. Several factors place limits on our ability to make judgments about the blameworthiness of agents—or at least the fairness of doing so. These factors include culturally induced moral ignorance, a changing circumstance in the specification of moral principles, and indeterminacy in an organization's division of labor and designation of responsibility. All were present to some degree in the AT&T case.

Judgments of exculpation depend, at least to some extent, on whether proper moral standards were acknowledged in the culture in which the events transpired—for example, in the professional ethics of the period. If we had possessed clear standards regarding the justice of hiring and promotion in the 1950s and 1960s, it would be easier to find AT&T officials culpable. The absence of such standards is a factor in our reflections about culpability and exculpation, but need not be part of our reflection on the wronging that occurred.

The fact of culturally induced moral ignorance does not by itself entail exculpation or a lack of accountability for states of ignorance. The issue is the degree to which persons are accountable for holding and even perpetuating or disseminating the beliefs that they hold when an opportunity to remedy or modify the beliefs exists. If such opportunities are unavailable, a person may have a valid excuse; but the greater the opportunity to eliminate ignorance, the less is exculpation appropriate. Persons who permit their culturally induced moral ignorance to persist through a series of opportunities to correct the beliefs thereby increase their culpability.

The more persons are obstinate in not facing issues, and the more they fail to perceive the plight of other persons who may be negatively affected by their failure to act, the more likely are we to find their actions or inactions inexcusable. No doubt culturally induced moral ignorance was a mitigating factor in the 1960s and early 1970s, but I believe history also shows that it was mixed with a resolute failure to face moral problems when it was widely appreciated that they were serious problems and were being faced by other institutions.

The central issue for my purposes is not whether discriminatory attitudes should be judged harshly in the pre-affirmative action situation at AT&T, but whether the affirmative action policy that was adopted itself involved wrongdoing or constituted, then or now, an activity for which we would blame persons who establish such policies. I do not see how agents could be blamed for maintaining and enforcing this program, despite its toughness. Given AT&T's history as well as the desperate situation of discrimination in American society, under what conditions could agents be culpable even if McAleer-type cases of reverse discrimination occasionally resulted? Even if we assume that McAleer and others were wronged in the implementation of the policy, it does not follow that the agents were culpable for their support of the policy.

Today, many corporate programs similar to the AT&T policy are in place. We can and should ask both whether persons are wronged by these policies and whether those who use the policies are culpable. The answer seems to me the same in the 1990s as it was in the 1970s: As long as there is persistent, intractable discrimination in society, the policies will be justified and the agents nonculpable, even if some persons are harmed and even wronged by the policies. To say that we should fight wrongs done by the policies is not to say that we should abandon the policies themselves.

Indeed, I defend a stronger view: Affirmative action was a noble struggle against a crippling social ill in the 1960s and 1970s, and those who took part in the struggle deserve acknowledgment for their courage and foresight. Those who failed to seize the opportunity to enact affirmative action policies or some functional equivalent such as companywide enforcement of equal opportunity are culpable for what, in many cases, were truly serious moral failures.

There is no reason to believe that, in this respect, the situation is changed today from the 1970s. Today persons in corporations, universities, and government agencies who are aware or should be aware that a high level of racism or sexism exists are culpable if they fail to move to counteract its invidious effects by affirmative policies or similarly serious interventions such as meaningful enforcement of fair opportunity. To say that we should judge the officers of these institutions culpable for their moral failures is not to say that there are no

mitigating conditions for their failures, such as the mixed messages they have received over the past fifteen years from federal officials and the general cultural climate of moral indifference to the problem. At the same time, the mitigating conditions are weaker today than in the 1970s because the excuse of culturally induced moral ignorance is weaker. In general, there are now fewer excuses available for not taking an aggressive posture to combat discrimination than ever before.

All of this is not to say that we are never culpable for the way we formulate or implement affirmative action policies. One aspect of these policies for which we likely will be harshly judged in the future is a failure of truthfulness in publicly disclosing and advertising the commitments of the policies—for example, in advertising for new positions.[23] Once it has been determined that a woman or a minority group member will most likely be hired, institutions now typically place advertisements that include lines such as the following:

> Women and minority-group candidates are especially encouraged to apply. The University of X is an equal opportunity, affirmative action employer.

Advertisements and public statements rarely contain more information about an institution's affirmative action objectives, although often more information might be disclosed that would be of material relevance to applicants. The following are examples of facts or objectives that might be disclosed: A department may have reserved its position for a woman or minority; the chances may be overwhelming that only a minority group member will be hired; the interview team may have decided in advance that only women will be interviewed; the advertised position may be the result of a university policy that offers an explicit incentive (perhaps a new position) to a department if a minority representative is appointed, etc. Incompleteness in disclosure and advertising sometimes stems from fear of legal liability, but more often from fear of departmental embarrassment and harm either to reputation or to future recruiting efforts.

The greater moral embarrassment, however, is our ambivalence and weak conceptions of what we are doing. Many, including academics, fear making public what they believe to be morally commendable in their recruiting efforts. There is something deeply unsatisfactory about a reluctance to disclose one's real position. This situation is striking, because the justification for the position is presumably that it is a morally praiseworthy endeavor. Here we have a circumstance in which the actions taken may not be wrong, but the agents are culpable for a failure to clearly articulate the basis of their actions and to allow those bases to be openly debated so that their true merits can be assessed by all affected parties.

Conclusion

During the course of the last thirty years, the widespread acceptance of racial segregation and sexual dominance in America has surrendered to a more polite culture that accepts racial integration and sexual equality. This discernible change of attitude and institutional policy has led to an imposing public opposition to preferential treatment on the basis of race and sex in general. In this climate what should happen to affirmative action?

As long as our choices are formulated in terms of the false dilemma of either special preference for groups or individual merit, affirmative action is virtually certain to be overthrown. Americans are now wary and weary of all forms of group preference, other than the liberty to choose one's preferred groups. I would be pleased to witness the defeat of affirmative action were the choice the simple one of group preference or individual merit. But it is not. Despite the vast changes of attitude in thirty years of American culture, the underlying realities are naggingly familiar. Perhaps in another thirty years we can rid ourselves of the perils of affirmative action. But at present the public good and our sense of ourselves as a nation will be well served by retaining what would in other circumstances be odious policies. They merit preservation as long as we can say that, on balance, they serve us better than they disserve us.

Notes

1. Executive Order 11246. C.F.R. 339 (1964–65).
2. See J. Angelo Corlett, "Racism and Affirmative Action," *Journal of Social Philosophy* 24 (1993): 163–75; and Cass R. Sunstein, "The Limits of Compensatory Justice" *Nomos XXXIII: Compensatory Justice,* ed. John Chapman (New York: New York University Press, 1991): 281–310.
3. See Thomas Nagel, "A Defense of Affirmative Action," testimony before the Subcommittee on the Constitution of the Senate Judiciary Committee, June 18, 1981; and Louis Pojman, "The Moral Status of Affirmative Action," *Public Affairs Quarterly* 6 (1992): 181–206.
4. See the analyses in Gertrude Ezorsky, *Racism and Justice* (Ithaca, NY: Cornell University Press, 1991); and Robert Fullinwider, *The Reverse Discrimination Controversy* (Totowa, NJ: Rowman and Allanheld, 1980).
5. Bob Woodward, *The Commanders* (New York: Simon and Schuster, 1991), p. 72.
6. Bron Taylor, *Affirmative Action at Work: Law, Politics, and Ethics* (Pittsburgh: University of Pittsburgh Press, 1991); Morley Gunderson, "Male-Female Wage Differentials and Policy Responses," *Journal of Economic Literature* 27 (March 1989), and Morley Gunderson, "Pay and Employment Equity in the United States and Canada," *International Journal of Manpower* 15 (1994):

26–43; Patricia Gaynor and Garey Durden, "Measuring the Extent of Earnings Discrimination: An Update," *Applied Economics* 27 (August 1995): 669–76; Marjorie L. Baldwin and William G. Johnson, "The Employment Effects of Wage Discrimination Against Black Men," *Industrial & Labor Relations Review* 49 (1996): 302–16; Franklin D. Wilson, Marta Tienda, and Lawrence Wu, "Race and Unemployment: Labor Market Experiences of Black and White Men, 1968–1988," *Work & Occupations* 22 (1995): 245–70; National Center for Education Statistics, *Faculty in Higher Education Institutions, 1988, Contractor Survey Report,* compiled by Susan H. Russell et al. (Washington, DC: U.S. Dept. of Education, March 1990), pp. 5–13; Betty M. Vetter, ed., *Professional Women and Minorities: A Manpower Data Resource Service,* 8th ed. (Washington, DC: Commission on Science and Technology, 1989); (anonymous) "Less Discrimination for Women but Poorer Prospects at Work than Men," *Management Services* 40 (1996): 6; Cynthia D. Anderson and Donald Tomaskovic-Devey, "Patriarchal Pressures: An Exploration of Organizational Processes that Exacerbate and Erode Gender Earnings Inequality," *Work & Occupations* 22 (1995): 328–56; Thomas J. Bergman and G. E. Martin, "Tests for Compliance with Phased Plans to Equalize Discriminate Wages," *Journal of Applied Business Research* 11 (1994/1995): 136–43.

7. Brent W. Ambrose, William T. Hughes, Jr., and Patrick Simmons, "Policy Issues Concerning Racial and Ethnic Differences in Home Loan Rejection Rates," *Journal of Housing Research* 6 (1995): 115–35; Gerald D. Jaynes and Robin M. Williams, Jr., eds., *A Common Destiny: Blacks and American Society,* Committee on the Status of Black Americans, Commission on Behavioral and Social Sciences and Education, National Research Council (Washington, DC: NAS Press, 1989), pp. I2–I3, 138–48; Sunwoong Kim, Gregory D. Squires, "Lender Characteristics and Racial Disparities in Mortgage Lending," *Journal of Housing Research* 6 (1995): 99–113; Glenn B. Canner and Wayne Passmore, "Home Purchase Lending in Low-Income Neighborhoods and to Low-Income Borrowers," *Federal Reserve Bulletin* 81 (February 1995): 71–103; Constance L. Hays, "Study Says Prejudice

in Suburbs is Aimed Mostly at Blacks," *New York Times,* November 23, 1988, p. A16; John R. Walter, "The Fair Lending Laws and Their Enforcement," *Economic Quarterly* 81 (Fall 1995): 61–77; Stanley D. Longhofer. "Discrimination in Mortgage Lending: What Have We Learned?" *Economic Commentary* (Federal Reserve Bank of Cleveland), August 15, 1996: 1–4.

8. As reported by Rudolf A. Pyatt, Jr., "Significant Job Studies," *Washington Post,* April 30, 1985, pp. D1-D2. See also Paul Burstein, *Discrimination, Jobs, and Politics* (Chicago: University of Chicago Press, 1985); Bureau of Labor Statistics, *Employment and Earnings* (Washington, DC: U.S. Department of Labor, January 1989); Jaynes and Williams, *A Common Destiny,* pp. 16–18, 84–88.

9. See Margery Austin Turner, Michael Fix, and Raymond Struyk, *Opportunities Denied, Opportunities Diminished; Discrimination in Hiring* (Washington, DC: Urban Institute, 1991).

10. See Laura Purdy, "Why Do We Need Affirmative Action?" *Journal of Social Philosophy* 25 (1994): 133–43; Farrell Bloch, *Antidiscrimination Law and Minority Employment: Recruitment Practices and Regulatory Constraints* (Chicago: University of Chicago Press, 1994); Joseph Sartorelli, "Gay Rights and Affirmative Action" in *Gay Ethics,* ed. Timothy F. Murphy (New York: Haworth Press, 1994); Taylor, *Affirmative Action at Work.*

11. *Fullilove v. Klutznick,* 448 U.S. 448 (1980); *United Steelworkers v. Weber,* 443 U.S. 193 (1979); *United States v. Paradise,* 480 U.S. 149 (1987); *Johnson v. Transportation Agency,* 480 U.S. 616 (1987); *Alexander v. Choate,* 469 U.S. 287, at 295.

12. *Firefighters v. Stotts,* 467 U.S. 561 (1984); *City of Richmond v. J. A. Croson Co.,* 109 S. Ct. 706 (1989); *Adarand Constructors Inc. v. Federico Pena,* 63 LW 4523 (1995); *Wygant v. Jackson Board of Education,* 476 U.S. 267 (1986); *Wards Cove Packing v. Atonio,* 490 U.S. 642.

13. In 1964 the New York Commission for Human Rights investigated the union and concluded that it excluded nonwhites through an impenetrable barrier of hiring by discriminatory selection. The state Supreme Court concurred and Issued a "cease and desist" order. The union ignored it. Eventually, in a 1975 trial, the U.S. District Court

found a record "replete with instances of bad faith" and ordered a "remedial racial goal of 29% nonwhite membership" (based on the percentage of nonwhites in the local labor pool). Another court then found that the union had "consistently and egregiously violated" the law of the land (Title 7, in particular). In 1982 and 1983 court fines and civil contempt proceedings were issued. In the early 1980s virtually nothing had been done to modify the discriminatory hiring practices after 22 years of struggle.

14. For a very different view, stressing inconsistency, see Yong S. Lee, "Affirmative Action and Judicial Standards of Review: A Search for the Elusive Consensus," *Review of Public Personnel Administration* 12 (1991): 47–69.

15. See Robert Ladenson, "Ethics in the American Workplace," *Business and Professional Ethics Journal* 14 (1995): 17–31; Gertrude Ezorsky, *Racism and Justice: The Case for Affirmative Action;* Thomas E. Hill, Jr., "The Message of Affirmative Action," *Social Philosophy and Policy* 8 (1991): 108–29; Jorge L. Garcia, "The Heart of Racism," *Journal of Social Philosophy* 27 (1996): 5–46.

16. For an interesting example in academia, see Penni Stewart and Janice Drakich, "Factors Related to Organizational Change and Equity for Women Faculty in Ontario Universities," *Canadian Public Policy* 21 (1995): 429–48.

17. Jerry T. Ferguson and Wallace R. Johnston, "Managing Diversity," *Mortgage Banking* 55 (1995): 32–36L; Joseph Semlen, "Opening the Utility Door for Women and Minorities," *Public Utilities Fortnightly,* July 5, 1990, pp. 29–31; Walter Kiechel, "Living with Human Resources," *Fortune,* August 18, 1986, esp. p. 100; Irene Pave, "A Woman's Place is at GE, Federal Express, P&G . . ." *Business Week,* June 23, 1986, p. 76; Peter Perl, "Rulings Provide Hiring Direction: Employers Welcome Move," *Washington Post,* July 3, 1986, pp. A1, A11.

18. See Jeanne C. Poole and E. Theodore Kautz, "An EEO/AA Program that Exceeds Quotas—It Targets Biases," *Personnel Journal* 66 (January 1987), pp. 103–105; Mary Thornton, "Justice Dept. Stance on Hiring Goals Resisted," *Washington Post,* May 25, 1985, p. A2; Pyatt, "The Basis of Job Bias," p. D2; Linda Williams, "Minorities Find Pacts with Corporations Are Hard to Come By and Enforce," *Wall Street Journal,* August 23, 1985, p. 13.

19. See Robert Fullinwider, *The Reverse Discrimination Controversy;* Nicholas Capaldi, *Out of Order* (Buffalo, NY: Prometheus Books, 1985); F. R. Lynch, *Invisible Victims: White Males and the Crisis of Affirmative Action* (Westport, CT: Greenwood Press, 1989); Barry R. Gross, ed., *Reverse Discrimination* (Buffalo, NY: Prometheus Books, 1977).

20. U.S. Equal Employment Opportunity Commission, "Petition to Intervene," Federal Communications Commission Hearings on AT&T Revised Tariff Schedule, December 10, 1970, p. 1.

21. *McAleer v. American Telephone and Telegraph Company,* 416 F. Supp. 435 (1976); "AT&T Denies Job Discrimination Charges, Claims Firm is Equal Employment Leader," *Wall Street Journal,* December 14, 1970, p. 6; Richard M. Hodgetts, "AT&T versus the Equal Employment Opportunity Commission," in *The Business Enterprise: Social Challenge, Social Response* (Philadelphia: W. B. Saunders, 1977), pp. 176–82.

22. According to a representative of the legal staff in AT&T's Washington, DC, office (phone conversation on March 10, 1982).

23. See Steven M. Cahn, "Colleges Should Be Explicit about Who Will Be Considered for Jobs," *Chronicle of Higher Education,* April 5, 1989, p. B3.

Study Questions for Section 10

1. Cahn argues that appeals to "diversity" are inherently problematic, because they are uninformative until one specifies which kind of diversity matters. Is he correct?

2. Where does Beauchamp's view of affirmative action fall with Cahn's distinction between procedural and preferential versions of the doctrine? How would Cahn reply to Beauchamp?

3. Both authors hold that affirmative action, if permissible at all, is a temporary measure, an instrument for achieving certain social results. How could we know when affirmative action policies have achieved their purposes and should be abandoned?

SECTION 11

IMMIGRATION

THE DISTRIBUTION OF MEMBERSHIP

Michael Walzer

Members and Strangers

The idea of distributive justice presupposes a bounded world, a community within which distributions take place, a group of people committed to dividing, exchanging, and sharing, first of all among themselves. It is possible to imagine such a group extended to include the entire human race, but no such extension has yet been achieved. For the present, we live in smaller distributive communities. Were the extension ever attempted, its success would depend upon decisions made within these smaller communities and by their members—who distribute decision-making power to one another and avoid, if they possibly can, sharing it with anyone else. When we think today about distributive justice, we think about independent states and commonwealths capable of arranging their own distributions, justly or unjustly. We assume an established group and a fixed population, and so we miss the first and most important distributive question: how is that group constituted?

I don't mean: how *was* it constituted? I am not concerned here with the historical origins of the different groups, but with the decisions they make in the present about their present and future populations. The primary good that we distribute to one another is membership in some human community. And what we do with regard to membership structures all our other distributive choices. It determines with whom we make those choices, from whom we require obedience and collect taxes, to whom we allocate goods and services.

Men and women without membership anywhere are stateless persons. That condition doesn't preclude every sort of distributive relation. Markets, for example, are often open to all comers. But nonmembers are vulnerable and unprotected in the marketplace. Although they participate freely in the exchange of goods, they have no part in those goods that are shared. They are cut off from the communal provision of welfare and security. Even those aspects of welfare and security that are, like public health, collectively distributed are not guaranteed to them, for they have no guaranteed place in the collectivity and are always liable to expulsion. As recent history has amply demonstrated, statelessness is a condition of infinite danger.

But membership and nonmembership are not the only, or for our purposes, the most important set of possibilities. It is also possible to be a member of a poor or a rich country, to live in a densely crowded or a largely empty country, to be the subject of a tyrant or the citizen of a liberal and democratic state. Since human beings are highly mobile, large numbers of men and women regularly attempt to change their residence and their membership, moving from unfavored to favored environments. Affluent and free countries are like elite universities; they are besieged by applicants. They have to decide on their own size and character. Whom should they admit? Ought they to have open admissions? Can they choose among applicants? What are the appropriate criteria for distributing membership?

These are hard questions, and perhaps they are not questions of justice at all. Perhaps, indeed, the positive obligations presupposed by theories of distributive justice exist only within established groups, among men and women already members of a single political community (however they came to be members), while toward outsiders we have only negative obligations—not to kill them, rob them, defraud them, and so on. The moral laws of commerce and war determine what we owe to outsiders, and no other laws apply. This is an attractive view because it matches a moral distinction to a political distinction and so, perhaps, it makes both more plausible then they might otherwise be. But I am inclined to think that the match is wrong. It would appear that at least one positive moral principle—mutual aid or Good Samaritanism—extends across political frontiers. . . .

The principle of mutual aid is most commonly recognized when there is no question of community at all, when two strangers meet at sea or in the desert or, as in the Good Samaritan story, by the side of the road. What precisely they owe one another is by no means clear, but it is commonly said of such cases that positive assistance is required if (1) it is needed or urgently needed by one of the parties, and (2) if the risks and costs of giving it are relatively low for the other party. Given these conditions, I ought to stop to help the injured stranger, wherever I meet him, whatever his membership or my own. This is, moreover, an obligation that can be read out in roughly the same form at the collective level. Groups of people ought to help necessitous strangers whom they somehow "discover" in their midst or in their path. But the limit on risks and costs is sharply drawn: I need not take the injured stranger into my home, except briefly, and I certainly need not care for him, or even associate with him, for the rest of my life.[1] My life cannot be shaped and determined by such chance encounters. Whether this right of refusal can also be read out at the collective level is a question that I shall come to only gradually. One of my purposes in this chapter is to explore the requirements of mutual aid upon political communities. Before that, however, I need to say something about the character of the communities and the meaning of membership within them.

If all human beings were strangers to one another, if we had no particular communities and all our meetings were like meetings at sea or in the desert or by the side of the road, then there would be no membership to distribute. Admissions policy would not be an issue. Where and how we lived, and with whom we lived, would depend upon our particular desires, moral understandings, and charitable impulses, and upon the relationships we individually formed.

Justice would be nothing more than non-coercion, good faith, and Good Samaritanism. If, by contrast, all human beings were members of a global society, then membership would already have been distributed (equally) and the distribution of other goods would be just so long as it reflected the universal application of whatever standards we had previously thought appropriate in particular communities. The first of these arrangements suggests a kind of global libertarianism, the second a kind of global socialism. These are the two conditions under which the distribution of membership would never arise. Either there would be no such status to distribute or it would simply come (to everyone) with birth. But neither of these arrangements is likely to be realized in the foreseeable future—and there are impressive arguments, which I will come to later on, against both of them. In any case, so long as members and strangers are, as they are at present, two distinct groups, admissions decisions have to be made, men and women taken in or refused. Given the indeterminate requirements of mutual aid, these decisions are not fixed or constrained by any widely accepted standards. That's why the admissions policies of countries are rarely criticized except in terms suggesting that the only relevant criteria are those of charity, not justice. It is certainly possible that a deeper criticism would lead one to deny the member/stranger distinction. But I shall try, nevertheless, to defend that distinction and then to argue that there are (sometimes) moral reasons for constraining the distribution of membership. . . .

Analogues: Neighborhoods, Clubs, Families

Admissions policies are shaped partly by arguments about economic and political conditions in the host country, partly by arguments about the character and "destiny" of the host country, and partly by arguments about the character of countries (political communities) in general. The last of these is the most important (in theory, at least), for our understanding of countries in general will determine whether particular countries have the right they commonly claim: to distribute membership for (their own) particular reasons. But few of us have ever had any direct experience of what a country is or of what it means to be a member. We often have strong feelings about our country, but we have only dim perceptions of it. As a political community (rather than a place) it is, after all, invisible; we can actually see only its symbols, its offices, and its representatives. I suspect that we understand it best when we compare it to other, smaller associations whose compass we can more easily grasp, whose entire membership, it may be, we can take in at a glance. For we are all members of formal and informal groups of many different sorts; we know their workings intimately. And all these groups have, and necessarily have, admissions policies. Even if we have never served as state officials, even if we have never emigrated from one country to another, we have all had the experience of accepting or rejecting strangers, and we have all had the experience of being strangers, accepted or rejected. I want to draw upon this experience. My argument will be worked through a series of rough comparisons, in the course of which the special character of the political community will, I hope, become increasingly apparent.

Consider, then, three possible analogues for the political community: we can think of countries as neighborhoods, clubs, or families. The list is obviously not exhaustive, but it will serve to illuminate certain key features of admission and exclusion. Universities and companies, though they have some of the characteristics of clubs, distribute social and economic status as well as membership; I will take them up separately. Many domestic associations are parasitic for their memberships, relying on the procedures of other associations. Unions depend upon the hiring policies of companies; parent-teacher organizations depend upon the openness of neighborhoods or the selectiveness of private schools. Political groups are generally like clubs; religious groups are often designed to resemble families. What should countries be like?

The neighborhood is an enormously complex human association, but it has an ideal form that is at least partially reflected (though also increasingly challenged) in contemporary American law. It is an association without an organized or legally enforceable admissions policy. Strangers can be welcomed or not welcomed; they cannot be admitted or excluded. Of course, being welcomed or not welcomed is sometimes effectively the same thing as being admitted or excluded, but the distinction is theoretically important. In principle, individuals and families move into a neighborhood for reasons of their own; they choose but are not chosen. Or rather, in the absence of legal controls, the market controls their movements. Whether they move is determined not only by their own choices but also by their ability to find someone to hire them and someone to rent or sell them a place to live. (The case would be the same in a socialist society, unless people were administratively assigned to jobs and residences. The hiring and renting might involve collective rather than individual decisions, but these would still be market decisions, "private" to the enterprise or the communal apartment building; they would not be neighborhood decisions.) Ideally, the market works independently of the existing composition of the neighborhood. The

state upholds this independence by refusing to enforce restrictive covenants and by acting to prevent or minimize discrimination in employment. . . .

It was a common argument in classical political economy that national territory should be as "indifferent" as local space. The same writers who defended free trade in the nineteenth century also defended unrestricted immigration. They argued for perfect freedom of contract, without any sort of political restraint. International society, they thought, should take shape as a world of neighborhoods, with individuals moving freely about, seeking private advancement. . . .

Perfect labor mobility, however, is probably a mirage, for it is almost certain to be resisted at the local level. Human beings, as I have said, move about a great deal, but this is not because they love to move. They are, most of them, emotionally prone to stay where they are unless their life is very difficult where they are. They experience a tension between love of place and the discomforts of particular places. While some of them leave their homes and become foreigners in new lands, others stay where they are and resent the foreigners in their own land. Hence, if states ever become large neighborhoods, it is likely that neighborhoods will become little states. Their members will organize to defend the local politics and culture against strangers. Historically, neighborhoods have turned into closed communities (leaving aside cases of legal coercion) whenever the state was open: in the cosmopolitan cities of multinational empires, for example, where state officials don't foster any particular identity but permit different groups to build their own institutional structures (as in ancient Alexandria), or in the receiving centers of mass immigration movements (early twentieth-century New York) where the country is an open but also an alien world—or, alternatively, a world full of aliens. The case is similar where the state doesn't exist at all or in areas where it doesn't function. Where welfare monies are raised and spent locally, for example, as in a seventeenth-century English parish, the local people will seek to exclude newcomers who are likely welfare recipients. It is only the nationalization of welfare (or the nationalization of culture and politics) that opens the neighborhood communities to whoever chooses to come in.

Neighborhoods can be open only if countries are closed, or rather, only if countries are potentially closed. Only if the state makes a selection among would-be members and guarantees the loyalty, security, and welfare of the individuals it selects, can local communities take shape as "indifferent" associations, determined only by personal preference and market capacity. Since we live most immediately at the local level, since individual choice is most dependent upon local mobility, this would seem to be the preferred arrangement. Moreover, politics and culture probably develop best if we do not have to defend them in our neighborhoods; they require the kind of largeness, and also the kind of boundedness, that states provide. I don't mean to deny the value of sectional cultures and ethnic communities, only to describe the rigid parochialism that would be forced upon them in the absence of inclusive and protective states. To tear down the walls of the state is not . . . to create a world without walls, but rather to create a thousand petty fortresses.

The fortresses too could be torn down, of course. All that is necessary is a global state sufficiently committed to labor mobility and sufficiently powerful to overwhelm the local communities. Then the result would be . . . a world of radically deracinated men and women. Neighborhoods might maintain some cohesive culture for a generation or two on a voluntary basis, but people would move in, people would move out; soon the cohesion would be gone. The distinctiveness of cultures and groups depends upon closure and cannot be conceived as a stable feature of human life without it. If this distinctiveness is a value, as most people (though some of them are global pluralists and others only local loyalists) seem to believe—more strongly, if individuals have a right to form distinct and stable communities—then closure must be permitted somewhere. At some level of political organization, something like the sovereign state must take shape and claim the authority to make its own admissions policy, to control and sometimes to restrain the flow of immigrants.[2]

But this right to control immigration does not include or entail the right to control emigration. The political community can shape its own population in the one way, but not in the other. This is a distinction that gets reiterated in different forms throughout the account of membership. The restraint of entry serves to defend the liberty and welfare, the politics and culture of a group of people committed to one another and to their common life. But the restraint of exit replaces commitment with coercion. So far as the coerced members are concerned, there is no longer a community worth defending. States can, perhaps, banish individual citizens or expel aliens living within their borders (if there is some place ready to receive them; I will consider this issue later on). Except in times of national emergency, when everyone is bound to work for the survival of the community, states cannot prevent such people from getting up and leaving. Once again, however, the right to leave one country does not entail the right to enter another (any other). Immigration and emigration are morally asymmetrical.[3] Here the appropriate analogy is with the club, for it is a feature of clubs in domestic society, as I have just suggested it is of states in international society, that they can regulate admissions but cannot bar withdrawals.

Like clubs, countries have admissions committees. In the United States, Congress functions as such a committee, though it rarely makes individual selections. Instead, it establishes general qualifications, categories for admission and exclusion, and numerical quotas (limits). Then admissible individuals are taken in, with varying degrees of administrative discretion, mostly on a first-come, first-served basis. This sort of thing seems eminently defensible, though that does not mean that any particular set of qualifications and categories ought to be defended. To say that states have a right to act in certain areas is not to say that anything they do in those areas is right. One can argue about particular admissions standards by appealing, for example, to the condition and character of the host country. Such arguments have to be judged morally and politically as well as factually. When defenders of restricted immigration into the United States claimed (in 1920, say) that they were defending a homogeneous white and Protestant country, they were involved in a pretense that can plausibly be called immoral as well as inaccurate—as if nonwhite and non-Protestant citizens were invisible men and women who didn't have to be counted in the national census! Earlier Americans seeing the benefits of economic and geographic expansion had created a pluralist society, and the moral realities of that society ought to have guided the legislators of the 1920s. If we follow the logic of the club analogy, however, we have to say that the earlier decision might have been different, and the United States might have taken shape as a homogeneous community, an Anglo-Saxon nation-state (assuming what happened in any case—the virtual extermination of the Indians, who, understanding correctly the

dangers of invasion, struggled as best they could to keep foreigners from their native lands). Decisions of this sort are subject to constraint, but what the constraints are I am not yet ready to say. It is important now to insist that the distribution of membership in American society, and in any ongoing society, is a matter of political decision. The labor market may be given free rein, as it was for many decades in the United States, but that does not happen by an act of nature or of God; it depends upon choices that are ultimately political. What kind of community do the citizens want to create? With what other men and women do they want to share and exchange social goods?

These are exactly the questions that club members answer when they make membership decisions, though usually with reference to a less extensive community and a more limited range of social goods. In clubs, only the founders choose themselves (or one another); all other members have been chosen by those who were members before them. Individuals may be able to give good reasons why they should be selected, but no one on the outside has a right to be inside. The members decide freely on their future associates, and the decisions they make are authoritative and final. Only when clubs split into factions and fight over property can the state intervene and make its own decision as to who the members are. When states split, however, no legal appeal is possible; there is no superior body. Hence, we might imagine states as perfect clubs, with sovereign power over their own selection processes.[4]

But if this description is accurate as to the law, it is not an accurate account of the moral life of political communities. Clearly, citizens often believe themselves morally bound to open the doors of their country—not to anyone who wants to come in, perhaps, but to a particular group of outsiders, recognized as national or ethnic "relatives."

In this sense, states are like families rather than clubs, for it is a feature of families that their members are morally connected to people they have not chosen, who live outside the household. In time of trouble, the household is also a refuge. Sometimes, under the auspices of the state, we take in fellow citizens to whom we are not related, as English country families took in London children during the Blitz, but our more spontaneous beneficence is directed at our own kith and kin. The state recognizes what we can call the family principle when it gives priority in immigration to the relatives of citizens. That is current policy in the United States, and it seems especially appropriate in a political community largely formed by the admission of immigrants. It is a way of acknowledging that labor mobility has a social price. Since laborers are men and women with families, one cannot admit them for the sake of their labor without accepting some commitment to their aged parents, say, or their sickly brothers and sisters.

In communities differently formed, where the state represents a nation largely in place, another sort of commitment commonly develops, along lines determined by the principle of nationality. In time of trouble, the state is a refuge for members of the nation, whether or not they are residents and citizens. Perhaps the lines of the political community were drawn years ago so as to exclude their villages and towns; perhaps they are the children or grandchildren of emigrants. They have no legal membership rights, but if they are persecuted in the land where they live, they look to their homeland not only with hope but also with expectation. I am inclined to say that such expectations are legitimate. Greeks driven from Turkey, Turks from Greece, after the wars and revolutions of the early twentieth century, had to be taken in by the states that bore their collective names. What else are such states for? They don't merely preside over a piece of territory and a random collection of inhabitants; they are also the political expression of a common life and (most often) of a national "family" that is never entirely enclosed within their legal boundaries. After World War II, millions of Germans, expelled by Poland and Czechoslovakia, were received and cared for by the two Germanies. Even if these states had been free of all responsibility in the expulsions, they would still have had a special obligation to the refugees. Most states recognize obligations of this sort in practice; some do so in law.

Territory

We might, then, think of countries as national clubs or families. But countries are also territorial states. Although clubs and families own property, they neither require nor (except in feudal systems) possess jurisdiction over territory. Leaving children aside, they do not control the physical location of their members. The state does control physical location—if only for the sake of clubs and families and the individual men and women who make them up—and with this control there come certain obligations. We can best examine these if we consider once again the asymmetry of immigration and emigration.

The nationality principle has one significant limit, commonly accepted in theory, if not always in practice. Though the recognition of national affinity is a reason for permitting immigration, nonrecognition is not a reason for expulsion. This is a major issue in the modern world, for many newly independent states find themselves in control of territory into which alien groups have been admitted under the auspices of the old imperial or colonial regimes. Sometimes these people are forced to leave, the victims of a popular hostility that the new government cannot restrain or can only inadequately restrain. More often, the government itself fosters such hostility and takes positive action to drive out "alien elements," invoking when it does so some version of the club or family analogies. Here, however, the analogies don't apply, for though no "alien" has a right to be a member of a club or family, it is possible, I think, to describe a kind of territorial or locational right. . . .

The state owes something to its inhabitants simply, without reference to their nationality. And the first place to which inhabitants are entitled is surely the place where they and their families have lived and made a life—if not this particular piece of land (or house or apartment), then some other within the same general "place." This claim is particularly powerful when, as in the cases I am considering, people have come where they have come illegally, if they have no other place to go. Then they can claim, as we shall see, the right of asylum. New states and governments, then, must make their peace with the old inhabitants of the land they rule. And countries are likely to take shape as closed territories dominated, perhaps, by particular nations (clubs or families), but always including aliens of one sort or another, whose expulsion would be unjust.

This common arrangement raises one important possibility—that many of the inhabitants of a particular country won't be allowed full membership (citizenship) because of their nationality. I will consider that possibility, and argue for its rejection, when I turn to the specific problems of naturalization. But one might avoid such problems entirely, at least at the level of the state, by opting for a radically different arrangement. Consider once again the neighborhood analogy. Perhaps we should deny to national states, as we deny to ward and

precinct organizations and to political parties generally, the collective right of territorial jurisdiction. Perhaps we should insist upon open countries and permit closure only in nonterritorial groups. Open neighborhoods *together with* closed clubs and families—that is the structure of domestic society. Why can't it, why shouldn't it be extended to the global society?

An extension of this sort was actually proposed by the Austrian socialist Otto Bauer, with reference to the old multinational empires of Central and Eastern Europe. Bauer would have organized nations into autonomous corporations, permitting them to tax their members for educational and cultural purposes, but denying them any territorial dominion. Individuals would have been free to move about in political space, within the empire, carrying their national memberships with them, much as individuals move about today in liberal and secular states, carrying their religious memberships and their partisan affiliations. Like churches and parties, the corporations could admit or reject new members in accordance with whatever standards their old members thought appropriate.[5]

The major difficulty here is that all the national communities that Bauer wanted to preserve came into existence and were sustained over the centuries on the basis of geographical coexistence. It isn't any misunderstanding of their histories that leads nations newly freed from imperial rule to seek a firm territorial status. Nations look for countries because in some deep sense they already have countries: The link between people and land is a crucial feature of national identity. Their leaders understand, moreover, that because so many critical issues (including issues of distributive justice, welfare, education, etc.) can be resolved only within geographical units, the focus of political life can never be established elsewhere. "Autonomous" corporations will always be adjuncts, and probably parasitic adjuncts, of territorial states, and to give up the state is to give up any effective self-determination. That's why borders, and the movements of individuals and groups across borders, are bitterly disputed as soon as imperial rule recedes and nations begin the process of "liberation." And, once again, to reverse this process or to repress its effects would require massive coercion on a global scale. There is no easy way to avoid the country (and the proliferation of countries) as we currently know it. Hence the theory of justice must allow for the territorial state, specifying the rights of its inhabitants, and recognizing the collective right of admission and refusal.

The Claim of Necessity

The argument cannot stop here, however, for the control of territory opens the state to the claim of necessity. Territory is a social good in a double sense. It is living space, earth and water, mineral resources and potential wealth, a resource for the destitute and the hungry. And it is protected living space, with borders and police, a resource for the persecuted and the stateless. These two resources are different, and we might conclude differently with regard to the kinds of claims that can be made on each. But the issue at stake should first be put in general terms. Can a political community exclude destitute and hungry, persecuted and stateless—in a word, necessitous—men and women simply because they are foreigners? Are citizens bound to take in strangers? Let us assume that they have no formal obligations; they are bound by nothing more stringent than the principle of mutual aid or Good Samaritanism. The principle must be applied, however, not to individuals directly but to the citizens as a

group, for immigration is a matter of political decision. Individuals participate in the decision-making, if the state is democratic, but they decide not for themselves, but for the community generally. And this fact has moral implications. It replaces immediacy with distance, and the personal expense of time and energy with impersonal bureaucratic costs. Mutual aid is more coercive for political communities than it is for individuals because a wide range of benevolent actions are open to the community that will only marginally affect its members considered as a body or even, with possible exceptions, one by one (or family by family, or club by club). These actions include, or may include, the admission of strangers, for admission to a country does not entail the kinds of intimacy that could hardly be avoided in the case of clubs and families. And if this is true, might not admission be morally imperative, at least for *these* strangers, who have no other place to go?. . .

I have put the argument in these forceful terms in order to suggest that the collective version of the mutual-aid principle might generate a kind of distributive justice. This is the only kind available to us in a world of members and strangers. Farther than this we cannot go. . . . To argue, for example, that living space should be distributed in equal amounts to every inhabitant of the globe would be to allow the individual version of the right to a place in the world to override the collective version. Indeed, it would deny that national clubs and families can ever acquire a firm title to a particular piece of territory. A high birthrate in a neighboring land would immediately annul the title and require territorial redistribution. The same difficulty arises with regard to wealth and resources. These too can be superfluous, far beyond what the inhabitants of a particular state require for a decent life (even as they themselves define the meaning of a decent life). Are those inhabitants morally bound to admit immigrants from poorer countries for as long as superfluous resources exist? Or are they bound even longer than that, beyond the limits of mutual aid, until a policy of open admissions ceases to attract and benefit the poorest people in the world? . . . But just how much of their wealth do they have to share? Once again, there must be some limit, short (and probably considerably short) of equality, else communal wealth would be subject to indefinite drainage. The very phrase "communal wealth" would lose its meaning if all resources and all products were globally common. Or rather, there would be only one community, a world state, whose redistributive processes would tend over time to annul the historical particularity of the national clubs and families.

If we stop short of equality, there will continue to be many communities, with different histories, ways of life, climates, political structures, and economies. Some places in the world will still be more desirable than others, either to individual men and women with particular tastes and aspirations, or more generally. Some places will still be uncomfortable for at least some of their inhabitants. Hence immigration will remain an issue even after the claims of distributive justice have been met on a global scale—assuming, still, that global society is and ought to be pluralist in form and that the claims are fixed by some version of collective mutual aid. The different communities will still have to make admissions decisions and will still have a right to make them. If we cannot guarantee the territorial or material base on which a group of people build a common life, we can still say that the common life, at least, is their own and that their comrades and associates are theirs to recognize or choose.

There is, however, one group of needy outsiders whose claims cannot be met by yielding territory or exporting wealth, but only by taking people in. This is the group of refugees whose need is for membership itself, a nonexportable good. The liberty that makes certain countries possible homes for men and women whose politics or religion isn't tolerated where they live is also nonexportable; at least we have found no way of exporting it. These goods can be shared only within the protected space of a particular state. At the same time, admitting refugees doesn't, or doesn't necessarily, decrease the amount of liberty the members enjoy within that space. The victims of political or religious persecution, then, make the most forceful claim for admission. "If you don't take me in," they say, "I shall be killed, persecuted, brutally oppressed by the rulers of my own country." What can we reply?

Toward some refugees, we may well have obligations of the same sort that we have toward fellow nationals. This is obviously the case with regard to any group of people whom we have helped turn into refugees. The injury we have done them makes for an affinity between us; thus Vietnamese refugees had, in a moral sense, been effectively Americanized even before they arrived on these shores. But we can also be bound to help men and women persecuted or oppressed by someone else—if they are persecuted or oppressed because they are *like us*. Ideological as well as ethnic affinity can generate bonds across political lines, especially, for example, when we claim to embody certain principles in our communal life and encourage men and women elsewhere to defend those principles. In a liberal state, affinities of this latter sort may be highly attenuated and yet still be morally coercive. Nineteenth-century political refugees in England, for example, were generally not English liberals. They were heretics and oppositionists of all sorts, at war with the autocracies of Central and Eastern Europe. It was chiefly because of their enemies that the English recognized in them a kind of kin. Or consider the thousands of men and women who fled Hungary after the failed revolution of 1956. It is hard to deny them a similar recognition, given the structure of the Cold War, the character of Western propaganda, the sympathy already expressed with East European "freedom fighters." They probably had to be taken in by countries like Britain and the United States. The repression of political comrades, like the persecution of coreligionists, seems to generate an obligation to help, at least to provide a refuge for the most exposed and endangered people. Perhaps every victim of authoritarianism and bigotry is the moral comrade of a liberal citizen; that is an argument I would like to make. But that would press affinity too hard, and it is in any case probably unnecessary. So long as the number of victims is small, the mutual-aid principle will generate similar practical results, and when the number increases, and we are forced to choose among the victims, we shall look, rightfully, for some more direct connection with our own way of life. If, on the other hand, there is no connection at all, antipathy rather than affinity, there can't be a requirement of any sort to take people in. Britain and the United States could hardly have been required, for example, to offer refuge to Stalinists fleeing Hungary in 1956, had the revolution triumphed. Once again, communities must have boundaries, and however these are determined with regard to territory and resources, they depend with regard to population on a sense of relatedness and mutuality. Refugees must appeal to that sense. One wishes them success, but in particular cases, with reference to a particular state, they may well have no right to be successful.

Since ideological (far more than ethnic) affinity is a matter of mutual recognition, there is a lot of room here for political choice—and that means, for exclusion as well as for admission. Hence it might be said that my argument doesn't reach to the desperation of the refugee. Nor does it suggest any way of dealing with the vast numbers of refugees generated by twentieth-century politics. On the one hand, everyone must have a place to live, and a place where a reasonably secure life is possible. On the other hand, this is not a right that can be enforced against particular host states. (The right can't be enforced in practice until there is an international authority capable of enforcing it, and were there such an authority, it would certainly do better to intervene against the state whose brutal policies were driving men and women into exile, and so enable them all to go home.) The cruelty of this dilemma is mitigated to some degree by the principle of asylum. Any refugee who has actually made his escape, who is not seeking but has found (at least a temporary) refuge can claim asylum, a right recognized today, for example, in British law, and then he cannot be deported so long as the only available country to which he might be sent "is one to which he is unwilling to go owing to well-founded fear of being persecuted for reasons of race, religion, nationality . . . or political opinion."[6] Though he is a stranger, and newly come, the rule against expulsion applies to him as if he had already made a life where he is; for there is no other place where he can make a life.

But this principle was designed for the sake of individuals, considered one by one, where their numbers are so small that they cannot have any significant or transforming effect upon the character of the political community. What happens when the numbers are not small? Consider the case of the millions of Russians captured or enslaved by the Nazis in World War II, and overrun by Allied armies in the final offensives of the war. All these people were returned, many of them forcibly returned, to the Soviet Union, where they were immediately shot or sent on to die in labor camps.[7] Those of them who foresaw their fate pleaded for asylum in the West, but for expediential reasons (having to do with war and diplomacy, not with nationality and the problems of assimilation), asylum was denied them. Surely, they should not have been forcibly returned—not once it was known that they would be murdered—and that means that the Western allies should have been ready to take them in, negotiating among themselves, I suppose, about appropriate numbers. There was no other choice; at the extreme, the claim of asylum is virtually undeniable. I assume that there are in fact limits on our collective liability, but I don't know how to specify the limits.

This last example suggests that the moral conduct of liberal and humane states can be determined by the immoral conduct of authoritarian and brutal states. But if that is true, why stop with the right of asylum? Why be concerned only with men and women actually on our territory who ask to remain, and not with men and women oppressed in their own countries who ask to come in? We seem bound to grant asylum for two reasons: because its denial would require us to use force against helpless and desperate people, and because the numbers likely to be involved, except in unusual cases, are small and the people easily absorbed (so we would be using force for "things superfluous"). But if we offered a refuge to everyone in the world who could plausibly say that he needed it, we might be overwhelmed. The call, "Give me . . . your huddled masses yearning to breathe free . . ." is generous and noble; actually to take in large numbers of refugees is often morally necessary; but the right to restrain the flow remains a feature of communal self-determination.

Alienage and Naturalization

The members of a political community have a collective right to shape the resident population, subject always to the limiting factors I have described: national or ideological affinity, the right to place, the claim of necessity. Given these factors, particular countries at particular times are likely to include among their residents men and women who are in different ways alien. These people may be members in their turn of minority or pariah groups, or they may be refugees, immigrants newly arrived. Let us assume that they are rightfully where they are. Can they claim citizenship and political rights within the community where they now live? Does citizenship go with residence? In fact, there is a second admissions process, called naturalization, and the criteria appropriate to this second process remain to be determined. I should stress that what is at stake here is citizenship and not (except in the legal sense of the term) nationality. The national club or family is a community different from the state, for reasons I have already sketched. Hence it is possible, say, for an Algerian immigrant to France to become a French citizen (a French "national") without becoming a Frenchman. But if he isn't a Frenchman, only a resident in France, has he any right to French citizenship?

One might insist, as I shall ultimately do, that the same standards apply to naturalization as to immigration, that every immigrant and every resident is a citizen too or at least a potential citizen. That is why territorial admission is so serious a matter. The members must be prepared to accept the men and women they admit as their own equals in a world of shared obligations; the immigrants must be prepared to share the obligations. But things can be differently arranged. Often, the state controls naturalization strictly, immigration only loosely. Immigrants become resident aliens and, except by special dispensation, nothing more. Why are they admitted? To assist the citizens, to free them from unpleasant work. Then the state is like a family with live-in servants.

That is not an attractive image, for a family with live-in servants is—inevitably, I think—a little tyranny. The principles that rule in the household are the principles of family life. They establish the underlying pattern of mutuality and obligation, of authority and obedience. The servants have no proper place in that pattern, but they have to be assimilated to it. Thus, in the premodern literature on family life, servants are commonly described as children of a special sort: children, because they are subject to command; of a special sort, because they are not allowed to grow up. Parental authority is asserted outside its sphere, over adult men and women who are not and can never be full members of the family. When this assertion is no longer possible, when servants come to be seen as hired workers, the great household begins its slow decline. The pattern of living in is gradually reversed; erstwhile servants seek households of their own.

It is not possible to trace a similar history at the level of the political community. Live-in servants have not disappeared from the modern world. As "guest workers" they play an increasingly important role in its most advanced economies. . . .

Guest Workers

I will not attempt a full description of the experience of contemporary guest workers. Laws and practices differ from one country to another and are constantly changing; the situation is complex and unstable. All that is necessary here is a schematic sketch (drawn chiefly from the practices of West European countries in the early 1970s) designed to highlight those features of the experience that are morally and politically controversial.[8] Imagine, then, a country called Fredonia, a capitalist democracy and welfare state, with strong trade unions and a fairly affluent population. The owners and managers of Fredonia find it increasingly difficult to attract workers to a set of jobs that are or have come to be regarded as exhausting, dangerous, degrading, and dirty. But these jobs are also socially necessary; someone must be found to do them. Domestically, there are only two alternatives, neither of them palatable. The constraints imposed on the labor market by the unions and the welfare state might be broken, and then the most vulnerable segment of the local working class driven to accept the jobs hitherto thought undesirable. But this would require a difficult and dangerous political campaign. Or the wages and working conditions of the undesirable jobs might be dramatically improved so as to attract workers even within the constraints of the local market. But this would raise costs throughout the economy and, what is probably more important, challenge the existing social hierarchy. Rather than adopt either of these drastic measures, the owners and managers, with the help of the Fredonian government, shift the jobs from the domestic to the international labor market, making them available to workers in poorer countries for whom they are less undesirable. The government opens recruiting offices in a number of economically backward countries and draws up regulations to govern the admission of guest workers.

It is crucial that the workers who are admitted should be "guests," not immigrants seeking a new home and a new citizenship. For if they come as future citizens, they would join Fredonia's labor force, temporarily occupying its lower ranks, but benefiting from its unions and welfare programs, and in time reproducing the original dilemma. Moreover, as they advanced, they would come into direct competition with local workers, some of whom they would outdo. Hence the regulations that govern their admission are designed to bar them from the protection of citizenship. They are brought in for a fixed time period, on contract to a particular employer; if they lose their job, they have to leave; they have to leave in any case when their visas expire. They are either prevented or discouraged from bringing dependents along with them, and they are housed in barracks, segregated by sex, on the outskirts of the cities where they work. Mostly they are young men or women in their twenties or thirties; finished with education, not yet infirm, they are a minor drain on Fredonia's welfare services (unemployment insurance is not available to them since they are not permitted to be unemployed in Fredonia). Neither citizens nor potential citizens, they have no political rights. The civil liberties of speech, assembly, association—otherwise strongly defended in Fredonia—are commonly denied to them, sometimes explicitly by state officials, sometimes implicitly by the threat of dismissal and deportation.

Generally, as it becomes clear that foreign workers are a permanent requirement of Fredonia's economy, these conditions are somewhat mitigated. For certain jobs, workers are given longer visas and permitted to bring their families with them, and so they are admitted to some of the benefits of the welfare state. But their position remains precarious. Residence is tied to employment, and the authorities make it a rule that any guest worker who cannot support himself and his family without repeated recourse to state welfare programs can be deported. Hence, in time of recession, many of the guests are forced to leave. In good times, however, the number who choose to come and who find ways to remain is high; soon some 15 percent of the industrial labor force is made up of foreigners. Frightened by this influx, various cities and towns within Fredonia establish residence quotas for guest workers (defending their neighborhoods against an open state). Bound to their jobs, the guests are in any ease closely confined in choosing a place to live.

Their existence is harsh and their wages low by the standards prevailing in Fredonia, less so by their own standards. What is most difficult is their homelessness: They work long and hard in a foreign country where they are not encouraged to settle down, where they are always strangers. For those workers who come alone, life in Fredonia is like a self-imposed prison term. They are deprived of normal social, sexual, and cultural activities (of political activity too, if that is possible in their home country) for a fixed period of time. During that time, they live narrowly, saving money and sending it home. Money is the only return Fredonia makes to its guests, and though they export most of it, they are still very cheaply had. The costs of raising and educating workers in Fredonia and paying them what the local labor market requires would be vastly higher than the amount remitted to the guest workers' home countries. So the relation of guests and hosts seems to be a bargain all around; for the harshness of the working days and years is temporary, and the money sent home counts there in a way it could never count in Fredonia.

But what are we to make of Fredonia as a political community? Defenders of the guest worker system might claim that the country is now a neighborhood economically, but politically still a club or family. As a place to live, it is open to anyone who can find work; as a forum or assembly, as a nation or a people, it is closed except to those who meet the requirements set by the present members. The system is a perfect synthesis of labor mobility and patriotic solidarity. But this account somehow misses what is actually going on in Fredonia. The state-as-neighborhood, an "indifferent" association governed only by the laws of the market, and the state-as-club-or-family, with political laws, authority relations, and police, don't simply coexist, like two distinct moments in historical or abstract time. The market for guest workers, while free from the particular political constraints of the domestic labor market, is not free from all political constraints. Indeed, state power plays a crucial role in its creation and then in the enforcement of its rules. Without the denial of political rights and civil liberties and the ever-present threat of deportation, the system would not work. Hence guest workers can't be described merely in terms of their mobility, as men and women free to come and go. While they are guests, they are also subjects. They are ruled . . . by a band of citizen-tyrants.

But don't they agree to be ruled? Certainly they choose to come knowing roughly what to expect, and they often return knowing exactly what to expect. But this kind of consent, given at a single moment in time, while it is clearly sufficient to legitimize many market transactions, is not sufficient in the political realm. Political authority is precisely the right to make decisions over periods of time, to change the rules, to cope with emergencies; hence it requires the ongoing consent of its subjects. And its subjects are all those men and women resident within the territory over which its rule-making power extends. On the other hand, guest workers really are free to come and go; they can always give up their residence if they find subjection painful. Though they are treated like

indentured servants, they are not in fact indentured. They can quit their jobs, buy train or airline tickets, and go home; they are citizens elsewhere. If they come voluntarily, to work and not to settle, and if they can leave whenever they want, why should they be granted political or civil rights while they stay? Ongoing consent, it might be argued, is required only from long-term residents. Aside from the explicit provisions of their contracts, the guest workers have no more rights than tourists have.

But guest workers are not, in the usual sense of the word, guests; and they are certainly not tourists. They are workers, above all, and they come (and generally stay for as long as they are allowed) because they need to work, not because they expect to enjoy the visit. They are not on vacation; they do not spend their days as they please. State officials are not polite and helpful to them, giving directions to the museums, enforcing the traffic and currency laws. These guests experience the state as a pervasive and frightening power that shapes their lives and regulates their every move—to which they have no access. Departure is only a formal option, deportation a continuous practical threat. As a group, they constitute a disenfranchised class. They are typically an exploited or oppressed class as well—and they are exploited or oppressed at least in part because they are disenfranchised, incapable of organizing effectively for mutual aid and advancement. Their material condition is unlikely to be improved except by altering their political status. Meanwhile, tyranny is the right name for their subjection. And surely political community requires something else.

The relevant principle here is not mutual aid but political justice. The guests don't need citizenship—not in the same sense in which they might be said to need their jobs. Nor are they injured, helpless, destitute; they are able-bodied and earning money. Nor are they standing, even figura- tively, "by the side of the road"; they are living among the citizens. They do socially necessary work and they are deeply enmeshed in the legal system of the coun- try to which they have come. Participants in economy and law, they ought to be able to regard themselves as potential or future participants in politics as well. And they must be possessed of those basic civil liber- ties the exercise of which is so much pre- paration for voting and office-holding. They must be set on the road to citizenship. They may choose not to become citizens, to return to their homes, or to stay on as resi- dent aliens. Many, perhaps most, will choose to return because of their emotional ties to their national family and their native land. This will be especially true insofar as the system is genuinely beneficial to them as well as to the people of Fredonia—if they are able to save or remit enough money to make a difference at home. But unless they have that choice, their other choices cannot be taken as so many signs of their acquies- cence to the economy and law of Fredonia. And if they do have that choice, the econ- omy and law of Fredonia are likely to look different than they currently do. A firmer recognition of the guests' civil liberties and some enhancement of their opportunities for collective bargaining would be difficult to avoid once they were seen as potential citizens.

I should add that something of the same sort might be obtained in another way. Fredonia might undertake to negotiate for- mal treaties with the countries from which the guest workers come, setting out in authoritative form a list of "guest rights"— the same rights, roughly, that the workers might win for themselves as union mem- bers and political activists in Fredonia.[9] The treaty could include a proviso stipulating its periodic renegotiation, so that the list of rights could be adapted to changing social and economic conditions. Then, even when

they were not at home, the original citizen- ship of the guests would work for them, and they would in some sense be repre- sented in Fredonia decision-making. In one way or another, they ought to be able to enjoy the protection of citizenship (or potential citizenship).[10]

Leaving aside international arrange- ments of the sort just described, the princi- ple of political justice is this: the processes of self-determination through which a ter- ritorial state shapes its internal life must be open, and equally open, to all those men and women who live in the territory, work in the local economy, and are subject to local law. Hence, second admissions (natu- ralization) depend on first admissions (immigration), and are subject only to cer- tain constraints of time and qualification, never to the ultimate constraint of closure. When second admissions are closed, the political community collapses into some- thing very different: a world of members and strangers, with no political bound- aries between the two groups, where the strangers are the subjects of the members. Among themselves, perhaps, the members are equal, but it is not their equality but their tyranny that determines the character of the state. Political justice is a bar to permanent alienage—either for particular individuals or for a class of changing individuals. There cannot be a fixed status between citizen and foreigner (though there can be stages in the transition from one of these political identities to the other). Men and women are either subject to the full force of the state's authority or they are not, and if they are subject they must be given a say, and ultimately an equal say, in what that authority does. The citizens of Fredonia, then, have a choice. If they want to bring in new workers, they must be prepared to enlarge their own membership; if they are unwilling to accept new members, they must find ways within the limits of the domestic labor market to get socially necessary work done. And those are their only choices. Their right to choose derives from the existence in this particular territory of a community of citizens, and it is not compatible with the destruction of the community or its transformation into yet another local tyranny.

Membership and Justice

The distribution of membership is not pervasively subject to the constraints of justice. Across a considerable range of the decisions that are made, states are simply free to take in strangers (or not)—much as they are free, leaving aside the claims of the needy, to share their wealth with foreign friends, to honor the achievements of foreign artists, scholars, and scientists, and to enter into collective security arrangements with foreign states. But the right to choose an admissions policy is more basic than any of these, for it is not merely a matter of acting in the world, exercising sovereignty, and pursuing national interests. What is at stake here is the shape of the community that acts in the world, exercises sovereignty, and so on. Admission and exclusion are at the core of communal independence. They suggest the deepest meaning of self-determination. Without them, there could not be *communities of character*, historically stable, ongoing associations of men and women with some special commitment to one another and some special sense of their common life.[11]

But self-determination in the area of membership is not absolute. It is a right exercised, most often, by national clubs or families, but it is held in principle by territorial states. Hence it is subject both to the claims of affinity and of place and, when territory is considered as a resource, to the claims of necessity too. These are the constraints imposed on immigration. The constraints on naturalization are more severe.

Every new immigrant, every refugee taken in, every resident and worker must be offered the opportunities of citizenship. If the community is so radically divided that a single citizenship is impossible, then its territory must be divided too, before the rights of admission and exclusion can be exercised; for these rights are to be exercised only by the political community as a whole (even if in practice some national majority dominates the decision-making) and only with regard to foreigners, not by some members of the community with regard to other members. No community can be half slave, half free, and claim that its admissions policies represent acts of self-determination.

The determination of ethnic minorities by all-powerful majorities, or of slaves by masters, or of aliens and guests by an exclusive band of citizens is not communal freedom but oppression. The men and women of the majority group, the masters, the band of citizens: these people are free, of course, to set up a club, make membership as exclusive as they like, write a constitution, and govern one another. But they can't claim territorial jurisdiction and rule over the people with whom they share the territory. To do that is to act outside their sphere, beyond their rights. It is a form of tyranny. Indeed, the rule of masters and citizens over slaves, aliens, and pariahs is probably the most common form of tyranny in human history. The theory of distributive justice, then, must begin with an account of membership rights. It must vindicate at one time the (limited) right of closure, without which there could be no communities at all, and the internal inclusiveness of the existing communities. For it is only as members somewhere that men and women can hope to share in all the other social goods—security, wealth, honor, culture, and political power—that communal life makes possible.

Notes

1. In an argument against free immigration to the new Puritan commonwealth of Massachusetts, John Wintrop stresses the limitations on mutual aid or, as he calls it, "mercy": "1st. A man is not a fit object of mercy except he be in misery. 2nd. We are not bound to exercise mercy to others to the ruin of ourselves. 3rd. . . . As for hospitality, that rule doth not bind further than for some present occasion, not for continual residence." *Puritan Political Idea: 1558–1794*, ed. Edmund S. Morgan (Indianapolis: Bobbs-Merrill, 1965), p. 146.

2. Obviously, the unit from within which closure is attempted can vary a great deal, but the most common alternative to the country is the city, which in classical, medieval, and early modern times always regulated immigration and, what was often more important, naturalization. See, for example, Henri Pirenne on communal exclusivism in the Middle Ages, *Medieval Cities* (Garden City, NY: Doubleday Anchor Books, n.d.), esp. p. 150.

3. Maurice Cranston on the traditional understanding of liberty as a right to move: "It is a tradition which recognizes the right to move in the most literal sense; it does not recognize a natural right to stop and permanently stay. In the language of the French Constitution of 1791, the right of movement is *libertè d'aller, de rester, de partir." What Are Human Rights?* (New York: Taplinger, 1973), p. 32.

4. Winthrop makes the point clearly: "If we here be a corporation established by free consent, if the place of our cohabitation be our own, then no man hath right to come into us . . . without our consent." *Puritan Political Ideas*, p. 145. I will come back to the question of "place" below.

5. *Austro-Marxism*, ed. Tom Bottomore and Patrick Goode (Oxford: Oxford University Press, 1978), pp. 102–25.

6. E. C. S. Wade and G. Godfrey Phillips, *Constitutional and Administrative law*, 9th ed., revised by A. W. Bradley (London: Longman, 1977), p. 424.

7. For the whole ugly story, see Nikolai Tolstoy, *The Secret Betrayal: 1944–1947* (New York: Scribner, 1977).

8. In my account of guest workers, I rely chiefly on John Berger, *A Seventh Man* (Hammondsworth, England: Penguin Books, 1975); Stephen Castles and Godula Kosack, *Migrant Workers and Class Structure in Western Europe* (Oxford: Oxford University Press, 1973); and Cheryl Bernard, "Migrant Workers and European Democracy," *Political Science Quarterly* 92 (Summer 1978): 277–99. I shall say nothing here about the condition of illegal immigrants (who often enough come in with the connivance of government officials). The illegality of their status obviously does not free them from subjection, but only makes it more difficult for them to defend themselves.

9. The argument can be made that the home states ought to insist upon such treaties— that is, they owe it to their citizens, who have every right to continued protection. But home states may not always be able to provide such protection in any effective way.

10. It has been suggested to me that this argument does not plausibly apply to privileged guests: technical advisers, visiting professors, and so on. I concede the point, though I am not sure just how to describe the category "guest workers" so as to exclude these others. But the others are not very important, and it is in the nature of their privileged positions that they are commonly able to call upon the protection of their home states if they ever need it.

11. I have taken the term "communities of character" from Otto Bauer, *Austro-Marxism*, p. 107.

MIGRATION AND MORALITY: A LIBERAL EGALITARIAN PERSPECTIVE

Joseph H. Carens

What must we do to treat all human beings as free and equal moral persons? That is the question that liberal egalitarianism demands we ask of all institutions and social practices, including those affecting citizenship, borders and migration.

Like any tradition of moral discourse, liberal egalitarianism is filled with conflicting arguments. The issue of movement across borders has only recently received any sustained attention, but already one can find major splits among liberal egalitarians. Some claim there should be no restrictions on freedom of movement, or almost none; others say that states are morally entitled to admit or exclude whomever they want with only a few qualifications; still others adopt some position in between.[1] In this chapter, therefore, I will not claim to represent the consensus of the tradition. Instead I will offer my current view of what anyone committed to liberal egalitarianism ought to think about migration, noting along the way the major points of disagreement within the tradition and indicating the places where I feel least certain about my own argument.

Overall, my position is this: liberal egalitarianism entails a deep commitment to freedom of movement as both an important liberty in itself and a prerequisite for other freedoms. Thus, the presumption is for free migration and anyone who would defend restrictions faces a heavy burden of proof. Nevertheless, restrictions may sometimes be justified because they will promote liberty and equality in the long run or because they are necessary to preserve a distinct culture or way of life.

I

Like all those in the liberal tradition, liberal egalitarians care about human freedoms.[2] People should be free to pursue their own projects and to make their own choices about how they live their lives so long as this does not interfere with the legitimate claims of other individuals to do likewise. In addition, liberal egalitarians are committed to equal opportunity. Access to social positions should be determined by an individual's actual talents and capacities, not limited on the basis of arbitrary native characteristics (such as class, race or sex). Finally, liberal egalitarians want to keep actual economic, social and political inequalities as small as possible, partly as a means of realizing equal freedom and equal opportunity and partly as a desirable end in itself.[3]

Freedom of movement is closely connected to each of these three concerns. First, the right to go where you want to go is itself an important freedom. It is precisely this freedom, and all that this freedom makes possible, that is taken away by imprisonment. Second, freedom of movement is essential for equality of opportunity. You have to be able to move to where the opportunities are in order to take advantage of them. Third, freedom of movement would contribute to a reduction of political, social and economic inequalities. There are millions of people in the Third World today who long for the freedom and economic opportunity they could find in affluent First World countries. Many of them take great risks to come: Haitians setting off in leaky boats, Salvadorians being smuggled across the border in hot, airless trucks, Tamils paying to be set adrift off the coast of Newfoundland. If the borders were open, millions more would move. The exclusion of so many poor and desperate people seems hard to justify from a perspective that takes seriously the claims of all individuals as free and equal moral persons.

Consider the case for freedom of movement in light of the liberal critique of feudal practices that determined a person's life chances on the basis of his or her birth. Citizenship in the modern world is a lot like feudal status in the medieval world. It is assigned at birth; for the most part it is not subject to change by the individual's will and efforts; and it has a major impact upon that person's life chances. To be born a citizen of an affluent country like Canada is like being born into the nobility (even

though many belong to the lesser nobility). To be born a citizen of a poor country like Bangladesh is (for most) like being born into the peasantry in the Middle Ages. In this context, limiting entry to countries like Canada is a way of protecting a birthright privilege. Liberals objected to the way feudalism restricted freedom, including the freedom of individuals to move from one place to another in search of a better life. But modern practices of citizenship and state control over borders the people to the land of their birth almost as effectively. If the feudal practices were wrong, what justifies the modern ones?

Some would respond to this challenge by drawing a distinction between freedom of exit and freedom of entry and arguing that the two are asymmetrical.[4] The former, the right to leave one's own state, ought to be virtually absolute, precisely because restrictions resemble the objectionable feudal practices. But that does not imply a right to enter any particular place. From a liberal egalitarian perspective this answer is clearly unsatisfactory if entry is so restricted in most states that most people who want to leave have no place to go. That is certainly the case in the modern world. The liberal egalitarian branch of liberalism is sympathetic to the charge that liberal freedoms can be empty formalities under some circumstances. Liberal egalitarians want to pay attention to the conditions (material and other) that make formal freedom meaningful and effective. So, a right of exit that does not carry with it some reasonable guarantee of entry will not seem adequate.

The initial allocation of citizenship on the basis of birthplace, parentage or some combination thereof is not objectionable from a liberal egalitarian perspective. Indeed it is morally required because children are born into a community with ties to others that should be acknowledged. In principle, however, individuals should be free to change their membership at will.

Finally, compare freedom of movement *within* the state to freedom of movement across state borders. Like every freedom involving human action, freedom of movement is not unlimited, but because it is an important liberty, limitations have to be justified in a way that gives equal weight to the claims of all. Some restrictions on movement are easy to justify, e.g. traffic regulations or a right to exclude others from one's home (assuming everyone has a home or a reasonable opportunity to obtain one). But imagine an attempt by officials in one city or county to keep out people from another. That sort of restriction is seen as fundamentally incompatible with a commitment to free and equal citizenship. Cities and provinces have borders, but not ones that can be used to keep people in or out against their will. Indeed freedom of movement *within* the nation-state is widely acknowledged as a basic human right, and states are criticized for restricting internal movement even by those who accept the conventional view of state sovereignty. People *are* generally free to change their membership in subnational political communities at will.

If it is so important for people to have the right to move freely within a state, is it not equally important for them to have the right to move across state borders? Every reason why one might want to move within a state may also be a reason for moving between states. One might want a job; one might fall in love with someone from another country; one might belong to a religion that has few adherents in one's native state and many in another; one might wish to pursue cultural opportunities that are only available in another land. The radical disjunction that treats freedom of movement within the state as a moral imperative and freedom of movement across state borders as merely a matter of political discretion makes no sense from a perspective that takes seriously the freedom and equality of all individuals.

II

The arguments in the preceding section create at least a presumption for freedom of movement from a liberal egalitarian perspective. Can this presumption ever be overridden? One possible approach is to argue that restrictions on free movement are necessary in order to promote freedom and equality in the long run. On this view, free movement is an aspect of the liberal egalitarian ideal which we should ultimately try to achieve but to adopt the practice of open borders now would jeopardize those liberal egalitarian institutions and practices that currently exist and slow their development elsewhere.[5]

This argument takes several related forms, most of them focusing on the need to protect existing liberal egalitarian cultures and institutions (however imperfectly realized). First, there is the question of national security. Presumably an invading army is not entitled to unopposed entry on the grounds of free movement. But that does not entail any real modification because the principle of free movement does not entitle citizens to organize their own armies to challenge the authority of the state either. What about subversives? Again, if it is against the law for citizens to try to overthrow the state, that kind of activity would presumably justify refusal of entry to outsiders. So, people who pose a serious threat to national security can legitimately be excluded.

A related argument concerns the danger to a liberal egalitarian regime posed by a large influx of people who come from nonliberal societies, even if they do not come with any subversive intent. To put it another way, are people committed to treating all individuals as free and equal moral persons obliged to admit people who are not so committed? This is close to the familiar question of the toleration of the intolerant in liberal regimes. One conventional answer (which I accept) is that liberal regimes are obliged to tolerate the intolerant and respect their liberties so long as they do not pose an actual threat to the maintenance of liberal institutions. When they do pose a threat, however, their liberties may be curtailed in order to preserve the regime.[6] Here that answer would imply that restrictions on non-liberal entrants would be justified only if one had good reason to believe that they would threaten the liberal character of the regime if admitted. This entails the conclusion that it could be legitimate to exclude people for holding beliefs and values that are also held by people who are already members but only because of the presumed cumulative effect of their presence.

Would it be justifiable to expel non-liberal members because of their beliefs and values if their numbers grew large enough to constitute a threat? No. I argued above that the radical disjuncture between freedom of entry and freedom of exit in conventional morality is not justified. Nevertheless, there is something to the claim of asymmetry. Under many circumstances, the right to leave is much more important than the right to enter any particular place. It is only in the limiting case where there is nowhere to go that the two become equivalent, although as I noted above that limiting case is closely approximated in the real world for many people. Similarly, under many, perhaps most circumstances the right to remain in a country where one is already a member is much more fundamental than the right to get in. All of the ties that one creates in the course of living in a place mean that one normally (though not always) has a much more vital interest in being able to stay where one is than in being able to get in somewhere

new. This is not a denigration of the importance of the freedom to move, but rather a claim that the freedom to remain is even more important. Thus, expulsions of members are almost never justified from a liberal egalitarian perspective.

Although it is a distraction from the threat to liberalism argument, it is worth pausing here to explore the implications of this point about expulsions for the issue of migrant workers and their families.[7] In the preceding paragraph, I deliberately used the term "members" rather than "citizens" because being a member of a society and having the moral claims of a member is not dependent upon having the formal status of a citizen. Indeed, one of the ways states may act unjustly is by denying citizenship to people who are members. When a state admits people to live and work in the territory it governs, it admits them to membership so long as they stay any significant period of time. It cannot do otherwise and still treat them as free and equal moral persons. Thus it is obliged to admit their immediate families as well and to open the doors to citizenship to them and their families. Even if they do not become citizens, they have a right to stay for all of the reasons discussed in the preceding paragraph. So, the state cannot rightly expel them even if circumstances have changed and it is no longer advantageous to have them. And again in parallel with the preceding paragraph, it is much worse to deport people who have already come and settled than to refuse entry to new workers.

These claims about membership and the right to remain are not altered even if the migrant workers were admitted under terms that explicitly provided for their return should circumstances change. Liberal egalitarianism places limits on freedom of contract, rendering void any agreements that are incompatible with equal respect for persons. And unlike most of the

claims I make in this chapter about what
liberal egalitarianism requires with respect
to migration, these claims about migrant
workers are generally reflected in the practices of contemporary liberal democratic
societies.

To return to the threat to liberalism
argument, another variant focuses not on
beliefs and values but on sheer numbers.
Given the size of the potential demand, if a
rich country like Canada or the United
States were to open its borders, the number
of those coming might overwhelm the
capacity of the society to cope, leading to
chaos and a breakdown of public order.[8]
The risk would be especially great if only
one or two of the rich countries were to
open their borders. One cannot assume
that the potential immigrants would see
the danger and refrain from coming
because of the time lag between cause and
effect, because of collective action problems, and so on. Call this the public order
problem. Note that the "public order" is
not equivalent to the welfare state or whatever public policies are currently in place.
It is a minimalist standard, referring only
to the maintenance of law and order.
A threat to public order could be used to
justify restrictions on immigration on
grounds that are compatible with respecting every individual as a free and equal
moral person, because the breakdown of
public order makes everyone worse off in
terms of both liberty and welfare. . . .

Even if one accepts all of the arguments
above as sources of possible constraint on
entry, the basic commitment to free movement as the fundamental goal and underlying principle remains intact. Just as those in
a lifeboat are positively obliged to take in as
many as they can without jeopardizing the
safety of the boat as a whole (a point that
those fond of this analogy often neglect), the
state is obliged to admit as many of those
seeking entry as it can without jeopardizing

national security, public order and the
maintenance of liberal institutions.

One obvious danger, however, is that an
expansive interpretation of the criteria in
the preceding arguments will open the
door to a flood of restrictions. For example,
the United States has used the national
security justification to deny entry (even
for temporary visits) to people identified
as homosexuals, as well as to all sorts of
people whose views do not conform to
the reigning American ideology. And if
national security is linked to the state's
economic performance (as it often is), any
economic costs connected with immigration can be seen as threatening national
security. Exclusionists in the nineteenth
century in the United States cited the dangers of immigration from non-liberal societies as grounds for keeping out Catholics
and Jews from Europe and all Asians and
Africans. Canada and Australia had comparable restrictions on similar grounds.
(Today Islamic fundamentalism seems to
be the main target of those worried about
non-liberal values.) And, of course, some
people see a threat to public order in any
new demand placed on a social system.
They want a safety margin of fifty empty
places in a lifeboat built for sixty.

Despite these sad examples, one should
not exclude proper concerns, at least at the
level of theory, because they are subject to
exaggeration and abuse in practice. The
task is to distinguish between reasonable
and unreasonable uses of these sorts of
arguments. As Rawls puts it in acknowledging that liberties may sometimes be
restricted for the sake of public order and
security, the hypothetical possibility of a
threat is not enough. Rather there must be a
"reasonable expectation" that damage will
occur in the absence of restrictions and the
expectation has to be based on "evidence
and ways of reasoning acceptable to all."[9]
The same strictures apply to all attempts to

justify restrictions on immigration along the lines sketched above, and none of the examples cited is really justified as a reasonable use of restrictive criteria.

A variation of the preceding arguments that is based on real concerns but is much more problematic from a liberal egalitarian perspective is what might be called the backlash argument.[10] On this view, the commitment to liberal egalitarian principles is not very secure even in liberal societies. Current citizens might object to the ethnic and cultural characteristics of new immigrants, fear them as competitors in the workplace, and perceive them as economic burdens placing excessive demands upon the social welfare system. At the least, this reaction might erode the sense of mutuality and community identification that makes egalitarian and redistributive programmes politically possible. At the worse, it might threaten the basic liberal democratic framework. A glance at current European politics makes it clear that this threat is all too real. In several countries, extreme right-wing parties, using veiled and not so veiled racist and neo-fascist appeals, have gained ground, primarily, it seems, by making opposition to current immigrants and future immigration a key element in their platforms. In this context, to open the borders more now might well provoke a political reaction that would quickly slam the doors shut and damage other liberal egalitarian institutions and policies as well.

Would this justify restrictions on immigration from a liberal egalitarian perspective? The answer must be "no" at the level of principle and "perhaps" at the level of practice. I am assuming here that the claims to exclude do not rest on some as yet unspecified valid argument. By hypothesis then we are dealing with a case in which restrictions on immigration would not be justified if one took a perspective in which all were regarded as free and equal moral persons. Those advocating exclusion are either putting forward claims that are intrinsically unjust (e.g. racist claims) or ones that are legitimate concerns (e.g. their economic interests) but outweighed by the claims of the potential immigrants (both in terms of their right to free movement and in terms of their own economic interests). The "justification" for restrictions is simply that if no concessions are made to the exclusionists they may make things even worse. Put that way it is clearly no justification at all at the level of principle though one cannot say that such concessions are never prudent in practice.

Compare this issue to such questions as whether slaveowners should have been compensated for the loss of their property when slavery was abolished, whether holders of feudal privilege should have been compensated when those privileges were abolished and whether segregation should have been ended gradually (with "all deliberate speed") rather than all at once. All of these questions were live issues once in political contexts where defenders of the old ways still had sufficient political power to resist change and perhaps even reverse it if pressed too hard. In none of these cases, it seems to me, were concessions required as a matter of principle, but in any of them they may have been defensible in practice as the best that could be achieved under the circumstances. The latter seems an appropriate moral guide to political action assuming a definition of the good that takes into account independent ethical constraints upon action. And so the backlash argument, too, may provide grounds of this limited sort for restrictions in some cases.

Finally, there are arguments for restriction that focus not on the protection of liberal egalitarian institutions and practices in states that currently have them but on their development elsewhere and on the reduction of global inequalities.[11] According to the "brain drain" hypothesis, the movement of people from the Third World to the First World actually increases global inequalities because the best educated and most talented are among the most likely to move in order to take advantage of the greater professional and economic opportunities in affluent societies. Even among the poor, it is the most energetic and ambitious who move, and usually people from the lower middle classes rather than the worst off because the latter do not have the resources needed for migration. Thus, migration actually involves a transfer of human resources from poor countries to rich ones. This often involves the loss of actual economic investments in the form of scarce and costly expenditures on education and training, but the greatest cost is the loss of people with the capacity to contribute to the transformation of their country's condition. Freer movement would only make the situation worse, making development in the Third World and a reduction of global inequalities even more unlikely than it is now.

A variant of this argument stresses politics rather than economics, drawing attention to the way in which easy exit may act as a safety valve for a repressive regime. It may be easier to silence domestic opposition by sending it abroad than by suppressing it internally. And if exit is an easy option, those living under a repressive regime may devote their energies to getting out rather than to transforming the system under which they live.

On the whole, I think these are the sorts of arguments that have given utilitarianism a bad name in some quarters, although, as is often the case, I do not think a clear thinking utilitarian would support them. What is particularly objectionable is the way they

propose to extract benefits for some people by, in effect, imprisoning others. As is so often the case in discussing migration, it is helpful to compare internal migration with migration across state borders. Many states suffer from severe regional inequalities and it is often suggested that these inequalities are made worse by the movement of the brightest, best-trained people from poor regions to rich ones—an internal brain drain. But what would we think if Canada tried to cope with its regional disparities by prohibiting people from moving from Newfoundland to Ontario, or if Italy limited migration from Naples to Milan? The regional differences are a serious problem that states have a duty to address, but they would be wrong to try to solve this problem by limiting the basic freedoms of their citizens.

So, too, with the international brain drain. International inequality is a serious moral problem, but restricting movement is not a morally permissible tactic for dealing with it. And that assumes that it would be a useful tactic. In fact, the benefits themselves are extremely problematic. Emigrants contribute in various ways to their communities of origin (often through direct financial remittances), and it is far from clear that making them stay home would lead to the desired economic and political transformation. On the other hand, the cost to those denied permission to leave is clear and direct. Limitations of important freedoms should never be undertaken lightly. In the face of great uncertainty about their effects they should not be undertaken at all.

What about financial compensation for the costs of education and training? Here it is important to distinguish between basic education and advanced education or training. For the former no compensation is due; Everyone is entitled to basic education, and children cannot enter into binding contracts. Whatever investments a society makes in its young, it cannot rightly require direct repayment. Advanced training is somewhat different both because it is provided only to a few and because those receiving it are normally old enough to assume responsibility for their choices. If it is subsidized by the state, especially a state with comparatively few resources, it may be reasonable to expect the recipients to commit themselves to a few years of service in the country or to repay the costs of the training. But these sorts of expectations must be limited and reasonable. Liberal egalitarianism is incompatible with any form of indentured servitude.

In arguing that the state may not normally limit migration as a way of enforcing a claim to the services of its citizens, I am not saying that people have no obligations to their communities of origin. It is a familiar feature of most liberal theories that the state should not enforce many sorts of moral duties or obligations not just on the prudential grounds that enforcement will be costly or ineffective but on the principle that individuals must have considerable scope to define their own lives and identities, including the moral worlds that they inhabit. This does not mean that all moral commitments are a matter of choice. From the individual's perspective, the moral ties may be experienced as given, a product of unchosen relationships with members of one's family, ethnic group, religious faith, or even political community. Take a black doctor in the United States. He or she might or might not feel a special obligation to work in the black community. If he or she does, he or she might or might not think that other black doctors have a comparable obligation. Liberal egalitarianism has nothing to say about these matters. It does not try to fill the whole moral world. It does not deny the existence of such obligations or imply that they are purely subjective and not subject to rational discussion. The only limit that liberal egalitarianism places on

such moral views and moral commitments is that they must not conflict with the rights and duties that liberal egalitarianism itself prescribes.

People from poor countries may feel a special obligation to use their talents at home, and they may think that their compatriots have the same obligation. Liberal egalitarianism does not deny or affirm this view. It only denies the moral propriety of enforcing it through restrictions on movement.

My arguments about the brain drain have focused on the countries of origin. What about the countries of destination? It would be both paternalistic and hypocritical for rich countries to say that they were closing their borders to help the poor ones out. Moreover, given my arguments above about the relationship between the right of exit and the right of entry, it would be wrong to do so with the goal of denying potential emigrants any place to go.

III

One objection to the line of argument I have been developing so far is that the whole problem of freedom of movement is essentially epiphenomenal. Other things being equal, one could expect that most people would not want to leave the land where they were born and raised, a place whose language, customs and ways of life are familiar. But other things are not equal. There are vast economic inequalities among states, and some states deny basic liberties to their own citizens. These are the circumstances that create such a vast potential for movement across borders and that make the issue of migration seem like an urgent moral problem. But from a liberal egalitarian perspective, these circumstances are at least as morally objectionable as restrictions on freedom of movement.[12] States have an obligation to respect their citizens' basic liberties, and rich states have an obligation to transfer resources and adopt other measures to reduce drastically the prevailing international economic inequalities. If they fulfilled these obligations, migration would no longer be a serious moral problem, because relatively few people would want to move and those who did could and would be accommodated somewhere.

If one replies that states will not meet these obligations, the response is that we gain nothing by focusing on another obligation which they are equally unlikely to fulfill. Most of the same practical and self-interested considerations that will prevent rich states from transferring significant resources to poor states will keep them from opening their borders wide to poor immigrants. In struggling against injustice, it is a bad strategy to make the admission of new immigrants to rich countries a priority, because restrictions are a symptom, not a cause, of the real problems, because immigration can never be a solution for more than a relatively small number, no matter how open the borders, and because this focus on people who want to move from the Third World to the First World may perpetuate neo-colonial assumptions about the superiority of the First World.

I think there is something to be said for this objection. International inequalities and political oppression are certainly more important moral and political problems than restrictions on migration. The sense that the latter is an urgent problem derives in large part from the size of the potential demand and that in turn derives from international inequalities and other forms of injustice that free movement will do little to cure. Nevertheless, we cannot entirely ignore the question of immigration. In the long run, the transformation of the international politico-economic order might reduce the demand for international migration and the resistance to it, but, as Keynes said, in the long run we are all dead. We have to consider the moral claims of those whom we confront here and now (as well as the claims of future generations). For example, refugees who have no reasonable prospect of a return to their homes in the near term need a place to settle if they are to have any chance of a decent life. Moreover, we lack knowledge as well as will when it comes to radically reducing international inequalities, as is illustrated by the failures of most attempts to eliminate regional inequalities *within* states. In terms of politics, it is not clear that increasing aid and increasing immigration are really incompatible. In general, the same political actors support or oppose both.

But the objection that the demand for free movement is essentially epiphenomenal poses a theoretical challenge as well as a practical one. To what extent does my earlier claim about the liberal egalitarian commitment to free movement rest upon the current realities of international inequalities and political oppression? Would people have the right to move freely in a world without the deep injustices of the one we live in, or might there be legitimate grounds for restricting free movement, say, for the sake of a certain kind of community? In other words, is free movement epiphenomenal at the theoretical level, not derived directly from fundamental principles but rather from the application of those principles to the circumstances in which we find ourselves?

To explore this question, I propose to focus in the next two sections on the question of movements across borders when the states in question enjoy comparable levels of affluence and comparable liberal democratic political institutions.

IV

The epiphenomenon argument raises questions about the consequences of focusing on possible changes in migration policies in abstraction from other issues, but it does not directly challenge the principle that free movement is good from a liberal egalitarian perspective. Are there any elements in the liberal egalitarian tradition that would give pause to this general embrace of openness?

One possible source is the liberal egalitarian commitment to pluralism, and the consequent respect for difference and diversity. Consider first the case of Japan. Should Japan's immigration policy be the same as that of the United States or Canada? A commitment to free movement seems to require a positive response to this question, except that the public order constraint might kick in sooner because of the high population density in Japan. But to answer that question positively seems counterintuitive, and not just because we assume that all states have the right to control their borders. Rather a positive response seems to imply that all states have a moral obligation to become like us—multicultural countries with large numbers of immigrants (or at least to open themselves to that possibility). (This sounds like a form of North American moral imperialism: our way is the only right way.)

Now that does not prove that the claim is wrong. Appeals to diversity and pluralism carry no weight when it comes to the violation of basic human rights. From a liberal egalitarian perspective all states are obliged to respect such rights regardless of their history, culture or traditions. As we have seen, it is possible to claim that freedom of movement is a basic human right from a liberal egalitarian perspective. But perhaps that claim does not pay sufficient attention to the costs that freedom of movement can impose.

To return to the Japanese case, Japan is a country with a highly homogeneous population. It is not completely homogeneous. There are religious differences and ethnic minorities in Japan as there are in every country. But most people in Japan share a common culture, tradition and history to a much greater extent than people do in countries like Canada and the United States. It seems reasonable to suppose that many Japanese cherish their distinctive way of life, that they want to preserve it and pass it on to their children because they find that it gives meaning and depth to their lives. They cannot pass it on unchanged, to be sure, because no way of life remains entirely unchanged, but they can hope to do so in a form that retains both its vitality and its continuity with the past. In these ways many Japanese may have a vital interest in the preservation of a distinctive Japanese culture; they may regard it as crucial to their life projects. From a liberal egalitarian perspective this concern for preserving Japanese culture counts as a legitimate interest, assuming (as I do) that this culture is compatible with respect for all human beings as free and equal moral persons.[13]

It also seems reasonable to suppose that this distinctive culture and way of life would be profoundly transformed if a significant number of immigrants came to live in Japan. A multicultural Japan would be a very different place. So, limits on new entrants would be necessary to preserve the culture if any significant number of people wanted to immigrate.

Would the limits be justified? That depends, I think, on why the people wanted to come. We have to weigh the claims of those trying to get in equally with the claims of those who are already inside, but to do that we have to know something about the nature of those claims. For example, suppose some non-Japanese person had married a Japanese citizen. It would clearly be wrong to exclude the non-Japanese spouse, even if mixed marriages were seen as subversive of Japanese culture. Here the fundamental right of individuals to marry whom they want and to live together, along with the fundamental right of the Japanese citizen not to be expelled from his or her home, should trump any communal concerns for the preservation of culture. (And, as far as I know, Japan does indeed admit spouses.)

Suppose, however, that people wanted to come to live and work in Japan as a way of pursuing economic opportunity. Should that trump the concern of the Japanese to preserve their culture? The answer might depend in part on the nature of the alternatives the potential immigrants face if Japan is closed. Recall that we have temporarily put to one side, by hypothesis, the problems of deep international inequalities and refugee-generating forms of oppression. Presumably, then, the potential immigrants have reasonable economic opportunities elsewhere, even if ones that are not quite as good. I do not see why an interest in marginally better economic opportunities should count more than an interest in preserving a culture.

One obvious rejoinder is that restricting immigration limits individual freedom, while cultural changes that develop as a by-product of uncoordinated individual actions do not violate any legitimate claims of individuals. The problem with this sort of response (which clearly does fit with some strains in the liberal tradition and even with some forms of liberal egalitarianism) is that it uses too narrow a definition of freedom. It excludes by fiat any concern for the cumulative, if unintended, consequences of individual actions. A richer concept of freedom will pay attention to the context of choice, to the extent to which background conditions make it

possible for people to realize their most important goals and pursue their most important life projects. That is precisely the sort of approach that permits us to see the ways in which particular cultures can provide valuable resources for people and the costs associated with the loss of a culture, while still permitting a critical assessment of the consequences of the culture both for those who participate in it and for those who do not.

But if we say that exclusion may be justified to preserve Japanese culture, does that not open the door to any other state that wants to exclude others, or certain kinds of others, to preserve its culture and its way of life? Doesn't it legitimate racist immigration policies? What about the White Australia policy, for example? That was defended as an attempt to preserve a particular culture and way of life, as were similar racial and ethnic policies in Canada and the United States.[14]

From some viewpoints every form of exclusion that draws distinctions based on race, ethnicity, or cultural heritage is morally objectionable. I think, however, that one cannot make such a blanket judgement. Difference does not always entail domination. One has to consider what a particular case of exclusion means, taking the historical, social and political context into account.[15] For example, the White Australia policy cannot be separated from British imperialism and European racism. That is why it was never a defensible form of exclusion.

Japan's exclusionary policy seems quite different. First it is universal, i.e. it applies to all non-Japanese. It is not aimed at some particular racial or ethnic group that is presumed to be inferior, and it is not tied to a history of domination of the excluded. Japan has a centuries-old tradition of exclusion based partly on fears of the consequences of European penetration. Of course, there is also the Japanese imperialism of the twentieth century, but that developed only after the West had forced Japan to end its isolation. Moreover, it was only during its period of imperialist expansion that Japan adopted a non-exclusionary policy, declaring all the subjects of the Japanese Empire to be Japanese citizens and bringing thousands of Koreans into Japan as workers. Both before and after this period, Japan strictly limited new entrants. Unlike much of Western Europe, for example, Japan rejected proposals for guest worker programmers to solve labour shortages in the 1960s and 1970s. I trust that it is clear that I am in no way defending or excusing Japanese imperialism. On the contrary, my point is that the Japanese policy of exclusion was not a product of, and was in important ways antagonistic to, Japanese imperialism. In that respect, at least, exclusion was not linked to domination.

But does not a policy of exclusion always imply that the culture and the people being protected through exclusion are superior to the ones being excluded? Not necessarily. It may simply reflect an attachment to what is one's own. Presumably it does entail the view that this way of life is worth preserving, that it is better than whatever would replace it under conditions of openness. But that is not necessarily objectionable in itself. Besides, having relatively open borders may also generate a sense of cultural superiority, as the American case reveals.

I do not pretend to have established the legitimacy of Japanese exclusion. That would require a much more detailed and careful examination than I can provide here. What I do hope to have established is that such an examination would be worthwhile, that exclusion for the sake of preserving Japanese culture is not self-evidently wrong, at least in a context where we have temporarily assumed away the most urgent

concerns (desperate poverty and fear of oppression) that motivate so many of those who actually want to move and that make their claims so powerful.

What if we let those concerns back in and at the same time assumed that the positive case for the preservation of a distinctive Japanese culture could be sustained? One possibility is that we would conclude that not all of the rich states should have precisely the same responsibilities regarding admission of new members and assistance to poor states. Perhaps it would be appropriate for Japan to meet most of its responsibilities through aid rather than through admissions. (I express these thoughts tentatively because I feel unsure about them.)

Even if one did follow this line of thought, however, Japan would face certain responsibilities regarding the admission and integration of "outsiders." For example, Japan should admit some reasonable number of refugees on a permanent basis. Their needs cannot be met by aid and Japan cannot rightly expect others to assume all the burdens of resettlement. Perhaps it would be acceptable to select among the refugees on the basis of their adaptability to or compatability with Japanese culture.

Even more important, Japan has a responsibility to treat its Korean minority differently. Most of the Koreans in Japan are people who were brought over to work in Japan during World War II or their descendants. They have lived in Japan for many years. Most of the children have never lived anywhere else, and many do not even speak any other language than Japanese. Japan has an obligation to treat these people as full members of society, to grant them citizenship easily if they wish it and to make their position as permanent residents more secure and more equitable if they prefer to retain their Korean citizenship.[16] In short,

Japan's desire to protect its cultural cohesiveness is outweighed in some cases by the legitimate claims of others to entry and integration.

The discussion of Japan makes a preliminary case for exclusion the sake of preserving a cultural tradition and way of life. In Japan this cultural tradition and way of life are closely associated with the political boundaries of a sovereign state. But this does not establish anything about the moral status of the state as such nor does it rule out the possibility that there may be other communities with cultures and ways of life worth preserving that do not exist as states. Take, for example, the case of native communities in North America who are trying to preserve a traditional way of life within some defined land area. Most of what has been said about the Japanese case could also be said about them: they are trying to maintain a distinctive culture and way of life that gives meaning to those who inhabit it and which they regard as highly preferable to the way of life that would be entailed if they mixed with others, they cannot maintain this culture if any significant number of outsiders come to settle on their land and the reasons the outsiders have for coming (e.g. to use the land for recreational purposes) generally seem far less compelling than the reasons the natives have for keeping them out.[17]

I accept these general claims. Indeed the control that native peoples exercise over their land provides a striking exception to the general right of free mobility within the modern state, and one that is entirely justified from a liberal egalitarian perspective in my view. So, it is not the state as such that gives rise to a claim to exclude, but rather the existence of a community with a distinctive and valuable way of life that would be threatened by immigration.[18]

V

Can a parallel argument be developed on behalf of the state as such, perhaps on the grounds that each (legitimate) state has a distinct political culture worthy of preservation and protection? By "political culture" I mean the collective self-understanding, the way citizens think of themselves and of their relationship with one another as this is reflected in their political institutions, policies and practices. One reason people have for wanting to restrict entry is their desire to protect the democratic autonomy of the community in which they live. This view presupposes that there is some significant space between what is morally required of all and morally prohibited to all so that different communities can legitimately make different choices about goals, institutions and policies, or, more broadly, about the ways they lead their collective lives. Call this the zone of the morally permissible. One need not think of this as a realm of mere preferences, however. The moral arguments that belong here (and are most apt to be used in real political debates) are ones about the history and character of the community rather than about universal rights and duties. Most forms of liberal egalitarianism do not pretend to settle all moral questions. So, different communities will make different decisions, adopt different policies and develop different characters. But these differences may be threatened by open borders.[19]

Let me offer a concrete example from a comparison between Canada and the United States.[20] (I write as someone born and raised in the United States who has lived in Canada for the past four years.) Canada has a national health insurance plan that pays for the medical care of all citizens and permanent residents. The United States does not. According to some estimates, 30 percent of the American population has no health insurance, and many more are underinsured. Should Americans with serious health problems be able to move to Canada to take advantage of its health care system? Take those with AIDS as an example. This is an illness that requires a lot of expensive medical care over a long period, care that may simply be unavailable in the United States if one has no insurance. People with AIDS and without insurance might well choose to move to Canada if they could do so. But Canada's population as a whole is only 10 per cent of that of the United States. If even a small proportion of the Americans with AIDS moved, it would put a severe strain on the Canadian health care system. At present, Canadian immigration requirements keep out potential immigrants with medical problems that seem likely to put an unusually high financial burden on the health care system. Is that an unjust restriction on potential American immigrants?

Canada's health care system is only one example of a pervasive difference between Canada and the United States in social welfare policy. In one area after another Canada provides greater benefits to those in need, and, of course, Canadians pay much higher taxes than Americans to fund these programmes. If the borders were open and if many of the needy moved across, both the capacity and the willingness to support the programmes would be in jeopardy. The capacity would be threatened by the relative size of the Canadian and American populations, the willingness by the sense that Americans were taking advantage of Canadians (not so much the needy Americans, who would probably arouse both sympathy and resentment, as the greedy ones who refused to bear the costs of caring for their own and tried to shift these costs onto others). Restrictions on immigration from the United States therefore may help to make it possible for

Canadians to take a different and more generous path from Americans when it comes to social policy. Does liberal egalitarianism require them to open the borders anyway?

If the questions in the last two paragraphs sound rhetorical, it is only because the presumption that states have the right to control entry is so deeply rooted in our thinking. One has only to shift the focus to intrastate movement to see why the questions are real and important. In the United States as in many federal systems, subunits bear much of the responsibility for social policy and they differ greatly in the ways they carry out these responsibilities. For example, Wisconsin's welfare policies are much more generous (or much less stingy) than those of the neighbouring state of Illinois. Some Wisconsin officials claim that people are moving from Illinois to Wisconsin for the sake of these benefits. These officials propose to discourage the influx by reducing benefits for new residents during a temporary waiting period—a strategy that may or may not pass legislative and judicial scrutiny. But not even the most ardent advocates of exclusion think that they can prohibit people from moving to Wisconsin from Illinois or keep them from gaining access to all of the state's social programmes after a waiting period. This is not just a quirk of the U.S. constitutional system. As we have seen, freedom of movement within the nation-state is widely regarded as a basic human right, and if this freedom is to be more than a mere formality, it necessarily entails that new arrivals have access to the rights and privileges that current residents enjoy, at least after the satisfaction of a modest residency requirement and, in some cases, immediately. But this freedom of movement has the same effect of eroding or at least limiting the democratic autonomy of Wisconsin as it would that of Canada.

Is that bad? Should Wisconsin have the right to keep out people from Illinois after all? Or should Canada be obliged to admit people from the United States? If the two cases are different, how and why are they different? I find these questions genuinely puzzling, but in the end I cannot see that sovereignty makes that much difference from a liberal egalitarian perspective. Despite my attachment to Canada's social welfare policies, I do not think they justify restrictions on movement. On the other hand, I do think that this commitment to free movement is compatible with short-term residency requirements so that one must live somewhere for a few months before becoming eligible for social pro-grammes, and that such requirements would do a great deal to protect against the erosion of social programmes. Living in Canada, one cannot help but be aware of the importance some people (especially in Quebec) attach to maintaining the distinct culture and way of life of their province. It turns out to be possible to do so even within a context of free migration within the state and considerable immigration from out-side. Despite its occasional effects on social policies, it is easy to exaggerate the impact of free movement within the state and also to ignore its importance to those who do take advantage of it. The same is true of movement across borders. Perhaps even the Japanese ought in principle to begin with a policy of open doors, closing them only if a substantial demand actually appears. Given the difficulties of fitting into Japanese society as an outsider, how many would actually want to settle there if they had reasonable opportunities elsewhere?

So, I return to the theme with which I began. Liberal egalitarianism entails a deep and powerful commitment to free-dom of movement which can be overrid-den at the level of principle only with great difficulty.

VI

Let me turn briefly now to the question of how the responsibilities of one state with regard to migration are affected by what other states do. In principle, the failures of one state should increase the obligations of the others since there are people out there with legitimate needs and moral claims that are not being met. And it actually seems to work this way with regard to refugees at first. Thus the very existence of refugees reflects a failure of the state from which they have fled, and other states gen-erally acknowledge that this imposes new obligations on them to care for people who were not previously their responsibility. But then by any reasonable specification of what a fair share of responsibility for refugees would require of each state, most states fail to live up to their responsibili-ties. (Except for the states that are next door to the refugees. They sometimes act admirably and in any event can rarely avoid bearing a disproportionate share of the burden.) Should we say that this sec-ond round of failures generates a new set of obligations for the few states that have acted responsibly? That seems an unpromising line, ratcheting up the level of responsibility until one is almost bound to fail. On the other hand, the needs of the refugees remain unmet. In practice, states, like people, tend to judge their own behav-iour by what others do, so that states feel proud if they do more for refugees than most (and especially than the ones with whom they compare themselves).

VII

I will conclude with a few remarks on cri-teria of inclusion and exclusion. Assuming that there will be some restrictions on entry, either for legitimate reasons like the public order constraint or for illegitimate ones like a desire to protect economic privilege, are there some criteria of inclusion and exclusion that are more (or less) objectionable than others from a liberal egalitarian perspective? Certainly need should be one important criterion for admission, and refugees seeking permanent resettlement rank very high on this score since they literally need a place to live. The claims of immediate family members (spouse, minor children) rank very highly as well. No one should be denied the right to live with his or her family. Other relatives also have some claim but not as strong as one.

To return to the criterion of need, if one accepts the brain drain hypothesis, it would seem appropriate to give priority to the least skilled and most needy among potential immigrants as this would have the least negative impact on the countries of origin. On the other hand, if one admits people with skills and education, it may reduce the backlash problem (which appears to be a real or potential problem in every country that accepts immigrants, especially refugees).

Are criteria that serve the interests of the receiving country always morally problematic in this way, defensible only on prudential grounds? Not necessarily. Taking linguistic and cultural compatibility into account does not seem objectionable if it is not a disguised form of racial or ethnic prejudice and if the cumulative effects of such policies by different countries do not leave out some groups altogether.

Criteria of selection that discriminate against potential immigrants on the basis of race, ethnicity, religion, sex or sexual orientation are particularly objectionable from a liberal egalitarian perspective. Can these criteria ever be used legitimately to give priority to some? Again, one crucial question is whether they constitute *de facio* forms of discrimination. Consider four recent or current policies with these sorts of factors (I oversimplify a bit, but I think I describe the main lines accurately):

1. Britain removed citizenship from holders of overseas passports and citizens of commonwealth countries, except for those whose grandfather was born in Great Britain.

2. Ireland grants an automatic right to citizenship to anyone with a grandparent born in Ireland, provided that the person comes to Ireland to live.

3. Germany grants citizenship (upon application in Germany) to anyone of ethnic German descent, no matter how long since the person's ancestors lived in Germany.

4. Israel grants automatic citizenship to any Jew who comes to live in Israel.

Of these, the British law is the most objectionable from a liberal egalitarian perspective and the Irish law the least, despite their formal similarity. The British law is a thinly disguised form of racism. It was designed to preserve the citizenship rights of as many descendants of white settlers as possible while depriving as many Asians and Africans as possible of theirs. The Irish grandfather clause, by contrast, has no hidden exclusionary goal. It is merely an attempt to lure back the descendants of some of those who left. The German law is troubling for two related reasons. First, the explicit link between ethnicity and citizenship raises questions about whether those German citizens who are not ethnic Germans are really regarded as equal citizens. Second, the easy grant of citizenship to people who have never lived in Germany before and some of whom do not even speak the language contrasts sharply with the reluctance to grant citizenship automatically to the children of Turkish "guest workers" even when the children were born and brought up in Germany (and sometimes speak no other language). Finally, the Israeli "Law of Return" raises questions about whether the Arab citizens of Israel whose friends and relatives do not have comparably easy access to citizenship are really regarded as equal citizens. On the other hand, the Israeli law is tied both to national security concerns and to the historic purpose of Israel as a homeland for Jews.

VIII

Liberal egalitarians are committed to an idea of free movement, with only modest qualifications. That idea is not politically feasible today and so it mainly serves to provide a critical standard by which to assess existing restrictive practices and policies. While almost all forms of restriction on movement are wrong from a liberal egalitarian perspective, some practices and policies are worse than others. Expulsion is worse than a refusal to admit. Racism and other forms of discriminatory exclusion are worse than policies that exclude but do not distinguish in objectionable ways among

those excluded. Ideals do not always translate directly into prescriptions for practice because of the second-best problems familiar from economic theory which have their analogue in moral theory. In theory this might seem to make it difficult to identify the policy implications of liberal egalitarianism with regard to free movement. One can doubtless imagine cases where the sudden opening of the borders of one country (with all the other circumstances of the modern world remaining unchanged) would do more harm than good from a liberal egalitarian perspective. In practice, however, we can usually ignore this concern because, in every polity, domestic political considerations will confine feasible policy options to a relatively narrow range, excluding alternatives that would entail major costs to current citizens. Given these political realities, liberal egalitarians should almost always press for more openness towards immigrants and refugees.

Notes

1. For a defence of few or no restrictions, see Joseph H. Carens, "Aliens and Citizens: The Case for Open Borders," *The Review of Politics*, 49 (Spring 1987), 251–73; Bruce Ackerman, *Social Justice in the Liberal State* (New Haven, CT: Yale University Press, 1980), pp. 89–95; Judith Lichtenberg, "National Boundaries and Moral Boundaries: A Cosmopolitan View," *Boundaries: National Autonomy and Its Limits*, ed. Peter Brown and Henry Shue (Totowa, NJ: Rowman & Little-field, 1981), pp. 79–100; and Roger Nett, "The Civil Right We Are Not Yet Ready For: The Right of Free Movement of People on the Face of the Earth," *Ethics*, 81 (1971), 212–27. For the state's right to control entry, see Michael Walzer, *Spheres of Justice* (New York: Basic Books, 1983), pp. 31–63. For the middle position, see Frederick Whelan, "Citizenship and Freedom of Movement: An Open Admission Policy," *Open Borders? Closed Societies?: The Ethnical and Political Issues*, ed. Mark Gibney (Westport, CT: Greenwood Press, 1988), pp. 3–39.

2. The arguments in this section draw upon Carens, "Aliens and Citizens" and Whelan, "Citizenship and Freedom of Movement."

3. This brief sketch necessarily covers over deep disagreements among liberal egalitarians with regard to many issues such as how much inequality is compatible with or required by the commitment to freedom, whether affirmative action for groups historically subject to discrimination is a violation of, or a means of realizing, liberal egalitarian principles, what are the foundations (if any) of liberal egalitarian commitments, and so on.

4. See Walzer, *Spheres of Justice*. For a detailed discussion of the right of exit, see Frederick Whelan, "Citizenship and the Right to Leave," *American Political Science Review*, 75 (1981), 636–53.

5. I have discussed these sorts of arguments previously in "Aliens and Citizens." For

other treatments see Ackerman, *Social Justice*; Whelan, "Citizenship and Freedom of Movement," and an unpublished paper by Whelan entitled "Freedom of International Movement: Some Reservations."

6. Here I follow John Rawls, *A Theory of Justice* (Cambridge, MA: Harvard University Press, 1971), pp. 216–21.

7. I develop the claims in the next two paragraphs at greater length in "Membership and Morality: Admission to Citizenship in Liberal Democratic States," *Immigration and the Politics of Citizenship in Europe and North America*, ed. William Rogers Brubaker (Lanham, MD: German Marshall Fund of America and University Press of America, 1989), pp. 31–49.

8. For one discussion of the potential demand, see Michael Teitelbaum, "Right versus Right: Immigration and Refugee Policy in the United States," *Foreign Affairs*, 59 (1980), 21–59.

9. Rawls, *A Theory of Justice*, p. 213.

10. For an explicit use of this argument, see Teitelbaum, "Right versus Right."

11. Whelan offers a clear presentation of these arguments in "Freedom of International Movement."

12. See, e.g., Charles Beitz, *Political Theory and International Relations* (Princeton, NJ: Princeton University Press, 1979); Brian Barry, "Humanity and Justice in Global Perspective," *Ethics, Economics, and the Law: Nomas XXIV*, ed. J. Roland Pennock and John W. Chapman (New York: New York University Press, 1982), pp. 219–52; and David A. J. Richards, "International Distributive Justice," in Pennock and Chapman, pp. 275–99.

13. For discussions of the ways in which liberal individualism is compatible with the view that people may have an interest in maintaining and passing on a culture, see Brian Barry, "Self-Government Revisited," *The Nature of Political Theory*, ed. David Miller and Larry Siedentop (Oxford: Clarendon Press, 1983) and Will Kymlicka, *Liberalism, Community and Culture* (Oxford: Oxford University Press, 1989).

14. For a fuller discussion of the White Australia policy, see Joseph H. Carens, "Nationalism and the Exclusion of Immigrants: Lessons from Australian Immigration Policy," *Open Borders? Closed Societies: The Ethical and Political Issues*, ed. Mark Gibney (Westport, CT: Greenwood Press, 1988), pp. 41–60.

15. For a fuller defence of this approach see Joseph H. Carens, "Difference and Domination: Reflections on the Relation between Pluralism and Equality," *Majorities and Minorities: NOMOS XXXII*, ed. John Chapman and Alan Wertheimer (New York: New York University Press, 1990), pp. 226–50.

16. The claims made here for Koreans in Japan parallel those made above for migrant workers.

17. I have explored these issues more fully in an unpublished paper entitled "Migration, Morality, and the Nation-State."

18. For a valuable discussion of minority rights, especially the rights of native people in liberal societies, see Kymlicka, *Liberalism, Community and Culture.*

19. This concern for the capacity of communities to define their own character lies at the heart of Walzer's defence of their right to closure. See note 1.

20. I explore the relevance of differences in social welfare policy between Canada and the United States in a similar way in "Immigration and the Welfare State," *Democracy and the Welfare State*, ed. Amy Gutmann (Princeton, NJ: Princeton University Press, 1988), pp. 207–30.

Study Questions for Section 11

1. Walzer explores the concept of political community by way of three analogies (neighborhood, club, family). Are these analogies apt? How do these analogies help us understand the issue of immigration?

2. Walzer contends that "immigration and emigration are morally asymmetrical," because the right to leave one country does not entail the right to enter any other. Carens rejects this asymmetry. Which view is more compelling?

3. Assuming that one's life chances are strongly influenced by the accidental circumstances of one's birth, how should this consideration affect our thinking about immigration?

SECTION 12

THE ENVIRONMENT

People or Penguins: The Case for Optimal Pollution

William F. Baxter

I start with the modest proposition that, in dealing with pollution, or indeed with any problem, it is helpful to know what one is attempting to accomplish. Agreement on how and whether to pursue a particular objective, such as pollution control, is not possible unless some more general objective has been identified and stated with reasonable precision. We talk loosely of having clean air and clean water, of preserving our wilderness areas, and so forth. But none of these is a sufficiently general objective: each is more accurately viewed as a means rather than as an end.

With regard to clean air, for example, one may ask, "how clean?" and "what does clean mean?" It is even reasonable to ask, "why have clean air?" Each of these questions is an implicit demand that a more general community goal be stated—a goal sufficiently general in its scope and enjoying sufficiently general assent among the community of actors that such "why" questions no longer seem admissible with respect to that goal.

If, for example, one states as a goal the proposition that "every person should be free to do whatever he wishes in contexts where his actions do not interfere with the interests of other human beings," the speaker is unlikely to be met with a response of "why." The goal may be criticized as uncertain in its implications or difficult to implement, but it is so basic a tenet of our civilization—it reflects a cultural value so broadly shared, at least in the abstract—that the question "why" is seen as impertinent or imponderable or both.

I do not mean to suggest that everyone would agree with the "spheres of freedom" objective just stated. Still less do I mean to suggest that a society could subscribe to four or five such general objectives that would be adequate in their coverage to serve as testing criteria by which all other disagreements might be measured. One difficulty in the attempt to construct such a list is that each new goal added will conflict, in certain applications, with each prior goal listed; and thus each goal serves as a limited qualification on prior goals.

Without any expectation of obtaining unanimous consent to them, let me set forth four goals that I generally use as ultimate testing criteria in attempting to frame solutions to problems of human organization. My position regarding pollution stems from these four criteria. If the criteria appeal to you and any part of what appears hereafter does not, our disagreement will have a helpful focus: which of us is correct, analytically, in supposing that his position on pollution would better serve these general goals. If the criteria do not seem acceptable to you, then it is to be expected that our more particular judgments will differ, and the task will then be yours to identify the basic set of criteria upon which your particular judgments rest.

My criteria are as follows:

1. The spheres of freedom criterion stated above.
2. Waste is a bad thing. The dominant feature of human existence is scarcity—our available resources, our aggregate labors, and our skill in employing both have always been, and will continue for some time to be, inadequate to yield to every man all the tangible and intangible satisfactions he would like to have. Hence, none of those resources, or labors, or skills, should be wasted—that is, employed so as to yield less than they might yield in human satisfactions.
3. Every human being should be regarded as an end rather than as a means to be used for the betterment of another. Each should be afforded dignity and regarded as having an absolute claim to an evenhanded application of such rules as the community may adopt for its governance.
4. Both the incentive and the opportunity to improve his share of satisfactions should be preserved to every individual. Preservation of incentive is dictated by the "no-waste" criterion and enjoins against the continuous, totally egalitarian redistribution of satisfactions, or wealth; but subject to that constraint, everyone should receive, by continuous redistribution if necessary, some minimal share of aggregate wealth so as to avoid a level of privation from which the opportunity to improve his situation becomes illusory.

The relationship of these highly general goals to the more specific environmental issues at hand may not be readily apparent, and I am not yet ready to demonstrate their pervasive implications. But let me give one indication of their implications. Recently scientists have informed us that use of DDT in food production is causing damage to the penguin population. For the present purposes let us accept that assertion as an indisputable scientific fact. The scientific fact is often asserted as if the correct implication—that we must stop agricultural use of DDT—followed from the mere statement of the fact of penguin damage. But plainly it does not follow if my criteria are employed.

My criteria are oriented to people, not penguins. Damage to penguins, or sugar pines, or geological marvels is, without more, simply irrelevant. One must go further, by my criteria, and say, penguins are important because people enjoy seeing them walk about rocks; and furthermore, the well-being of people would be less impaired by halting use of DDT than by giving up penguins. In short, my observations about environmental problems will be people oriented, as are my criteria. I have no interest in preserving penguins for their own sake.

It may be said by way of objection to this position that it is very selfish of people to act as if each person represented one unit of importance and nothing else was of any importance. It is undeniably selfish. Nevertheless I think it is the only tenable starting place for analysis for several reasons. First, no other position corresponds to the way most people really think and act —i.e., corresponds to reality.

Second, this attitude does not portend any massive destruction of nonhuman flora and fauna, for people depend on them in many obvious ways, and they will be preserved because and to the degree that humans do depend on them.

Third, what is good for humans is, in many respects, good for penguins and pine trees—clean air, for example. So that humans are, in these respects, surrogates for plant and animal life.

Fourth, I do not know how we could administer any other system. Our decisions are either private or collective. Insofar as Mr. Jones is free to act privately, he may give such preferences as he wishes to other forms of life: he may feed birds in winter and do less with himself, and he may even decline to resist an advancing polar bear on the ground that the bear's appetite is more important than those portions of himself that the bear may choose to eat. In short my basic premise does not rule out private altruism to competing life-forms. It does rule out, however, Mr. Jones' inclination to feed Mr. Smith to the bear, however hungry the bear, however despicable Mr. Smith.

Insofar as we act collectively on the other hand, only humans can be afforded an opportunity to participate in the collective decisions. Penguins cannot vote now and are unlikely subjects for the franchise—pine trees more unlikely still. Again each individual is free to cast his vote so as to benefit sugar pines if that is his inclination. But many of the more extreme assertions that one hears from some conservationists amount to tacit assertions that they are specially appointed representatives of sugar pines, and hence that their preferences should be weighted more heavily than the preferences of other humans who do not enjoy equal rapport with "nature." The simplistic assertion that agricultural use of DDT must stop at once because it is harmful to penguins is of that type.

Fifth, if polar bears or pine trees or penguins, like men, are to be regarded as ends rather than means, if they are to count in our calculus of social organization, someone must tell me how much each one counts, and someone must tell me how these life-forms are to be permitted to express their preferences, for I do not know either answer. If the answer is that certain people are to hold their proxies, then I want to know how those proxy-holders are to be selected: self-appointment does not seem workable to me.

Sixth, and by way of summary of all the foregoing, let me point out that the set of environmental issues under discussion—although they raise very complex technical questions of how to achieve any objective—ultimately raise a normative question: what ought we to do. Questions of ought are unique to the human mind and world—they are meaningless as applied to a non-human situation.

I reject the proposition that we ought to respect the "balance of nature" or to "preserve the environment" unless the reason for doing so, express or implied, is the benefit of man.

I reject the idea that there is a "right" or "morally correct" state of nature to which we should return. The word "nature" has no normative connotation. Was it "right" or "wrong" for the earth's crust to heave in contortion and create mountains and seas? Was it "right" for the first amphibian to crawl up out of the primordial ooze? Was it "wrong" for plants to reproduce themselves and alter the atmospheric composition in favor of oxygen? For animals to alter the atmosphere in favor of carbon dioxide both by breathing oxygen and eating plants? No answers can be given to these questions because they are meaningless questions.

All this may seem obvious to the point of being tedious, but much of the present controversy over environment and pollution rests on tacit normative assumptions about just such nonnormative phenomena: that it is "wrong" to impair penguins with DDT, but not to slaughter cattle for prime rib roasts. That it is wrong to kill stands of sugar pines with industrial fumes, but not to cut sugar pines and build housing for the poor. Every man is entitled to his own preferred definition of Walden Pond, but there is no definition that has any moral superiority over another, except by reference to the selfish needs of the human race.

From the fact that there is no normative definition of the natural state, it follows that there is no normative definition of clean air or pure water—hence no definition of polluted air—or of pollution—except by reference to the needs of man. The "right" composition of the atmosphere is one which has some dust in it and some lead in it and some hydrogen sulfide in it—just those amounts that attend a sensibly organized society thoughtfully and knowledgeably pursuing the greatest possible satisfaction for its human members.

The first and most fundamental step toward solution of our environmental problems is a clear recognition that our objective is not pure air or water but rather some optimal state of pollution. That step immediately suggests the question: How do we define and attain the level of pollution that will yield the maximum possible amount of human satisfaction?

Low levels of pollution contribute to human satisfaction but so do food and shelter and education and music. To attain ever lower levels of pollution, we must pay the cost of having less of these other things. I contrast that view of the cost of pollution control with the more popular statement that pollution control will "cost" very large numbers of dollars. The popular statement is true in some senses, false in others; sorting out the true and false senses is of some importance. The first step in that sorting process is to

achieve a clear understanding of the difference between dollars and resources. Resources are the wealth of our nation; dollars are merely claim checks upon those resources. Resources are of vital importance; dollars are comparatively trivial.

Four categories of resources are sufficient for our purposes: At any given time a nation, or a planet if you prefer, has a stock of labor, of technological skill, of capital goods, and of natural resources (such as mineral deposits, timber, water, land, etc.). These resources can be used in various combinations to yield goods and services of all kinds—in some limited quantity. The quantity will be larger if they are combined efficiently, smaller if combined inefficiently. But in either event the resources stock is limited, the goods and services that they can be made to yield are limited; even the most efficient use of them will yield less than our population, in the aggregate, would like to have.

If one considers building a new dam, it is appropriate to say that it will be costly in the sense that it will require X hours of labor, Y tons of steel and concrete, and Z amount of capital goods. If these resources are devoted to the dam, then they cannot be used to build hospitals, fishing rods, schools, or electric can openers. That is the meaningful sense in which the dam is costly.

Quite apart from the very important question of how wisely we can combine our resources to produce goods and services is the very different question of how they get distributed—who gets how many goods? Dollars constitute the claim checks which are distributed among people and which control their share of national output. Dollars are nearly valueless pieces of paper except to the extent that they do represent claim checks to some fraction of the output of goods and services. Viewed as claim checks, all the dollars outstanding during any period of time are worth, in the aggregate, the goods and services that are available to be claimed with them during that period—neither more nor less.

It is far easier to increase the supply of dollars than to increase the production of goods and services—printing dollars is easy. But printing more dollars doesn't help because each dollar then simply becomes a claim to fewer goods, i.e., becomes worthless.

The point is this: many people fall into error upon hearing the statement that the decision to build a dam, or to clean up a river, will cost $X million. It is regrettably easy to say, "It's only money. This is a wealthy country, and we have lots of money." But you cannot build a dam or clean a river with $X million—unless you also have a match, you can't even make a fire. One builds a dam or cleans a river by diverting labor and steel and trucks and factories from making one kind of goods to making another. The cost in dollars is merely a shorthand way of describing the extent of the diversion necessary. If we build a dam for $X million, then we must recognize that we will have $X million less housing and food and medical care and electric can openers as a result.

Similarly, the costs of controlling pollution are best expressed in terms of the other goods we will have to give up to do the job. This is not to say the job should not be done. Badly as we need more housing, more medical care, and more can openers, and more symphony orchestras, we could do with somewhat less of them, in my judgment at least, in exchange for somewhat cleaner air and rivers. But that is the nature of the

trade-off, and analysis of the problem is advanced if that unpleasant reality is kept in mind. Once the trade-off relationship is clearly perceived, it is possible to state in a very general way what the optimal level of pollution is. I would state it as follows:

People enjoy watching penguins. They enjoy relatively clean air and smog-free vistas. Their health is improved by relatively clean water and air. Each of these benefits is a type of good or service. As a society we would be well advised to give up one washing machine if the resources that would have gone into that washing machine can yield greater human satisfaction when diverted into pollution control. We should give up one hospital if the resources thereby freed would yield more human satisfaction when devoted to elimination of noise in all cities. And so on, trade-off by trade-off, we should divert our productive capacities from the production of existing goods and services to the production of a cleaner, quieter, more pastoral nation up to—and no further than—the point at which we value more highly the next washing machine or hospital that we would have to do without than we value the next unit of environmental improvement that the diverted resources would create.

Now this proposition seems to me unassailable but so general and abstract as to be unhelpful—at least unadministerable in the form stated. It assumes we can measure in some way the incremental units of human satisfaction yielded by very different types of good . . . . But I insist that the proposition stated describes the result for which we should be striving—and again, that it is always useful to know what your target is even if your weapons are too crude to score a bull's-eye.

READING

24

IDEALS OF HUMAN EXCELLENCE AND PRESERVING NATURAL ENVIRONMENTS

Thomas E. Hill, Jr.

I

A wealthy eccentric bought a house in a neighborhood I know. The house was surrounded by a beautiful display of grass, plants, and flowers, and it was shaded by a huge old avocado tree. But the grass required cutting, the flowers needed tending, and the man wanted more sun. So he cut the whole lot down and covered the yard with asphalt. After all it was his property and he was not fond of plants.

It was a small operation, but it reminded me of the strip mining of large sections of the Appalachians. In both cases, of course, there were reasons for the destruction, and property rights could be cited as justification. But I could not help but wonder, "What sort of person would do a thing like that?"

Many Californians had a similar reaction when a recent governor defended the leveling of ancient redwood groves,

From Thomas E. Hill, Jr., "Ideals of Human Excellence and Preserving Natural Environments," *Environmental Ethics* 5 (1983): 211–24.

reportedly saying, "If you have seen one redwood, you have seen them all."

Incidents like these arouse the indignation of ardent environmentalists and leave even apolitical observers with some degree of moral discomfort. The reasons for these reactions are mostly obvious. Uprooting the natural environment robs both present and future generations of much potential use and enjoyment. Animals too depend on the environment; and even if one does not value animals for their own sakes, their potential utility for us is incalculable. Plants are needed, of course, to replenish the atmosphere quite aside from their aesthetic value. These reasons for hesitating to destroy forests and gardens are not only the most obvious ones, but also the most persuasive for practical purposes. But, one wonders, is there nothing more behind our discomfort? Are we concerned solely about the potential use and enjoyment of the forests, etc., for ourselves, later generations, and perhaps animals? Is there not something else which disturbs us when we witness the destruction or even listen to those who would defend it in terms of cost/benefit analysis?

Imagine that in each of our examples those who would destroy the environment argue elaborately that, even considering future generations of human beings and animals, there are benefits in "replacing" the natural environment which outweigh the negative utilities which environmentalists cite.[1] No doubt we could press the argument on the facts, trying to show that the destruction is shortsighted and that its defenders have underestimated its potential harm or ignored some pertinent rights or interests. But is this all we could say? Suppose we grant, for a moment, that the utility of destroying the redwoods, forests, and gardens is equal to their potential for use and enjoyment by nature lovers and animals. Suppose, further, that we even grant that the pertinent human rights and animal rights, if any, are evenly divided for and against destruction. Imagine that we also concede, for argument's sake, that the forests contain no potentially useful endangered species of animals and plants. Must we then conclude that there is no further cause for moral concern? Should we then feel morally indifferent when we see the natural environment uprooted?

II

Suppose we feel that the answer to these questions should be negative. Suppose, in other words, we feel that our moral discomfort when we confront the destroyers of nature is not fully explained by our belief that they have miscalculated the best use of natural resources or violated rights in exploiting them. Suppose, in particular, we sense that part of the problem is that the natural environment is being viewed exclusively as a natural *resource*. What could be the ground of such a feeling? That is, what is there in our system of normative principles and values that could account for our remaining moral dissatisfaction?[2]

Some may be tempted to seek an explanation by appeal to the interests, or even the rights, of plants. After all, they may argue, we only gradually came to acknowledge the moral importance of all human beings, and it is even more recently that consciences have been aroused to give full weight to the welfare (and rights?) of animals. The next logical step, it may be argued, is to acknowledge a moral requirement to take into account the interests (and rights?) of plants. The problem with the strip miners, redwood cutters, and the like, on this view, is not just that they ignore the welfare and rights of people and animals; they also fail to give due weight to the survival and health of the plants themselves.

The temptation to make such a reply is understandable if one assumes that all moral questions are exclusively concerned with whether *acts* are right or wrong, and that this, in turn, is determined entirely by how the acts impinge on the rights and interests of those directly affected. On this assumption, if there is cause for moral concern, some right or interest has been neglected; and if the rights and interests of human beings and animals have already been taken into account, then there must be some other pertinent interests, for example, those of plants. A little reflection will show that the assumption is mistaken; but, in any case, the conclusion that plants have rights or morally relevant interests is surely untenable. We do speak of what is "good for" plants, and they can "thrive" and also be "killed." But this does not imply that they have "interests" in any morally relevant sense. Some people apparently believe that plants grow better if we talk to them, but the idea that the plants suffer and enjoy, desire and dislike, etc., is clearly outside the range of both common sense and scientific belief. The notion that the forests should be preserved to avoid *hurting* the trees or because they have a *right* to life is not part of a widely shared moral consciousness, and for good reason.[3]

Another way of trying to explain our moral discomfort is to appeal to certain religious beliefs. If one believes that all living things were created by a God who cares for them and entrusted us with the use of plants and animals only for limited purposes, then one has a reason to avoid careless destruction of the forests, etc., quite aside from their future utility. Again, if one believes that a divine force is immanent in all nature, then too one might have reason to care for more than sentient things. But such arguments require strong and controversial premises, and, I suspect, they will always have a restricted audience.

Early in this century, due largely to the influence of G. E. Moore, another point of view developed which some may find promising.[4] Moore introduced, or at least made popular, the idea that certain states of affairs are intrinsically valuable—not just valued, but valuable, and not necessarily because of their effects on sentient beings. Admittedly Moore came to believe that in fact the only intrinsically valuable things were conscious experiences of various sorts, but this restriction was not inherent in the idea of intrinsic value.[5] The intrinsic goodness of something, he thought, was an objective, nonrelational property of the thing, like its texture or color, but not a property perceivable by sense perception or detectable by scientific instruments. In theory at least, a single tree thriving alone in a universe without sentient beings, and even without God, could be intrinsically valuable. Since, according to Moore, our duty is to maximize intrinsic value, his theory could obviously be used to argue that we have reason not to destroy natural environments independently of how they affect human beings and animals. The survival of a forest might have worth beyond its worth *to* sentient beings.

This approach, like the religious one, may appeal to some but is infested with problems. There are, first, the familiar objections to intuitionism, on which the theory depends. Metaphysical and epistemological doubts about nonnatural, intuited properties are hard to suppress, and many have argued that the theory rests on a misunderstanding of the words *good, valuable,* and the like.[6] Second, even if we try to set aside these objections and think in Moore's terms, it is far from obvious that everyone would agree that the existence of forests, etc., is intrinsically valuable. The test, says Moore, is what we would say when we imagine a universe with just the thing in question, without any effects or accompaniments, and then we ask, "Would its existence be better than its nonexistence?" Be careful, Moore would remind us, not to construe this question "Would you *prefer* the existence of that universe to its nonexistence?" The question is, "Would its existence have the objective, nonrelational property, intrinsic goodness?"

Now even among those who have no worries about whether this really makes sense, we might well get a diversity of answers. Those prone to destroy natural environments will doubtless give one answer, and nature lovers will likely give another. When an issue is as controversial as the one at hand, intuition is a poor arbiter.

The problem, then, is this. We want to understand what underlies our moral uneasiness at the destruction of the redwoods, forests, etc., even apart from the loss of these as resources for human beings and animals. But I find no adequate answer by pursuing the questions, "Are rights or interests of plants neglected?" "What is God's will on the matter?" and "What is the intrinsic value of the existence of a tree or forest?" My suggestion, which is in fact the main point of this paper, is that we look at the problem from a different perspective. That is, let us turn for a while from the effort to find reasons why certain *acts* destructive of natural environments are morally wrong to the ancient task of articulating our ideals of human excellence. Rather than argue directly with destroyers of the environment who say, "Show me why what I am doing is *immoral*, "I want to ask, "What sort of person would want to do what they propose?" The point is not to skirt the issue with an *ad hominem*, but to raise a different moral question, for even if there is no convincing way to show that the destructive acts are wrong (independently of human and animal use and enjoyment), we may find that the willingness to indulge in them reflects the absence of human traits that we admire and regard morally important.

This strategy of shifting questions may seem more promising if one reflects on certain analogous situations. Consider, for example, the Nazi who asks, in all seriousness, "Why is it wrong for me to make lampshades out of human skin—provided, of course, I did not myself kill the victims to get the skins?" We would react more with shock and disgust than with indignation, I suspect, because it is even more evident that the question reveals a defect in the questioner than that the proposed act is itself immoral. Sometimes we may not regard an act wrong at all though we see it as reflecting something objectionable about the person who does it. Imagine, for example, one who laughs spontaneously to himself when he reads a newspaper account of a plane crash that kills hundreds. Or, again, consider an obsequious grandson who, having waited for his grandmother's inheritance with mock devotion, then secretly spits on her grave when at last she dies. Spitting on the grave may have no adverse consequences and perhaps it violates no

rights. The moral uneasiness which it arouses is explained more by our view of the agent than by any conviction that what he did was immoral. Had he hesitated and asked, "Why shouldn't I spit on her grave?" it would seem more fitting to ask him to reflect on the sort of person he is than to try to offer reasons why he should refrain from spitting.

III

What sort of person, then, would cover his garden with asphalt, strip mine a wooded mountain, or level an irreplaceable redwood grove? Two sorts of answers, though initially appealing, must be ruled out. The first is that persons who would destroy the environment in these ways are either shortsighted, underestimating the harm they do, or else are too little concerned for the well-being of other people. Perhaps too they have insufficient regard for animal life. But these considerations have been set aside in order to refine the controversy. Another tempting response might be that we count it a moral virtue, or at least a human ideal, to love nature. Those who value the environment only for its utility must not really love nature and so in this way fall short of an ideal. But such an answer is hardly satisfying in the present context, for what is at issue is *why* we feel moral discomfort at the activities of those who admittedly value nature only for its utility. That it is ideal to care for nonsentient nature beyond its possible use is really just another way of expressing the general point which is under controversy.

What is needed is some way of showing that this ideal is connected with other virtues, or human excellences, not in question. To do so is difficult and my suggestions, accordingly, will be tentative and subject to qualification. The main idea is that, though indifference to nonsentient nature does not *necessarily* reflect the absence of virtues, it often signals the absence of certain traits which we want to encourage because they are, in most cases, a natural basis for the development of certain virtues. It is often thought, for example, that those who would destroy the natural environment must lack a proper appreciation of their place in the natural order, and so must either be ignorant or have too little humility. Though I would argue that this is not necessarily so, I suggest that, given certain plausible empirical assumptions, their attitude may well be rooted in ignorance, a narrow perspective, inability to see things as important apart from themselves and the limited groups they associate with, or reluctance to accept themselves as natural beings. Overcoming these deficiencies will not guarantee a proper moral humility, but for most of us it is probably an important psychological preliminary. Later I suggest, more briefly, that indifference to nonsentient nature typically reveals absence of either aesthetic sensibility or a disposition to cherish what has enriched one's life and that these, though not themselves moral virtues, are a natural basis for appreciation of the good in others and gratitude.[7]

Consider first the suggestion that destroyers of the environment lack an appreciation of their place in the universe.[8] Their attention, it seems, must be focused on parochial matters, on what is, relatively speaking, close in space and time. They seem not to understand that we are a speck on the cosmic scene, a brief stage in the evolutionary process, only one among millions of species on Earth, and an episode in the course of human history. Of course, they know that there are stars, fossils, insects, and ancient ruins; but do they have any idea of the complexity of the processes that led to the natural world as we find it? Are they aware how much the forces at

work within their own bodies are like those which govern all living things and even how much they have in common with inanimate bodies? Admittedly scientific knowledge is limited and no one can master it all; but could one who had a broad and deep understanding of his place in nature really be indifferent to the destruction of the natural environment?

This first suggestion, however, may well provoke a protest from a sophisticated anti-environmentalist.[9] "Perhaps *some* may be indifferent to nature from ignorance," the critic may object, "but *I* have studied astronomy, geology, biology, and biochemistry, and I still unashamedly regard the nonsentient environment as simply a resource for our use. It should not be wasted, of course, but what should be preserved is decidable by weighing long-term costs and benefits." "Besides," our critic may continue, "as philosophers you should know the old Humean formula, 'You cannot derive an *ought* from an *is*.' All the facts of biology, biochemistry, etc., do not entail that I ought to love nature or want to preserve it. What one understanding is one thing; what one values is something else. Just as nature lovers are not necessarily scientists, those indifferent to nature are not necessarily ignorant."

Although the environmentalist may concede the critic's logical point, he may well argue that, as a matter of fact, increased understanding of nature tends to heighten people's concern for its preservation. If so, despite the objection, the suspicion that the destroyers of the environment lack deep understanding of nature is not, in most cases, unwarranted, but the argument need not rest here.

The environmentalist might amplify his original idea as follows: "When I said that the destroyers of nature do not appreciate their place in the universe, I was not speaking of intellectual understanding alone, for, after all, a person can *know* a catalog of facts without ever putting them together and seeing vividly the whole picture which they form. To see oneself as just one part of nature is to look at oneself and the world from a certain perspective which is quite different from being able to recite detailed information from the natural sciences. What the destroyers of nature lack is this perspective, not particular information."

Again our critic may object, though only after making some concessions: "All right," he may say, *"some* who are indifferent to nature may lack the cosmic perspective of which you speak, but again there is no *necessary* connection between this failing, if it is one, and any particular evaluative attitude toward nature. In fact, different people respond quite differently when they move to a wider perspective. When *I* try to picture myself vividly as a brief, transitory episode in the course of nature, I simply get depressed. Far from inspiring me with a love of nature, the exercise makes me sad and hostile. You romantics think only of poets like Wordsworth and artists like Turner, but you should consider how differently Omar Khayyam responded when he took your wider perspective. His reaction, when looking at his life from a cosmic viewpoint, was 'Drink up, for tomorrow we die.' Others respond in an almost opposite manner with a joyless Stoic resignation, exemplified by the poet who pictures the wise man, at the height of personal triumph, being served a magnificent banquet, and then consummating his marriage to his beloved, all the while reminding himself, 'Even this, shall pass away.' "[10] In sum, the critic may object, "Even if one should try to see oneself as one small transitory part of nature, doing so does not dictate any particular normative attitude. Some may come to love nature, but others are moved to live for the moment; some sink into sad resignation; others get depressed or angry. So

indifference to nature is not necessarily a sign that a person fails to look at himself from the larger perspective."

The environmentalist might respond to this objection in several ways. He might, for example, argue that even though some people who see themselves as part of the natural order remain indifferent to nonsentient nature, this is not a common reaction. Typically, it may be argued, as we become more and more aware that we are parts of the larger whole we come to value the whole independently of its effect on ourselves. Thus, despite the possibilities the critic raises, indifference to nonsentient nature is still in most cases a sign that a person fails to see himself as part of the natural order.

If someone challenges the empirical assumption here, the environmentalist might develop the argument along a quite different line. The initial idea, he may remind us, was that those who would destroy the natural environment fail to *appreciate* their place in the natural order. "Appreciating one's place" is not simply an intellectual appreciation. It is also an attitude, reflecting what one values as well as what one knows. When we say, for example, that both the servile and the arrogant persons fail to *appreciate* their place in a society of equals, we do not mean simply that they are ignorant of certain empirical facts, but rather that they have certain objectionable attitudes about their importance relative to other people. Similarly, to fail to appreciate one's place in nature is not merely to lack knowledge or breadth of perspective, but to take a certain attitude about what matters. A person who *understands* his place in nature but still views nonsentient nature merely as a resource takes the attitude that nothing is *important* but human beings and animals. Despite first appearances, he is not so much like the pre-Copernican astronomers who made the intellectual error of creating the Earth as the "center of the universe" when they made their calculations. He is more like the racist who, though well aware of other races, treats all races but his own as insignificant.

So construed, the argument appeals to the common idea that awareness of nature typically has, and should have, a humbling effect. The Alps, a storm at sea, the Grand Canyon, towering redwoods, and "the starry heavens above" move many a person to remark on the comparative insignificance of our daily concerns and even of our species, and this is generally taken to be a quite fitting response.[11] What seems to be missing, then, in those who understand nature but remain unmoved is a proper humility.[12] Absence of proper humility is not the same as selfishness or egoism, for one can be devoted to self-interest while still viewing one's own pleasures and projects as trivial and unimportant.[13] And one can have an exaggerated view of one's own importance while grandly sacrificing for those one views as inferior. Nor is the lack of humility identical with belief that one has power and influence, for a person can be quite puffed up about himself while believing that the foolish world will never acknowledge him. The humility we miss seems not so much a belief about one's relative effectiveness and recognition as an attitude which measures the importance of things independently of their relation to oneself or to some narrow group with which one identifies. A paradigm of a person who lacks humility is the self-important emperor who grants status to his family because it is *his*, to his subordinates because *he* appointed them, and to his country because *he* chooses to glorify it. Less extreme but still lacking proper humility is the elitist who counts events significant solely in proportion to how they affect his class. The suspicion about those who

would destroy the environment, then, is that what they count important is too narrowly confined insofar as it encompasses only what affects beings who, like us, are capable of feeling.

This idea that proper humility requires recognition of the importance of nonsentient nature is similar to the thought of those who charge meat eaters with speciesism. In both cases it is felt that people too narrowly confine their concerns to the sorts of beings that are most like them. But, however intuitively appealing, the idea will surely arouse objections from our antienvironmentalist critic. "Why," he will ask, "do you suppose that the sort of humility I *should* have requires me to acknowledge the importance of nonsentient nature aside from its utility? You cannot, by your own admission, argue that nonsentient nature *is* important, appealing to religious or intuitionist grounds. And simply to assert, without further argument, that an ideal humility requires us to view nonsentient nature as important for its own sake begs the question at issue. If proper humility is acknowledging the relative importance of things as one should, then to show that I must lack this you must first establish that one *should* acknowledge the importance of nonsentient nature."

Though some may wish to accept this challenge, there are other ways to pursue the connection between humility and response to nonsentient nature. For example, suppose we grant that proper humility requires only acknowledging a due status to sentient beings. We must admit, then, that it is logically possible for a person to be properly humble even though he viewed all nonsentient nature simply as a resource. But this logical possibility may be a psychological rarity. It may be that, given the sort of beings we are, we would never learn humility before persons without developing the general capacity to cherish, and regard important, many things for their own sakes. The major obstacle to humility before persons is self-importance, a tendency to measure the significance of everything by its relation to oneself and those with whom one identifies. The processes by which we overcome self-importance are doubtless many and complex, but it seems unlikely that they are exclusively concerned with how we relate to other people and animals. Learning humility requires learning to feel that something matters besides what will affect oneself and one's circle of associates. What leads a child to care about what happens to a lost hamster or a stray dog he will not see again is likely also to generate concern for a lost toy or a favorite tree where he used to live.[14] Learning to value things for their own sake, and to count what affects them important aside from their utility, is not the same as judging them to have some intuited objective property, but it is necessary to the development of humility and it seems likely to take place in experiences with nonsentient nature as well as with people and animals. If a person views all nonsentient nature merely as a resource, then it seems unlikely that he has developed the capacity needed to overcome self-importance.

IV

This last argument, unfortunately, has its limits. It presupposes an empirical connection between experiencing nature and overcoming self-importance, and this may be challenged. Even if experiencing nature promotes humility before others, there may be other ways people can develop such humility in a world of concrete, glass, and plastic. If not, perhaps all that is needed is limited experience of nature in one's early, developing years; mature adults, having overcome youthful self-importance, may

live well enough in artificial surroundings. More importantly, the argument does not fully capture the spirit of the intuition that an ideal person stands humbly before nature. That idea is not simply that experiencing nature tends to foster proper humility before other people; it is, in part, that natural surroundings encourage and are appropriate to an ideal sense of oneself as part of the natural world. Standing alone in the forest, after months in the city, is not merely good as a means of curbing one's arrogance before others; it reinforces and fittingly expresses one's acceptance of oneself as a natural being.

Previously we considered only one aspect of proper humility, namely, a sense of one's relative importance with respect to other human beings. Another aspect, I think, is a kind of *self-acceptance*. This involves acknowledging, in more than a merely intellectual way, that we are the sort of creatures that we are. Whether one is self-accepting is not so much a matter of how one attributes *importance* comparatively to oneself, other people, animals, plants, and other things as it is a matter of understanding, facing squarely, and responding appropriately to who and what one is, e.g., one's powers and limits, one's affinities with other beings and differences from them, one's unalterable nature and one's freedom to change. Self-acceptance is not merely intellectual awareness, for one can be intellectually aware that one is growing old and will eventually die while nevertheless behaving in a thousand foolish ways that reflect a refusal to acknowledge these facts. On the other hand, self-acceptance is not passive resignation, for refusal to pursue what one truly wants within one's limits is a failure to accept the freedom and power one has. Particular behaviors, like dying one's gray hair and dressing like those twenty years younger, do not *necessarily* imply lack of self-acceptance, for there could be reasons for acting in these ways other than the wish to hide from oneself what one really is. One fails to accept oneself when the patterns of behavior and emotion are rooted in a desire to disown and deny features of oneself, to pretend to oneself that they are not there. This is not to say that a self-accepting person makes no value judgments about himself, that he likes all facts about himself, wants equally to develop and display them; he can, and should feel remorse for his past misdeeds and strive to change his current vices. The point is that he does not disown them, pretend that they do not exist or are facts about something other than himself. Such pretense is incompatible with proper humility because it is seeing oneself as better than one is.

Self-acceptance of this sort has long been considered a human excellence, under various names, but what has it to do with preserving nature? There is, I think, the following connection. As human beings we are part of nature, living, growing, declining, and dying by natural laws similar to those governing other living beings; despite our awesomely distinctive human powers, we share many of the needs, limits, and liabilities of animals and plants. These facts are neither good nor bad in themselves, aside from personal preference and varying conventional values. To say this is to utter a truism which few will deny, but to accept these facts, as facts about oneself, is not so easy—or so common. Much of what naturalists deplore about our increasingly artificial world reflects, and encourages, a denial of these facts, an unwillingness to avow them with equanimity.

Like the Victorian lady who refuses to look at her own nude body, some would like to create a world of less transitory stuff, reminding us only of our intellectual and social nature, never calling to mind our affinities with "lower" living creatures. The "denial of death," to which psychiatrists call attention, reveals an attitude incompatible with the sort of self—acceptance which philosophers, from the ancients to Spinoza and on, have admired as a human excellence.[15] My suggestion is not merely that experiencing nature causally promotes such self-acceptance, but also that those who fully accept themselves as part of the natural world lack the common drive to disassociate themselves from nature by replacing natural environments with artificial ones. A storm in the wilds helps us to appreciate our animal vulnerability, but, equally important, the reluctance to experience it may *reflect* an unwillingness to accept this aspect of ourselves. The person who is too ready to destroy the ancient redwoods may lack humility, not so much in the sense that he exaggerates his importance relative to others, but rather in the sense that he tries to avoid seeing himself as one among many natural creatures.

V

My suggestion so far has been that, though indifference to nonsentient nature is not itself a moral vice, it is likely to reflect either ignorance, a self-importance, or a lack of self-acceptance which we must overcome to have proper humility. A similar idea might be developed connecting attitudes toward nonsentient nature with other human excellences. For example, one might argue that indifference to nature reveals a lack of either an aesthetic sense or some of the natural roots of gratitude.

When we see a hillside that has been gutted by strip miners or the garden replaced by asphalt, our first reaction is probably, "How ugly!" The scenes assault our aesthetic sensibilities. We suspect that no one with a keen sense of beauty could have left such a sight. Admittedly not everything in nature strikes us as beautiful, or even aesthetically interesting, and sometimes a natural scene is replaced with a more impressive architectural masterpiece. But this is not usually the situation in the problem cases which environmentalists are most concerned about. More often beauty is replaced with ugliness.

At this point our critic may well object that, even if he does lack a sense of beauty, this is no moral vice. His cost/benefit calculations take into account the pleasure others may derive from seeing the forests, etc., and so why should he be faulted?

Some might reply that, despite contrary philosophical traditions, aesthetics and morality are not so distinct as commonly supposed. Appreciation of beauty, they may argue, is a human excellence which morally ideal persons should try to develop. But, setting aside this controversial position, there still may be cause for moral concern about those who have no aesthetic response to nature. Even if aesthetic sensibility is not itself a moral virtue, many of the capacities of mind and heart which it presupposes may be ones which are also needed for an appreciation of other people. Consider, for example, curiosity, a mind open to novelty, the ability to look at things from unfamiliar perspectives, empathetic imagination, interest in details, variety, and order, and emotional freedom from the immediate and the practical. All these, and more, seem necessary to aesthetic sensibility, but they are also traits which a person needs to be fully sensitive to people of all sorts. The point is not that a moral person must be able to distinguish beautiful from ugly people; the point is rather that unresponsiveness to what is beautiful, awesome, dainty, dumpy, and otherwise aesthetically interesting in nature probably reflects a lack of the openness of mind and spirit necessary to appreciate the best in human beings.

The anti-environmentalist, however, may refuse to accept the charge that he lacks aesthetic sensibility. If he claims to appreciate seventeenth-century miniature portraits, but to abhor natural wildernesses, he will hardly be convincing. Tastes vary, but aesthetic sense is not *that* selective. He may, instead, insist that he *does* appreciate natural beauty. He spends his vacations, let us suppose, hiking in the Sierras, photographing wildflowers, and so on. He might press his argument as follows: "I enjoy natural beauty as much as anyone, but I fail to see what this has to do with preserving the environment independently of human enjoyment and use. Nonsentient nature is a resource, but one of its best uses is to give us pleasure. I take this into account when I calculate the costs and benefit of preserving a park, planting a garden, and so on. But the problem you raised explicitly set aside the desire to preserve nature as a means to enjoyment. I say let us enjoy nature fully while we can, but if all sentient beings were to die tomorrow, we might as well blow up all plant life as well. A redwood grove that no one can use or enjoy is utterly worthless."

The attitude expressed here, I suspect, is not a common one, but it represents a philosophical challenge. The beginnings of a reply may be found in the following. When a person takes joy in something, it is a common (and perhaps natural) response to come to cherish it. To cherish something is not simply to be happy with it at the moment, but to care for it for its own sake. This is not to say that one necessarily sees it as having feelings and so wants it to feel good nor does it imply that one judges the thing to have Moore's intrinsic value. One simply wants the thing to survive and (when appropriate) to thrive, and not simply for its utility. We see this attitude repeatedly regarding mementos. They are not simply valued as a means to remind us of happy occasions; they come to be valued for their own sake. Thus, if someone really took joy in the natural environment, but was prepared to blow it up as soon as sentient life ended, he would lack this common human tendency to cherish what enriches our lives. While this response is not itself a moral virtue, it may be a natural basis of the virtue we call "gratitude." People who have no tendency to cherish things that give them pleasure may be poorly disposed to respond gratefully to persons who are good to them. Again the connection is not one of logical necessity, but it may nevertheless be important. A nonreligious person unable to "thank" anyone for the beauties of nature may nevertheless feel "grateful" in a sense; and I suspect that the person who feels no such "gratitude" toward nature is unlikely to show proper gratitude toward people.

Suppose these conjectures prove to be true. One may wonder what is the point of considering them. Is it to disparage all those who view nature merely as a resource? To do so, it seems, would be unfair, for, even if this attitude typically stems from deficiencies which affect one's attitudes toward sentient beings, there may be exceptions and we have not shown that their view of nonsentient nature is itself blameworthy. But when we set aside questions of blame and inquire what sorts of human traits we want to encourage, our reflections become relevant in a more positive way. The point is not to insinuate that all anti-environmentalists are defective, but to see that those who value such traits as humility, gratitude, and sensitivity to others have reason to promote the love of nature.

Notes

1. When I use the expression "the natural environment," I have in mind the sort of examples with which I began. For some purposes it is important to distinguish cultivated gardens from forests, virgin forests from replenished ones, irreplaceable natural phenomena from the replaceable, and so on; but these distinctions, I think, do not affect my main points here. There is also a broad sense, as Hume and Mill noted, in which all that occurs, miracles aside, is "natural." In this sense, of course, strip mining is as natural as a beaver cutting trees for his dam, and, as parts of nature, we cannot destroy the "natural" environment but only alter it. As will be evident, I shall use *natural* in a narrower, more familiar sense.

2. This paper is intended as a preliminary discussion in *normative* ethical theory (as opposed to *metaethics*). The task, accordingly, is the limited, though still difficult, one of articulating the possible basis in our beliefs and values for certain particular moral judgments. Questions of ultimate justification are set aside. What makes the task difficult and challenging is not that conclusive proofs from the foundation of morality are attempted; it is rather that the particular judgments to be explained seem at first not to fall under the most familiar moral principles (e.g., utilitarianism, respect for rights).

3. I assume here that having a right presupposes having interests in a sense which in turn presupposes a capacity to desire, suffer, etc. Since my main concern lies in another direction. I do not argue the point, but merely note that some regard it as debatable. See, for example, W. Murray Hunt, "Are *Mere Things* Morally Considerable?" *Environmental Ethics* 2 (1980): 59–65; Kenneth E. Goodpaster, "On Stopping at Everything," *Environmental Ethics* 2 (1980): 288–94; Joel Feinberg, "The Rights of Animals and Unborn Generations," in William Blackstone, ed., *Philosophy and Environmental Crisis* (Athens: University of Georgia Press, 1974), pp. 43–68; Tom Regan, "Feinberg on What Sorts of Beings Can Have Rights," *Southern Journal of Philosophy* (1976); 485–98; Robert Elliot, "Regan on the Sort of Beings that Can Have Rights,"

Southern Journal of Philosophy (1978): 701–5; Scott Lehmann, "Do Wildernesses Have Rights?" *Environmental Ethics* 2 (1981): 129–46.

4. G. E. Moore, *Principia Ethica* (Cambridge: Cambridge University Press, 1903); *Ethics* (London: H. Holt, 1912).

5. G. E. Moore, "Is Goodness a Quality?" *Philosophical Papers* (London: George Allen and Unwin, 1959), 95–7.

6. See, for example, P. H. Nowell-Smith, *Ethics* (New York: Penguin Books, 1954).

7. The issues I raise here, though perhaps not the details of my remarks, are in line with Aristotle's view of moral philosophy, a view revitalized recently by Philippa Foot's *Virtue and Vice* (Berkeley: University of California Press, 1979), Alasdair McIntyre's *After Virtue* (Notre Dame: Notre Dame Press, 1981), and James Wallace's *Virtues and Vices* (Ithaca and London: Cornell University Press, 1978), and other works. For other reflections on relationships between character and natural environments, see John Rodman, "The Liberation of Nature," *Inquiry* (1976): 83–131 and I. Reinhardt, "Some Gaps in Moral Space: Reflections on Forests and Feelings," in Mannison, McRobbie, and Routley, eds., *Environmental Philosophy* (Canberra: Australian National University Research School of Social Sciences, 1980).

8. Though for simplicity I focus upon those who do strip mining, etc., the argument is also applicable to those whose utilitarian calculations lead them to preserve the redwoods, mountains, etc., but who care for only sentient nature for its own sake. Similarly the phrase "indifferent to nature" is meant to encompass those who are indifferent *except* when considering its benefits to people and animals.

9. For convenience I use the labels *environmentalist* and *anti-environmentalist* (or *critic*) for the opposing sides in the rather special controversy I have raised. Thus, for example, my "environmentalist" not only favors conserving the forests, etc., but finds something objectionable in wanting to destroy them even aside from the costs to human being and animals. My "anti-environmentalist" is not simply one who wants to destroy the environment; he is a person who has no qualms about doing so independent of the adverse effects on human beings and animals.

10. "Even This Shall Pass Away," by Theodore Tildon, in *The Best Loved Poems of the American People*, ed., Hazel Felleman (Garden City, NY: Doubleday Co., 1936).

11. An exception, apparently, was Kant, who thought "the starry heavens" sublime and compared them with "the moral law within," but did not for all that see our species as comparatively insignificant.

12. By "proper humility" I mean that sort and degree of humility that is a morally admirable character trait. How precisely to define this is, of course, a controversial matter; but the point for present purposes is just to set aside obsequiousness, false modesty, underestimation of one's abilities, and the like.

13. I take this point from some of Philippa Foot's remarks.

14. The causal history of this concern may well depend upon the object (tree, toy) having given the child pleasure, but this does not mean that the object is then valued only for further pleasure it may bring.

15. See, for example, Ernest Becker, *The Denial of Death* (New York: Free Press, 1973).

Study Questions for Section 12

1. Baxter contends that natural objects ("geological marvels") and nonhuman animals (such as penguins) do not have intrinsic value but are important only insofar as humans enjoy them. Do you agree?

2. Hill suggests that we view environmental policies as expressions of personal attitudes toward nature. How would Baxter reply?

3. What role should considerations about future generations play in our moral thinking about environmental policy?

CREDITS

William F. Baxter, "People or Penguins: The Case for Optimal Pollution" from *People or Penguins* by Baxter. Copyright 1974 Columbia University Press. Reprinted with Permission.

Tom L. Beauchamp, "In Favor of Affirmative Action" *Journal of Ethics,* Volume 2, 1998.

Hugo Adam Bedau, "Capital Punishment" from *Matters of Life and Death,* edited by Tom Regan, McGraw Hill 1993.

Steven M. Cahn, "Two Concepts of Affirmative Action" from *Academe*, Volume 83, No. 1, 1997. Reprinted with the permission of the author.

Joseph H. Carens, "Migration and Morality: A Liberal Egalitarian Perspective" by Joseph H. Carens. Reprinted with the permission of the author.

Noël Carroll, "Can Government Funding of the Arts Be Justified Theoretically?" from *Journal of Aesthetic Education*, Volume 21, No. 1, Spring 1987, pp. 21–35.

Ronald Dworkin, "Can a Liberal State Support Art?" from *A Matter of Principle* by Ronald Dworkin, pp. 221–233, Cambridge, Mass. Harvard University Press. Copyright © 1985 by Ronald Dworkin. Reprinted by permission of the publisher.

Joel Feinberg, "The Feminist Case against Pornography" from *Offense to Others* by Joel Feinberg, Oxford University Press 1985.

Samuel Freeman, "Liberalism and Rights of Drug Use" from *Drugs and the Limits of Liberalism*, edited by Pablo DeGrieff, Cornell University Press, 1999.

Ernerst van den Haag, "In Defense of the Death Penalty" *Criminal Law Bulletin*, Volume 14, No. 1, 1978, pp. 51–68.

Jeffrey R. Henig, "Rethinking School Choice" from *Rethinking School Choice* by Jeffrey R. Henig, Princeton University Press, 1994.

Daniel J. Hill, "Ticking Bombs, Torture and the Analogy with Self-Defense" *American Philosophical Quarterly*, Volume 44, No. 4, 2007.

Thomas E. Hill, Jr. "Ideals of Human Excellence and Preserving Natural Environments" *Environmental Ethics*, Volume 5, 1983.

Todd C. Hughes and Lester H. Hunt, "The Liberal Basis of the Right to Bear Arms" *Public Affairs Quarterly*, Volume 14, No. 1, 2000.

Douglas N. Husak "Liberal Neutrality and Drug Prohibitions" *Philosophy and Public Affairs*, Volume 29, Issue 1, 2000, pp. 43–80.

Jeffrey Jordon, "Is it Wrong to Discriminate on the Basis of Homosexuality?" *Journal of Social Philosophy*, Volume 26, No. 1, Spring 1995.

Hugh LaFollette, "Gun Control" by Hugh LaFollette. Copyright 2000, The University Chicago Press.

Helen E. Longino, "Pornography, Oppression, and Freedom: A Closer Look" by Helen E. Longino. Reprinted with permission of Helen Longino. Copyright © 1980.

Lionel K McPherson, "Is Terrorism Distinctively Wrong?" *Ethics*, Volume 117, April 2007, pp. 524–546.

Henry Shue, "Torture" *Philosophy and Public Affairs*, Volume 1, Winter 1978.

Joseph S. Spoerl, "Justice and the Case for School Vouchers" *Public Affairs Quarterly*, Volume 9, No. 1, January 1995.

Michael Walzer, "The Distribution of Membership" from *Boundaries: National Autonomy and its Limits*, edited by P. Brown and H. Shue, Rowan & Littlefield, 1981.

Michael Walzer, "Terrorism: A Critique of Excuses" by Michael Walzer. Reprinted with the permission of the author.

Ralph Wedgwood, "Same-Sex Marriage: A Philosophical Defense" by Ralph Wedgwood. Reprinted with permission of Ralph Wedgewood.